Scientific Method in Psychology

McGRAW-HILL SERIES IN PSYCHOLOGY

HARRY F. HARLOW, *Consulting Editor*

John F. Dashiell was Consulting Editor of this series from its inception in 1931 until January 1, 1950. Clifford T. Morgan was Consulting Editor of this series from January 1, 1950 until January 1, 1959.

Scientific Method in Psychology

Clarence W. Brown

Professor, Department of Psychology
University of California at Berkeley

Edwin E. Ghiselli

Professor, Department of Psychology
University of California at Berkeley

McGRAW-HILL BOOK COMPANY, INC.

New York   Toronto   London

1955

SCIENTIFIC METHOD IN PSYCHOLOGY

VII
08125

To
Betty · Bill · Dick
and
David · Jack · Bill

Preface

This book is a systematic description of the use of the scientific method in studying behavior. Although the study of behavior is as old as man, its systematic formulations have usually taken the form of pseudoscientific systems, each purporting to have the keys to the understanding of man's problems. Relatively few attempts have been made to put forth in simple language a description of the scientific method, which has been utilized so successfully in other areas. The past hundred years have seen remarkable progress in evolving scientific procedures for studying behavior, but it is questionable whether these advances have appreciably reduced the extent to which pseudoscientific systems are accepted. In systematically describing how the scientific method can be applied to human responses, this book will help to counteract false approaches to the study of man's behavior.

For many years there has been a need in the field of psychology for a textbook on the scientific method. The present book gives the student a systematic description of the many concepts with which the scientific psychologist must deal. The aim of the book is to present the characteristics and concepts of the scientific method as a set of tools with which the student can embark on a serious attempt to learn about, and to experiment with, human behavior. It is common practice, early in his training, to expose the student of psychology to the experimental literature. There is no question that a knowledge of this literature is essential, and that absorbing it is a continuous process in the life of the student. It is the experience of the authors, however, that many students begin their study of the literature before they have sufficient background to enable them to understand, evaluate, and absorb the important concepts they are expected to learn. The student will find the experimental literature in psychology more meaningful if he can approach it with a well-formulated set of tools, even though these tools are not forged to the precision that characterizes those used by the mature scientist.

The field in psychology showing the most promise for future development is research in the problems of behavior. There are many forms of research, extending from simple methods of fact gathering to combined rational and empirical explorations of highly conceptualized theories about "human nature." Psychology has reached a stage of maturity when it can discard, for the most part, mere collecting of information about human responses and can get down to the more profitable business of exploring theoretical frameworks applicable to the various kinds of human behavior. In recent years many investigators have shown that it is not only feasible but very profitable to examine scientifically even the most molar types of human response.

In presenting a systematic account of the concepts widely used by scientific psychologists, the authors have not attempted to present all possible interpretations of any given concept. At first, the serious student of psychology can readily be overwhelmed by the wide variation with which scientific concepts are interpreted. It has been necessary at times to give very precise meanings to some of the concepts. This is done, not with the intent of persuading the student to adopt the interpretations suggested, but rather to avoid clouding the issues with variations in interpretation that will prevent him from learning the nature of the principal arguments being advanced. At this stage in learning it is much more important to find the common thread that runs through all scientific psychology than to become confused about divergencies of meaning that have proved so difficult to resolve even by mature scientists. After having gained an understanding of the common methods and goals of scientific psychology, the student is better prepared to engage in polemic discussions on psychological theory.

The book is written with the expectation that the student will approach the study of scientific psychology as a scholar. It is, then, not a compilation of experimental studies, written in recipe style for easy mastery. The aims and methods of scientific psychology are treated as principles to be learned at a generalized level so they can be applied to any problem within any particular field. Concreteness is given to the principles by means of illustrations drawn from many special areas of psychological research. There has been an attempt to make the book evenly difficult throughout, without omitting any concepts that are thought important for the beginning student in scientific psychology.

The nature of the content of the book and the particular method of presentation utilized make it adaptable to the needs and special interests of a wide variety of college courses. In mimeographed form it has served the authors in beginning courses in experimental psychology. It has been used in courses that have included a weekly 3-hour laboratory period and in courses consisting only of lectures or lecture-demonstrations. With the omission of certain chapters, the mimeographed edition has been adapted to courses carrying only two units of college credit. It has also served as supplementary reading for upper-division experimental courses and for graduate courses in research methodology and design.

The book is divided into three parts. Part One explains certain general concepts of the scientific method and particularizes them in terms of the problems of psychology. Part Two discusses the principal steps of the method, beginning with the formulation of a problem that initiates a study and ending with the formulation of the generalizations that terminate it. In Part Three, many of the special procedures of scientific psychology are presented. Here the student comes to grips with some of the particular tools he will need to master if he intends to perform scientific research of any kind in the area of human behavior.

Suggested readings are given at the end of each chapter. These are not included for the purpose of documenting the arguments of the text, but rather to assist the interested reader in initiating further exploration of those general areas that appeal to him. The number of selections is purposely kept small. The student will find of interest in these references many chapters that are not specifically cited.

The authors are indebted to many of their colleagues and graduate students in psychology for advice and criticism. Particular thanks are expressed to Professors D. G. Ellson, L. J. Postman, and T. R. Sarbin. The following graduate students, who over the years assisted in the teaching of demonstration and laboratory sections in which earlier versions of the text materials were used, made many valuable suggestions: Richard Barthol, Richard Christie, Samuel Fillenbaum, Theodore Kroeber, Frank Meeker, Donavon Morrison, Herbert Naboisek, Harvey Peskin, Carlos Quadra, Benjamin Rosenberg, Harold Sampson, William Sickles, George Stone, Frank Vanasek, and Everett Wyers.

The authors wish to express their appreciation for permission to reproduce the following materials: quotation in Chap. 4 from A. A. Brill, "The Basic Writings of Sigmund Freud," Modern Library, Inc., and George Allen & Unwin, Ltd.; scaled statements in Chap. 12 from "A Scale for Measuring Attitude toward War," by D. D. Droba, The University of Chicago Press; Fig. 12, Chap. 15, from Report No. 1, The Aviation Psychology Program in the Army Air Forces; material for Tables 6 and 7, Chap. 15, from Treatment of Schizophrenia by J. S. Gottlieb and Paul E. Huston, *Archives of Neurology and Psychiatry;* Fig. 13, Chap. 15, from Overcoming Resistance to Change, by L. Coch and J. R. P. French, *Human Relations;* Table 8, Chap. 15, from Assessment of Persons through a Quasi Group-interaction Technique, by R. S. Crutchfield, *Journal of Abnormal and Social Psychology.*

CLARENCE W. BROWN

EDWIN E. GHISELLI

Contents

Contents

PART ONE

Some General Concepts about the Scientific Method

Every discipline has an underlying rational basis, and in this respect science does not differ from other disciplines. There are certain fundamental philosophical notions about natural phenomena that we should examine early in our study of the scientific method. In addition, there are several basic problems that must be dealt with by every scientist regardless of what type of subject matter he chooses to study. These problems should also be surveyed early, and consideration given to how they are solved in the field of psychology.

Chapter 1 briefly reviews the ways in which the word science is used. The point of view is developed that science is primarily a method and as such it has applications to all kinds of natural problems. Successful execution of the method, of course, demands a scientist who must be willing to learn its intricacies and abide by its rules. Being human, the scientist is subject to errors, and therefore scientific findings can never be interpreted as infallible.

In dealing with natural phenomena, the scientist must take certain things for granted. These presuppositions are described in Chap. 2. They concern in part the nature of the physical universe with which the scientist deals and in part the nature of the psychological processes that are involved in his role as scientist. Knowledge of how he contributes as part of the scientific method enables the scientist to minimize bias and achieve a high degree of objectivity.

The aims and methods of science are discussed in Chap. 3. The most general aim of science is understanding, but there are several more specific aims that we achieve on the way to understanding. As a method, science can be described at such a general level that it encompasses all subject-matter disciplines. When applied to particular problems, however, the method becomes a very large number of specific procedures.

The concept of cause and effect has been central to man's thinking both as a scientist and as a nonscientist. It is a particular way of describing relationships among natural events. In Chap. 4 we examine this concept in a pragmatic way to determine what we actually are able to observe in a relationship that we refer to as causal. For the purpose of the scientist, the concept of functional relationship seems sufficient and squares with the facts.

Two very fundamental problems faced by every scientist are the problem of controlling the variables relevant to his project and the problem of quantitatively describing these variables. Control of variables is discussed in Chap. 5. The first psychologists followed closely the lead of the natural scientists in attempting to control variables by procedures of physical manipulation. They soon learned, however, that differences between phenomenal changes in human beings and phenomenal changes in inanimate physical objects were so great as to require procedures especially designed for the variables operating in human behavior. Much of the scientific psychologist's time is spent in the development of procedures for achieving the degree of control needed by his particular kinds of hypotheses.

Describing changes in behavior is a core procedure in all science. As explained in Chap. 6, the highest possible accuracy is obtained in quantitative description. The scientist has continually appealed to the number meanings of mathematics as a means of improving his descriptions. The application of these number meanings to human behavior is subject to many errors. It is necessary for us to realize fully the increased precision that mathematical and statistical procedures afford the psychologist, but at the same time we must be aware of the fundamental assumptions underlying these procedures. Only when the behavior data to be analyzed meet the assumptions underlying the formulas or equations we desire to use are we justified in availing ourselves of these procedures.

CHAPTER 1

Some Characteristics of Science

Without expending any great effort we can collect many divergent statements on what constitutes science. These statements will vary so widely in their emphases that an aspect held important by one authority will not be included in the definition of science as given by another authority. If we are to study scientific method in psychology, it is essential for us to make a beginning toward defining that method. The following sections are directed toward establishing, in a preliminary way, a concept of science.

SOME CURRENT INTERPRETATIONS OF THE TERM SCIENCE

As is true of most words, the word science has come to have a variety of meanings. Let us briefly review some of the more frequently used interpretations that have stemmed from notions about the scientist and his work.

Science and Subject-matter Fields. The word science is often used in a generic sense to refer to the so-called "sciences" or fields of scientific subject matter, such as physics, geology, astronomy, and the like. In high school this meaning is used in designating a certain class of courses, the so-called "science courses," as contrasted with other kinds of courses, such as those in history, civics, and economics, which are called the humanities, or courses in literature, drama, and music, which are called the arts. Science is, then, conceived as a term to be applied to only the "hard" things of nature and is not to include the less tangible phenomena of human behavior. This interpretation of science is widely held by the general populace.

Science and Complicated Gadgets. The word science is also applied to activities in which such intricate instruments as microscopes, electric meters, complexly arranged glass tubes, etc., are used. Such gadgets are considered too difficult for most people to understand and use. Presum-

3

ably, science is reserved for the select few who have the inclination and ability to deal with such complex things.

Science and Universal Laws. Sometimes the word is used to refer to theories and laws that have been evolved to explain natural phenomena. Almost everyone has heard of the law of gravity and the law of relativity, and somehow science comes to stand for these and other principles and theories by which the scientist explains the workings of the natural universe. Thus, to many, science means abstruse descriptions of how the universe operates.

Science and Systematic Procedures. A further use of the term science associates it with what is called the scientific point of view. This is given a variety of interpretations, sometimes referring to the making of a purposeful search, sometimes to the trusting of only facts, sometimes to the use of prolonged deliberation, sometimes to the application of involved mathematics, or to the use of some other supposed unique characteristic. There is no unanimity as to what is meant by being scientific about a problem except the idea that the scientific approach is somehow superior to any other approach.

Science as Technical Methodology. Lastly, science is looked upon as comprising technical methods for solving problems. This is one of the most widely held meanings. Presumably, years of training are required to master the techniques. There are some who think that these scientific techniques are applicable only to the physical or material elements of nature.

Pseudoscientific Schemes. Mention should be made here of the fallacious application of the term in connection with certain pseudoscientific schemes devised for understanding and predicting human behavior. Astrology, phrenology, physiognomy, chirognomy, chiromancy, palmistry, chemotypology, graphology, and other kindred systems are presented as scientifically derived methods for explaining and controlling human behavior. It is not necessary here to evaluate these pseudoscientific approaches. Rather, it is more important that the reader do this for himself after he has gained an understanding of the scientific method. It is necessary to state, however, that proponents of each approach appeal to facts to gain support for their point of view. Furthermore, it must be affirmed that in some instances these facts are as well supported as the facts in use by the scientist.

The statement that the above-named approaches to the study of behavior are pseudosciences results from the authors' judgments about each one as a total system. No claim is being made that all parts of every system are pure fancy. Neither is it held that those parts that are supported by facts should be denied because a scheme as a whole is declared unscientific.

SCIENCE AS BOTH GENERAL AND SPECIFIC METHODS

The intensive cultivation of science in the narrow fields of physical subject matter has resulted in the development of a seriously retarding influence, viz., it has tended to encourage the idea that there is only one method of science and that this method is that of the physical sciences. Actually, as method, science can be interpreted either as a single general method or as many specific methods. It is fallacious to restrict the term to the procedures used in the study of physical phenomena.

Science as a General Method. When we study the wide variety of situations considered scientific, examining their similarities and their differences, the one feature that is most common, that stands out most prominently, and that seems to form the essence of science is its general method. Starting, then, with this as a premise, we can ask the question: Is there one general method of science? The answer is that on a highly conceptual level science may be considered a general method. When scientists study specific problems, however, this general method is modified in numerous ways, and many of these adaptations are of sufficient importance and sufficiently general in nature to be considered methods within themselves. Science, then, is a very general method, modified in various ways into many less general methods that are utilized in the study of specific problems.

Science as a Multiplicity of Methods. The scientific method has been varied in a tremendous number of ways. No two problems are exactly alike, and no one method can be applied in an invariable manner to different types of problems. Every investigator has had to adapt existing methods to the specific conditions of his projects. One of the frequent mistakes of the young scientist is his failure to recognize the need for modifying available methods to suit his particular problem, with the result that the methods he uses are sometimes inappropriate. He later finds that such carelessness either produces totally invalid results or greatly reduces the precision of his interpretations and generalizations.

Factors Underlying the Modification of the Method. It is not necessary here to consider specific modifications of the scientific method. Many illustrations will be found throughout the text. Mention should be made, however, of several factors that underlie modifications in the method. Three of these are as follows: the nature of the subject matter, the nature of the specific problem, and the stage of the inquiry.

Variation in method due to difference in subject matter may be illustrated by contrasting physiological psychology and social psychology. The study of brain mechanisms in learning demands histological and experimental methods; the determination of racial prejudice in minority groups demands survey and population sampling methods.

The nature of the problem very definitely conditions the method to be used. Inquiry starts, not from a method, but rather from a problem, and thus from the beginning the problem will condition the steps taken to solve it. Different types of problems raise different types of questions and require different kinds of procedures to achieve the answers. Let us consider two problems concerned with the relationship between ability in arithmetic and success in clerical work. One problem involves vocational selection, the other vocational guidance. The first problem requires information about the relationship between arithmetic ability and clerical success in order to determine if an arithmetic test should be used as a device for selecting clerks. The second requires similar information in order that vocational advice can be given to a graduating high school student who thinks he would like to become a clerk in a banking firm. In the first problem we would need to learn if applicant clerks scoring high on an arithmetic test will manifest superior performance when hired and trained as clerks. In the second problem we would need to know how performance on an arithmetic test, when combined with other information known about a graduating high school student, assists in prognosticating his success in the clerical profession. Even though the information needed appears to be similar, the problems are radically different, and different methods would be required to solve them.

Variation in methodology associated with the stage of the inquiry may be exemplified in the use of logic, experiment, and statistics as individual procedures within a scientific study. Logic enters the picture early during the formulation of the inquiry; experiment enters later when the empirical steps are being designed to collect the data; statistical methods enter at this stage and also at a later period when the data are being analyzed; and logic again enters when the implications of the findings are being evolved and formulated as generalizations.

THE NATURE OF FACTS

If we cast about for a single word by which to epitomize the most essential element in science, we can do no better than to select the word *fact*. If this burden is assigned to the word fact in scientific circles, then it should be obvious that the meaning of the *concept* of fact will not be a simple one.

The Use of Facts by Both Layman and Scientist. Facts perform a yeoman service for the nonscientific individual, who frequently uses them in the form of pragmatic tests to settle differences. Such phrases as "Let's appeal to the facts," "But the facts in the case are . . . ," and "The facts speak for themselves," are frequently heard when differences are to be reconciled or decisions are to be made in the affairs of the workaday world. Facts are compelling aspects of experience to which everyone must adjust.

To the nonscientific person, there seems to be inherent in his concept of fact "a given" or "a finality" characteristic that brooks no opposition. "A fact is a fact and that is all there is to it." This is not the interpretation of the scientist, who, more than any other person, has the task of discovering and identifying facts for all of us. Facts are not *given* but are discovered through inquiry. Facts do not possess the characteristic of *finality* but are continually undergoing change as inquiry proceeds.

The essential task of the scientist is to identify facts with the highest possible precision, for they form the stock in trade of all of his work. He discovers facts, he describes facts, he relates facts, he makes judgments about facts, he explains facts, and he generalizes from his facts. The center of focus of all of his activities, whether they are concerned with empirical search or with rational manipulation, is facts.

Facts Defined. A general definition of the term fact is as follows: an experience, event, change, or occurrence for which there is substantial evidence. As with most definitions, there is need of further elaboration. We should keep in mind that the word fact is a generalized concept and therefore may be assigned more than one meaning. One way of interpreting fact is to conceive it to be a continuum of experience, from experience that is immediate to experience that is highly conceptual. The one essential characteristic of all facts is the substantiation of their existence through evidence. In the following discussion, three levels of fact are outlined. It is to be understood that these levels are chosen arbitrarily to highlight three points along the continuum of fact.

Facts of Immediate Experience. One kind of immediate experience is called "raw" or "brute" experience. It refers to experiences that are "uncluttered" even by names. Such would be the experiences of a young infant. These can be called the most "factual of facts" because they have not been subjected to change through the individual's thinking about them.

It is questionable whether a person is capable of having raw or brute experience once he has learned to assign names to his experiences. The assignment of a name to an experience is the first step in conceptualization. The individual's intellectual processes are brought into play immediately upon the presence of a stimulus, to identify, interpret, and assign meanings to the new experience. Thus his experiences have a conceptual component and are no longer the immediate "naked" experiences that a young infant might have.

Facts Describing Immediate Experience. These facts are abstract and conceptual in nature, and describe and interpret immediate experience. They involve the combining of several meanings into a composite. Meanings directly aroused by sensory stimuli are combined with meanings dependent upon the arousal of previous experience. Regardless of the complexity of the psychological genesis of this composite type of experience, it is readily considered a fact. This kind of fact is exemplified by such words as house, tree, rock, table, book, muscle, head, etc.

The least conceptualized experience is primarily sensory in nature. Some examples are touches, smells, sounds, and pains. More conceptualized in nature are the thought or rational experiences exemplified by ideas, memories, and images. Sensory facts may be referred to either external or internal sources; rational experiences are referred only to internal conditions. This distinction between external and internal is made because of the difference in ease with which agreement can be attained about facts of these two types. Suppose we present a small box to two individuals, allowing each one to see and lift it. We then ask each to describe his visual and his kinesthetic experiences of the box. We shall find much more agreement in the descriptions of the visual box than in the descriptions of the kinesthetic box.

Conceptual experiences are one of man's greatest assets because they are the only ones that he can mentally manipulate. They enable him to perform three functions, namely, to represent the past in the present, to react in the present with implicit or covert responses, and to carry the past and the present into the future in the form of foresight and planning. An illustration of the first function should prove sufficient. The simple recall of a sports event will be used. We can recall and think about yesterday's baseball game by manipulating the names of the players, the numbers of the innings, the words that depict the plays that were made, the decisions of the umpires, etc. We reconstruct the game by the use of conceptual facts.

Facts describing immediate experience are not highly conceptualized. Counterparts in sensory experience are usually readily found, and the conceptualization is primarily associated with the recall of past meanings.

Facts Remote from Sensory Experience. It is obvious that meanings may transcend sensory experience. Some meanings are never displayed to view in any sensory manner. They never exist in a form in which they are open to sensory inspection. These meanings are evolved primarily through the use of reason. Despite the fact that they are highly conceptual in nature, when they are supported by sufficient empirical evidence, they are accepted as fact.

One way of arriving at a fact of this type is through generalization. An example is represented in the following statement: All sharp objects strongly pressed against the skin will cause pain. It is not possible to have a sensory experience of such a general proposition. Through reasoning, we form the general proposition from many specific sensory experiences with sharp objects. When supported with sufficient evidence, such a generalized proposition is considered a fact.

Another example of this type of fact is the relationship between two concepts. Such a relationship is not observable in sensory experience, but there may be sufficient evidence of its existence to compel its acceptance as a fact. That arithmetic ability is positively related to spelling ability is accepted as a fact. Both abilities are concepts and are never actually experienced. They are inferred from the concrete performance of individuals in solving problems and in spelling words. Likewise, the relationship between the abilities is experienced only on a conceptual level. However, there is a sufficient amount of evidence traceable to various forms of sensory experience to justify accepting as fact the conclusion that a positive relationship exists between the two abilities.

THE SCIENTIST'S ROLE IN SCIENCE

Scientific generalizations are the joint product of two factors, namely, the scientific method and the scientist. The scientific method is the product of man's ingenuity, and its successful application depends upon a continuous exercise of this ingenuity. Sometimes the point of view is expressed that science is too difficult ever to find widespread use. This proposition requires further examination.

The Concept of the Scientist. Peculiar notions have arisen concerning the traits and characteristics possessed by the scientist. Popular accounts of scientific discoveries may conceive the scientist to be an elderly gentleman with bushy gray hair, peering from behind horn-rimmed spectacles. Or they may conceive him to have a goatee and always be wearing a white laboratory coat. These conceptions about the scientist extend into his working space and are concerned with certain "gear and trappings" that command awe and respect from the uninitiated. Sometimes the necessary accoutrements consist of a laboratory room with benches on which there are long, twisted tubes of glass, gas burners, beakers, and bottles of mysterious chemicals. Sometimes they consist of motors, gears, wires, and meters accompanied by characteristic whirrings, grindings, and crackles. Sometimes, but not very frequently, they may include an ordinary room with a desk on which there are sheets of printed materials.

Regardless of what the popular conception of the scientist is or what kind of trappings are thought required for his "trade," there is a proneness to accept him uncritically as a peculiar individual engaged in a mysterious calling that has to do with analyzing the nature of things, such as stars, rocks, chemicals, forces, and the like. Although in very recent years there has been an increased understanding of the importance of the contribution of scientists, seldom have questions been raised concerning the use of the scientific method as a possible and workable method for attacking the everyday problems of the "ordinary" man.

A definition of a scientist that is readily understood can be stated as follows: He who rigorously applies the scientific method is a scientist. It follows that any individual can be scientific by rigorously applying the scientific method. This interpretation is not difficult to understand because it stems directly from the most widely accepted definition of science. Furthermore, there is nothing new about this conception, for it has been championed over the years by those individuals most qualified to speak, namely, the scientists. Despite its acceptance by critical minds, however, this conception runs counter to most of the mystery and superstition which beclouds current popular understanding of science.

If this conception is correctly interpreted, it means that an individual can be scientific without the characteristics of bushy hair, horn-rimmed spectacles, goatee, or white laboratory coat. It means that scientific results can be achieved in the absence of a room full of test tubes, gas flames, whirring motors, and crackling electric sparks. A further interpretation of the conception means that scientific results are not limited to a study of stars, chemical elements, cosmic rays, and the like, but that a scientific attack can be directed on problems of a more mundane nature, such as the frustrations and failures, the confusions and conflicts, and the prejudices and perversities of ordinary people.

The Nature of the Scientist's Contribution. Dame Nature is somewhat reluctant to reveal her secrets and does so only when prodded. The scientist acts as a probe; his task is to prod nature into displaying her workings. His search, then, must be an active one. He is not a mere passive recorder, registering successions of sensory impressions as events occur before him, but he busies himself in devising all manner of procedures, gadgets, and techniques by means of which he can push into the greater vistas that lie beyond the scope of superficial observation. The scientist plays an active role in all phases of the scientific method, and it is important that the manner and extent of his contribution be considered.

The starting point of any scientific investigation is the scientist's problem. His study of the problem takes directions imparted to it by questions that require answers. Questions do not appear spontaneously; they are the product of the scientist's thinking. Right from the beginning, then, the investigator contributes to his study. The hypothesis he frames as the proposition to be investigated is a product of his interest, knowledge, training, motivation, and other similar personal characteristics. As a method, science provides a means for studying his hypothesis. Some kind of investigation, such as a survey, interview, case history, or experiment, is organized through which empirical evidence pertinent to the hypothesis can be collected.

In the conduct of the investigation, regardless of its nature, the primary method that will be followed will be observation. Obviously, the scientist must be the observer.

With the data collected, the next task is that of analysis. There are no analytical procedures available that can be applied automatically. The scientist must not only carefully select the appropriate procedures, but it is his responsibility to see that those selected are executed with high fidelity.

Following the discovery of all the facts there comes the task of interpretation. This is a stage of high subjectivity, in which the pitfalls are both numerous and subtle. To do the job adequately the investigator must utilize his scientific acumen to the utmost in order to discover all of the hidden meanings and still adhere steadfastly to the facts. Seldom will he complete his study without discovering some "loose ends" that affect his generalizations and that escaped notice despite his attempt to control rigorously all of the pertinent variables. Never will he reach conclusions that will be wholly free of ambiguity.

SCIENTIST AND NONSCIENTIST COMPARED

In spite of the aura of magic and mystery with which the layman surrounds the scientist, it is actually found that in many respects the scientist's labors are not very different in kind from those characterizing a nonscientific person reacting in the ordinary situations of everyday living.

The Approach of the Scientist. The stimulus that goads the scientist into action is a problem. Some question is raised for which there is no immediate answer. He is provoked into thinking about it and into pondering about possible answers to it. As he mulls over the problem, the question at stake becomes clarified, and he verbalizes it as accurately as he can. Often this verbalization is formed into a hypothesis that can be empirically studied. He then devises situations from which he can collect facts that will be pertinent to the problem and from which he might be able to construct a solution. He is persistent in this search for facts and continues until he can establish a good case either for or against the hypothesis. He is careful, however, not to exclude any facts because of personal bias, but allows every fact to contribute its share to the total picture. Thus, he establishes a sound factual basis from which he can devise generalizations about the problem that initiated the study.

The Approach of the Nonscientist. The various steps outlined above, at least in a very general way, find their counterparts in the behavior of the nonscientific person. To begin with, he encounters a wide variety of problems, and a large proportion of them merit the sound and careful attack used by the scientist. Likewise, the nonscientific person frequently thinks about his problems, but often in an ineffective way that can best be described as "stewing" or "fretting." He is usually not so successful as the scientist in reaching the kernel of the problem, in stating it in the form of an answerable question, or in devising a workable hypothesis. His failure, however, is not due to the impossibility of applying a more rigorous analysis but rather to his ignorance or lack of experience in using a more rigorous method.

Failure to state the problem accurately markedly handicaps his subsequent attempts to devise an answer. He frequently will seek out facts that are not pertinent to the problem. Here again his ineffectiveness is often due to lack of discipline and training. He may not continue his search long enough, and he may be content to formulate generalizations prematurely, before sufficient facts have been collected to justify them.

Again, in his search he may allow some bias to influence his selection of the facts, and this will result in an invalid base on which to establish his generalizations. Frequently this biased selection of the facts is not known to the individual, and in many cases, if it were known, he would take steps to counteract it.

Having made a generalization, the nonscientific person is less willing subsequently to check it as further facts become known. He persists in arguing for his generalization, either because he has strong feelings concerning the certainty of it, or because he is fearful of the changes he would have to face were he to give it up.

A Comparison in Terms of Individual Flexibility. One of the chief characteristics of the scientist is his flexibility. His purpose is to improve his beliefs rather than to defend them. He is suspicious of his generalizations. He is forever questioning their validity and deliberately seeking further facts in order to test them. His creed calls for a continuous revision of all phases of his work as additional knowledge is accumulated, whether method or result, whether hypothesis or generalization. Of all people he is the most expert in changing his mind; that is, he is continually vigilant to bring his findings up to date in terms of trustworthy evidence.

The attitude of the nonscientific person is in sharp contrast with this. As he grows up, he forms habitual ways of responding and becomes accustomed to rely on them most of the time. He is schooled to take for granted whatever is familiar, traditional, or customary. He stabilizes his behavior in an attempt to resist change, and comes to accept a certain amount of frustration and failure as inevitable. He enters the school of hard knocks and there builds up tolerance for various forms of social and personal dislocation. A little confusion, anxiety, and worry can prove profitable experiences along the road to understanding, but he accepts them as a continuing necessity. He actually becomes adjusted to a certain amount of maladjustment. He not only tolerates maladjustment but he accepts it as a necessary steppingstone to tranquillity. Such beliefs form a powerful barrier to modifications in behavior and are handicaps to his discovering adequate solutions to his problems.

The Scientist's Tolerance of Change. The scientist thrives on change. He is progressive because he is never too certain of his facts. He encourages systematic doubt. Critical thinking results only when there is doubt. When there is no doubt, there can be no science. Progress is achieved by modifying the findings and techniques of the past and thus making possible a continuous adjustment to the changing conditions of the present.

Instead of tolerating failure, the scientist endeavors to evolve methods for avoiding it. In the face of failure, he demands a change. When old procedures begin to lose their usefulness, when they are no longer adequate for satisfying current needs, he demands that they be modified or that new methods be devised. He does not admit that past methods will continuously measure up to the problems of the present and the future.

Although the scientist welcomes change, he does not abandon the concepts of the past upon the first revelation of new findings. He trains himself to be an expert in changing his mind. He fires everything in the crucible of experience and accepts it only when it has demonstrated its serviceability. He critically evaluates all of the facts and changes only when the weight of the evidence demands change. He is conservative in that he first wants to be convinced by facts. He is progressive in that he will readily accept change when the facts warrant it.

SELECTED READINGS

Churchman, C. W., and R. L. Ackoff: "Methods of Inquiry," chaps. 1 and 8, Educational Publishers, 1950. The first eight chapters provide a brief but comprehensive description of the historical development of the antecedents of the scientific method. Chapter 8 describes the pragmatic method, which of all earlier points of view in philosophy approaches most closely the scientific method.

Conant, J. B.: "On Understanding Science," Yale University Press, 1947. (Also published in Mentor Book series.) The nature of the scientific method is described by way of examples selected from the natural sciences. In chap. 4 on Certain Principles of the Tactics and Strategy of Science, principles are presented that have wide applicability to the development of science in various subject-matter areas.

Preston, M. G.: Methodological Considerations, in H. Helson (ed.), "Theoretical Foundations of Psychology," chap. 1, D. Van Nostrand Company, Inc., 1951. This chapter introduces the student to various concepts and methods in the field of scientific psychology. Although written at a more difficult level than the present text, it furnishes the student with an excellent preview of some of the problems confronting the psychologist in his use of the scientific method.

CHAPTER 2

Presuppositions of the Scientific Method

All of us take for granted certain characteristics of the objects and activities we experience. For example, we take for granted the continuity of events in time. We live today expecting that there will be a tomorrow. Tomorrow we expect to encounter about the same conditions as today, that is, the same people, the same objects, the same kinds of relationships, etc. We expect these people to manifest about the same kinds of behavior when confronted with about the same kinds of situations. We expect the objects to occupy about the same points in space and to be serving us in about the same ways as they do today.

We also take for granted the accuracy of the activities of knowing, those activities by which we come to understand ourselves and our environment. Few of us take the time to examine the accuracy of our perceptions, memories, and reasonings concerning the world around us. For example, if I see a dress as red, I do not question that the dress is red. If I recall that I mailed a letter yesterday, then the letter was mailed yesterday. If I reason that today is my birthday and my wife has baked a cake for me on my birthday every year of our married life, then I do not even question my conclusion that there will be a cake awaiting me when I return home tonight. In the foregoing examples involving the primary knowing activities of perception, memory, and reasoning, full trust is placed in the final outcome of the psychological processes utilized. As a matter of fact, we are not even aware most of the time that there is a need for questioning the trustworthiness of these activities and so we remain wholly ignorant of the subtle ways in which inaccuracy in these responses may influence our day-to-day reactions.

For the scientist's scientist, ignorance about any matters that bear upon the correct execution of the scientific method is not to be tolerated. It is necessary then to consider some of these presuppositions that the scientist must accept as a basis for his procedures, and to learn how they may influence the execution of these procedures. The propositions that deal with the fundamental nature of the universe of objects and

15

events with which the scientist works are primarily the concern of the philosophy of science. The propositions that directly affect the application of scientific procedures are the immediate concern of the individual scientist, both in his conduct of an investigation and in his subsequent theorizing about the findings.

THE UNIFORMITY OF NATURE

Most of the presuppositions concerning the nature of objects and events can be subsumed under the topic of the uniformity of nature. This concept is an old one in scientific thought and, of course, a much older one in philosophical speculation. As a consequence, there are numerous interpretations and points of view concerning the concept. It is not the purpose here to attempt a comprehensive account of the development of the concept, but only to make clear the fact that the scientist never begins an investigation from "scratch." In other words, there are certain propositions concerning the universe to which the scientist must subscribe in order that he can go to work.

These propositions may not be found in the forefront of the scientist's thinking, and, in fact, he may not even be aware of them as logical necessities. Regardless of how the concept is considered by the individual scientist, however, it nevertheless remains true that unless nature is assumed to be uniform there can be no science. It is not necessary to assume that nature is rigidly uniform in all respects, but to the extent that nature is uniform to that extent science is possible.

For the purposes of the present discussion, the general concept of the uniformity of nature will be divided into the individual propositions or postulates of natural kinds, of permanence, and of determinism.

THE POSTULATE OF NATURAL KINDS

The Meaning of the Postulate. In his observation of natural phenomena, man observed that objects seemed to go together in groups, the members within a group showing more resemblance to others in that group than they showed to objects in other groups. When resemblances became numerous, he gave a name to the group. This observation—that objects may have many common characteristics—was a rather compelling one, and led to the postulate of natural kinds. This postulate says that among natural phenomena resemblances occur in large numbers. Resemblances can be of any kind, that is, any element, aspect, occurrence, characteristic, item, function, structure, process, etc., by which a phenomenon can be described. There seem to be no restrictions on the nature of the associations occurring among these resemblances. Resemblances between material or structural elements may be associated, as when we associate blond hair with a fair, delicate skin. Resemblances between functional aspects may be associated, as when we associate poor ability to drive a car at night with a slow recovery rate of the retina of the eye following a bright light stimulation. Resemblances between structural elements and functional aspects may be associated, as when we associate a short, stocky physique with slowness of movement.

Resemblances as the Basis of Scientific Classification. This process of discovering resemblances between natural phenomena underlies one of the scientist's most important procedures, that of classification. Once the scientist has found some resemblances among objects, the postulate leads him to expect and to look for additional resemblances among these objects. This expectation of further resemblances leads to the postulation of resemblances that are in need of investigation. The investigation may demonstrate that the postulated resemblances actually exist, or it may demonstrate the existence of differences or dissimilarities which in themselves may be very important items of knowledge.

When resemblances are sufficiently numerous to treat the objects as a group by themselves, the scientist forms a class and gives the group a class name. Some examples of common class names are igneous rock, radio tube, poisonous gas, cosmic ray, visual perception, personality trait, physiological drive, etc. The delineation of a class is based on the number of resemblances or the degree of resemblance, since members of any given class do not resemble each other in every possible respect.

The Importance of the Postulate for Science. The postulate is important for science in terms of the effect it may have on the scientist's thinking. Regardless of whether or not the scientist actually verbalizes the postulate, he does have the expectation of finding additional resemblances when he is conducting a study. It is the effect that this expectation may have on his reasoning that is important. It may lead him to attribute significance to resemblances that are unimportant. Thus his reasoning and the subsequent inferences that he makes will be in error. Generalizations based on unimportant resemblances usually are fallacious.

The resemblances on which any reasoning is based should be pertinent to the nature of the element or aspect being inferred. Both the number and the importance of the resemblances determine the accuracy of the inference. The reader can call to mind examples like the following, in which the resultant inference based on analogical reasoning is in error. Certain primitive tribes make a wax figure of the enemy in the belief that as the figure melts away, the body of the enemy will waste away. These aborigines believe that figures that have the same shape are somehow physically associated. Similarly we find that in some tribes the warriors eat the heart of the wild game killed in order to become stout-hearted. Zulu tribesmen chew wood to soften the heart of their enemy. These examples illustrate the fact that error results when the inference is based on superficial resemblances.

The scientist is subject to these errors and must maintain a critical attitude in making his inferences. When human individuals are his concern, the chances of error greatly increase because the number of potential resemblances are legion and the intricacy of their interrelationships continue to defy understanding. We should be reminded that much of the reasoning underlying the pseudoscientific schemes referred to in the last chapter is based on superficial resemblances.

THE POSTULATE OF PERMANENCE

The Meaning of the Postulate. The presupposition of permanence affirms that nature is relatively stable in time. "That which has been will be." Most characteristics change slowly, so that year after year a tree, a house, a person, a community, seems not to vary perceptibly. Although change is always occurring, it is often so gradual that it falls below the threshold of our perception. We learn early in life to accept and expect permanence; seldom do we question the matter.

Variable Rates of Change. In accepting the postulate of permanence, we are not denying differences in the rate at which natural phenomena change in time. On the contrary, different kinds of phenomena demonstrate different rates of change. From an examination of history it is clear that the postulate of permanence originated from man's dealings with the physical universe. On the whole, change in the physical world is slow, and the sequences and relationships discovered among physical phenomena have been found to endure over long periods of time.

In dealing with people, we must introduce a more skeptical attitude concerning the slowness of the rate of change. Human beings do not remain constant in time, and on occasion they show high rates of change. Man's behavior is the outcome of many factors, not the least of which is the changing environment to which he must respond. Small changes in this environment may produce marked and rapid changes in a given individual.

In the social world we are occasionally confronted with very rapid and unpredictable changes which result in relatively sudden social disturbances. Under such conditions the prescriptions of the past cannot be applied in unmodified form to the new situations. Social changes incident to the discovery, development, and use of the atomic bomb are a case in point. Because of the atomic bomb, rapid changes are called for in the social thinking of today; changes so marked that at times it appears man is failing to adjust rapidly enough to avert social disaster.

The Importance of the Postulate for Science. In the logic of science, the postulate of permanence must be accepted or science is impossible. Obviously, without permanence natural phenomena would show no consistency in time, and this consistency is basic to the procedures of science. Without permanence the aims of control and prediction would become meaningless. It is difficult to imagine just how the objectives of science could be achieved if the predictions of the future rested solely upon chance, which is the alternative we must accept if we deny the postulate of permanence.

In accepting the postulate, science does not demand absolute permanence. Rather it is implied that natural phenomena change so slowly that the scientist can learn about them, and that in spite of his slow rate of progress what he learns remains usable long enough to be put to profitable application.

THE POSTULATE OF DETERMINISM

The Meaning of the Postulate. Science accepts the postulate that all phenomena are determined. All of nature's manifestations are resultants of fundamentally stable processes at work and do not issue from caprice. "Things don't just happen." Each occurrence has a beginning in the events that have preceded it and to which, at least theoretically, it eventually can be traced. There is a temporal relationship between an event and its precursors, and this relationship supplies us with information about the occurrence of the event. The postulate of determinism, then, affirms that every event has a history in the events that have preceded it.

Opposed to this supposition is the postulate of indeterminism or non-determinism, which states that events just happen. Events are not related temporally to other events. The idea of spontaneous generation illustrates indeterminism.

The concept of determinism is very widely accepted, most persons being strongly opposed to the idea that events occur by chance. We not only apply the postulate to our individual behavior but also consider it a fundamental assumption underlying all of the social institutions that have been established.

Kinds of Determinism. The interpretation of the nature of determinism varies widely among different groups of thinkers. There are three general types of interpretation, as follows: spiritual determinism, self-determinism, and natural determinism.

In *spiritual determinism,* forces different from those known to exist among natural phenomena are credited with determining behavior. They are referred to as supernatural and are sometimes considered to be the attributes of a higher Being. The phrase *self-determinism* is used to refer to two very distinctly different types of determinants. It is used to denote changes in the bodily mechanisms that contribute to behavior, such as, for example, the contractions of the walls of the stomach in hunger. This type of factor is a phenomenon of nature and should be classified under natural determinism. We shall use the phrase self-determinism in a narrower sense, to refer to what certain philosophers call an unseen force or power which expresses itself through the activities of the individual.[1] The antecedents of this force are not clearly described, but they seem in some way to be a part of a larger creative impulsion responsible for the universe and its endless development. This force has not been identified or described empirically, and so it cannot be classified as a natural phenomenon.

The type of determinism characteristic of science is called *natural determinism*. Natural events form the subject matter studied by the scientist. Each natural event is related to preceding natural events, and in turn is related to subsequent natural events. Determinism in science refers to natural events associated in time, thus the name natural determinism. As we shall presently see, the term natural event is not to be restricted to occurrences in the physical universe. Psychological events in the form of urges, drives, appetites, loves, hates, and the like are natural events although differing very fundamentally from physical events such as molecular forces, electrical currents, or magnetic fields. These psychological events are found related in temporal sequences in nature and are therefore to be classified under natural determinism.

The Importance of the Postulate for Science. As interpreted above, determinism is essential to science. In attempting to control the variables of his experiment, the scientist discovers the time relations among these variables so that at some given point in the experiment he can establish those conditions that will bring about an appropriate expression of the variables. If there are no stable sequences among the variables it is impossible to exercise control over them.

In making his predictions, the scientist again depends upon the stability of the sequences that he has discovered among his variables. If the sequences are not stable, if there is no evidence that one variable consistently precedes another under some definite set of conditions, there is no basis for prediction. In fact, without the postulate of determinism there would be no problem of prediction because there then would be no basis for thinking that the future could be foretold from a knowledge of the past.

It would appear that if there are undetermined events, they fall outside the domain of scientific investigation.

[1] H. L. Bergson, "Creative Evolution," translated by Arthur Mitchell, Henry Holt and Company, Inc., 1911.

THE CONCEPT OF IMMUTABLE LAWS

Some of the early scientists interpreted the concept of the uniformity of nature as meaning that nature is governed by a set of general laws that have the characteristics of being both universal and changeless. It was sometimes maintained that once these laws were understood the divergent and multifarious expressions seen in natural phenomena could be readily explained. Underlying this conception of universal laws was a very strict interpretation of the immutability or changelessness of natural phenomena.

There is so much evidence now available to show that natural phenomena are not constant that the concept of absolute immutability is no longer widely accepted. It is not essential to science that the laws governing nature be immutable in any absolute sense. As already pointed out, it is only necessary that the changes be slow enough to allow the scientist to make profitable use of his findings. Furthermore, it can be shown that so-called "changeless" laws are not true in any absolute sense, but are only approximations of the truth. They can be considered as correct only within the range of approximation set by the limits of accuracy of the measuring instruments. In reference to their universal nature, it should be pointed out that, logically speaking, they are not really universal laws because they have not been tested over the complete range of the variables that they are intended to encompass. They are, then, only probable truths.

For our purposes the important point is that natural phenomena, in the main, change slowly, and consequently the laws governing their expression need to be changed only infrequently. We need to recall that science allows for, expects, and encourages change of any kind. Even the laws issuing from previous scientific studies must come under further scrutiny and be changed if the evidence so indicates.

SOME PRESUPPOSITIONS CONCERNING THE RELIABILITY OF THE KNOWING ACTIVITIES

In the foregoing discussions it was pointed out that in the logic of science certain presuppositions about natural objects and events must be accepted before science becomes possible. We shall now consider certain general notions concerned with the knowing activities of perceiving, remembering, and reasoning, which are the psychological processes used by man in gaining knowledge about the universe. These processes are subject to error. Because they are a bona fide part of the scientific method, error introduced through them will be reflected in the generalizations of any study. Presuppositions concerning the reliability of these knowing activities should receive the attention of every worker in science.

The term *reliability* is here being used in the sense of accuracy. It is concerned with the degree to which we can trust our perceptions to give us correct pictures of the stimuli we experience, our remembrances to represent accurately the past, and our reasonings to evolve correct inferences.

THE POSTULATE OF THE RELIABILITY OF PERCEIVING

The Problem. All of us have experienced some of the common illusions in the field of visual perception. These illusions clearly illustrate the unreliability of perceptual processes. For example, when we look down a railroad track into the distance, our eyes tell us that the rails come together. From other knowledge about railroad tracks and railroad cars we know the rails do not come together, and so we are able to make correct responses despite the misinformation given to us in perception. The fact is, however, that in the perception of the tracks the two rails do come together, and we can make no adjustment with our eyes that will enable us to see the rails otherwise. Our perceptual processes must, then, be considered as providing us with erroneous information.

Similarly, if we draw a perfect square and then look at it from a distance, it will appear "squatty," that is, wider than it is high. The proofreader's illusion is another example. Despite the fact that in reading proof we direct our attention to the detection of typographical errors, we still see as correctly spelled many words that actually are misspelled.

The question can be raised: If some of our perceptions are correct and some incorrect, then how can we tell which ones are to be trusted? Actually, we decide that some perceptions are in error by finding that they disagree with other perceptions, but how do we know that these other perceptions are not also in error? The skeptic enters the argument here and concludes that sense perceptions are not to be trusted. He reasons that because we have found many of our perceptions in error it is not possible to know just when they provide us with accurate information, and so we can never trust them.

Logically speaking, the fact must be accepted that perception is not completely trustworthy. The skeptic must be reminded, however, that the method he applies to show that certain perceptions are in error involves the use of other perceptual processes. Here is a paradox: He shows that perceiving is not trustworthy by utilizing perceptual processes. The solution to this paradox is simple. We must accept perceptual processes as fundamentally trustworthy, but, knowing that errors are possible, we must be willing to subject our perceptual findings to whatever checks will aid us in maintaining the highest possible degree of accuracy.

The Nature of Perception. In order to discriminate the true from the false among perceptual experiences, the scientist should understand the nature of perceptual processes. An act of perception involves sense-organ activity, attentive adjustments in the muscles and in thought, and the consequent arousal of meanings.

During waking life the individual is being continuously stimulated in a variety of ways, hence various kinds of sensory activity are occurring simultaneously. In the resulting sensory experience, however, stimulating objects are not observed as a jumble of isolated events but as events in relation. Nature has provided us not only with sensory structures keyed to different types of energy change in the environment, i.e., eyes, ears, taste buds, etc., but with a nervous system through which the diverse sensory stimuli are brought together and integrated into various complex arrangements. As we introspect upon our experience at any given moment, this experience appears to us to be unitary in nature.

The responses of an individual are being channeled or directed to some degree all of the time. Even when we think a person's behavior is aimless, it is actually being channeled toward certain ends, but in ways that we either have not discovered or do not understand. Channeling of response involves three general kinds of sets. First, there is the direction of the sense organs. To obtain a clearer experience of a stimulus we adjust the sense organs involved; e.g., we adjust the eyes to see an object. This is a receptor set. Movements of the sense organs and other parts of the body that may be involved in perception are accomplished by means of muscles; therefore there are motor or muscular sets. A third type of set involves the channeling of thought activities, i.e., mental sets. For example, when we pick up a book to read, our purpose sets us to look for the meanings of the printed words. If upon reaching the bottom of a page we find we do not have the faintest notion of what we supposedly have just read, then the mental set has not been focused on the meanings of the printed symbols even though the sensory and motor sets may have been appropriately made.

As we learned in the preceding chapter, facts are often composite experiences in which meanings obtained directly from the stimulus are combined with meanings rearoused from past experience. We find these two kinds of meanings in all perception. Meanings which originate directly from the functioning of a sense organ are called sensory meanings. Meanings which involve the rearousal of past experience are called inferential meanings. We can distinguish these two types of meaning by supposing that we are looking at a block of ice. When we say the ice is transparent, square, or has height, we are verbalizing sensory meanings. When we say the ice is cold, smooth, or wet, we are verbalizing inferential meanings. If we now touch the ice, the meanings of cold, smooth, and wet are then sensory in nature. Perceptual experiences are always made up of both sensory and inferential meanings.

Perception in the Work of the Scientist. It is not necessary here to describe how perception enters into the work of the scientist. It should be obvious that he constantly uses perception in all phases of his work. Accuracy in both sensory and inferential meanings is a prime requirement for his success.

The scientist's present perceptions are, of course, conditioned by the perceptual experiences of earlier occasions. We must remember that the inferential meanings of present experience originate in the sensory meanings of earlier experiences. Inaccuracy in these previous sensory meanings may, then, have both profound and prolonged effects upon later experiences. In regard to the scientist's work, this means that the meanings he manipulates in connection with any given experiment are conditioned by the accuracy of the perceptions he has had during many preceding years.

Sources of Error in Perception. Some errors of perception may be traced to a failure to make accurate discriminations. All perception involves discrimination. Perceiving an object requires that it be discriminated from its background and from surrounding objects. Different stimuli are often very similar in many of their characteristics and so may be reacted to with the same inferential meanings and thus confused. A good example of this type of error is the incorrect identification of identical twins. Unless a person is aware of a difference in the twins and can correctly perceive that difference on a given occasion, the chances are 50 to 50 that he will commit an error in identification.

Error may result from a failure to react to all of the direct stimulus contents that are significant for our purpose. This is a source of error particularly important for the scientist. It refers to the very common tendency of an individual to direct his attention to such a narrow field that much significant stimulation fails to be appreciated and thus fails to influence him. Many meanings are possible in any perceptual situation because many details are present to the senses and there are many relevant meanings in the perceiver's past experiences. There is interaction between the different stimulating aspects of any given situation, and sometimes one aspect may dominate and prevent response to some other aspect. Some of the factors that condition this failure to respond to all pertinent aspects of a situation are strong goals, preconceived mental sets, intellectual biases, emotional prejudices, distractions of the moment, etc. For example, distractions of the moment in large measure dominate the stimulating situation created by a ventriloquist. Paying attention to only the actions of Charlie McCarthy and not allowing certain other sensory stimuli to enter the perceptual activity produce a very real illusion.

Error in perception may result from a failure to identify the source of the meaning. Sometimes we mistake an inferential for a sensory meaning. Inferential meanings, of course, have many of the characteristics possessed by meanings gained directly from sensory stimulation. They involve color, shape, sound, warmth, movement, and the like. It is not difficult to see, then, why at times the two types of meaning are confused. If the inferential meanings dominate the perceptual experience, then the individual may not adequately react to the sensory stimuli present and thus may lose the correcting influences that these stimuli might otherwise contribute. In hallucination the inferential meanings are dominant in controlling the perceptual situation. They are so intense that they are interpreted as sensory meanings by the individual. Thus to the hallucinated alcoholic the spiders, pink elephants, or snakes he sees on the wall appear real and are not interpreted as merely figures on the wallpaper.

Means for Preventing Errors in Perception. The scientist should train himself in specific perceptual skills. Perception is not a general process but many specific processes. It involves many specific sensory, attentive, and thought reactions. Training in a certain area cannot be expected to spread over and affect perceptual responses in all other areas. Training should be directed to specific types of problems and involve the development of specific anticipatory sets. For example, if the scientist's problem is going to involve the use of the microscope, then he had better spend some time learning the many little perceptual tricks involved in operating this particular aid to vision. If the individual is going to work in the field of labor-management relations, he had better train himself in the specific perceptual situations of this field.

Training in background meanings is important. When one is searching for something new, as is the scientist, his success is directly predicated upon his being able to bring to bear many past experiences through the manipulation of inferential meanings. The new has to come from recombinations of the old. It is, then, very important that there be a rich and full store of relevant information. The more information the scientist has concerning the general area containing his problem, the greater are his chances of hitting upon a recombination of the old that will solve the problem.

Errors in meaning or failure to get all the significant meanings in a situation may result from the functioning of emotional and intellectual biases. Emotional biases are based on the personal feelings of the individual and are very likely to distort his perceptual activities. Whenever an individual supports his beliefs in the face of overwhelming facts to the contrary, an emotional bias is to be suspected. Such a bias acts as a selective agent in perception. Consequently, the person will be inclined to develop and retain those meanings that agree with his bias, and ignore meanings in disagreement with the bias despite any truth that they may contain.

The scientist should train himself against harboring intellectual biases. He usually is not a person who becomes emotionally involved in the defense of his findings, but at times he may take his theories too seriously and allow them to blind him to the possibilities of alternative concepts. This is an example of intellectual bias. Darwin is reported to have purposely formed an intellectual bias against his theory of evolution in order that he would not fail to include any and all facts that were contrary to his views.

The scientist can take several simple steps to reduce the possible influence of emotional and intellectual biases. He can thoroughly acquaint himself with all the points of view concerning his problem and know particularly well those views which are in opposition to his own. He can purposely examine his own thinking for bias and encourage his colleagues to be free with their criticism. He can purposely restrain himself from "overworking" the theory that he is championing, and refrain from over-generalization even when the theory is richly supported by empirical findings.

THE POSTULATE OF THE RELIABILITY OF REMEMBERING

The Problem. We are all familiar with the tricks that memory is forever playing on us. The failure of the busy husband to remember the groceries correctly, bringing home beans when peas were wanted; the failure of the student to remember the right material to study for a quiz, spending most of his time studying irrelevant content; the failure of the physician to remember correctly the symptoms of the familiar disease of diphtheria, diagnosing it as eczema; these are examples of a frailty to which the scientist also is heir.

Here again we have a problem that delights the skeptic. He asks: Can we ever determine when the recall of an event is true? Answering his own question in the negative, he decides that all memory is untrustworthy. This is another paradox. We must call the skeptic's attention to the fact that the psychological processes by which he judges a remembered event as fallacious are memory processes. To determine if a remembered event is true he must compare it with the original event, and memory is involved in the identification of the original event.

The scientist must admit that he is liable to make mistakes in recalling past events, but in spite of this limitation he must postulate the fundamental reliability of memory. He would make little progress if he seriously questioned the accuracy of recall of every event. Knowing that memory may be in error, however, he can devise aids by which to increase the accuracy of remembering and thus minimize possible errors.

Remembering Dependent upon Learning and Retention. Remembering is part of a larger response. When an individual remembers that the diagonal of a square is equal to the square root of twice the square of one side, two other conditions must previously have been met. First, learning must have occurred—the rules about square figures, powers, roots, hypotenuses, and the like, were acquired. This process of learning the rules involved changes in the physiological mechanisms of the body, principally in the nervous system and particularly in the brain. Secondly, the neurological changes must have persisted over a period of time in such a form that when appropriate stimuli were subsequently presented the mechanisms were rearoused to activity. This second phase, the temporal persistence of the neurological changes, is called retention. Remembering may, then, be adversely affected by factors that adversely affect either the original learning or the retention. Whether or not some item of the past will be remembered, to what extent it will be remembered, and in what form it will be remembered are, therefore, dependent upon a variety of factors.

Remembering in the Scientist's Work. As with the activity of perception, remembering enters into all phases of the scientific method. The scientist is continuously manipulating the meanings of the past. Throughout an investigation, whether it is an experiment, a simple interview, or a complex survey, he is recalling information to apply to his current needs. Although the scientist has constructed many successful mnemonic aids, his work is still greatly dependent upon the effectiveness of his memory.

Recall of the ideas of others and of his own from previous occasions is especially important in the beginning of a study, when he is trying to devise new concepts. The new always comes as a reconstruction of the old, and therefore it is important that he have at his finger tips a large background of information. During the conduct of the study, memory may prove very vital even to "making or breaking" all previous accomplishment. For example, during a crucial run in an experiment the apparatus may start to falter and just a small item of technical information may be all that is necessary to keep it functioning. Without this bit of information the crucial run might fail, resulting in the loss of all of the experimental data up to that point. Again, in the final interpretative phases of a study, when the scientist is extracting all the meanings he can from the data, his work is greatly facilitated if he can readily recall the background meanings that are relevant to his findings.

Errors of Remembering. Defects of remembering may be classified under two headings; namely, failure to remember, which refers primarily to the quantitative aspects of recall; and change in fidelity of the recalled response, which refers to qualitative differences between the remembered response and the originally learned response. Psychologically, this is an artificial separation. Actually, the same processes that underlie *what* is recalled also underlie *the degree* to which it is recalled. Some errors can, then, be classified under both headings.

Failure to Remember. Failure to remember is in part due to poor initial learning. The more efficient the original learning, the higher the chances will be for effective recall.

Failure to remember may be due to the fact that the patterns in the nervous system, basic to the response, have not been kept intact over the period of disuse when no recall was attempted. Competing responses, learned later, may act to prevent the desired recall, that is, some more recently learned item may inhibit the recall of the desired item. We have all had the experience of trying to recall someone's name and of failing because of the persistent remembrance of another name that we know is incorrect. Later learned responses, of course, may also facilitate the recall of an earlier learned response.

Failure to recall may be due to a lack of sufficient stimulation at the time recall is attempted. Learning of an event does not occur in isolation; it is initiated and enhanced by a large number of associated stimulating conditions. The more adequately these associated stimulating conditions are represented in the recall situation, the higher the chances that the recall will be successful. The associated stimuli will vary in kind, in number, and in intensity, and therefore the recall will be a function of the pertinence, number, and intensity of the associated stimuli that are reproduced.

One further reason for failure to remember may be offered, and that is that remembering is selective in nature. Not all aspects of a response are remembered on a given occasion because not all of them are congruous with the particular purposes and motives of the individual at the time of recall. We suspect that the "tall tales" heard around the campfire after a day of fishing contain elements that are meant primarily to impress the listener rather than to adhere to the truth. Here memory is selective because of the purposes of the teller, and as a consequence the remembered events do not represent all aspects of the experiences being described.

Selectivity of remembering is also traceable in part to the selectivity present in the original learning, where not all aspects of the experience may have been equally well learned.

Errors in Fidelity of Recall. These errors are of several kinds and stem from different sources. The most characteristic feature of these errors is a change in the meanings involved. This change seems to arise from the influence of strong mental sets and purposes on the part of the individual. The remembered event is made to harmonize with some other thought or feeling. There is ample evidence that the interests, attitudes, and expectations of the individual do determine the nature of the meanings elicited in later recall. The error usually is one of distortion, the recalled meanings being different from those established at the time of the original learning.

In his effort to confirm a theory, a scientist, in recalling the relevant findings of other scientists, may recall clearly those facts that support his own notions but may hazily and inaccurately recall those facts that are contrary. Thus a false interpretation is placed on the works of other scientists, which may be carried forward to influence his work right up to the completion of the project. The scientist faces a situation similar to that of a witness in a courtroom. It is clear that when a witness is before the court describing a former experience, say his observation of an accident, he is not describing the accident, nor is he describing his perception of the accident—he is describing what he can remember of his perception of the accident. Similarly, when a scientist refers to the findings of another investigator from memory, he does not reproduce the written descriptions of the experiment as furnished by this investigator, nor does he reproduce exactly his actual perceptions of the investigator's report. He gives a description of those impressions of the other investigator's report that his own selective perception and his own selective and limited memory make available. Thus there is considerable opportunity for distortion.

Obviating the Errors of Remembering. To reduce or to eliminate errors in remembering, sound psychological principles must be followed during the learning, during the intervening interval, and during the recall situation. Some of these principles are expressed in the following rules: (1) get an accurate and comprehensive perception of the event to be learned; (2) learn all of the aspects of the event that are judged to be important and necessary; (3) learn with the intent to recall and later utilize; (4) overlearn; (5) make a record of those parts that are particularly difficult; (6) review; and (7) reproduce at the time of recall the stimuli that were present in the original and review situations.

The first two principles assist in getting thorough coverage in the original learning and in putting the various aspects in their proper perspective. Selective learning can then be so controlled that bias and distortion do not enter the learning. Adherence to these two rules will aid in get-

ting higher fidelity in later recall. In the third step, the event is assimilated into the purposes, needs, and expectations of the scientist. As a result, the event has more significance for the scientist, who thus benefits
from the fact that it becomes an important element in his motivational
schemes. This enhances recall.

The fourth rule refers to the need of learning well whatever is learned,
that is, not stopping the learning process at the point when an immediate
recall is deemed satisfactory. The event must be overlearned if recall
following long delays is to be satisfactory. Overlearning clarifies and intensifies the meanings of the event and presumably intensifies and makes
more stable the neurological changes occurring during the learning.
This increases the chances that future relevant stimuli will prove adequate for reexciting the underlying nervous mechanisms. The fifth rule
deals with the strengthening of those aspects which are particularly difficult and which, if not given this special attention, might result in the
complete forgetting of the whole event. The sixth rule demands a brush-
ing up or relearning of the event. This step serves, as no other step does,
to preserve intact the changes in the neurological mechanisms which
underlie the event and which make recall possible.

The seventh rule is concerned with the stimuli present at the time recall
is attempted. As already stated, the success of recall is a function of the
current stimuli, inasmuch as they serve to elicit the rearousal of the past
experience. At the anticipated time of recall, the scientist should reproduce all the aids he can muster in the form of sensory and ideational
stimulation. These aids include written notes, records of data, photographs of apparatus, and similar helps that will contribute to eliciting
the desired response.

A final statement should be made concerning the use of memory aids.
All of the many types of recording gadgets employed by the scientist are
aids to memory. Polygraphs, photographs, recording meters, recording
clocks, calibrated containers, written records of subject's responses such
as test booklets, written accounts logging the progress of the study, diaries,
interview records, and other kinds of records of observations aid in re-
constructing with high fidelity the particular situation being subjected
to analysis. Some of these aids get their value from the fact that they
result in an immediate record of the occurrences (e.g., sound recording
of conversations in an interview), which in most instances is superior to
the descriptions obtainable at a later time by means of recall. Many of
these aids provide a more accurate picture of the particular aspect they
encompass than the scientist can provide from memory, e.g., the photo-
graph of a microscopic slide depicting the reproduction of bacteria. Certainly, the scientist should avail himself of any aid that will increase the
fidelity of his remembrances.

THE POSTULATE OF THE RELIABILITY OF REASONING

The Problem. Thinking and reasoning are frequently used as synonymous terms. Of the two, thinking is the more inclusive, reasoning being one form of thinking. Other general forms of thinking have been given the names of recollecting and imagining. Our primary concern is with the trustworthiness of reasoning.

The problem is reduced to the question: Is the reasoning of the scientist trustworthy? As the reader must suspect, the answer is similar to those given for perception and memory. Reasoning is not completely trustworthy, being subject to many kinds of error and sometimes resulting in false products even in the hands of the expert. Despite its limitations, however, we cannot accept the skeptic's view that reasoning cannot be trusted. His point is untenable because it is through reasoning that he arrives at his conclusion that all reasoning is untrustworthy. We must accept reasoning as fundamentally trustworthy but be willing to subject it to any checks that will assist in preventing inaccuracy.

The Nature of Reasoning. Reasoning is a form of problem solving in which the manipulation of ideas is substituted for the manipulation of real objects, as, for example, in overt trial-and-error behavior. It is the process of attacking a problem by means of concepts rather than by means of overt responses. Reasoning involves the use of many psychological processes, including symbolizing, remembering, imagining, comparing, analyzing, synthesizing, abstracting, inferring, generalizing, etc.

If the individual is going to respond to an object when it is absent as a sensory stimulus, or if he is going to manipulate thought objects not even having perceptual counterparts, he must have some mechanism for representing these objects to himself. The mechanism that has proved most effective for most individuals is language. Objects and relations are represented in thought by means of words. The word becomes a sign of the meaning that the object has for the individual and serves as an adequate surrogate.

Reasoning is made very effective through language because of the apparently limitless possibilities for meanings of the latter. The objective of all reasoning is to re-form past meanings into new combinations. The result is new meanings. Language offers, through its alphabetical symbols, almost limitless possibilities for representing the new meanings as they are developed.

Through concepts we can manipulate objects in ways that are impossible in terms of actual objective movements. For example, we can think of pushing over the Golden Gate Bridge. We can think of an object out of its concrete context, as when we think about dogs without referring to specific dogs, in specific locations, on specific days, belonging to specific people. Again, we can change and elaborate meanings of objects beyond those known in perception. One of our highest achievements in thinking is to form meanings that are so far removed from our perceptual experience that it is impossible to find any perceptual counterparts for them. Such ideas of this higher order are represented by the concepts of an endless progression, *n*-dimensional space, infinite time, and the like.

The concepts in thinking may issue directly from percepts, as when we note the relationship between parts of a mechanical puzzle; or stem from recollections, as when we remember the destruction caused by the big flood last spring; or involve imagination, as when we think about creating a device for automatically registering man's thoughts.

Reasoning in the Scientific Method. As is true for the activities of perceiving and remembering, there can be no science without reasoning. In the beginning, reasoning aids in delimiting and framing a problem. Through it the irrelevant elements are eliminated and the relevant factors are organized in the most meaningful arrangements. After the problem is stated, reasoning is necessary and essential in framing the solution. Here begins the effortful task of discovering, applying, fitting, modifying, and finally of rejecting or accepting potential solutions.

Once a solution is tentatively accepted there follows a similar complex and varied attack in devising methods and techniques for obtaining data that will test the validity of the potential solution. During the conduct of a study, many problems arise for which there are no ready-made solutions. The scientist faces problems about the order of experimental conditions, of apparatus design, of types of control, of statistical analysis, and the like.

In the stage of generalization when the scientist has the data before him and is contemplating their significance, he again appeals to reasoning. The significance of the data for the solution, the significance of the solution for the problem with which he began his study, and the significance of his findings for other related problems are worked out through the use of reasoning.

Sources of Error in Reasoning. Reasoning is beset with many kinds of errors. Those that are infractions of the formalized rules of logic are treated systematically in books on logical thinking. Some of these errors are the concern of the scientist, and he should become familiar with them. Our concern here is to point out some of the psychological sources of error. The line of demarcation between the psychology and the logic of errors of reasoning will be found to be rather indistinct.

Errors in reasoning may be due to bias. An intense desire to confirm a hypothesis may result in the scientist's placing an incorrect interpretation on some item of information pertinent to his problem. This mistake may then be projected into all of his subsequent reasoning. Bias may result in errors of selection, errors of interpretation, and errors of inference, all of which are important in scientific reasoning.

Errors in reasoning may be due to inaccurate judgments pertaining to the appropriateness and use of statistical and experimental techniques. A striking example of an error in experimental procedure was brought to the attention of one of the authors during the Second World War. In a government-sponsored project conducted by a reputable biochemist, large groups of individuals were exposed to the administration of certain vitamins. There was a small change observed in their visual efficiency subsequent to the use of the drugs; a result that was predicted and desired by the investigator. Whether the change was significant or not could be determined only by comparing the behavior of the tested subjects with that of a control group. For some unknown reason, in the design of the experiment no provision had been made for a control group; consequently, the findings had no general value. This was indeed a serious error in judgment.

Errors in reasoning may result from assigning incorrect meanings to words or from allowing the same word to carry more than one meaning during a series of logical deductions. The following familiar example from logic illustrates change in word meaning:

> Light is given off by the sun,
> Feathers are light,
> Therefore, feathers are given off by the sun.

Although the error is very obvious in this example, at times word-meaning changes occur that are not readily discernible and escape detection by the scientist.

Suggestions for Avoiding Errors in Reasoning. Certain rather immediate checks can be used by the scientist in detecting and removing errors in his reasoning. One is the formal check of logic. Much of the scientist's reasoning can be subjected to the formalized pattern of syllogistic reasoning. Having arranged his facts and arguments in the appropriate form, he can subject them to the rules of logic and thus learn if they fulfill the demands of correct reasoning.

Several other checks should be made routinely. The scientist should examine the nature of the assumptions that underlie his problem and note what bearing they have on the specific outcome that he anticipates from his study. He should carefully examine the relevance to his problem of the evidence already available. He should make certain that he has included all of the known facts in his own statement of the problem. Before being satisfied with his own interpretation of his findings, he should explore other possible hypotheses. Each of these checks will reduce his chances of making errors in his generalizations.

Errors due to bias are reduced by developing appropriate attitudes. For example, the scientist should exercise an impersonal point of view. His acceptance of any evidence should not depend upon its agreeing with his hypothesis. Again, the scientist should be tolerant of change. Stereotyped thinking is not scientific thinking, and it will not occur when the scientist develops an attitude to look for and accept change.

Errors of judgment are directly dependent upon the scientist's understanding in the area in which he is working. They are a function of his insightfulness and are reduced as his knowledge is increased. In all areas where his experience or knowledge is restricted or limited, the chances of error in judgment are increased. There is no substitute for wisdom in the area of the problem under study.

SELECTED READINGS

Black, M.: "Critical Thinking," 2d ed., chaps. 17 and 18, Prentice-Hall, Inc., 1952. Chapter 17 presents specimens of scientific method and discusses their relative strengths and weaknesses. Chapter 18 describes the nature of scientific observation and experiment and obstacles that are confronted in executing them.

Peirce, C. S.: Notes on a Scientific Philosophy, in D. J. Bronstein, Y. H. Krikorian, and P. P. Wiener (eds.), "Basic Problems of Philosophy," pp. 292–316, Prentice-Hall, Inc., 1947. This reference includes short papers on the following topics: laboratory and seminary philosophies, axioms, the observational part of philosophy, the first rule of reason, and fallibilism, continuity, and evolution. They present the reasoning of pragmatism in dealing with some of the fundamental propositions about nature that are faced by both the philosopher and the scientist.

Bronstein, D. J.: Introduction to chap. 5, Theory of Knowledge, *ibid.*, pp. 354–362. This is a brief introduction to the problems treated in the next four papers, in which different points of view concerning the nature of knowledge are given in articles by Berkeley, Hume, Santayana, and Woodbridge.

CHAPTER 3

The General Aims and Methods of Science

From our consideration of various characteristics of science, we gained some knowledge about its aims and methods. A more thorough treatment of these aspects is now in order.

The objective of the scientist is to understand the phenomenon with which he is working. He considers that he understands it when he can successfully predict its expressions under circumstances somewhat different from those used in studying it, or when his knowledge enables him to control its expressions to achieve certain ends.

FOUR FUNDAMENTAL QUESTIONS

The scientist asks himself four questions. In connection with any phenomenon he may query: Is it so? He is here concerned with the existence of the phenomenon, that is, whether or not what he has experienced has any degree of permanence. He wants to know if he can experience it repeatedly and if other observers can also experience it, or if the phenomenon is an illusion, a fantasy, or a delusion. A second and closely related question is: To what extent is it so? This requires an estimate of the magnitude, amount, frequency, or some other quantitative characteristic of the phenomenon. These two questions fall primarily in the province of description.

Having satisfied himself on these questions, the scientist then asks: Why is it so? He is now required to do some "speculating," to reason beyond the facts that he has collected; to get behind the facts, so to speak. Related to this third question is a further one, viz., What are the conditions that bring about the phenomenon? In certain respects, the answering of this question provides some of the necessary information for answering the third question; that is, to determine the conditions that bring about a phenomenon is to take a first step toward understanding why it is so. These last two questions fall primarily in the realm of explanation and theory.

UNDERSTANDING AS THE GENERAL AIM OF SCIENCE

Understanding and the Search for Truth. One of the most general statements of the aim of science is: to discover truth about natural events. To do this requires knowledge about the events, and this knowledge comes from the experiencing of the events. Experiencing natural phenomena gives the scientist his facts, and his aim is to discover, accumulate, and interpret facts and relationships among facts.

Facts about the natural universe are not isolated events but are patterned and related in diverse ways that in most instances are unknown to the scientist. Sometimes facts are initially experienced in ways that are meaningful, but most of the time the scientist's effort is expended in arranging the known facts in new patterns in an effort to discover unknown meanings and relationships. Through rational analysis he organizes the facts into more and more abstract and general systems. The end result is the formulation of general principles or laws under which all of the facts and relationships within some restricted domain of experience can be subsumed. The word understanding best expresses the end result of this "search for truth," and it expresses more accurately than any other word the general aim of all scientific work.

A Continuum of Understanding. Experience, knowledge, and understanding are closely related. They should be placed on a common continuum with experience at the beginning and understanding at the end. From experience we pass through knowledge on our way to attaining understanding. There are no sharp lines of demarcation between them. They are really three different points or levels on a common axis.

It is obvious that understanding is more than experiencing. Sometimes, having experienced a phenomenon on several occasions, an individual will declare that he understands it. He may be in error, and this type of error frequently occurs in everyday life. Mere repetition of the experience of an event does not necessarily result in an understanding of the event. We all can recall having experienced some phenomenon many times, and of knowing little more about it after the last experience than we knew after the first one. Most housewives do not understand electricity although they have used it in many ways over many years. Experience is a first step, and an important step, toward understanding—but it is not understanding.

Understanding is more than knowledge. Knowledge is a second step toward understanding. By manipulation of experience through the thought processes old meanings are reinterpreted and new meanings are discovered. The end result is knowledge. This knowledge is then further enlarged, organized, and systematized, and the end result is understanding. Knowledge, then, must be integrated and ordered before we have understanding.

The Continuous Expansion of Understanding. Understanding is characterized as continuously growing and expanding. At the beginning it waits upon experience and knowledge, but after it comes into being in its own right it does not remain static. Additional experiences and further knowledge increase understanding, so it is continuously evolving. Gaining understanding is a never-ending process, because with each increment of understanding further doubt arises, and this doubt, in turn, creates a need for more experience and knowledge. In some individuals, understanding begets complacency; in others, uncertainty. If we were forced to classify the scientist, we would, of course, place him among those whose understanding causes them continually to question the *status quo* and thus to seek further experience and knowledge.

PREDICTION AS AN AIM OF SCIENCE

The Meaning of Prediction. No scientist is content to stop after he has made a discovery, confirmed a hypothesis, or explained a complex phenomenon. He wants to make some use of his results. He therefore projects his generalizations to situations in which he believes they will hold; he makes predictions concerning the way the principles he develops will operate in new situations.

Suppose that in studying the intelligence of a class of eighth-grade children we learn that the brightest child obtains a score twice the amount of the lowest score achieved. Such a large discrepancy might lead us to conclude that the progress in school attainable by the children getting the highest and lowest scores would differ considerably if differences in intelligence were reflected in school achievement. We might predict that the brightest child could progress faster if given more work, or that the social adjustment of the dullest child would improve if he were not forced to compete with the brightest child. Thus on the basis of this present knowledge we are forecasting what would take place if we used this knowledge in a given specific way.

Prediction and Understanding. Prediction is based on understanding. Understanding forms the springboard from which prediction into the unknown is made. In turn, prediction contributes toward the further testing and verification of understanding. One check we can apply to our understanding of a phenomenon is the success with which we can use that understanding in new situations. If our prediction is unsuccessful, then our understanding of the phenomenon is to be questioned and challenged in reference to the particular predicted situation.

In the aforementioned example, our predictions concerning the improvement in the rate of progress of the brightest child or the improvement in social adjustment of the dullest child might turn out to be successful, thus verifying the application of our findings. We might then recommend the segregation of students in school in terms of their intelligence-test scores. We could make a broad prediction that the school progress and social adjustment of all children would be improved if they were allowed to work with children of their own intelligence level. Our prediction might then be found in error. The social adjustment of children might be more closely associated with their ages than with their intelligence-test scores. Equalizing the children in terms of intelligence would exaggerate differences in the ages of the children occupying the same classroom. If there were a very close relation between age and social adjustment, we would have to revise our notion about segregating all of the children in terms of their intelligence. Regardless of whether our prediction turned out to be correct or incorrect, the result of our prediction would have a direct effect upon our understanding of the problem involved.

Tentative Nature of a Prediction. The predicted situation always differs from the predictor situation. Sometimes the difference is small, as when a given situation is being duplicated with a minimum of change. For example, having determined the learning scores of rats in an alley maze, we might predict a similar distribution of scores for these rats on an elevated maze. Sometimes the difference is large, as when several factors are allowed to vary between the predictor and predicted situations. Having determined the distribution of scores of some rats on a brightness-discrimination problem, we might then destroy different parts of the visual areas of the brain and predict that the brightness-discrimination function would be lost. In this instance the brain damage may produce differences in health and differences in motivation as well as differences in learning ability, and consequently our prediction has more likelihood of failure than if only differences in learning ability were present.

Regardless of whether the difference between the predictor and predicted situations is large or small, in a prediction we set up a relationship which cannot be completely verified by a utilization of knowledge from the past. The unknown factors that are present force us to accept the prediction as only tentatively correct. Our confidence in the prediction will, of course, vary with the degree to which the predicted situation corresponds to the predictor situation. The wider the discrepancies between the two situations, the less confidence we shall have that the prediction will turn out successfully.

The Testing of Predictions. We must include a testing situation as part of prediction. A prediction that cannot be tested is of no value. It forever remains an unknown.

The test may be either rational or empirical in nature. In a rational test we may show, through reasoning, that the outcome of our particular explanation or theory ought to be of a certain kind or have particular characteristics. If our prediction concerns relationships that are only partially understood, we may be able, through reasoning, to increase this understanding by introducing into the relationships additional meanings that at first were thought to be irrelevant.

Suppose we are interested in explaining how we see color. We recall that there are two kinds of retinal structures, the rods and the cones, and that the latter are color-sensitive. We also know from our color-mixing experiments that the spectral colors can be obtained from variations in the mixture of three colors, viz., a certain red, a certain yellow, and a certain blue. Associating these facts together might lead us to the notion that there are three color-sensitive structures in the retina, one for each of these colors. We now can explain how we see color by stating that the light rays differentially activate one or more of these three color-sensitive structures in the retina. With this explanation we can now proceed to predict what might happen if there were radical changes in these structures. We might, for instance, predict that if a person were born without any one of them he would be color-blind to certain hues. Or again, if the color-sensitive structures were not evenly and uniformly distributed in the retina, a person might see certain hues and fail to see certain other hues in some given part of the visual field. We are pleased with our explanation because it enables us to give plausible predictions about other events in which we are interested.

Tests of the rational kind are one of the most valuable tools of the theoretical scientist. Although he may not be interested in knowing if his ideas have practical value in everyday-life situations, he nevertheless is concerned with any forward reference that his data, explanations, or theories may have. Consequently, he finds prediction a valuable aid in forecasting in "conceptual space" what can be expected from his ideas.

In an empirical test, the prediction is applied to conditions in the natural world. The relationships stipulated in the findings are projected to natural phenomena and these phenomena are then carefully observed to determine if these relationships occur according to the demands of the prediction.

Let us consider again the example of the predictive value of our explanation of how we see color. After having predicted that if people were born without one of these sensitive color processes in their retina they would be blind to certain particular colors, we could then explore the possibility that there are color-blind persons who fit our predicted descriptions. We would first describe (predict) the types of color blindness that would occur, depending on which color process or combinations of color processes were absent in the retina. For example, if the retina contained no red-sensitive process the person should not see red hues, or if all three sensitive processes were absent the person should be totally color-blind. Having calculated the various types of blindness, we would then study color-blind people and learn if their actual blindness corresponded to the blindness predicted by our color-vision explanation. If we found a relatively high correspondence, we would have empirical evidence supporting our explanation.

Eventually, all predictions should be brought to some kind of empirical test. Empirical conditions offer the most easily understood types of situation. They usually allow for the coincident observation of the phenomena by many individuals, and therefore increase the probability of reaching agreement among different investigators.

CONTROL AS AN AIM OF SCIENCE

The Meaning of Control. As an aim of science, control refers to the manipulation of the conditions determining a phenomenon in order to achieve some desired end. In utilizing present understanding to control the functioning of any factor, we are thus testing and verifying this understanding.

Ready examples of the use of control are to be found in the area of vocational guidance. Aptitude-test scores have been found to correlate rather highly with success in college. From this finding we can now exercise a more intelligent control over the admission of students to college training. We can advise an individual who has very low aptitude scores that he should not attempt college work. In such an instance we might save the person from many serious frustrations and direct his activities to areas where he would achieve marked success. We would be exercising control over his behavior, and the resulting achievement would serve to verify the understanding gained concerning the relation between aptitude-test scores and college success.

Control and Prediction. Control is a corollary aim to prediction. Actually, the two are inseparable when interpreted as general aims of science. To achieve any prediction, regardless of how simple it might be, some control of the determinants of the behavior is required. In the problem of predicting college success from aptitude-test scores, we have exercised control by permitting only certain kinds of behavior to be expressed, i.e., those behaviors that are elicited by the particular tests used. Likewise, regardless of the behavior we desire to control, there is always an uncertainty about the end result, so whether we consciously make a prediction or not the conditions characteristic of prediction are present. When we speak of the relationship between aptitude and college success in connection with the advice we give a high school graduate who is considering going to college, there is implied a predictive relation between the two types of variables.

Control and Application. Sometimes the term control is restricted to situations of a practical nature, such as the example of segregating school children in terms of their intelligence-test scores. This is a narrow interpretation of the term. Control serves equally well at the abstract and theoretical levels on which the "pure" scientist works. His task is to form inferences from his theory and to devise new conceptual situations to which the theory can be applied. He must logically show how an end result of a given kind can be produced by controlling the conceptual situations according to the implications of his theory. For example, the concept of control can be found throughout Einstein's theory of relativity, although what Einstein did can in no sense be construed to be control of practical situations.

THE EMPIRICAL AND RATIONAL PHASES OF SCIENCE

The scientist capitalizes on any type of approach that he thinks will enhance his chances of gaining knowledge. Some of these involve the direct manipulation of the natural phenomena he is studying, whereas some of them involve the use of the higher mental processes by which he thinks about these phenomena. There are then both empirical and rational phases, and the scientific method is an intelligent combination of these two types of procedures.

The Empirical Phases of Science. The meaning of empirical should not be restricted to the meaning of "that which is sensed." Experiences of natural phenomena are the first facts the scientist collects. The original experiences he gains in collecting the facts are of great significance because they are the "stock" with which he "sets up housekeeping."

In addition to the sensory experiences themselves, empirical refers to the techniques and procedures in which sensory experience plays an important role. Beyond the original observations, empirical features are to be found in all of the subsequent steps in which sensory experience is present. For example, the experimentalist, in the designing, constructing, and operating of apparatus, depends heavily upon empirical procedures. This is also true for various types of analysis of the data. Frequently the scientist reduces his data to graphic form and through the examination of diagrams, figures, and drawings he discovers many new meanings. These are empirical procedures.

Empirical facts are the point of origin of evidence. The scientist tests his ideas under natural conditions. These tests thus provide the means for confirming and justifying all of his work. They are the court of final appeal where he must be content to rest his case.

In the realm of the production of hunches, ideas, and hypotheses, empirical procedures by themselves are strictly limited in scope. Alone, raw sensory experience provides us with only a rather elemental type of meaning. Mere awareness of an object is very limited. We add little to knowledge if we terminate our activity at this point. The full import and significance of an experience results from various intellectual manipulations of the sensed data gained in the experience. Rational phases, then, are essential to higher-order meanings.

The Rational Phases of Science. Whether or not the facts of experience eventually add significantly to our knowledge depends upon the kind of rational manipulations we perform and the accuracy with which we perform these manipulations. We can study the data statistically or logically; we can analyze them into more elemental structures or combine them into complex patterns; we can note their similarities or their differences. These rational manipulations of sensory and inferential meanings are the "heart" processes of our descriptions, explanations, generalizations, and theories. Through these manipulations we learn about the relationships between other variables and the phenomena under study and the significance that these relationships have for future understanding.

The rational phases of the scientific method include all procedures in which higher-order meanings are involved and include such individual processes as memory, abstraction, inference, reasoning, generalization, judgment, and the like.

Certainly, as scientists, we must use rational procedures from the beginning of an investigation right through to the end. Science particularly requires rational processes in the setting up of the problem, in the analysis of the results, and in the interpretation of the findings.

The rational procedures of formal logic are a valuable part of the scientific method. As indicated earlier, scientists must practice "straight" or "sound" reasoning. Logic sets up patterns of reasoning for us to follow, patterns which, if followed, will lead us to what are considered logically correct conclusions. Logic aids in the accurate formulation of propositions so they can be evaluated against other possible alternatives. It enables us to state our postulates so their full implications can be developed through further reasoning. "Straight" thinking is required in every stage of a scientific inquiry, and therefore we should not depreciate or ignore a procedure that has as its fundamental purpose the description of the conditions for accurate thinking.

THE MAJOR METHODS OF SCIENCE

In an earlier discussion it was pointed out that science can be interpreted as a very general method composed of many important but less general procedures. Some of these procedures deserve separate treatment because they form the solid core of the scientific method. These major methods are symbolization, description, explanation, and theorizing.

SYMBOLIZATION AS A METHOD OF SCIENCE

The Meaning of Symbolizing. Symbolization has to do with translating experience into symbols. Experience is fleeting; it is here, then gone. There is little time for pondering its nature while its sensory components are still manifest. If we are to deal with an experience after its disappearance, some change caused by the experience must be carried over in time and must be of such a nature that it can be rearoused in memory and manipulated by means of various thought processes. This is accomplished through symbols or words. Experiences are given names. Every event, and every characteristic of every event, is given a symbol or word-tag by which it is known from that time forward. It is this word-tag that, so to speak, makes the experience "immortal."

Symbolization includes the assignment of names to objectively observed events, e.g., tables, rocks, houses; the assignment of names to subjective events, e.g., joys, pains, thoughts; and the assignment of words and other symbols to conceptual events created through the thought processes, e.g., infinity, purposes, theories, relativity.

Language is stressed in symbolization because it is the most widely used type of sign. It is not sufficient for all purposes, however, and an investigator may need to adopt or invent some other forms of symbolization. Two other systems of signs that are of great service are mathematics and symbolic logic.

The Characteristic of Correspondence in Symbolizing. The most important characteristic of symbolization concerns the degree of accuracy with which the symbols represent the facts they stand for. The objective in science is to develop symbols which can accurately substitute for the particular aspects of the events we want to represent; that is, to devise symbols that will faithfully signify the meanings of these events. It is important, then, that there be some form of correspondence between the world of events, on the one hand, and the system of symbols, on the other. An ideal arrangement is one in which there is a distinct symbol for each of the attributes, phases, qualities, aspects, elements, etc., that can be found in a given class of events. Actually we must be content with much less than this perfect "co-relationship."

Symbolizing in Science. We find that symbolization contributes to the scientist's work in two very significant ways; namely, (1) it makes possible a permanent record of experience, and (2) it furnishes a vehicle or mechanism for the rational manipulation of past experience.

By means of symbols, experiences are retained in varying degrees by the individual, so that through his memory he can later reproduce them for further examination and use. Experiences also are retained through written records. Both of these methods enable the scientist to call back again the meanings of a previous experience. He thus gains an unlimited number of opportunities to study the experience.

It will be recalled that the manipulation of symbols in thinking is one of the essential procedures in science. The scientist, by mentally manipulating the word that stands for an event, is doing the next best thing to manipulating the event itself. In fact, dealing with an event in thought by manipulating its word meanings is in some respects superior to manipulating the event as an experience. The actual experienced event occupies a single precise point in time and space; the recalled event does not, and can therefore be manipulated indefinitely without respect to temporal and spatial contexts.

The Demands to Be Met by Symbolization. It will help us to understand what we should expect from symbolization as a method in science if we briefly review three characteristics of natural phenomena that set the demands that must be met by a successful system of symbols.

The tremendous complexity of natural phenomena sets the most severe demand. There is no apparent limitation to the extent to which natural phenomena can be subdivided and differentiated. Each event studied, upon closer examination, is found to be composed of parts, and, similarly, each part is found to be composed of other parts, ad infinitum. Truly, on the face of it, we are here confronted with what we can call an infinite progression. To be successful, our system of symbolization must have unlimited possibilities in regard to the number of signs it can supply.

A second demand to be met by our system of symbols is referable to the characteristic of change. Never is the "same" event exactly the same. It is merely treated as constant in order to fulfill some particular purpose. Our system of symbols must be flexible enough to accommodate itself to changes in meanings occurring in time.

A third characteristic is summed up in the word relationship. Not only is an object found to be divisible into parts, and the object and its parts found to undergo continuous change, but the object and its subdivisions are found to be related in very complex ways with each other and with other objects and their subdivisions. For the want of exact knowledge and a more precise symbol, we shall use the word infinite to characterize both the number and diversity of the relationships that exist among natural phenomena. We must make our symbols accurately express the nature and degree of these relationships.

The Deficiency of Words as Symbols of Natural Phenomena. Keeping in mind the foregoing demands placed upon symbolization, let us consider the handicap under which we are working in trying to force natural phenomena into the system of signs called language—a system that we have poorly mastered even at best. We need not question the fact that language is one of the most valuable tools that man has invented, but there is need for questioning man's failure to make a more accurate use of the language he possesses. In meeting the demand for increased numbers of meanings, we have not exploited language to the fullest. We have been content to allow the same word to do double duty—actually, many times more than double duty. We also have been negligent in another way; we have assigned the same meaning to more than one word. Certainly, when we are in need of accurate representation of such a tremendous number of meanings, it is most inefficient to use the same word to stand for several meanings and to make several words function as representatives of the same meaning.

Language is deficient in representing changes in time. In many instances natural phenomena change faster than the words with which we describe them. Much of our language is still in the "horse-and-buggy" era. In fact, we persist in refusing to accept the innovations that crowd in upon us, and even ridicule the individual who dares to "coin" a new word.

Language, in the strict meaning of the term, is most deficient in regard to the symbolization of relationships. Here there is a severe limitation on the number of words that are available, so the scientist has had to look elsewhere to find a more exact and comprehensive system. This he has found in the symbolization of mathematics. Seldom does *a* scientist nowadays rely solely upon words for representing the relationships he wishes to describe. Numbers and their relationships are now a prime necessity in science.

Science has demonstrated through its use of mathematics and tabular and pictorial techniques that meanings can be represented with precision. It likewise has improved the precision of its descriptions through a more careful use of language as a vehicle for meanings. Some of this increased precision has come from the invention of new words, but much has been achieved through correct choice and use of familiar words. This is a step we all can take to achieve greater accuracy in our language. We are not expected to invent a new term every time we encounter difficulty in expression. It can be expected, however, that we shall exercise increasingly greater care in the selection of the words we use.

DESCRIPTION AS A METHOD OF SCIENCE

The Meaning of Description. As already noted, the function of symbolization is to assign word meanings to experiences of natural phenomena. But word meanings left as isolated events serve no useful purpose. Description is a systematic attempt to symbolize the obvious relationships that are found among the natural phenomena under study. By manipulating the name-tags, description creates a word picture of the orders that are readily observable among the phenomena. The term description, then, is usually applied to the ordering of natural events in ways that issue immediately and directly from the facts themselves. The organizations and relationships dealt with are of a simple nature. An important feature of the new meanings formed in description is that the characteristics and relationships evolved can be readily traced to sensory experiences and involve little or no abstraction from these experiences.

Description serves a bookkeeping function. At the time of the occurrence of an experience, there is never time for us to analyze it into its constituent determiners and to note all of the relationships it bears with other experiences. Through description, an account of the experience is put in a more or less permanent written form. With the written record available, we are able to examine the data at will. The written record does not consist merely of a listing of symbols; rather, the patterns and arrangements experienced in the data are recorded. It is then that description as a simple rational process comes into play.

Description as Classification. Classification has to do with the discovery of relatively stable associations among properties or characteristics and with the symbolizing of these associations. Classificatory schemes serve the purpose of organizing and grouping large numbers of facts into smaller numbers of divisions which then can be manipulated as units in further analyses. Events or processes that have the same characteristics are grouped together and these groups or categories are given names. Classes of familiar common objects are exemplified by ants, people, buildings, books, games, etc. The tendency is to make the classificatory categories as specific and precise as possible. Highly abstract classes which tend to go far beyond the empirical facts are not considered description. Some examples of these are categories of reason, n-dimensions of space, brain models, types of personality organizations, and the like.

The classification assigned a given event or process is to be considered as somewhat tentative in nature. Classificatory schemes gradually undergo change as more and more knowledge is gained about the events or processes being classified. What appears on first inspection to be a certain kind of property upon a more thorough examination may turn out to be quite a different kind of property.

Description as Seriating. A second form of description is called simple ordering or seriating. Seriating requires more knowledge about the events than does classification. It requires not only some common characteristic or feature in all of the events but that this characteristic or feature be known to exist in degrees or amounts, or be arrangeable on some form of continuum in a consistent way. If we are studying the reading ability of individuals then we can arrange our subjects in an order according to their speed of reading. The subjects are not only classified as being capable of reading, but are arranged in order on a continuum of reading speed. Another example, in which the ordering is of a little different kind, is the arrangement of geometric figures constructed from straight lines. We can arrange the following figures on a continuum in terms of the number of their sides: triangle, quadrangle, pentagon, hexagon, heptagon, and octagon. When the characteristic being described is a magnitude and is measurable, a basis is available for accurately determining differences between the objects or events and thus a more precise classification scheme can be developed.

Description as Correlation. A third application of description is called correlation. In examining a group of objects it is sometimes noted that two different characteristics are associated in such a way that when one is present the other is present and when one is absent the other is also absent. The two characteristics are said to occur concomitantly and such a relationship is referred to as correlation. As an example, the concomitant variation of eye color and hair color in man can be cited. In the case of individuals with blond hair, the eyes are more frequently light in color than dark, while the reverse of this tends to be true for individuals possessing brown or black hair.

Quantitative characteristics may also be found correlated, as in the relationship between the variables of height and weight. Such a correlation can be expressed in numerical terms, and thus its variation in degree or amount can be expressed quantitatively.

It will be noted that, in general, the correlation form of description goes somewhat beyond classification and seriating; that is, the facts are first classified and arranged in order of magnitude before an attempt is made to correlate them.

In the forms of description discussed above, it is to be remembered that the feature or characteristic used as a basis for classifying, seriating, or correlating must be discoverable in the facts or events themselves. What actually can be observed or what can be empirically demonstrated becomes the basis on which the description proceeds. No recourse is made to knowledge that lies beyond the events or to inferences or theories that transcend the knowledge gained directly from the events.

EXPLANATION AS A METHOD OF SCIENCE

The Meaning of Explanation. As already stated, one of the fundamental objectives of science is to find the reasons for the occurrence of events. The scarcity of facts may compel us to resort to higher-order conceptual meanings in order to account for the phenomena we are studying. In searching for the possible conditions giving rise to an event, we are trying to answer the question: Why is it so? Explanation is the fundamental method through which we discover the answer to this type of question.

Explanation proceeds to the discovery of higher-order meanings by means of the manipulation of concepts. Symbolization, then, is necessary for explanation. The sensed experiences and the meanings derived from them must be symbolically represented in verbal or other form and thus made available for mental manipulation.

Explanation involves abstraction. Conceptual meanings depend upon the process of abstraction. As we attempt to create new patterns and relationships among the facts, reasoning takes us further and further away from the factual meanings of description to meanings at higher and higher levels of abstraction and generalization. Meanings in the form of postulated entities, processes, or relations, which the scientist conceptually invents to account for his results, are called logical constructs.

At higher levels of abstraction, explanation becomes theorizing. When an explanation effects a pattern of logical constructs as a conceptual framework into which all the facts relevant to some phenomenon can be fitted, it is usually called a theory.

Let us again refer to the example of explaining how we see color. The three most important empirical meanings are that we see variations in color, that the retina of the eye is not structurally uniform but contains at least two structures, namely, the rods and cones, and that the cones are the sensitive structures responding when colors are seen. Explanation now enters in the postulation that there are three color-sensitive retinal structures, each sensitive to a different band of wave lengths. These three structures are not distinguishable in the retina and therefore are conceptual in nature. They are at least one step removed, through abstraction, from the observable structures of rods and cones. They are conceptually devised to supplement our knowledge about the responses of rods and cones. In attempting to learn about the various kinds of color blindness, we manipulate these conceptualized retinal structures. They are logical constructs that we use to push beyond the empirical facts that we now possess about color seeing.

Explanation and Description. There is general agreement that there is no sharp dividing line between description and explanation. Explanation begins where description leaves off. Both have the fundamental function of discovering the meanings of experienced events through the manipulation of symbols. The primary feature that distinguishes the two is the relative amount of conceptualizing involved. As already pointed out, the purpose of description is to discover the meanings that are observable in the sensed data themselves. The manipulation of the data is done in ways that issue directly from an observation of the facts available to experience. In explanation, the meanings are less observable in the data and are discovered through some process of mental manipulation of the data. The meanings derived at the descriptive level are further manipulated in explanation in an attempt to discover additional meanings. In our example of color vision, the empirical meanings about the functions of rods and cones were manipulated and gave rise to the postulation of three different retinal structures sensitive to color stimuli. The meanings of these three conceptual structures were then further manipulated to discover additional meanings about how we see colors.

Compared to the meanings of description, the meanings of explanation are more flexible, that is, they can be more easily changed to suit the purposes of the investigator. As a consequence, the meanings of explanation are more controversial. Procedures of mental manipulation are private to each thinker, and it is often difficult to get these manipulatory processes sufficiently similar in two or more individuals to achieve correspondence in the final meanings devised. In the experiencing of concepts, individuals do not see eye to eye as readily as in the experiencing of percepts.

Referring again to our example, the exact colors which presumably result from the activation of the three postulated retinal structures cannot be established to everyone's satisfaction. Different investigators postulate different structures because they use different criteria for defining them. One investigator may define the retinal structures in terms of the three colors which, through mixture, give only the spectral colors. Another may use as his criterion the three colors which, when mixed, give both spectral and nonspectral colors. In these two instances the three postulated color structures would not be exactly the same.

The meanings of explanation are subject to less control than the meanings of description. Being removed by several steps from the empirical facts, explanatory meanings also are further removed from the controlling influence of experience. This is apparent in the explanations of the chemical changes in the cone and rod responses. We know that in rod stimulation there is a bleaching of a substance called rhodopsin. In cone response we are not certain about the existence of a similar substance and therefore our explanations of cone response are more variable. Broad explanations of behavior, like the instinct hypothesis, are difficult to dislodge from the layman's thinking because they are far removed from the actual concrete facts known about behavior.

Compared to descriptive meanings, explanations are more tentative in nature. In general, an explanation contains so much meaning that is guessed that it must be accepted only as a possible truth. As it receives verification through logic and experience it can be expressed as a probable truth, and sometimes the degree of probability can be accurately stated, depending on the amount and accuracy of the empirical data available.

The Purposes Served by Explanation. Explanation is directed toward increasing our understanding of natural phenomena. It is like description in that it results in the formation of classificatory schemes into which sensed data may be meaningfully organized, but the schemes of explanation are not readily observable in the data and depend primarily upon the reasoning processes. Through manipulation of their conceptual meanings, explanation relates variables in terms of their less obvious features. It results in the discovery of the more subtle orders that characterize the relations among natural phenomena.

Explanation enables us to carry knowledge forward. Explanation reveals the gaps existing in our understanding and sets about to devise the necessary conditions that will bridge these gaps. Explanations built on past experiences make easier the understanding of present and future experiences. Knowledge from the past has to be put on trial. Through postulation, this knowledge is modified and formed into explanation, which then is subjected to empirical testing. Knowledge is then carried forward in time through explanation and is thus used in the gaining of further knowledge.

THEORIZING AS A METHOD OF SCIENCE

In his attempt to understand nature, man has never been content with merely gathering and ordering existential facts. He seems always to have a burning curiosity to discover some supposed "final explanation." An examination of the explanations that he has conjured up to account for his behavior will show that he has run the full gamut of the explanatory continuum, from the factual at one end to the highly imaginary at the other. What he has lacked in fact he has readily made up with fiction. The suppositions used by older generations seem a bit incredible to us today, but in our own ways we "moderns" continue to call upon little understood postulated entities or principles—pixies—to fill in the gaps of knowledge, thus giving the appearance that our intellectual armor is impervious.

Older Fallacious Theories of Behavior. One of the earlier explanations of the behavior of the feebleminded and insane is illustrative of the pre-scientific theories man has held. The early diagnosticians believed that a mentally deficient person was possessed of an evil spirit or of a good spirit, according to the nature of his behavior. If the diagnosis was of an evil spirit, all manner of exorcisms, magic rituals, physical punishments, and the like were practiced in an effort to banish the supposed demon. More fortunate was the person who was judged possessed of a saintly spirit, as he was considered a messenger of the Deity, and his every want was administered to by those who curried his favor.

Another example of this fallacious explanation of abnormal behavior is seen in the early New England conceptions of witchcraft. Hysterical symptoms in the form of anesthesias were declared to be of the devil and merited the harshest of treatment. Many persons displaying such symptoms were put to death by hanging.

Fairy tales are rich in the use of personified concepts as determiners of events. Giants, dwarfs, brownies, elves, goblins, and similar imaginary persons, who have all of the traits of human beings, are conjured up as explanatory devices to allay the questioning fears of children or to free the parent of the task of giving valid explanations to the thousand-and-one questions of his offspring.

Current Fallacious Theories of Behavior. Modern man has not freed himself of the use of imaginary entities in his attempts to account for his behavior. Modern pixies, however, are not always personified, and they are more abstract in nature. But they are still products of the imagination constructed to serve as ready answers for difficult questions, and often serve in the same uncritical way as did the pixies of earlier generations. For many individuals, these modern pixies satisfactorily account for behavior, and, after all, that is their function.

Fate is a modern pixy frequently used to explain behavior. If a person has come through several dangerous situations unscathed when others have been injured or killed, his good fortune is attributed to fate—it "just wasn't his time to go." *Lady Luck* is another explanation offered to account for the nature of results. If the individual has good fortune, Lady Luck is on his side; if he experiences ill fortune, then the "Good Lady" has forsaken him.

One of the current overworked pixies of uncritical psychological thinking is *human nature.* This concept has had wide application in the explanation of group behavior. For example, war is a form of social behavior that has never been adequately explained. It can readily be dismissed from the minds of some thinkers, however, by being attributed to human nature. *Instinct* is another tired, overworked old pixy. It seems that every type of behavior of which man is capable has at one time or another been attributed to instinct. *Heredity* and *environment* are always available as explanatory devices and are frequently called in to settle disputes about the determination of behavior. The *unconscious* is another modern pixy of questionable repute, seemingly charged with about every function that the human individual possesses.

We must recognize that these latter concepts are in use today, some of them playing a prominent role in current explanations of behavior. Thus the censor mechanism of psychoanalysis has become the "little man" who guards the portals to the dungeons of the unconscious. This pixy is most mortal in his behavior; and his frailties, so humanlike, explain in turn the behavior of the individual in which he dwells. To characterize concepts such as these as modern pixies is to bring into relief their uncritical use as end explanations of human response. It is to level criticism against those users of concepts who, when they announce that a given concept is applicable to some behavior, consider that thereby they have fully accounted for that behavior. We do not suggest that their concepts are entirely useless to psychology. Rather, we wish to indicate the need for clearer thinking with regard to the manner in which their concepts are formulated, interpreted, and used.

Scientific Pixies. A scientist devises theories to understand better that which he observes. He does not engage in theorizing merely to satisfy some intellectual curiosity. By the use of logical reasoning he deduces and formulates from present knowledge postulates through which common features and relationships or underlying principles and laws can be discovered, thereby rendering more understandable the phenomena he is investigating. He devises a rule that states the common conditions of a group of events, and then under this rule he subsumes the new event to be explained. This step of bringing forward knowledge in the form of hypotheses to be verified is an essential step in his program to discover truth. He makes progress because the insufficiency of old explanations stimulates him to evolve new hypotheses. These, in turn, lead to new modes of experiment and analysis and thus to the discovery of additional knowledge.

The thalamic theory of emotion is a good illustration of this procedure. The familiar association between physiological changes in the body and emotional experiences required explanation. If the physiological changes were to be accepted as components of emotion, then the widespread occurrence of these physiological changes in emotion had to be explained. Furthermore, what is called emotional control, by which is meant the simple fact that the individual can develop means for preventing impulsive, explosive, and intense emotional expressions, needed to be explained. In the thalamic theory the physiological changes are considered a bona fide part of the emotional experience. The thalamic region of the brain was postulated as a controlling center from which issued the nervous impulses that evoked the emotion. Impulses from the thalamus excite the sympathetic nervous system and through it elicit widespread bodily changes. The cortex of the brain was postulated as containing the higher centers through which the thalamic region was kept under control. The cortex of the brain is involved in the reasoning and evaluative processes by which emotion-provoking situations are assessed. Through these processes the thalamus is brought under control. Following the enunciation of this theory a large number of experiments were conducted that have greatly increased our knowledge concerning the nature of emotional responses.

Scientific Compared with Nonscientific Pixies. It is interesting to note that the pixies of the scientist and the nonscientist are alike in one point; namely, they are born of the imagination—they are beyond apprehension by the senses. By the process of assumption, these imaginary factors are assigned explanatory powers. The scientist postulates entities, structures, relations, mechanisms, and the like, which he cannot sense, that is, see, hear, or feel. He employs constructs that do not refer to things that are actually observable or that are representative duplications of former sensory experiences. These constructs refer to entities or relationships the existence of which he postulates in order to understand better the things that he actually observes. In a similar way, through his imagination, the nonscientific individual postulates his ghosts, spirits, elves, and gremlins.

More important for our consideration are the points on which the pixies of the scientist differ from those of the nonscientist. To begin with, scientific theories are not personified. They are not imaginary people, big or little, good or evil. They do not have the characteristics of people. They do not have desires, feelings, or intentions. They do not have to be placated as do the gods of primitive tribes.

Theories of science are not reified concepts. They do not come alive and act, working toward ends and accomplishing purposes. For example, in the hands of some psychoanalysts the concept of the unconscious has been reified. In their thinking it is no longer a simple rational idea that helps to explain man's behavior. It is described as if it were another person on the inside of the individual, a person with desires and ambitions at variance with those of the individual. Such an interpretation is not far removed from ghosts and demons.

Scientific theories stem from facts. Although a theory involves entities or constructs that are not observable, the propositions through which the theory was devised stem from facts. The scientist defines his theories very carefully, assigning them the characteristics that they have in order that they may explain the observed events. He is aware that they are products of his imagination which he projects into reality. The non-scientist is usually unaware of the linkages through which his pixies have evolved from empirical situations.

To the scientist, a theory is a tool of research. It is not an end in itself but a means to further understanding, a form of lever by means of which he can pry loose more facts. A theory to him is something to be tested. It provides various postulates, and from these postulates the scientist is able to devise theorems for empirical testing. If he is unable to devise testable theorems the theory is abandoned as unproductive. The pixies of the nonscientist are accepted uncritically; they are accepted without challenge. He does not feel the need of questioning them and sees no need of subjecting them to any analysis or test. They do not serve as useful tools because they do not lend themselves to investigation.

A scientific theory has a predictive character through which the scientist seeks to improve his control over new phenomena. The pixies of the non-scientist offer hindsight, not foresight. They are conjured up to account for past events and are used by the witch doctor and his modern counterparts as portents of the future. They are unpredictable. For example, the censor of the Freudian psychoanalyst has its own whims to satisfy and its "behavior" cannot be foreseen. Being unpredictable, such pixies offer no control over future events.

The scientist controls his theory. He keeps it subservient to his problems and purposes and makes it work for him. In many respects the pixies of the nonscientist control him much as the rabbit's foot controls the behavior of the superstitious person. They function to stifle and channelize thought, facilitating the acceptance of stereotypes, and discouraging the entertainment of new ideas.

SELECTED READINGS

Feigl, H.: Operationism and Scientific Method, in H. Feigl and W. Sellars (eds.), "Readings in Philosophical Analysis," pp. 498–509, Appleton-Century-Crofts, Inc., 1949. This article considers the problem of definition and argues that the meaning of "operational" should be confined to the definition of empirical concepts. Operationism is considered to be "a set of regulative or critical standards" that may be used in appraising the meaningfulness of scientific concepts.

Feigl, H.: Some Remarks on the Meaning of Scientific Explanation, *ibid.*, pp. 510–514. Description is restricted to "singular statements representing fully specific facts, events or situations." Explanation is defined as "a procedure of inference." Several levels of explanation are described.

Marx, M. H.: The General Nature of Theory Construction, in M. H. Marx (ed.), "Psychological Theory: Contemporary Readings," chap. 1, The Macmillan Company, 1951. The basic assumptions and elements of theory construction are discussed as these are found in the science of psychology. Both reductive and constructive types of explanations are considered.

CHAPTER 4

Functional Organization among Natural Phenomena

A knowledge of the functional relationships among variables is basic to man's understanding of nature. Particularly with the scientist does this concept of functional organization play a central role in the attack upon "unknowns." His task is to find and describe order in the world of natural phenomena. The consistent and stable functional relationships that he finds among events he calls laws of nature. These laws are descriptions of the sequences of events that he has found to recur regularly. Knowledge of these relationships enables him to predict the occurrences of new instances of such relationships and thus gives him a hold upon the future.

The utilization of functional relationships by both the layman and the scientist is predicated upon the postulate of the uniformity of nature. Our knowledge of the relational meanings of events gives us assurance that phenomena will continue to happen in an orderly fashion. Thus the concept of functional organization, generalized to all phenomena, is basic to man's every activity, and it is particularly important in the work of the scientist.

SOME FUNDAMENTAL RELATIONSHIPS

When we examine experience, we find many kinds and many degrees of relationships. We find relationships in space, including such meanings as adjacency, inside, outside, above, below, under, over, left, right, and other similar meanings. Relationships involving time include simultaneity, antecedent, consequent, sequentiality, regularity, and others. Additional relationships underlie the meanings we assign to various sensory attributes, such as quality, intensity, size, complexity. In the realm of thinking, concepts are related in a tremendous number of ways. Each of the following words refers to a relationship: logical, dependent, connect, union, equal, affiliated, ratio, comparable. There is a plethora of patterns, schemata, linkages, concatenations, transitions, etc., observable among event processes whether these are sensory experiences or rational experiences.

The terms *event process* and *event sequence* are used in order to place emphasis upon the dynamic or process characteristic of experience. The argument is that experiencing is a function, a process, an activity; and therefore what we call our experiences are not static cross sections of unrelated events but are ongoing events in dynamic relation. The word event can be substituted for these terms as long as an event is looked upon as an activity.

At any one instant we are aware of only a limited number of the relationships of a given event process. Purpose and interest dictate our attending to specific aspects or contexts and our disregarding those relationships of the event process that are not involved in our particular problem.

Temporal and Spatial Organization of Perceptions. Probably the most dominant organizational dimension we experience is that of time. All of our perceptions of objects are temporally related in some way or another. Several event processes may be perceived simultaneously or as one following another in a sequence. The experiences of the past, when represented in the present through memory, make possible a comparison of past and present. Furthermore, the perceived sequences noted in the present arouse expectations of their continuance or of their recurrence. Thus we extend the time meaning forward and experience the idea of the future. The meanings of time and of duration are then readily induced from our experiences of event relationships. These common psychological experiences of past, present, and future can be accepted as facts regardless of the particular way in which we might wish to define time.

Event processes are also experienced as related in space. Almost as soon as we are able to respond to an object we experience that object as occupying space and being in relation with other objects in both its immediate and remote environs.

These characteristics of time and space are two of the most important relationships with which we as scientists must deal. In order to accomplish any given end we must arrange in relation in both time and space those events that we think determine the end event we are pursuing. We must deal with event processes that are both prior to and current with the desired event process, and that are both juxtaposed to and spatially remote from this event process.

Organization among Concepts. Both layman and scientist inquire and reflect about the characteristics of experience and devise relationships among conceptual categories in order to make nature more intelligible. Concepts arise from the meanings of previous perceptions. By a process of abstraction we develop meanings that are not tied to the concrete reference points in space and time that bind our perceptions to the here and now. Conceptual meanings are then freed from the perceptual events that gave them birth, and through reasoning they are combined and recombined in all the diverse relational ways that human imagination can conceive.

A homely illustration will help to make clear this process of conceptualization. Let us consider the concept of "dog." In perception we experience many dogs, all of which are in some way tied to concrete temporal and spatial environments, and each of which has definite characteristics of shape, size, color, speed, noise, usefulness, and other traits. In thought, however, we can respond with meanings that are not referred to a given dog occupying a specific space at a given time and with a given set of characteristics. We can talk about just large dogs, or just short-haired dogs, or just those dogs we saw last week at the dog show, or just the dogs that we intend sometime to buy for hunting. In various ways we can abstract "dog meanings" from the specific perceptual relationships within which they were first experienced. Having abstracted these meanings, we can then proceed to recombine them in many new and different relationships.

Man has conceptualized a tremendous number of meanings, and he has arranged each of these meanings in a vast number of relationships. It is difficult to comprehend the number and complexity of the organizations among concepts that are now available to him. Suffice it to state that the activity of organizing conceptual experiences is a continuing one, and that one of the primary contributions of science is the enlargement of the organizational structure of man's concepts about nature.

The Causal Type of Relationship. One of the most significant relationships developed and used by man is the cause-and-effect sequence. It occupies a predominant position among organizing principles because of the important role it plays in practical experience. For most people it is basic to explanation, a description of the causes of an event being accepted as a valid and complete explanation.

Although the concept of causality is one of the most pervasive principles of organization, there is not complete agreement concerning its meaning. Over the years there has been an uncritical acceptance of it by the layman. Among philosophers and scientists it has been the center of continuous controversy. There is a theory of cause for every school of philosophy, and apparently no common ground has been advanced by which the diversity of viewpoints can be reconciled. The scientist has found that most of the meanings assigned the concept are unresolvable in terms of empirical observation. He has, therefore, redefined the concept in terms of observable phenomena and is leaving the resolution of the older meanings to his philosopher friends.

INTERPRETATIONS OF THE CONCEPT OF CAUSALITY

In the following pages, some of the more widely used meanings of causality are presented. It is important that we understand how these meanings are supported by evidence. Certainly, the scientist should champion any meaning confirmed by empirical findings. These are the meanings that will be useful in his attempt to discover and describe further orderly relationships among natural phenomena. The three major interpretations of the causal sequence are the animistic, the mechanistic, and the correlational.

The Animistic Interpretation of Cause. The animistic interpretation is expressed in the statement "All things are full of gods." The ancients ascribed to their gods the responsibility for the changes they observed in the world around them. The gods were the creators and the producers of events. They behaved as agents. Acting as the cause, the agent produced the effect. In later time agents took on other forms, such as elves, goblins, spirits, demons, werewolves, and the like.

This primitive animistic interpretation of cause has almost disappeared from scientific writings. To some extent it is still found in the literature of psychiatry and psychoanalysis, two disciplines concerned with the treatment and cure of abnormal forms of behavior. Following is a representative description from psychoanalytic literature.[1] It purports to explain the causes for the mental ill-health of a young lady.

To make ourselves more explicit, it will be necessary to say something about the elements of the psychic apparatus. According to Freud's formulation the child brings into the world an unorganized chaotic mentality called the id, the sole aim of which is the gratification of all needs, the alleviation of hunger, self-preservation, and love, the preservation of the species. However, as the child grows older, that part of the id which comes in contact with the environment through the senses learns to know the inexorable reality of the outer world and becomes modified into what Freud calls the ego. This ego, possessing awareness of the environment, henceforth strives to curb the lawless id tendencies whenever they attempt to assert themselves incompatibly. The neurosis, as we see it here, was, therefore, a conflict between the ego and the id. The ego, aware of the forces of civilization, religion and ethics, refused to allow motor discharge to the powerful sexual impulses emanating from the lawless id, and thus blocked them from attainment of the object towards which they aimed. The ego then defended itself against these impulses by repressing them. The young lady in question seemingly forgot this whole episode. Had the repression continued unabated, she would have remained healthy. But the repressed material struggled against this fate, finally broke through (as a

[1] A. A. Brill, "The Basic Writings of Sigmund Freud," p. 12, The Modern Library, Random House, Inc., 1938.

substitutive formation on paths over which the ego had no control), and obtruded itself on the ego as symptoms. As a result of this process, the ego found itself more or less impoverished, its integrity was threatened and hurt, and hence it continued to combat the symptom in the same way as it had defended itself against the original id impulses.

It is obvious that in this description the "id" and the "ego" do not remain as concepts descriptive of empirical events. They are mystical entities performing as personalities, clothed with awareness, wishes, strivings, repressions, and the like. Reified in this manner, they do not greatly differ from the animistic concepts of primitive people.

The Mechanistic Concept of Cause. As the name implies, this interpretation reduces the cause-and-effect sequence to a mechanical system. Objects and events are tied together in a mechanical relationship wherein forces are transmitted from the beginning, the cause, to the end, the effect. Knowing the objects, relations, and forces, it is possible to reconstitute the antecedent conditions and thus produce the same end results. For example, if several bricks are set on end in a row with the distance between adjacent bricks being less than a brick's length, then if one of the end bricks is toppled over toward the next adjacent one, the whole row of bricks will be made to fall.

It is not difficult to understand why force became an important aspect of the mechanistic interpretation of causality. In the field of common work, where the individual is required to exert force in lifting, pushing, pulling, jerking, and the like, he identifies force with his own feelings of exertion. Seeing similar work performed by machines, he readily transfers the concept of force to the machines concerned. Thus the cause of the acceleration of one body is ascribed to the force transmitted to it from another body. In the study of levers, gears, pulleys, and the like, we are concerned with the amount of force that can be transmitted from one point to another. Here there is a physical medium extending from the cause to the effect. In the field of light, where no visible medium is found, the ether is postulated as the means by which the energy change can be transmitted from the sun to the earth. This postulate resulted from the mechanical notion that there must be some intervening medium through which the sun's influence, as a force, can be transmitted.

Seventeenth- and eighteenth-century physical science championed mechanistic causality. The relationships among events were interpreted in terms of mechanical models. Accordingly, transmission of an impersonal physical force is a necessary condition for a cause-and-effect relation between two events. The mechanistic concept also includes the meaning of production or generation. The cause produces or generates the effect.

For some scientists, then, nature's ways are mechanical and are to be explained in mechanistic terms. Causality is interpreted mechanistically.

The Correlational Concept of Cause. *The Meaning of the Concept.* This interpretation of the causal concept was developed by scientists of the nineteenth and twentieth centuries. Science developed as an empirical study of nature, and the scientist directed his attention to characteristics that were observable. He devised various concepts by which he could classify these characteristics in terms of their similarities, coexistences, and sequential relationships. He sought the causes for a given event process in the associated occurrences of other event processes. The concept of causality was then applied to the concomitant variations observed to occur among event processes. It became identified with correlation.

True to his empirical approach, the scientist refers all of his meanings to the experienced phenomena from which they are derived. This he did with the meanings of causality. He considered it futile to speak of causality at a general level without being able to refer its meanings to empirical events. Correlational relations among variables were the only observable relationships he could find for justifying causal meanings.

Correlations without a Temporal Sequence. The nature of a phenomenon is exhibited in, and consists of, the correlational relations that this phenomenon has with other phenomena. This viewpoint includes relations as sequences or as temporal organizations, but it also includes relationships that do not exhibit the sequential characteristic. For example, the physicist has worked out the relationships among current strength, electromotive force, and resistance so that if the values of any two of these variables are given, the value of the third can be determined. In such an example, the idea of the variables being in a temporal sequence is of little consequence. The correlational point of view allows for causal relations between events that exhibit no sequential arrangement.

Correlation and the Concepts of Production and Force. Although the ideas of production and force were essential in the mechanistic interpretation of causality, they are not important in the correlational interpretation. These concepts are considered as inferences the empirical equivalents of which cannot be observed among natural phenomena. Correlational relationships do not manifest some peculiar power under which nature is compelled to follow a set form in which the cause is the generator of the effect. So-called causal relationships are simply descriptions of the ways in which nature is observed to be ordered. Event processes are observed to be related, and these relations can be adequately represented or expressed in the form of correlations.

EXAMINATION OF THE CAUSAL CONCEPT IN TERMS OF THE DATA OF EXPERIENCE

That we can manipulate event sequences in order to attain certain ends is a fact that cannot be controverted. Disagreement and controversy arise, however, concerning the way in which the manipulation of certain given factors brings about a desired end in some other factors. The question is: How does one event sequence influence another? We have presented three general interpretations purporting to answer this question. Most laymen accept the mechanistic viewpoint, but there are an appreciable number of them who still utilize causal concepts in a way that is reminiscent of the older animistic interpretations. The correlational point of view appeals to most scientists, although, again, many scientists use causal concepts in the mechanistic sense. With disagreement still prevalent among reputable scientists, an appeal to the actual facts of experience will help us evaluate the concepts now in dispute.

The Concept of Continuity. *The Concept of a Necessary Connection between Events.* The traditional mechanistic point of view concerning cause and effect refers to events as being separate entities bound together through the principle of causality. There is a necessary connection between the causal entity and the effectual entity. An event is produced by having a necessary connection with some other event, the two events forming a temporal sequence. Such common phrases as "the cause is the necessary condition for the effect," "the effect is always dependent for its occurrence upon the cause," and "the cause always precedes the effect," reflect this meaning of necessary connection.

Causality expresses this intimate connection between the two events of a causal sequence. Theories of causality are concerned with explaining the nature of this connection. As we have noted in earlier discussions, some of the more common meanings given this tie between cause and effect are creation, production, generation, and transmission of force.

Continuity as Found in Primary Experience. When we examine primary experience, we do not observe events as entities. We do not observe concatenations of events. Rather, we observe a continuous flow of event processes. Relatedness and organization are the warp and woof of experience. Our first experience is not of separate entities which we then relate with one another by superimposing some kind of continuity "glue" which binds them together. Continuity is not a fiction imposed from without; it is the essence of primary experience itself.

Any sharp separation in time between event processes is introduced through our own reflective analysis. We gain knowledge of the relations between events by a process of abstracting the events from a continuum of experiences. We then react to these artificially abstracted phases of a continuous process as if they are observable static occurrences. Actually, a given event process flows gradually from its predecessors and, in turn, it melts gradually into the event processes which follow it.

With event sequences dynamically interrelated in primary experience, there is no problem of tying events together by causality. We are not dealing with static events that we must "glue" together with some mysterious "causal tie." The problem of how a causal event brings about its effectual event is not a valid problem. It is not necessary, then, to explain the meanings of such concepts as production, generation, and transmission of force, which are advocated to account for this fictitious tie by which an effect is bound to its cause.

Generalizing the Concept of Causality. *The Principle of Causality.* This principle is inferred from the relationships observed among specific event sequences. It stipulates that causal laws are applicable to all natural phenomena. We learn from experience that when certain conditions are present, certain events occur. From this finding, we incorrectly generalize that whenever these prior conditions are present the particular events "must" follow. Sometimes the phrase "will always" is substituted for the word "must." One terse way in which this generalization is frequently stated is: Same cause, same effect. If, as in the mechanistic interpretation, the cause generates or enforces the effect, then in order to be consistent we must conclude that a given cause must always give rise to the same effect.

Although repetition of the same sequences of events is basic to the establishment of this generalization, mere regularity in the occurrences of the sequences does not express the full meaning intended by the principle. Regularity is interpreted as a sign of some more fundamental connection or intimacy that exists between a cause and its effect. This intimacy is referred to as a characteristic of the causal event, but it is abstracted from the specific temporal and spatial characteristics of the event and generalized to all future occurrences of the event. Thus, having determined the cause of a particular event, we conclude that we have discovered a fundamental and intimate connection that will hold true for the entire class of events of which our specific event is a member. Our generalization then carries the certainty of this connection to all future occurrences of events of this class.

Generalizing Relationships from Primary Experience. Let us again examine primary experience and seek empirical evidence for generalizing the causal concept. From practical experience we learn to expect the recurrence in the future of the patterns and relations we have discovered among event processes. We readily learn that certain actions need to be performed in order to accomplish certain ends. Experiences are carried over from the past and duplicated in the present. Memory elicits in us anticipations concerning the future. We count on the patterns of past events occurring again and operating in the future as we have known them to operate in the past. We do not expect exact duplications of these events in all of their spatial and temporal relationships, but experience gives us considerable assurance that for many events we can often achieve close approximations to many of their temporal, spatial, and other relationships.

We may say that given certain antecedent organizations of event processes we may expect the occurrence of certain consequent event processes. This is not to say that, given similar situations, similar consequences "must" or "will" follow. Rather, it means that within given similar situations we can expect to find similar event processes related in similar ways. What we observe when we closely examine a so-called cause-and-effect sequence is regularity of occurrence. This is the only empirical meaning that we can find. Thus, we are dealing with complexes of event processes manifesting definite dynamic relationships which are found to recur frequently in nature.

Our generalizations for the future are based on the anticipation of the continuance of the regularities already discovered. This means that if the same regularities in the dynamic relations among certain event processes can be reconstituted in some other place at some other time, we can expect the course of certain other event processes to be the same. We have here a dynamic relationship that has been abstracted from its spatial and temporal settings. This generalization seems to be the only one we can justify from the knowledge we derive from primary experience.

The Separation of Scientific and Philosophical Problems. In the foregoing discussions of the concept of causality, it was noted that radical differences exist between the mechanistic view championed by earlier scientists and the correlational view championed by scientists today. These differences developed parallel with the growth of the empirical phases of science and the relinquishing of philosophical problems which occupied so much of the attention of the earlier scientists.

The problem of the nature of causality is a philosophical problem. The philosopher asks such questions as: What is existence? What is an event? What is space? What is time? These questions deal with the concepts which form the framework within which any principle of causality must develop. The meaning of the phrase "because of" must wait upon a resolution of the meanings of these basic concepts of the framework. Of course, in the meantime, no philosopher denies that events are determined, and that by using the relations we find among event processes we can explain and predict natural phenomena.

The use of the concept of causality by the scientist must involve the particulars of his empirical studies. The scientist is interested in describing nature through observation. He seeks the solution to pragmatic questions through empirical studies and experiments. The beginning and end of science are found in the observable relationships among phenomena. Through his studies, he seeks knowledge that directly or indirectly helps to predict the occurrence of a given event process through the manipulation of antecedent and coexistent event processes related to it. What the philosopher calls the "real" meaning or the "ultimate basis" of causality is not of primary concern to the scientist.

SOME MEANINGS OF FUNCTIONAL RELATIONSHIPS

A Definition of Functional Relationship. Let us begin with a general definition of a functional relationship and wait for later sections for an explanation of the detailed meanings. A functional relationship is a relationship among given event processes expressible as a mathematical proposition that provides the basis for a prediction of subsequent instances of the relationship. Any event process occurs in relation with many other event processes, and it is through these relationships that we are able to assign meanings to the particular event process that we are endeavoring to understand. These relationships are dynamic, not static. They form the larger organization of event sequences wherein we can observe the genetic history of the given event process.

Functional Relationships Rest on the Uniformity of Nature. The use that can be made of any functional relationship rests primarily on its application to subsequent situations. Correlations between event processes hold not only for the relational sequences that have been observed but are presumed to hold as well for relational sequences yet to be observed. Correlations evolved in past experience gain in value in proportion to the extent to which they provide us with means for dealing with future situations. As scientists, we are forced to accept the fundamental postulate of the uniformity of natural processes upon which these expectations rest. An overwhelming amount of our experience leads us to believe that the universe is not ruled by caprice, but that all events are relational in nature. We must count on functional relationships operating in the future much as we have found them to operate in the past. We must trust that the organization and categorical relations we discover are enduring characteristics of the event processes of nature.

The Functional Interpretation and the Concept of Cause. *Some Similarities and Differences.* Both functional relationships and so-called causal sequences are founded on the postulate of a determinate nature. In each instance, the concept has been induced from observations of the regularity of temporal sequences between event processes. In the use of the concept of causality man has imposed a special kind of order upon nature, as shown by such statements as "Every cause has its effect," and "Given the same cause, the same effect must occur." Accordingly, nature "must" or "will" follow a certain prescribed pattern of organization.

The functional interpretation differs from causality in that it quantitatively describes the relationships observed and applies the particular function discovered to—but does not impose it upon—subsequent natural processes. The function is interpreted as merely describing how event processes might be related in the future if and when they occur again. The functional interpretation emphasizes the need of checking any given relationship to determine if and how it will occur in the future.

Let us contrast the two interpretations through an example. We know that there is a rather high relationship between reading ability and college grade-point average. This could be interpreted to mean that reading ability is the cause of college grade points, and that whenever the reading ability is high the college grade-point average must be high and whenever the reading ability is low the grade-point average must be low. According to the functional interpretation, the correlation indicates a high statistical probability that a high reading ability will be associated with a high grade-point average, but it does not require that this always be true. Rather, it invites the use of this correlational function in empirical situations to determine just what degree of confidence can be placed in it as a predictive tool.

The Meaning of Dependency in Functional Relationships. Many scientists have rejected the concept of cause because they have failed to discover any empirical meanings by which agreement can be reached on the significance of the concept. In its place they have substituted the terms *dependent* and *determined*. Scientific experiments demonstrate that the occurrence of a given variable depends upon certain other variables; that certain specific occurrences are determinned by certain experimental conditions.

Using these terms appears to be merely substituting the words dependent or determined for the term cause. This, however, is not the case. The meaning of dependent and determined stems directly from the empirical relationships in which a particular event process is found. The scientist expects that the temporal sequences discovered for a given event process will recur. If he can set up the earlier event processes in a given sequence he expects that the later event processes will occur. The dependency of one process upon another merely refers to an empirically described sequence of processes; an organization of interrelated processes in which the particular event process being studied occurs late in the series.

The empirical meanings to be given to the terms dependent and determined are the meanings of predictable and calculable. The scientist is willing to say that a given event process depends upon or is determined by other processes if he can successfully predict the occurrence of this process from his knowledge of its relationships with the others. He describes those conditions among the other processes that must be met in order to expect the occurrence of the given event process. The meaning of calculable is similar to that of predictable. The scientist is willing to say that B is dependent on or is determined by A if through his functional equation he can calculate the value of B when given a certain value of A. Functional equations will be discussed in later sections.

Functional and Nonfunctional Relationships. *Contextual Relationships.* Any given event process which we desire to study will be related with many other event processes. It will be found functioning in a context of interacting variables in which the relationships will be both varied and intricate. We shall find many of these relationships of little consequence. Those of greatest concern will be the relationships bearing directly on the special problem we are endeavoring to solve. To control and predict our event process requires the manipulation of many other related variables. We shall find it difficult to isolate simple sequences of event processes for experimentation.

Nonfunctional Relationships. For a given event process, some of the relationships in which it occurs will be found to be nonfunctional in nature; that is, they can be classified as nondependent or nondeterminate. We must be able to distinguish functional relationships from nonfunctional ones. This is done by the use of the "rule of exceptions." If in a relationship A → B, B frequently occurs when we have evidence that A has not occurred, or if A frequently occurs without being followed by B, the relationship would be suspected of being nondeterminate.

There is an additional check we can make. Through rational comparisons we can discover incongruities or discrepancies in the nature of the event sequences being related which will lead us to regard them as nonfunctional. For example, night following day is a temporal sequence without exception, at least in areas distant from the poles of the earth. We do not, however, consider this sequence a functional relationship. The darkness of night is a function of certain particular relationships between the earth and the sun, but it is not a function of the day that precedes it.

The Certainty of Functional Determination. Successful prediction rests upon duplicating the past in the future. This duplication, in turn, is a function of the accuracy with which we are able to describe the determinants of the event process being predicted. In neither of these activities are we likely to be completely successful. Only if the event process is extremely simple can we successfully describe most of its determinants.

Having accomplished this, we can never be assured that the future will not present variations from the special conditions upon which our prediction rests.

When event sequences are not simple in nature, we must be reconciled to error, both in our description of the determinants and in our prediction of the future functioning of these determinants. The meanings of functional relationships are established in empirical situations and are subject to the changes that these empirical situations may undergo. We are always in the process of making them more and more precise, but never can we make them completely stable. It follows that our strength of belief in the validity of a function, even when it is supported by dramatic verifications, should not prevent us from anticipating possible changes that would invalidate the function.

The Empirical Verification of Functional Relationships. The dependability and predictive effectiveness of a functional relationship is known as its precision. In the process of verification, the scientist learns how dependable the functional relationship is and how accurately it can be expected to predict under a variable set of conditions.

From his analyses of the empirical data, the scientist determines the particular function that best expresses the relationship between the event processes studied. He may also devise a mathematical formula for expressing the relationship. He will not, however, be content with having merely discovered and mathematically stated the function but will use the function to predict the type of relationships that are expected to occur among subsequent event processes under the set of conditions stipulated by the function. The scientist will then set up the necessary conditions and proceed to verify this prediction by applying the function to data that were not used in the original determination of the function.

After several tests of this kind, if the predictions are successful, he states the function in the form of a natural law. This law can then be applied in all future situations that are expected to duplicate the conditions demanded by the function. Like the function, this law is not considered "absolutely" valid. In science, there is no way of "proving" that a function is valid in any given instance except by actually trying it out in that instance. This is not a severe handicap to the scientist, however, as long as he is able to discover and describe situations for which the probability is high that the given function will predict successfully. Continued application of the function to new situations makes it possible to describe with continually increasing accuracy the particular set of conditions upon which the successful use of the functional relationship is predicated. In this way the scientist may eventually achieve a high level of precision in his predictions.

THE QUANTITATIVE NATURE OF FUNCTIONAL RELATIONSHIPS

The most accurate description is attained when the different amounts of expression of a variable are represented by means of numbers. Functional relationships involve the changes in amount of one variable associated with the changes in amount of one or more other variables. A functional relationship is quantitatively described when it is expressed as the correlation between the amounts of the associated variables.

The Use of Mathematical Equations. Describing variables by means of numbers makes possible the use of mathematical equations for representing functional relationships. Such equations are of particular service to the scientist because they can be used to describe both the kind and the amount of the relationship. Despite the tremendous variety of functional relationships discovered among natural events, it is possible to devise a mathematical formula for representing every type of relationship. Two general classes of relation are the rectilinear and the curvilinear. In the first the function can be represented by a straight line, in the second by some type of curved line. In psychology, the relation between abilities, such as between arithmetic and reasoning abilities, is usually rectilinear. This means that for a given increase in value of one of the variables there is found to occur an increase of a constant amount in the other variable. The relation between improvement and practice is usually curvilinear, e.g., the learning curve for poetry. In the learning situation, a given increase in value of the practice variable is associated with decreasing amounts of increase in the achievement variable.

In addition to depicting the kind of relationship, a mathematical equation also expresses the extent or amount of the relationship. For example, there is a higher degree of relationship between the ability to add and the ability to multiply than there is between the ability to add and the ability to reason. If we quantified each relationship by means of some index like the coefficient of correlation, thus expressing the degree of relationship between each pair of variables, we would find the index between the ability to add and the ability to multiply to have a higher value than the index between the ability to add and the ability to reason.

The Close Relationship between Mathematical Theory and Empirical Knowledge. Science does not tolerate a substitution of theory for the facts of experience. Either the theory expresses meanings that are applicable to event processes in nature or it merely expresses the relationships of the symbols which comprise it. If the latter, then the theory is sterile as a procedural tool of science.

In expressing functional relationships in the form of abstract mathematical equations, it is important that the meanings of these equations and any statistical manipulation we perform on them be continually referred back to the natural event processes from which the equations originally were derived. To be useful, the meanings of any formal set of numerical propositions must be applicable to the corresponding sequence of determinant event processes. There is nothing inherent in the logic of mathematics, however, that enables us to determine the applicability of a mathematical or numerical meaning to a natural process. The possibility always exists that the mathematical operations we use on our numbers are not applicable to the empirical facts. The meanings derived from an equation are then not necessarily assignable to the event processes under study.

Mathematical equations have been demonstrated to have great power for discovering new meanings for the sciences. The mathematical manipulation of quantities affords us a tremendous leverage over "the unknown" because of the very abstract nature of numerical symbols. The fact that we cannot compel empirical processes to jump through the hoop of the calculus does not mean that this mathematical tool is useless for deriving meanings for our functional relationships. It is necessary, however, once we have derived meanings from a mathematical equation, to justify the application of these meanings to the empirical determinant processes to which we desire to assign them.

Mathematical Equations and Scientific Laws. Mathematical equations make possible the most accurate statement of scientific laws. A scientific law is a functional relationship that has high predictive value in a wide variety of situations. Such laws have their beginning in empirically observed relationships among natural event processes. To be usable under a variety of conditions, a functional relationship must be abstracted from many of the specific contexts in which it occurs. By repeated testing of the function under a variety of conditions, it is possible to learn in what way and to what degree the function can be described without reference to particular specific conditions. Gradually, the function can be generalized into a law. This law merely refers to the statistical regularity of the functional relationship. Mathematical equations are particularly appropriate for representing a generalized functional relationship because mathematical symbols can be assigned whatever meanings are required to represent the function at that level of generality where it will have high predictive value.

THE STUDY OF FUNCTIONAL RELATIONSHIPS IN BEHAVIOR

The Complexity of Psychological Determinants. The most consistent characteristic of human behavior is the complexity of its determinants. We must think of every behavior sequence as stemming from many determinants. Some of these initiate their influence at the time of the conception of the individual, others come into play just prior to the occurrence of the observed behavior, while numerous others arise in between these two extremes on the time axis. Behavioral processes do not function independently but ineract with each other in many intricate and complex ways. Combinations of determinants act over various intervals: sometimes forming genetic series occupying hours, days, months, or years; at other times acting for merely a second or as a simultaneous flash occurrence.

Some determinants of behavior are little understood at present, and the names applied to them are lacking in empirical significance. Others, however, are accurately described and the nature of their contribution is fairly well understood.

There is little justification for oversimplifying our conception of the determination of human behavior. Seldom can a behavior process be completely represented as a simple response unit; nor can the determinant conditions be adequately analyzed into simple stimulus situations. The psychologist can muster little confidence in the logical reduction of behavior determinants to a state of abstracted simplification expressed in the form of simple stimulus-response sequences.

Narrowing the Area of Functional Relationships in a Study. One of the first steps we take in studying particular behavior processes is to discover the area of functional relationships in which we think the processes can be found. As we have previously learned, no process is ever found in isolation; it is always discovered intricately interwoven with a large number of other processes. Primary experience consists of sequences, systems, totalities, and organizations of processes. From among these multifarious spatial and temporal contextual relationships we must discover those that are pertinent to the behavior process we wish to understand.

We seek the determinants of a given behavior process among the many interrelationships that it exhibits with other behavior processes. To be able to predict the process accurately we must understand its relationships and be able to reconstruct these relationships. The contribution of any one of these relationships as a determinant will be conditioned by many factors. The question of just how many relationships must be reconstructed and just which ones of the many relationships will be required must be discovered by empirical investigations.

One factor that will restrict the area of relationships needing investigation is the nature of the problem being studied. We can disregard those relationships that seem not to come within the general purview of the problem. This, however, may not place sufficiently narrow limits on the known relationships to make an empirical analysis feasible. Additional limitation of the field for empirical investigation can be achieved by carefully examining the nature of the relationships and selecting only those sequences in which, from the standpoint of logic, there seems to be a close determinant relation. Further restriction can be obtained by centering our attention on systems of relationships that are temporally and spatially close to the behavior process under study. The more closely contiguous in time and space the determinant is to the process, the greater its contribution is likely to be.

An Example. Let us illustrate some of the foregoing points with a problem concerned with the determinants of an automobile accident. Suppose that Mr. Smith, in trying to pass the car ahead of him, had a very harrowing experience. This vividly brought to his attention the dangers inherent in unsafe driving, and is presently stimulating him to give a great deal of thought to the analysis of why he did what he did. He wishes to discover an order of events that will explain why he had the harrowing experience. He surveys the situation and brings to light the following facts which might bear on the problem: his erratic driving may have resulted from his not feeling well because of a protracted head cold; his attitude about safe driving may have become lax from just having been delayed at an intersection during an unwarranted traffic snarl; he may not have been actively attending to the driving task because he was thinking of the bawling out his boss gave him at noon; his car may have been at fault in not accelerating fast enough as he passed the other car, etc. We now have for consideration several areas where determining conditions may be found. These are relevant behavior processes that need further study.

All of the foregoing reasons appear to have relevancy for the near-accident situation, and thus they all come under the purview of the problem. There is need, however, for restricting the variables to some degree in order to facilitate the discovery of an acceptable explanation. Continuing his analysis, Mr. Smith remembers that the car was recently repaired and was presumably in excellent mechanical condition, a fact that he had momentarily forgotten. One of the relevant areas can now be passed over. The area of driver attitude appears to hold promise. Further study reveals that Mr. Smith had been delayed at the office and was getting home late, that there is often a family altercation when he arrives late for dinner, that he was hurrying to avoid being late, that the traffic jam at the intersection had frustrated him and had stimulated him to make up time, and that not only was he going to be late but he would have to tell his wife about the trouble with the boss. We find in this area of attitude events which are logically closely associated with the near-accident behavior, and which are also closely contiguous to this behavior in both temporal and spatial contexts.

Approximating the Determinants of a Behavior Process. The solutions to most psychological problems are obtained only after many empirical studies. The procedure is one of approximating more and more closely to an accurate description of the specific determinant conditions. The procedure to be followed bears repeating. We first must discover and describe those behavior systems that appear to contain important determinants. Then those systems that are relevant to our problem must be carefully analyzed. Next, particular behavior sequences that are logically pertinent to our problem must be discovered and further examined. Finally, these behavior sequences must be studied under empirical conditions with the expectation that behavior processes containing the solution will be found.

It is not necessary to achieve an accurate description of a behavior sequence before we hazard a judgment concerning its pertinence for our problem. From the first few approximation studies enough knowledge will be gained to justify the complete elimination of many relationships that at first appeared relevant. Likewise, our knowledge of some relationships will be sufficient to tag them as meriting more intensive examination.

According to our findings in these early studies, we proceed to eliminate those sequences that do not contribute to our problem and to sharpen our description of those that contain usable functional relationships. By repeating this procedure several times we gradually improve our description of the determinant conditions.

In later studies, our attention is focused on determining the relative importance of the several relationships still remaining. This is a difficult task. The contribution of any given variable is determined, in part, by its relationships with other variables, even relationships with those variables that have been eliminated earlier in the investigation. Therefore, as we proceed with the approximation studies it is important to note how the contribution of any given behavior process changes with the elimination and retention of other processes.

Once we have made a final selection of the behavior processes to be retained, further studies are required in order to assess accurately the functional relationships involved. This is especially true when we desire to abstract the relationships from the concrete characteristics of the empirical testing situations. The process of abstraction does not affect each of the several determinant relationships equally, and the differential effects of the abstraction must be known before an accurate generalization of the functional relationships can be made.

Psychological Functions Stated as Statistical Laws. The verification of a psychological function in a variety of situations enables us to determine its predictive effectiveness as a statistical law. A statistical law states the expectations of successful prediction in the form of a probability statement. The evidence favorable to a prediction is weighed against the evidence unfavorable to the prediction. The statistical statement is derived from the successes and failures obtained in empirical verification studies. The functional relationship is then expressed in terms of the probability of making a successful prediction.

The statement of probability should take account of the contribution of all of the known determinants. A statistical law attempts to summarize the findings of the past. This is very difficult to do, especially in global behavior situations where many determinants, varying in importance, are functioning. Only when the contributions of the determinants are accurately quantified, however, can a high level of precision be achieved in the over-all probability statement.

Accounting for Failures. In a deterministic world, failures, like successes, are to be traced to specific sequences of events. The failure of a behavior process to occur as we predict it is frequently ascribed to chance or accident. This is another way of saying that we do not know why the prediction failed. If we compare the behavior processes occurring during the failures with those occurring during the successes, we frequently can learn about differences that are critical. We can then attribute the failures to a particular organization of behavior processes and do not need to refer them to chance or accident.

There are two primary reasons why failures might occur. They may be attributed to our not reproducing all of the event sequences that our earlier analyses show are necessary for the prediction. They may be attributed to the operation of interfering or inhibitory variables that were never encountered in our earlier analyses and were thus not isolated and described. In the first instance, if we learn what the missing event sequences are, we can modify our procedures where necessary and reduce the probability of subsequent failures. In the second instance, if we can discover and isolate the interfering or inhibitory variables we may be able to devise control procedures that will prevent their occurrence in subsequent predictions.

SELECTED READINGS

Cohen, M. R., and E. Nagel: "An Introduction to Logic and the Scientific Method," chap. 13, Harcourt, Brace and Company, Inc., 1934. This is a brief evaluation of the methods of experimental inquiry as described by Francis Bacon and elaborated by John Stuart Mill. The methods are presumed to be useful designs for detecting causal relationships. The exposition covers the method of agreement, the method of difference, the method of concomitant variation, and the method of residues.

Feigl, H.: Notes on Causality, in H. Feigl and M. Brodbeck (eds.), "Readings in the Philosophy of Science," pp. 408–418, Appleton-Century-Crofts, Inc., 1953. This article reviews a number of the meanings associated with the concept of cause and effect and points up how the uses of these meanings are or are not justified. It is brief and somewhat difficult, but well worth the attention of the serious student.

Reichenbach, H.: "The Rise of Scientific Philosophy," chap. 10, University of California Press, 1951. This chapter briefly traces the historic change that occurred in the interpretation of the concept of causality. The idea of *if-then always* has for science become *if-then in a certain percentage.*

CHAPTER 5

The Control of Psychological Variables

One of the most important problems facing the scientific psychologist in his attempt to discover the fundamental orders underlying human behavior is that of controlling variables. It should be obvious that if any relationship is to be discovered, regardless of its nature, it is necessary to separate the variables thought to be related from other variables, at least to the extent that the variables under study can be observed and classified independently of other variables that are not of immediate concern. If we are to realize the aim of prediction, it is necessary to separate and control the effects of the several variables considered pertinent to our prediction.

THREE OBJECTIVES OF CONTROL

As psychologists, we are faced with a very difficult task in achieving control of the complex of variables that condition even the most simple expressions of behavior. To discover the factors underlying any human activity we must analyze the variation in numerous determiners, discover the nature and importance of combinations of these determiners, and, when possible, measure the interaction among individual determiners and among combinations of determiners. We seek to control variables for the following purposes: (1) to isolate the determiners individually and in combinations; (2) to vary them as magnitudes either singly or in combinations; and (3) to describe quantitatively the extent of their expression and their interacting effects, again, either as single determiners or as combinations of determiners.

Control to Achieve Isolation. In its simplest form, this level of control is used when it is desirable to rule out or keep constant the effects of a variable. This would occur in the isolation and elimination of extraneous noises in an experiment involving a study of auditory thresholds. Isolation in this instance might be accomplished by performing the experiment in a soundproof room.

Isolation may involve estimating the magnitudinal changes in a variable. For instance, sometimes in isolating a variable we need to know when the effect of the variable has been reduced to zero or has been made constant in amount. We can readily determine this if we can measure the expressions of the variable.

Control to Achieve Changes of Magnitude. This refers to a degree of control sufficient to enable us to change directly the expression of the variable. In most investigations we are not simply interested in learning if a variable has an effect on the outcome; we desire also to know how much effect the variable is contributing. To achieve this it is necessary that we be able to vary the magnitude of the pertinent variables under study. For example, in studying the relationship between high school preparation and college success we want to know how much contribution high school training makes to the student's work in college.

Control to Achieve Quantitative Evaluation. This is the highest level of control. We must not only know that a variable is large or small but must be able to express the magnitude of the variable in terms of some numerical value. We are not simply interested in knowing that one expression of a variable is larger or smaller than another; we want to know how much larger or smaller. We desire a quantitative statement of the difference. Similarly, we are not simply interested in knowing that two variables are functionally related, either positively or negatively; we want to know the extent or the amount of the relationship. We desire a numerical estimation that will indicate at what point the relation falls on a continuum that varies from zero relation at the one end to perfect relation at the other.

A majority of the variables in psychology are fundamentally continuous in nature or can be considered to operate as if they were continuous in nature, and therefore we can assume they are measurable. Their complexity, however, makes the problem of measurement difficult. Much of the time and effort of the psychologist is spent in evolving measuring devices by which he can obtain the precision of control that will enable him to make quantitative evaluations of his variables and their relationships.

A STUDY ILLUSTRATING PROBLEMS OF CONTROL

The Problem to Be Investigated. The project now to be described arose from practical problems involved in driving an automobile at night. A form of visual response that has bearing on night-driving performance is called glare blindness. On the highway at night the driver faces the bright headlights of oncoming cars. If he fixates on the highway ahead of his car, which he must do to drive safely, he cannot escape this source of intermittent bright stimulation. The eyes are forced to adapt alternately to brightness and dimness of illumination. Glare blindness refers to the experience immediately following the bright headlight stimulation when the driver's eyes are not dark-adapted, and when, as a consequence, he cannot accurately discriminate the objects along the road. This temporary blindness from glare stimulation disappears when his eyes have had time to adapt to the dimmer light conditions of the road ahead.

For many years it has been known that vitamin A is associated with the retina's power to adapt to dark conditions of illumination. Increased amounts of vitamin A in the retina are associated with higher rates of recovery from glare stimulation. The question arises as to whether changes in the vitamin A intake through diet regulation would have any effect upon the driver's ability to withstand the glare of oncoming headlights. The question selected for study was framed as follows: Do changes in vitamin A intake through regulation of the diet affect the individual's rate of recovery from exposure to bright light stimulation?

The Principal Experimental Procedures. College students were used as subjects. Variation in the dietary intake of vitamin A was accomplished by having the students go on a special dietary regimen: three weeks on a normal diet, three weeks on a diet high in vitamin A content, and three weeks on a diet low in vitamin A.

The response of the eyes was measured by means of a glare recovery test. This consisted of a lighttight box 12 by 12 by 18 inches in size. The headlamp of an automobile was placed at one end of the box behind an opalescent glass plate. At the opposite end there was a viewing aperture through which the subject could perceive the bright light. In front of the glass plate was a test object in the form of an arrow. This object was withdrawn from view during the bright light stimulation and returned to the field of vision at the instant the light was turned off. The arrow could be rotated in the four quadrants of space as seen by the subject.

In the testing situation the subject held his head tightly against the edge of the visor of the viewing aperture. The bright light was turned on for 20 seconds. The subject then reported the direction of the arrow as soon as he could see it. The arrow was rotated to a second and again to a third position, and the subject reported the direction he thought it pointed to at each setting. The time was recorded from the instant that the bright light was turned off to the instant the subject correctly reported the position of the arrow.

The Control of the Variables. *Controlling the Diet Variable.* A list of staple foods, high and low in vitamin A content, was given to the subject. During a given experimental period he varied the food he ate in accordance with the requirements of the experimental condition, in one phase concentrating on foods rich in vitamin A, and in another concentrating on foods low in vitamin A content. The divergence of the special diets from the normal diet of the subjects was very extreme, the subjects frequently commenting on the difficulty of maintaining the special dietary regimen for as long a period as three weeks.

Controlling Light-exposure Variables. The time of exposure of the subject to the bright light stimulation was held relatively constant through use of a stop watch. Variation in the intensity of the bright light stimulation was minimized by periodically checking the brilliance of the light by means of a light meter. The subject's pretest level of light adaptation was made approximately constant by having him remain in the testing room for a period of 20 minutes preceding the administration of the test. The subject was cautioned during the test to keep his head tightly against the visor of the viewing aperture in order to minimize the infiltration of stray light into the testing box.

Controlling Individual Differences. Individuals differ in respect to their ability to withstand glare stimulation and also in their ability to assimilate vitamin A. If a different group of subjects had been used in each of the three experimental conditions, we would have had to make sure that the three groups were equal in respect to these two variables. To circumvent this difficult problem each subject took part in each phase of the experiment. Any individual differences were then introduced equally into each of the three experimental conditions.

Controlling Interphase Effects. It is a well-documented fact that when an individual participates in every phase of an experiment, the effects of a given phase may continue forward in time to determine in part what he will do in a later phase. In the glare recovery experiment, the effect of the low vitamin A diet might be due in part to whether the subject had previously been on a normal diet or on a diet high in vitamin A. In the absence of knowledge of how one phase affects another phase, it is necessary to control these effects by equalizing them. This is accomplished by arranging the experimental conditions in several sequences and having different subjects participate in the different sequences. In the glare recovery experiment, the conditions were arranged so that each experimental condition preceded every other condition, different subjects being randomly assigned to the different sequences or orders of conditions.

Controlling Chance Factors. In addition to the variables mentioned above, there were many others operating to affect an individual's responses to light stimulation. Day-to-day fluctuations in physical efficiency, changes in the room temperature and illumination due to variations in the outside weather conditions, variation in the subject's willingness to cooperate in subscribing to the requirements of the experimental conditions, fluctuations in the attention and in the precision of response of the experimenters, and other such factors were operating. It was impossible to eliminate all of these factors, but an attempt was made to equalize their effects. This was done by arranging the experimental procedure so that each factor operated equally in every phase of the experiment. For example, in the experimental situation, every experimenter followed the same testing procedures, participated in testing every subject, and operated the test in each of the experimental conditions. Thus, any variation attributable to experimenters tended to be distributed in all phases of the testing.

The Experimental Findings. Although we are not here particularly concerned with the experimental results, the reader may be interested in the outcome of the experiment. Significant differences in the time of recovery from glare stimulation were found for the three conditions. The fastest recovery was achieved under the high vitamin A condition, the slowest under the low vitamin A condition. This was true for all subjects. Responses under the normal diet were never faster than under the high diet, but were not always faster than under the low diet. The high-vitamin-diet regimen was much more severe than one would want to undertake for any protracted length of time, indicating that supplementation by vitamin capsules would probably prove less objectionable than supplementation by diet regulation.

COMMON VARIABLES NEEDING CONTROL IN PSYCHOLOGICAL INVESTIGATIONS

Some General Areas of Behavior Determiners. Any factor that functions as a determiner of behavior at some time may require control. Below are listed some general areas of determinants of human behavior, and within each area some subareas are given. No attempt is made to be exhaustive of the possible areas or of the subareas within any area. The areas are sufficiently general in nature so that determiners from most of them will play a role in nearly every study in which human subjects are used. The purpose for listing the variables at this point is to remind ourselves of the breadth and kind of factors for which controls are needed, and to add some concreteness of meaning to our thinking about problems of control.

Examples of General Areas and Subareas of Determiners

SCHOOLING

Incentive to work with books
Level of success in school—general average
Level of success in school—in different subjects

Amount of training received—estimate of over-all average
Amount of training received—averages for specific subjects
Specific subjects liked
Specific subjects disliked
Speed of work in different subjects
Accuracy of work in different subjects
Specialized training received, e.g., skilled trades

SKILLS

Sports played—kinds and amounts
Hobbies practiced—kinds and extent
Musical instruments played—extent of skill
Mechanical skills—kinds and extent
Physical deficiencies affecting skills

FACTORS RELATED TO MATURITY

Chronological age
Physiological maturity
Psychological maturity—interests, drives, emotions
Amount of experience in special areas of development

CULTURAL FACTORS

Exposure to foreign language
Exposure to foreign culture and ideologies
Degree of assimilation of American culture
Exposure to particular regional cultural patterns

SOCIAL EXPERIENCE

Preferred social activities
Social activities disliked
Participation in social activities at school—
    kinds and extent
Participation in social activities at home—
    kinds and extent
Participation in group sports—kinds and extent
Participation in group hobbies—kinds and extent
Social activities connected with vocational interests

PHYSIOLOGICAL FACTORS

Physiological development
Emotional development
General physical well-being

Specific physical impairments
Susceptibility to particular diseases
Level of energy output

Some Examples of Specific Behavior Determiners. In conducting a particular study, more specific factors will be encountered than those considered above. These will vary widely with the nature of the problem being investigated. Suppose the study involves the administration of a group intelligence test, then specific factors would have to be considered in connection with the subjects taking the test, with the test itself, and with the testing procedures. A few examples of such specific factors follow:

Subject's degree of cooperation
Subject's anxiety relative to rate of work
Validity of test items
Adequacy of test instructions
Accuracy of norms and standards
Adherence to testing procedures
Prevention of distractions during the test
Accuracy of scoring of test responses

PROCEDURES FOR ACHIEVING CONTROL OF VARIABLES

Over many years of research, scientists have developed and adapted control procedures to meet a large variety of specific problems. It is a difficult task to find a simple classification scheme into which all of the individual procedures can be fitted. Three categories are selected that are sufficiently comprehensive to encompass all of the many diverse types of control procedures available today. According to the nature of the individual procedure applied to the variable, control can be achieved through physical manipulation, through procedures of selection, and through statistical manipulation.

Control by Some Form of Physical Manipulation. This refers to procedures in which there is a more or less direct manipulation of the determiner itself or the immediate conditions that give rise to the determiner.

Mechanical Means. One form of manipulation comprises mechanical methods. Here we may cite the familiar apparatus controls of the laboratory, such as the exposure drums for presenting memory materials, the insulating materials for soundproofing rooms, the tachistoscopes for exposing perceptual stimuli, and the problem boxes and mazes for measuring learning responses.

Electrical Means. A second form of physical manipulation utilizes electrical means to effect the control. This procedure has very wide application in the generation of sounds in experiments in hearing and in the use of telechron and other constant speed motors for driving apparatus, controlling relays, and measuring time intervals.

Surgical Means. The use of operative surgery also effects a direct control over the physical mechanisms determining behavior. Experiments on the brain are a case in point. Another would be the surgical removal of glands, such as the thyroid or the adrenals. Experiments on gonadectomized animals are an application of this procedure.

Pharmacological Means. A fourth type of procedure uses drugs, change of diet, feeding of gland extracts, etc., to effect control over certain biochemical determiners of behavior. Studies of the use of dilantin in the treatment of epilepsy and the use of pentobarbital in the release of the repressed fears of veterans suffering battle fatigue are illustrative of the controls that the use of drugs can effect.

Reasons for Not Using Physical Manipulation. Control through the physical manipulation of the variable itself or its immediate determiners may not be utilized for one of three reasons; namely, physical manipulation may be undesirable, it may be difficult to achieve, or it may be impossible to achieve with available techniques.

Obviously there are regions of human behavior, such as those of sex and inheritance, where we are woefully in need of additional knowledge, but in which direct physical manipulation of the variables is ruled out.

There are problems in social behavior in which manipulation of the variables is possible but very difficult for an individual investigator to achieve. An example is the study of the effects of physiological growth on the social behavior of children. Such a problem would require the genetic study of many children over several age levels, and would not only involve a long-term study but would be a highly expensive undertaking. Most individual investigators would not command the facilities required to undertake such an investigation.

Some variables are not amenable to control through physical manipulation. The variable of age is one; the variable of past experience, for the most part, is another. In studies of learning, variations in the past experience of the subjects are always present, but they can seldom be directly manipulated. We cannot equate the past experience of different subjects merely by some kind of condensed course of training in which each individual is schooled in the types of experience that the other individuals possess but that he lacks.

The Need for Other Methods of Control. Although physical manipulation of variables has played the primary role in the development of control procedures in the physical sciences, this method leaves unsolved a large number of the control problems of the psychological and social sciences. We must remember, however, that it is not necessary to be able to manipulate our variables physically in order to study them scientifically. Astronomy is a good example of a science that has no power of physical manipulation over most of the variables with which it is concerned. The psychologist similarly finds himself without direct manipulatory control in many behavior situations involving the adjustment of the individual. It is therefore necessary for him to effect and utilize other forms of control procedures.

Control by Procedures of Selection. *The Importance of Control through Selection.* Control by means of selection proves of great value in psychology because it can be applied to so many different phases of a scientific investigation. Variables which would otherwise go uncontrolled have been subjected to rigorous indirect manipulation, which should in no way be considered less effective than the procedures of direct physical manipulation. Control through selection has enabled the psychologist to study composites of determiners as they function in global units, a problem in control that the method of physical manipulation is not adapted to solve.

The Selection of Materials. An important means of effecting control over psychological variables is through the selection of experimental materials. The field of learning is replete with control problems solved by this procedure. For example, in studying the relation between the amount of material to be learned and the time required for learning, the investigator must use a large number of units of material that are comparable in terms of the ease of learning. The several conditions of the experiment require that differing amounts of material be learned. Of course, there can be no duplication of materials in the several conditions. Obviously, once a subject learns the material of one of the conditions, that material cannot be used again in any of the other conditions. There then is introduced the possibility that a spurious factor might affect the speed of learning, namely, differences in the difficulty of the material utilized in the several experimental conditions.

Referring to our example, suppose that our study involves a comparison of the amount of time required per syllable to learn lists of 8, 10, 12, and 14 syllables. If the 8-syllable list contains more difficult learning units than the 10-syllable list, more time for learning might be required for the 8-syllable list. Difficulty of material is then a factor spuriously affecting the relationship between amount of material and time required for learning. By means of a careful evaluation of the difficulty of all units of material and a selection for utilization of only those units that are comparable in difficulty, the spurious factor is minimized as a determiner of the learning time.

The Selection of Subjects. In the selection of the particular individuals to act as subjects in a study, we can manipulate indirectly many of the variables that are beyond direct physical manipulation, such as past experience, age, inherited dispositions, and the like. Suppose, as directors of operations in a factory, we are interested in studying the relative effectiveness of two different work procedures. We wish to investigate the relative effectiveness of two methods of operating a lathe when the lathe experience of the workers is held constant. If differences in the amount of lathe-operating experience were allowed to enter the experiment, we would not be justified in attributing the results to differences in the methods of work. We gain control over past lathe-operating experience by selecting workers who have equal amounts of such experience. We can arrange the workers in pairs having equal experience and then randomly assign a worker of each pair to each of the experimental conditions. In a similar way, such global factors as ability, interest, attitude, etc., can be brought under control.

The Selection of Data. A further application of selection procedures is found in the selection of the data to be analyzed. When this method is used, the problem to be investigated is so designed that data already available can be utilized in discovering possible solutions. This is exemplified in some of the problems of social psychology where such primary sources of data as the records of public institutions, various collections of vital statistics, government census reports, and the like, may provide an investigator with the facts he needs for studying certain social factors contributing to behavior. Similarly, this procedure may be used when the behavior to be studied is controlled in some manner by a federal or state institution, as in a reform school or a state prison. Here we might not be allowed to interfere with the behavior routine of the inmates but might be furnished records from which we could select data pertinent to our problem.

Although the method of selection of data may give the investigator an excellent leverage on the global composites of behavior that are represented by the categories used in the primary sources of the data, the procedure does not make possible the isolation and evaluation of every factor that conditions the behavior being investigated. Only those factors can be separated for study that are separately measured in the data. For example, juvenile delinquency can be studied in reference to the single factor of divorce of parents only if the records provide information concerning the marriage status of the parents of the delinquents. Furthermore, the quality of control that can be achieved is directly conditioned by the completeness and accuracy of the records. The degree of confidence that can be placed in the data and thus in any generalizations made from analyzing the data is a direct function of the completeness and accuracy of the facts recorded.

Control by Statistical Manipulation of the Data. This procedure extends control beyond that which is obtainable through the other two procedures. Statistical analyses, of course, are used in conjunction with other scientific procedures, but as a method for controlling variables they have a unique contribution to make that deserves our attention.

Statistical Control in Complex Behavior. Statistical controls are particularly adapted to the multiple variable situations found in psychology because they enable us to discover the determiners of behavior when these determiners are not amenable to direct physical manipulation. Furthermore, they enable us to approximate the relative importance of the contribution of each of several factors in the determination of an event, a problem that neither of the other two methods has adequately solved.

In the laboratory situation, where it is possible to isolate and vary each determiner independently of the others, the tracing and evaluation of functional relationships can readily be achieved. When we move out of the laboratory situation to seek functional relationships in the global behavior that characterizes everyday life, the problem is made exceedingly difficult. Here the techniques of physical manipulation are severely limited in their applicability. The procedures of selection involving materials, subjects, and data sometimes enable us to isolate and evaluate many of these global factors. We find, however, that these procedures seldom are sufficient to carry us all of the way to an evaluation of the relative significance of several global factors simultaneously functioning in complex combinations. It is in such problems as this that statistical control has proved of outstanding value.

An Example. The consideration of a concrete situation will assist us in comprehending the power found in statistical procedures of control. Let us consider the problem of predicting success in college from a knowledge of the experience and abilities of students. College success is a global complex of phenomena that results from the functioning of several other global complexes of factors such as ability to read, high school training, amount of time devoted to study, abstract intellectual ability, and the like. Such determiners are beyond physical manipulation and their complex interactions are not amenable to separation by procedures using selection. Statistical procedures, however, are available by which the effects of each of the global units can be isolated and evaluated. Furthermore, an estimation of the relative importance of the several complexes of determiners can also be made.

In a study by the authors of a group of college students containing a large number of students on probationary status, the global factors of high school preparation, reading ability, and scholastic aptitude were analyzed as possible determiners of scholarship deficiency. High school preparation was measured by translating course grades into grade points and averaging them. A special reading test was used involving subject matter from several of the common areas of college instruction. A widely used test of intellectual capacity provided a measure of scholastic aptitude. The grade-point index served as the criterion of success in college.

The scores on the three predictor variables were correlated with the grade-point indices, providing three coefficients of correlation. As was expected, each coefficient had a rather high positive value, as is shown in column 2 of Table 1. These generally high relationships are a signifi-

Table 1. Determination of Individual Differences in College Scholarship by Each of the Variables of High School Achievement, Reading Ability, and Scholastic Aptitude

Variable	Correlation of variable with college scholarship	
	Other predictors not controlled	Other predictors controlled
High school preparation.....	.67	.55
Reading ability............	.51	.23
Scholastic aptitude........	.46	.13

cant fact, indicating that each variable is probably functionally associated in a positive manner with every other variable. This means that in a situation where every variable is positively operating, the functional relationship between any given predictor and the criterion is conditioned by two factors, namely, the relation this predictor has with the other predictors and its relation, in turn, with the criterion.

Before we can determine the exact correlation between any given predictor and the criterion, we must find a method for holding constant the effects of the other predictor variables. By applying such a method to each predictor, in turn, it is possible to determine the functional relationship holding between this predictor and the criterion when the effects of other predictor variables are held constant.

Although it is beyond the scope of this book to develop the significance of the methods by which this can be accomplished, the student should be aware of the fact that there are several statistical formulas for holding constant the effects of several variables while analyzing the functional relationship between other variables. In the example of the college students, the method used is called partial correlation. Like the simple coefficient of correlation, the coefficient of partial correlation expresses the degree of relation between two variables. It differs from the simple coefficient in that it measures the degree of relationship between two variables when the effects of other relevant variables are held constant. In our example there were three partial correlation coefficients as presented in Table 1. It will be noted that the three predictor variables correlate with the criterion in order of magnitude from greatest to least as follows: high school preparation, reading ability, and scholastic aptitude. High school preparation seems to have contributed far more to the college success of these particular students than did their reading ability or their scholastic aptitude. Obviously, such findings as these have significance for the supervision and control of behavior in important college scholarship situations.

Two Conditions Essential to the Use of Statistical Controls. Two conditions must be met before we can use statistical procedures of control, namely, the variables to be controlled must be measured, and the investigation must be so planned as to make available a measure of unsystematic variation or error. In statistical control procedures, the score values are manipulated; that is, the numbers representing the quantitative characteristics of the variables are the units manipulated. If the characteristic being studied cannot be described numerically, then it cannot be controlled statistically. Designing the study to provide a measure of unsystematic errors is required in order to evaluate the contribution that these errors make toward the production of the phenomena being examined. An accurate determination of the contribution of the pertinent variables is impossible when the part played by unsystematic error variables cannot be estimated.

At this point the student may have difficulty getting an accurate understanding of error variables. To use the term loosely, an error variable is any variable which operates to introduce inaccuracy in the functioning of the particular variables under study. Unsystematic error, chance error, sampling error, and experimental error are different terms used to refer to the effects of some or all of these error variables. Further reference will be made to these variables in subsequent discussions, but it is beyond the scope of this book to develop the statistical formulas and their meanings by which these error variables can be understood.

Two Statistical Control Procedures. Two of the most frequently used statistical procedures for effecting an analysis of the functional relationships underlying complex behavior are the method of partial correlation, already mentioned, and the method of the analysis of variance. The reader will find the concepts involved in these methods treated in advanced texts in statistical methods. It is sufficient for our purposes to realize that there are control procedures available through statistical manipulation that open up large areas of psychological problems formerly closed to scientific study.

Choosing Control Procedures for an Investigation. The control procedures we have considered—physical manipulation, selection of experimental materials, subjects, and data, and statistical analyses—are available for controlling any of the multifarious variables with which the psychologist must deal. Of course, they will not control every variable equally well. The nature of the control procedures to be used on a given occasion will vary with the nature of the variables to be studied and the purposes of the investigation. Sometimes the best control procedures that can be devised will fall short of attaining the desired degree of control.

Inasmuch as we control variables to achieve definite purposes related to the objectives of our study, we should avail ourselves of any control procedure through which we can get answers to the questions being investigated. We should not control variables just to be controlling variables, as occasionally seems to be the case even in some current scientific studies. Neither should we restrict the controls to some one particular kind because of an "idolatrous" concern for that particular kind of control procedure. There are experimentalists who do not take seriously the control procedures offered by statistical methods; and there are statisticians who seem unaware of experimental techniques that they could use to advantage. The criterion for selecting a given control procedure should be the extent to which it will enable us to solve the problem under investigation.

SYSTEMATIC AND UNSYSTEMATIC DETERMINERS

Our success in controlling the variables of an experiment depends upon our knowing the kind of effect the variables have on the end results. The same variable may play different roles at different times. To learn the particular nature of the effect of a variable at a given time and under a particular set of conditions is the difficult task we face as scientists. According to the general effect that a variable has on a phenomenon under a given set of conditions, it is classified as a systematic or an unsystematic variable.

Systematic Variables. Variables that have a constant effect upon the end results are called systematic. By "constant effect" is meant that the final average values obtained from our analyses will be either larger or smaller than they would have been had the variable been inoperative during the investigation. Among the systematic factors will be found the variables pertinent to the purpose of our investigation, that is, those variables we have elected to study. These are often called the experimental variables.

There will be other factors which, if not controlled, will have constant effects upon the complex of variables to be studied. Potentially, they are systematic variables. These variables may be controlled in order either to eliminate entirely any effects that they may have, or to force them to contribute equally to all phases of the investigation. In the latter case the factors will not have a differential effect upon the end results. These potentially systematic variables, which should be prevented from contributing a constant effect to the end results, we shall call unwanted systematic variables.

Unsystematic Variables. Unsystematic determiners produce variation in the complex of variables under study, but they contribute equally in both positive and negative directions. They will sometimes increase and sometimes decrease the values of the complex of variables, but in the long run the final average values will be neither larger nor smaller than they would have been had the unsystematic variables been eliminated.

We should not think that the effect of unsystematic factors is ruled out just because the chances are high that the final average values will be disturbed. The increased variation introduced into an experiment by unsystematic factors increases the difficulty of discovering and accurately evaluating the effects of the experimental variables. This problem will receive further attention in later sections.

In any given experiment, there will be unsystematic factors that are completely unknown to the investigator. Furthermore, the nature and extent of the effects of the unsystematic factors that are known may be so poorly understood and thus so inadequately controlled that their contribution may outweigh the contribution of the systematic factors under study. It is apparent, therefore, that the control of unsystematic variables is a significant problem in all psychological research.

THE CONTROL OF EXPERIMENTAL VARIABLES

The Problem. The problem of controlling experimental variables is one of isolating, manipulating, and measuring one or more variables that form the precursor sequences related to one or more other variables that are wholly or partially unknown and about which information is desired. When the consequent sequences are wholly unknown, the study is designed in a way that will allow for detecting and recording the changes that would be expected if certain notions or hypotheses of the experimenter were true. When the nature of the expected changes is partially understood, the study is designed to get a more accurate description of the quantitative aspects of these changes as they relate to the quantitative aspects of the antecedent sequences.

The manipulation of experimental variables is planned to achieve one of three general levels of control. One purpose is to produce expressions of the experimental variable, at such times as they can be observed, when the amount of the variable is not determinable. The effects of the variable are then compared with findings from situations in which the experimental variable is nonfunctional. A situation requiring more precise control over the experimental variable is demanded when it is necessary to have several levels of expression of the variable, the amounts of the expression being unquantifiable or only roughly quantifiable. It is known that the two or more levels of expression vary in amount but the amount of the differences between levels is not known. A still higher degree of control is attained when the various levels of magnitude of the experimental variable are measured. It is then possible to describe quantitatively the amounts of expression and to measure the amount of difference between various expressions.

All of the control procedures that the scientist has devised are available for use in the controlling of experimental variables. The primary considerations that determine the kinds of control procedures that should be used in any given study are the nature of the variables involved, the nature of the functional relations suspected to hold among the variables, and the particular questions that the investigator proposes to answer.

In the glare recovery problem, the experimental variable was the amount of vitamin A in the retina. It was varied in reference to the power of the eyes to adapt to a reduction in illumination. These two variables were known to be functionally related, the rate of adaptation to reduced illumination depending upon the amount of vitamin A in the retina. The object of the experiment was to determine if this functional relationship could be affected by the manipulation of a person's dietary regimen. Although the results of the study might have had significance for the practical problem of driving an automobile at night, it was not necessary to design the experiment with the view of directly applying the findings to this situation.

Control through Physical Manipulation. This procedure involves a more or less direct manipulation of the experimental variables. In the glare recovery experiment, the vitamin A intake was regulated by adjusting the dietary regimen of the subjects. A quantitative change in the vitamin A content in the retina was effected by having the subject submit to very extreme dietary conditions. This procedure did not quantify the amount of vitamin A in the retina, nor did it provide an accurate description of the amount of vitamin A being assimilated under the several dietary conditions. Neither of these more precise measures of vitamin A was considered necessary to achieve the information needed for answering the question: Will changes in the assimilated amount of vitamin A resulting from changes in the daily diet affect the recovery time from glare stimulation?

The control procedure adopted for quantitatively varying vitamin A illustrates one of the cardinal principles of experimental design, namely, that the precision of control effected for any variable should be gauged in terms of the purposes of the experiment. Precision over and above what is required to accomplish the experimental objectives is usually unproductive, although this added precision seldom affects the findings detrimentally. Occasionally, when more precise procedures than are actually required are used, additional factors or characteristics are disclosed which less precise procedures would not reveal.

In the glare recovery experiment, the consequent variable of the recovery of the retina following glare stimulation was evaluated by measuring the time of recovery to the point when the target object was identified. The use of a stop watch was adequate. Of course, the experimenters varied in their reaction times in manipulating the watch, but these variations were extremely small in comparison with the very long recovery times that were being measured. More precise measures could have been obtained by an electric timing device which would have been operated by the same switch that turned off the stimulus light. This greater precision appeared to promise no information beyond that which could be obtained by the use of the stop watch.

A more critical problem was the determination of that instant when the subject recognized the target object. The particular level of distinctness in perception of the target—that is, whether the outline of the arrow was vague or clear—at which instant the stop watch was to be turned off, was not important. The important problem was to determine the recovery time in different subjects or in the same subject at different testings when recovery had reached approximately the same point or level in so far as the capacity for recognizing objects is concerned. It will be remembered that the target object was made in the shape of an arrow, and the subject was required to tell the direction the arrow was pointing. In this manner it was thought that the measurement would be taken at approximately the same point in the recovery process of the eyes. Recognition of the target object itself was a variable, because subjects differed in their judgments of that instant when the target changed from unidentified to identified. There was considerable variation in willingness of different subjects to report the instant the target object was identified. Some subjects reported as soon as the outline of the arrow was recognized, whereas others waited until they could identify the pointed end of the arrow. In the case of the former, the direction of the arrow was guessed rather than observed. This variation, of course, was not one of the experimental variables, but it is obvious that if uncontrolled it would directly affect the experimental variable of time of recovery. By rotating the arrow and requiring the subject to identify correctly its direction in three successive positions, the effect of this potentially disturbing variable was minimized and probably completely eliminated.

A problem in which very precise control through physical manipulation would be effected is the determination of intensity thresholds in hearing. The problem might be limited to pure tones and involve the intensity thresholds of pure tones of different pitch. Control of these variables involves the use of such electrical devices as resistances, capacitors, inductances, etc. Through these devices we are able to produce pure tones of selected frequencies which can be varied systematically in respect to their intensity.

Control through Procedures of Selection. Examples will be given in which experimental variables are controlled by selecting materials, selecting subjects, and selecting data. In later discussions on control of unwanted systematic factors and unsystematic factors, further details on selection methods of control will be presented.

Control through Selection of Material. Let us consider the question of whether or not the white rat can discriminate patterned stimuli. This problem could have arisen from arguments that the rat does not have pattern vision (ability to distinguish patterned stimuli) but only brightness vision (ability to discriminate differences between light and dark). To study the question, we would have to select stimulus cards that varied in the pattern of light and dark areas while presenting equal relative amounts of these light and dark areas. For example, a black triangle on a white background could be paired with a black circle on a white background, the rat being required to learn that the circle meant a correct choice and the triangle an incorrect one. The triangle and circle would be made equal in the amount of the blackened area. Pairs of triangles and circles varying in the absolute amount of the blackened area could be used. By appropriately selecting the materials the experimental variable could be put to a test.

Control through Selection of Subjects. Control by this procedure is found in testing the effect of educational background on the ability to learn to pilot an airplane. The argument may have arisen that individuals with two years of college training learn piloting faster than those of less education because of superior intellectual ability and not because of any technical knowledge learned in their college courses. One procedure of studying the problem would be to obtain college and noncollege populations of equal intellectual caliber and train them to fly. Another way would be to use only college students, but separate them into groups that differ in general intellectual ability but which have been exposed to the same content in college courses. Although directed to the same problem, these two procedures would not be getting at the same question. In either procedure, the only method for setting up variation in the experimental variable would be that of selecting the subjects. The task would not be an easy one, because a rather complete knowledge of the intellectual capacity and specific educational achievements of potential subjects would be required as a basis for correctly selecting and assigning them.

Control through Selection of Data. We can illustrate this control procedure by a study of the relationship between brightness of illumination of highways and frequency of occurrence of night accidents. One suggestion that has been made for decreasing the frequency of night accidents is to improve highway illumination, particularly at hazardous points along the roadway. Here we can appeal to Dame Nature, who during most months of the year provides us with some nights on which the highways are dimly illuminated and other nights on which the highways are moderately well illuminated, such as when the moon is in full phase. The motor-vehicle department of most states keeps a permanent record of night accidents. By selecting nights that were known to be very dark and nights when there was considerable illumination from the moon and tabulating accident data for these nights, we could set up a test of the experimental problem of the relationship between illumination of highways and frequency of night accidents.

Control through Statistical Procedures. As previously noted, in many situations in psychology it is either impossible or undesirable to manipulate the variables physically or to accomplish control through selection procedures. If the experimental variables can be left to function under natural conditions and can at the same time be measured, then much valuable information can be obtained that is lost under control conditions in which the variables are rigorously isolated. Under methods of physical manipulation, the interrelations of several variables within a complex situation cannot be adequately varied under controlled conditions, and this means that the nature of interactive effects between variables cannot be studied. Such interaction often yields to analysis by statistical procedures.

Suppose that the problem set for investigation is the hypothesis that the superiority of the distributed method of learning is independent of the factors of age, sex, and the meaningfulness of the subject matter. Here there are three factors the interactive relationships among which need to be investigated in connection with the problem of distributed versus massed practice. Each factor could be studied by itself, but under natural conditions all three factors are functioning at the same time, and it is more productive of information if we can study each factor when the others are operating. Suppose that learning scores under massed and distributed practice conditions were obtainable on meaningful and nonsense material for groups of male and female students at several age levels. The scores could then be arranged under the following headings:

Age level	Massed practice				Distributed practice			
	Meaningful material		Nonsense material		Meaningful material		Nonsense material	
	Male	Female	Male	Female	Male	Female	Male	Female
10–11 12–13 14–15 16–17								

A brief inspection of the arrangement will reveal that a very large number of comparisons can be made. In turn, each variable can be the object of study. We can compare learning achievement under distributed and massed practice:

For one or more of several age groups
For the same or different sex
For either meaningful or nonsense material

These comparisons are made possible because statistical methods enable us to pool the scores in the necessary ways. In addition, interaction among the variables can be estimated and taken into account when interpreting the functional relationships that are discovered.

THE CONTROL OF UNWANTED SYSTEMATIC VARIABLES

The Problem. We are here concerned with the systematic effects that might be contributed by factors that are not part of the complex of variables specifically under investigation. As previously pointed out, many of these disturbing systematic factors that are known cannot be controlled through direct means. It should be added that in investigations involving the study of global responses, many of these factors remain wholly unknown. When these unwanted variables are known, it is sometimes possible to eliminate them entirely by using physical manipulation, procedures of selection, or procedures of statistical control. But if we cannot completely remove these factors and if we are unable to measure their separate effects at the time we measure the effects of our experimental variables, the next best method for us to follow is to hold their contribution constant throughout all phases of the study. Under this controlled variation the factors will not function in a manner that will produce systematic changes in the final average values.

Control through Physical Manipulation. This type of control can be illustrated by reference to the glare recovery study. A potentially systematic factor affecting the recovery time was stray light entering the testing box through the view aperture. If uncontrolled, this stray light would directly affect the level of illumination in the testing box and thus the relative brilliance of the stimulus light during test runs. Entrance of stray light into the box should then be prevented. This was accomplished by compelling the subject to hold his head tightly against the visor of the aperture.

In an experiment on the intensity threshold of pure tones, extraneous noises would have the systematic effect of raising the threshold values. By mechanically soundproofing the test room this factor would be brought under control.

Control through Selection of Materials. In the early studies on memory it was found that the subject's acquaintance with the experimental materials often entered as a disturbing variable. The material to be memorized was not equally familiar to all subjects, therefore the learning of it was more difficult for some individuals than for others. This factor of difficulty then affected the rate of learning in experiments in which other variables were the object of study. Nonsense syllables were devised to control the factor by making the material equally unfamiliar to all subjects. Nonsense syllables are combinations of vowels and consonants that do not make sense. They provide material for memory experiments in which individual differences in familiarity with the material can be made to approach zero, as careful selection of the syllables makes them equally unfamiliar to most experimental subjects.

Control through Random Selection and Assignment of Subjects. *Logic of the Procedure.* Control over unknown factors and over known but unwanted relevant factors for which there are no measures can be obtained by planning the study so that these factors will be given equal opportunity to vary in all phases or conditions of the investigation. Obtaining equal distribution of the effects of these factors is accomplished at the time the individual subjects are selected for the investigation and is achieved by using the method of random selection of subjects. In the use of this control procedure the assumption is made that the factors to be controlled are randomly distributed in variable amounts and in variable combinations in the different experimental subjects. Selecting the subjects and assigning them to the several conditions of the experiment by some method that distributes them randomly in these conditions will thereby automatically distribute the factors at random within these conditions. Consequently, the unwanted factors will tend to contribute in the same way and to the same degree in each of the phases of the investigation. Such unsystematic variation will not then differentially affect the final average values.

An Example. Let us consider the common problem of determining a difference between two variables. Suppose the problem is to investigate two methods of performing a motor task such as assembling a pump. Two classes of individuals are available as subjects; therefore we teach method A to class I, and method B to class II. The results show that class I using method A assembled 50 per cent more pumps than class II. From these findings it cannot be concluded that method A is better than or even as good as method B until it can be shown that other factors not part of the two methods were operating unsystematically or in a nondeterminate manner between the two groups of subjects.

One such factor would be the mechanical ability of the subjects. It is very probable that regardless of methods of assembling, individuals with high mechanical ability would assemble more pumps than individuals with mediocre mechanical ability. In the example, the mechanical ability of the subjects was an unwanted systematic variable, but in the procedure used for selecting the subjects no attempt was made to determine the relative amount of mechanical ability represented in the two classes. It is obvious that it is neither desirable nor necessary—nor even possible —to eliminate mechanical ability from the experiment, but it is important that this ability be forced to vary equally within the conditions of the two methods so it will not operate to determine the relative assembling achievements of the two groups.

One way of equalizing the effect of mechanical ability is to measure all of the subjects in this particular ability, arrange them in pairs of equal ability, and then randomly assign the individuals of each pair so that the two groups will have approximately the same average mechanical ability. This selection, however, might not equate some other unwanted factor that would have a systematic effect upon the results. The best method to use when several unwanted systematic factors are present and cannot be measured is to assign the subject to the two methods according to some random or chance method, but without reference to any particular ability. In this way all of the unwanted factors will have an equal opportunity of getting into the two groups to the same degree, and so their general effect upon the two methods will be equalized. Any systematic difference in performance of the two groups cannot then be ascribed to these factors and will have to be attributed to the variables on which a difference between the groups was purposely arranged.

Measuring Unwanted Variables as Unsystematic Variables. When by a random selection and assignment of the subjects we force unwanted systematic variables to operate equally in all conditions of an investigation, we actually make these variables contribute unsystematically to the final average values. Their contribution then cannot be separated from the effects of "bona fide" unsystematic factors, and are evaluated through the use of special statistical procedures devised for measuring unsystematic variation. What is accomplished then is not a complete elimination of these disturbing factors, but a forcing of them into a form in which their contribution can be evaluated statistically.

Control through Selection of Data. Suppose we set up a research project to study the relationship between restriction of side vision and accident frequency, utilizing data available in the files of the motor-vehicle department of some state government. It is obvious that we must be able to study accident drivers with restricted fields of vision. We would also need to select a group of accident drivers with normal side vision. By examining driver accident record cards on which side-vision test scores are recorded we could prepare a roster of accident cases with and without restricted side vision. In examining the accident records of these cases we would find that some of the accidents would be referable to excessive speed, slow reaction time, or some other similar driver characteristic. Such factors might operate differentially between the two groups, and thus as systematic variables they would contaminate the end results. To control these unwanted systematic factors we could select accident situations in which side vision was favored as a possible determinant factor. Two such situations would be intersectional accidents and cutting-in accidents, in both of which side vision is an important driver qualification for safe driving. Selecting accidents for study that occur in such restricted situations would tend to emphasize side-vision factors and to minimize the effects of unwanted systematic determiners.

Control through Statistical Analysis. When means are available for measuring an unwanted systematic variable, it is sometimes advantageous to control it through statistical analysis. This requires that the factor be allowed to vary systematically and that measurements be made of these variations. Suppose that in the investigation on the factors conditioning college success our purpose was to study the contribution of scholastic aptitude to college success. We would then classify high school preparation and reading ability as unwanted systematic factors, and we would be required to eliminate their contribution from the end results. As explained earlier, in such a problem the procedures of partial correlation enable us to study the effect of a given variable when the effects of other variables are held constant. We would then learn the contribution of scholastic aptitude when the effects of high school preparation and reading ability were held constant.

THE CONTROL OF UNSYSTEMATIC VARIABLES

The Problem. It will be recalled that an unsystematic factor is one that influences a given phenomenon both positively and negatively in about equal amounts, and so in the long run it presumably does not change the final average values. Unsystematic factors, however, do increase the variability of the expressions of the phenomenon. Suppose we administer a research aptitude test to a group of 1,000 college sophomores. We test them in small groups during one semester, giving the test at different hours of the day on different days of the week, in different experimental rooms, and using several test administrators. Under these conditions test performance will be affected by variations in hourly efficiency, by variations in efficiency from day to day and from week to week, by variations in the room heat, ventilation, and light, and by any variations in the testing procedures of the different administrators. Some students will do better than their "true" average, others will do poorer. In the long run with a group of this size the number doing better is assumed to offset the number doing poorer, and so it is assumed that the mean performance of the group will not be changed. The variability of the group, however, will be increased above what it would be with the unsystematic factors eliminated. With variation in these factors eliminated, every individual would perform nearer to his average ability, and therefore the total variability of the group would be smaller.

The variation in an individual's performance that occurs from unsystematic factors increases the difficulty of finding in the systematic variable the most representative or "true" measure of performance of the individual. It is then said that a less accurate or reliable measure of the "true" performance is obtained when unsystematic variation is present, and that the accuracy decreases as the amount of unsystematic variation increases. This same logic is applicable to the measurement of the average performance of a group of individuals. The greater the amount of unsystematic variation the less reliable the determination of the value of the "true" average performance of the group. It is obvious then that the effects of unsystematic factors are in need of control and should be eliminated whenever possible.

So many of the factors producing unsystematic variation are unknown that it is difficult to know just what kind or degree of control is effected by any given procedure. The general objective is to reduce as much as possible the variation in the subject's responses that seems to be determined by factors not part of the experimental variables under study.

Control through Physical Manipulation. If the investigator has knowledge concerning a possible unsystematic factor, he may be able to eliminate it by direct manipulation of the physical characteristics of the experimental conditions. Suppose we become embroiled in an argument about the difference in speed of running of football players. We maintain that the backfield players are about 10 per cent faster than linemen, while our opponents argue that the difference is about 30 per cent in favor of the backs. We want to set up an experiment and collect empirical data for settling the dispute. We decide that a dash-run over a short distance would be a fair test, and then go about to measure the speed of running of a large number of individuals who classify themselves as backs and a large number who classify themselves as linemen.

The experiment is conducted at different schools, the running being over distances varying from 50 to 75 yards, on variable running surfaces (turf, gravel, asphalt), and the subjects wearing a variety of track, football, and everyday shoes and clothes. Obviously, under such variable conditions, many unsystematic factors would be functioning, which might not affect the final mean running times, but which certainly would greatly increase the variability of these times. To eliminate these factors a standard set of conditions could be established. These would include a course of 50 yards, the running to be done on turf, the subjects to wear regulation football clothes and shoes, the running to start from a standardized crouching position, etc.

Control through Selection of Materials. By careful selection of materials, the experimental situation can be made more homogeneous through controlling factors that might produce unsystematic variation. This can be illustrated in experiments on the attention value of advertisements.

Suppose the problem is to investigate the effect on attention value of variation in the size of advertisements. The attention value of advertisements can be measured by the degree to which they are recognized or recalled some time subsequent to the original exposure. A procedure sometimes followed is to select the materials from popular magazines. We select advertisements that vary in the following page sizes: $\frac{1}{8}, \frac{1}{4}, \frac{1}{2},$ $\frac{3}{4}$, and full page. It is obvious that when we select advertisements according to size there will also be variation in such factors as number of words, nature of type, over-all composition, nature of message, color, illustrations, and so on. Some of these variables can be removed entirely. For instance, color can be removed by using only black-white advertisements. The nature of the message would be very difficult to control. Meanings aroused by the message and later remembered provide a measure of the attention value. These meanings would change with variation in the message. We would not want to use the same message in all of the advertisements, however, as a given subject would be used to react to advertisements of different sizes. To control the effect of message on attention value we would introduce the same kinds of variations in message in each of the different sizes of advertisements. We would also endeavor to keep variation in the message as small as possible consistent with getting an accurate measure of the attention value.

Control through Selection of Subjects. Here the objective is to obtain a homogeneous group of individuals—the factors on which the homogeneity is based being those factors that would operate to produce unsystematic errors.

In our experiment on the speed of running of football backs and linemen we could use subjects widely varying in their football ability and experience. We could include players from junior high schools, high schools, preparatory schools, junior colleges, colleges, universities, amateur teams sponsored by business establishments, and professional teams. We could include those who had just learned the game, those at the height of their success as players, those who are almost through with active participation, and those who had long since hung up their "moleskins." We could include those who are "eager beavers" and those who take the game "in stride"; those who are in condition and those who are not, etc. Including representatives from such widely varying groups would introduce many unsystematic factors. Again, these factors might not affect the final average running times determined for backfield and linemen, but they would greatly increase the variability of these times.

By accurately selecting the subjects we could make the groups homogeneous in reference to many unsystematic factors without making them unrepresentative of backs and of linemen in respect to speed of running. In our experiment this might mean that we would select only individuals having certain definite characteristics, such as being college players who like the game, who have had at least two years of experience in a major college, who are currently playing and are in good physical condition, etc.

Control through Selection of Data. The controlling of unsystematic factors by this procedure can be illustrated in the study of the relationship between restriction of side vision and frequency of accidents. Having selected the two groups of accident cases, that is, drivers with restricted side vision and drivers with normal side vision, our next task is to determine the frequency of accidents of the two groups. In examining the accident records of these drivers we would find many accidents recorded that are not attributable to these drivers, that is, accidents brought about by other drivers, or by car, road or weather conditions over which our selected drivers had no control. In selecting the accidents to be used in the analysis we want to make sure that accidents referable to these other factors are not included, because of the possibility of introducing unsystematic variation. We would select for study only accidents for which our drivers were responsible. In doing so we would reduce the heterogeneity of the accident determiners and thus minimize the operation of unsystematic variables.

Control through Statistical Procedures. When examined closely it is found that the frequency of occurrence of the effects of unsystematic factors follows a well-established law. We have learned that, on the average, unsystematic factors increase and decrease the values of the experimental variable in about equal amounts. Furthermore, it is known that the effects of unsystematic factors on the experimental variable vary in amount from small to large. Small changes from these factors occur more frequently than large changes, and as the amount of the unsystematic effect gets larger the frequency of its occurrence gets smaller, following a definite form of decrease in frequency. The distribution of these unsystematic error effects above and below the "true" value of the experimental variables is often called the "law of error" or the "curve of error." It has definite properties that are computable through the use of appropriate mathematical formulas. We can then estimate the possible quantitative contribution of unsystematic factors to the experimental results.

An example will further clarify the distribution of these unsystematic errors. Suppose we desire to learn the reading rate of a particular individual for a particular type of reading material. We want this rate to be independent of the time of day, the cooperative efforts of the subject, his interest in the outcome, the lighting and ventilation of the room, and other similar factors which we assume will operate to produce unsystematic errors. On any given day, each of these factors will have a particular influence on the reading rate, but the end effect will differ from day to day; one time being positive, another time being negative; occasionally being large but more often being small. The reading rate will then fluctuate from day to day, and if other factors are constant, these fluctuations will be due to the unsystematic factors.

The results of such a study are represented in Fig. 1. The reading rate varies from 235 to 265 words per minute. The rates of medium size occur more frequently, the rates of extreme size less frequently, there being a definite curvilinear relationship between the size of the rate and its frequency.

We can evaluate the magnitude of variation represented in the reading-rate distribution curve and can estimate the contribution to this variation of unsystematic factors. Statisticians have provided precise procedures for this purpose.

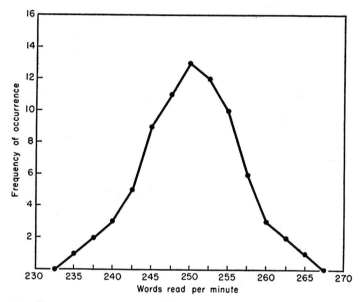

Fig. 1. Distribution curve representing variation in rate scores of one individual on a reading test.

The average reading rate is 250 words per minute. We can feel fairly confident that this value accurately represents the individual's ability to read under the conditions that we presented him. This conclusion is based on several facts, one of which is that the positive variations in rate offset the negative variations and therefore the average value remains representative of the individual's "true" reading ability for the set of conditions imposed on him.

Explanation of the exact statistical procedures for evaluating the contribution of unsystematic errors is beyond the scope of this book. It is important, however, that we know that accurate means are available for estimating the effects of these errors. Such statistical procedures provide a very important control over unsystematic variables.

The Control of Errors of Sampling. The scientist usually is required to study samples of his phenomenon because of the difficulty—and in most instances the impossibility—of studying all of its expressions. Errors may arise because the sample studied is not representative of the population. These are known as "sampling errors" and are classified as one form of unsystematic error. They are evaluated by the statistical procedures referred to above.

SELECTED READINGS

Andrews, T. G.: An Introduction to Psychological Methodology, in T. G. Andrews (ed.), "Methods of Psychology," chap. 1, John Wiley & Sons, Inc., 1948. Several types of experimental and differential methods are discussed, with descriptions given as to how these methods can be used in the control of psychological variables.

Jahoda, M., M. Deutsch, and S. W. Cook: "Research Methods in Social Relations," vol. 1, chap. 3, The Dryden Press, Inc., 1951. In this chapter the reader is introduced to problems of research design in the area of social science. Three types of approaches are discussed: formulative or exploratory studies, descriptive and diagnostic studies, and experimental studies. The differing objectives of these three approaches are achieved by appropriately tailoring the design of the research to the specific kinds of questions needing to be answered.

Underwood, B. J.: "Experimental Psychology," chap. 1, Appleton-Century-Crofts, Inc., 1949. In this introductory chapter the author discusses some of the basic concepts of experimental psychology, the nature of psychological dimensions, the origin of experimental problems, and the steps involved in conducting an experiment.

CHAPTER 6

Some Facts and Principles of Psychological Measurements

The most rigorous kind of description involves the assignment of number meanings to the variables under study. When accurately assigned, number meanings make possible greater precision in description and provide the basis for exact quantitative comparisons.

With the growing application of scientific methodology in the study of behavior, there has been a corresponding increased demand for quantitative description and for mathematical treatment of psychological data. But adoption in unmodified form of the analytical procedures of mathematics and statistics has seldom been completely successful. Psychological variables have unique properties which make a blind use of the procedures dangerous. The application of statistical methods to psychological data has had a short history, but when we keep in mind the complexity of psychological determinants, we are justified in concluding that remarkable progress has been made toward the goal of describing behavior quantitatively.

THE ORDERING OF VARIABLES BY MEANS OF MEASUREMENT

Past discussions have emphasized the importance of finding order in any data that have been collected by means of the scientific method. Through the process of ordering, many meanings are discovered or evolved that are not apparent in the first examination of the data. In the procedures of quantitative description we have available additional devices for ordering data and for discovering many significant meanings. It is important that we consider the ways in which psychological variables can be ordered in terms of the principles of measurement.

The Use of Frequency of Occurrence in Ordering Variables. In the procedure of counting the frequency of occurrence of a phenomenon, we have a ready means of introducing quantitative description into our analysis. The importance of a phenomenon very often is reflected in the number of times it takes place, and its relations with other phenomena are bound up with its frequency of occurrence. It is possible, by the simple mathematical process of counting, to discover important quantitative meanings of the phenomenon.

The Number within a Class. In an earlier chapter, description in the form of classification was discussed. To classify, we must be able to recognize in each event being studied the presence or absence of the particular characteristic on which the classification is made. This enables us to place each event either within or without the class. By applying the counting process to the number that is within the class, we are able to increase the precision of our description. The total number within the class is a new meaning that we can apply to the class as a whole. It is a quantitative description of the size of the class.

Suppose we are interested in studying the attendance of children at the motion picture *Quo Vadis.* We can separate all individuals attending the show into those below the age of twelve and those above this age. This is readily done by sorting the tickets by color, the tickets for children being a different color from those for adults. We can now count up the number of children's tickets and thus obtain the number of children attending the show.

Additional Meanings through Comparisons. Sometimes the number within a class does not tell us all we need to know. We oftentimes wish to know whether this number is large or small, and so we need to evaluate its size in terms of some other number related to it. This other number may be either the number of individuals classified as not falling in the class, or the total number of individuals being classified. We can get a more accurate understanding of the size of the class by comparing the number in the class with either of these other numbers.

In our example, the meaning or importance we can assign the number within the class is strikingly different for the situation of 50 children and 450 adults than for the situation of 50 children and 50 adults. In other words, the number of individuals not in the class gives us additional quantitative information about the class itself. We now have a quantitative meaning based on *relative* frequency, that is, the frequency within the class compared with the frequency not in the class.

Comparisons Using Per Cent Frequency. By stating the numbers in the classes as percentages, it is sometimes easier for us to make a judgment about relative frequency. The total number of individuals considered is given the value of 100, and the number in the class is expressed as a proportion of this value. In our example, the per cent of children attending the show in the first situation is 10 and the per cent of adults attending is 90.

One of the reasons for using percentages is that we have a common base in terms of which the numbers of several situations can be expressed. Suppose we conduct our study of attendance at *Quo Vadis* on three consecutive days and obtain the count shown in the table below. A compari-

Day	Children attending	Adults attending	Per cent children attending
1	391	34	80
2	230	20	80
3	290	25	80

son of the frequencies in column 2 with those in column 3 tells us that many more children than adults attended the show on each of the three days. For this conclusion we do not need to use percentages. The comparison of the attendance on the three days, however, is more difficult to make when we use the original numbers. In column 4 we have expressed the numbers of the second column in terms of per cent. It is seen that the per cent of children attending was the same on all three days. Per cent scores make it possible, then, to express in terms of the same base the relative frequencies of different situations. When the original numbers in the different situations vary in magnitude, as in our example, the per cent relative frequency greatly facilitates the comparisons we desire to make.

Examples of Ordering in Terms of Frequency. Ordering by means of frequency of occurrence is a common procedure in science. The physicist has the Geiger counter by which he measures the amount of radiation in studies of atomic energy. The physiologist counts the number of blood cells seen on a calibrated slide under a microscope and from his count makes quantitative statements about the content of an individual's blood. The psychologist uses this procedure when he evaluates individual performance in terms of the units of work achieved, such as the number of trials to learn a maze, the number of pages of text read in an hour, the number of examination questions correctly answered, the number of items forgotten after a given time interval, etc. When behavior is evaluated in terms of accuracy, ordering is then done in terms of the number of correct responses or the number of error responses. Following are some examples of measures of error performance: the number of misspelled words in a spelling test, the number of mistakes in typing ten pages, the number of entrances into blind alleys of a maze, the number of false leads attempted in the solution of a reasoning problem, etc.

It should be emphasized that in this very simple mathematical procedure of counting we possess the means for discovering very important quantitative meanings in our data.

The Use of Relative Amounts in Ordering Variables. To order by frequency of occurrence, we first needed to be able to recognize the presence and absence of the particular characteristic on which the events were to be classified, and then we needed to be able to count. Nothing was said about the relative amounts of the characteristic possessed by the events to be ordered. With knowledge of the relative amount of the characteristic we are able to increase further the precision of our description.

The Problem. Suppose we are interested in knowing who the best player on a baseball team is, or which employee in a factory turns out the most work, or which student at a university should be given a special scholarship. In these examples we need to go beyond the procedure of counting and ordering by frequency. In order to make the judgments indicated in these cases we must know more than just which players, or employees, or students are in a given class and how many there are in this class. We need to have information about the relative amount of the characteristic—that is, we need to be able to detect differences in amount of the characteristic possessed by the members falling within a class.

The Procedure. First, for any given problem, we must classify the individuals. For example, the students eligible for university fellowships are separated from those who are ineligible. As we have already seen, this step is prerequisite for any type of ordering. Next we must have information concerning the relative amount of the characteristic. Obviously, the characteristic must exist in varying amounts, and we must be able to detect at least in a rough way the amounts possessed by each individual in the class. In our three examples, there must be information about the players' effectiveness in the game, the employees' production in the firm, and the students' productivity as scholars.

Before we can arrive at a decision as to who is the best player, or most productive employee, or most scholarly student, we must rank some of the classified individuals in terms of the amount of the characteristic being studied. Actually, for any one of our specific examples we would not need to rank every individual who was classified. We could first select only the ones having high amounts of the characteristic and rank these cases in order from poorest to best. We would then be able to discover the person showing the best performance.

In some problems, we are required to rank all of the individuals in a class. In preparing a list of eligible persons for a civil-service job, it is necessary to rank all of the eligible applicants from poorest to best. Seniority lists for promotions usually require that all eligible candidates be placed in rank order. In psychological experiments, the rank ordering of all the participating subjects is usually necessary. In these problems reliable information must be obtained on every member of the group under study.

In order to rank individuals in terms of the amount of some characteristic possessed by them, it is not necessary actually to make a measurement of the amount of the characteristic possessed by each one. We must only be able to tell that one individual has more or has less of the characteristic than another individual. We must be able to state that A > B > C > D, etc. This judgment demands that we merely be able to observe differences in amount between individuals; it therefore need not be based on an actual measurement of these amounts. For example, we can rank the individuals of a group in order of their heights by comparing one with another without first measuring the actual height of any individual.

Ordering by Relative Amount in Terms of Categories. Sometimes in working with large numbers of data we find it convenient to classify them into categories according to relative amount. Each category differs from those adjacent to it in terms of average amount, but its limits are not precisely determined in reference to the limits of these adjacent categories. A good example of this procedure is the letter-grade system of the schools. For instance, in a given class in history the teacher learns through class discussions and essay examinations that some students are better than other students. A crude estimate of the amount of knowledge of every student is expressed in one of the following categories: A (very high), B (high), C (average amount), D (low), F (very low). The categories are placed in rank order, and thus students in different categories fall at different ranks. The students within a category are not arranged in rank order. This rough ranking of the students is all that is justified when exact differences in the amounts of the characteristic are not available.

Sometimes an ordering of the individuals is made in terms of scores expressed as per cents. There are two general procedures. One procedure has few facts to justify its use; the other is supported by sound empirical tests. The first is exemplified by a teacher who distinguishes the performance of his students on an essay examination in terms of very small percentage differences. Perfect performance is given the value of 100, and the performance of each student is judged in reference to this value. The examination papers are not merely judged to fall in one of several large related categories but are distinguished in some absolute sense and assigned exact per cent values, such as 70, 71, 72, or 92.5, 96.4, 98.8. It has been demonstrated that examiners are not capable of distinguishing very small differences in this type of examination performance. Assigning per cent values that differ by very small amounts gives the appearance of attaining a high precision. This is not justified by the facts.

In the second procedure, a few large categories are defined in terms of the proportions of the group that they are to include. For example, in grading classes in college the instructor might use the following per cent categories: 8 per cent A's, 20 per cent B's, 44 per cent C's, 20 per cent D's, and 8 per cent F's. In assigning certain proportions of the students to letter-grade categories it is not argued that we have in any way increased the precision of our measurements. The number of categories to be used should be determined by the accuracy with which the discriminations among individuals can be made.

Comparisons Using the Relative Amount Ordering Procedure. When we have sufficient knowledge about the amount of the characteristic possessed by every individual in a group so that we can place them in rank order, we can then make comparisons between each individual and every other individual in the group. If our measures are somewhat crude, we may not be confident of the accuracy of our estimate of the difference between adjacent ranks. That is, we may not feel confident that rank 1 is better than rank 2, rank 2 better than rank 3, or rank 3 better than rank 4. We may still be confident, however, that ranks which are two or three steps apart are sufficiently accurately assigned to accept the difference between them as significant. That is, we may feel confident that rank 1 is better than rank 3, or that rank 1 is better than rank 4. The confidence we have in our comparisons, whether the individuals are one step or more than one step apart, is dependent upon the accuracy of judging the relative amounts of the characteristic possessed by the individuals.

When categories are used, we can compare the performance of the individuals falling in the different categories. The further apart the categories in which the individuals fall, the greater confidence we can have in our comparisons. It should be obvious that errors will occur even when categories are used. For instance, an individual who is just barely good enough in his statistics course to be given a B grade is not much better than the individual who barely misses a B grade and is therefore given a C.

Ordering Involving the Measurement of the Amount of Difference in the Characteristic. In our previous discussion, we were concerned primarily with judging whether one individual had more of a given characteristic than did another individual. We were not concerned with the question of how much more. This question, however, is important in all types of scientific measurement. To get an answer to it requires a high level of precision in our measuring tools.

The Problem. We have previously observed that individuals in a group can be ranked in terms of the magnitude of some characteristic without measuring the amount of the characteristic possessed by each one. We need to know merely that A > B, B > C, C > D, etc. There is nothing in this procedure that enables us to tell whether the distances between the adjacent ranks are of equal size. The difference between A and B might be many times greater than, or merely a fraction of the size of, the difference between B and C, or the difference between any other two adjacent ranks. Greater precision in description results when we know the relative sizes of the differences between ranks. Even though these differences are not equal, knowledge of their relative sizes greatly increases the accuracy of our comparisons.

Suppose we have sufficient information about five individuals to be able to rank them on some trait X as indicated on the line below:

A	B	C	D		E

Under these conditions, our comparisons of any one with any other one are more accurate than if we merely know that A > B, B > C, and so on. Obviously, this greater precision in measurement can be achieved only with a more accurate estimate of the differences in amount of the characteristic possessed by the individuals under study.

The Meaning of Amount of Difference. To realize the type of description now under consideration, it is necessary to measure the amount of the difference in the characteristic. The question goes beyond that of: Is A greater than B? to the question: How much is A greater than B? It should be noted that we are not asking the question: How much is A? We are concerned here with finding, not the absolute amount of A or the absolute amount of B, but the best estimate of the absolute amount of the difference between A and B.

The amount of difference between individuals in terms of a common characteristic can be realized without knowing the exact amount possessed by each of the individuals. It is true, of course, that if we know the exact amounts of a characteristic possessed by two individuals it is a simple matter to compute the exact difference in amount between the two. We should note, however, that it is not necessary to know the exact amount possessed by each individual in order to measure the amount of the difference between them. This becomes obvious when we consider a simple problem in determining the difference in heights of two persons. We stand them close together and measure from the top of the head of one to the top of the head of the other. We can state the exact difference without knowing the position along the height dimension at which either individual falls.

Comparisons Possible with This Procedure. When we can measure amounts of difference in a characteristic, we can compare in a more precise manner individuals who differ in the amount of the characteristic. Referring to the illustration on page 111 of the amounts of performance of five individuals represented as A, B, C, D, and E, it will be noted that the differences between adjacent individuals are not the same. The graph was prepared so that the distance from A to B is twice that between B and C, three times that between C and D, and equal to the distance between D and E. Suppose that the performance scores of the five individuals were separated by amounts of score differences comparable to the linear differences of the illustration. It is then possible for us to make several comparative statements about the individuals, such as the following:

The difference in performance between A and B is twice the difference between B and C.

The difference in performance between B and C is one-third greater than the difference between C and D.

The difference in performance between B and C is half the difference between D and E.

Other similar statements are possible.

Order Involving the Measurement of the Absolute Amount of the Characteristic. As indicated in the preceding two sections, ordering of the expressions of a variable can be achieved without the measurement of the absolute amount of the expressions. The highest level of quantitative description is obtained, however, when it is possible to measure the absolute amount of these expressions.

The Problem. Sometimes we desire to know more than that one person's behavior is superior to another's by a given amount. We want to know what the level of superiority of each individual is; that is, we want to know how well each person performs. This knowledge requires measurement of the absolute amount of the characteristic under consideration.

Suppose we are placed in charge of the production of an assembly line in which electrical wall switches are being assembled. It is important that we keep account of the absolute number of switches assembled by each worker during some constant time interval such as a week. One purpose for which such knowledge is needed is for determining the cost of manufacture of the switches. This information may be fundamental to decisions concerning the effectiveness of the workers and the methods of work.

Type of Comparisons. With knowledge of the absolute amount of performance, it is possible to compare different individuals in absolute terms. For example, suppose worker X assembled 75 switches and worker

Y, 50. We not only know that the performance of X is better than that of Y and that the difference between the two performances is 25 switches, we also know that the performance of X is 1½ times greater than that of Y. By measuring every person's performance in absolute terms, any individual's performance can be taken as a standard and the achievements of the others expressed in terms of it. This type of ordering can be done in psychological measurements when we are ordering the actual performances. When we are concerned with the ability basic to the performances, we find that procedures are not yet available for expressing the ability in absolute terms. Further consideration will be given to this problem in subsequent discussions.

Need of Absolute Zeros. In order to measure in absolute terms we must have an absolute zero as a point from which to make the measurements. The nature of and need for zero points in measurement in general and in psychological measurements in particular are discussed in later sections of this chapter.

Four Levels of Precision in Measurement. It should be apparent that the precision of the measuring procedure available determines the accuracy with which we can quantitatively describe the order discovered in the characteristic. Ordering by frequency requires only classification and counting. It might be considered a form of ordering by amount, but the amount is represented by the frequency of occurrence of some complete unit, i.e., event, phenomenon, individual. Ordering by differences in the amount of some characteristic of the event, phenomenon, or individual requires measurement. If the procedure of measurement allows us to differentiate crudely differences in amounts possessed by the members of a class, we can place them in order of rank. If the procedure of measurement makes possible an estimate of the amount of the difference between members of the class, we can perform a more meaningful and exact ordering of the relative amounts of the behavior. If absolute amounts of the behavior being measured are available, it is possible to compare individuals by selecting the performance of one as a standard and expressing the performances of all other persons in terms of this standard.

THE USE OF NUMBER MEANINGS IN DESCRIPTION

As discussed in the foregoing sections, numerical description is accomplished by assigning number meanings to the characteristic of some event. There are several different kinds of number meanings. The precision of any measurement is a function of the accuracy with which the number meanings are assigned, and events differ in respect to the particular number meanings applicable to them.

Kinds of Number Meanings. Numerical symbols are readily used to represent different amounts of any behavior characteristic under consideration. Furthermore, as abstract symbols, they can be subjected to all of the manipulatory operations of mathematics. It is not always easy to establish that the meanings assigned to the symbols are applicable to the characteristic, and this is a point at which errors often are introduced in the measurement of psychological variables.

Assigning the Meaning of Magnitude. Numbers are concepts and are characterized by variations in the meaning called magnitude. As we have seen, experienced events also vary in this meaning or dimension of magnitude. We achieve measurement by assigning a number to some characteristic of an event. The fundamental condition that we must meet is that the number must correspond in magnitude with the amount of the characteristic. This requires that our knowledge go beyond the mere fact that the characteristic varies in amount. We must be able to determine, either roughly or with precision, the amount of the characteristic possessed by the particular event to be described. Measurement, then, requires special procedures by which we can determine the magnitude of the characteristic that we desire to describe quantitatively. We then assign to the characteristic a number that corresponds with this magnitude.

Assigning Complex Number Meanings. Besides the meaning of magnitude, numbers have other characteristics that allow us to manipulate them in the familiar ways of addition, subtraction, multiplication, and division. Under certain conditions, these more complex meanings can also be applied to the particular psychological event being described. This is what we do in a spelling test when we subtract 50 words spelled correctly from 75 words tried in order to learn the number of words missed.

Of course, it is not possible to submit every event and its characteristics to all of these operations. There is, then, the problem of determining and interpreting the relationship between the meanings of the numerical symbols and the meanings of the events.

Necessary Conditions for Assigning Number Meanings. In order to use the meanings of numbers accurately in describing events, it is necessary that the events be of such a nature that the particular number meanings are appropriate. Some meaning that is assignable to the events must be congruent with the number meaning that we desire to apply.

A homely illustration involving the meaning of addition should help make this point clear. If 12 oranges are added to 12 apples, the answer is not 24 apples, nor 24 oranges, nor 24 apple-oranges. The meaning must correspond to a characteristic that fits both oranges and apples, such as the meanings "pieces of fruit" or "object" or "thing," e.g., 24 objects. If a meaning peculiar to each fruit is retained, then the description must contain the conjunction "and," e.g., 24 oranges and apples. In either instance, the meaning assigned the totality suffers a reduction in precision because the specific meaning of 12 assigned to both oranges and apples before the addition is performed is not either implicit or explicit in the meaning assigned the totality. In other words, the phrase "24 oranges and apples" does not include the meaning 12 of one and 12 of the other. Twenty-four oranges and apples means combinations of oranges and apples in any numbers that will add to 24, as, for example, 1 orange and 23 apples. Although this point seems obvious and may appear inconsequential in the example given, in the application of measurement to psychological phenomena a real and significant problem is involved.

Advantages from Assigning Number Meanings. *Singleness of Meaning.* In general, numbers have singleness of meaning; that is, there is little disagreement in the meaning assigned a number by different persons. Freedom from ambiguity in meaning is one of the necessary conditions for accurate description. With singleness of meaning established in the number series, our task of achieving a high fidelity of correspondence between the numerical meanings and the event meanings is made much easier. Our attention can be focused primarily upon obtaining singleness of meaning in the magnitudinal aspects of the events.

Increase in Precision. Numbers are peculiarly appropriate as symbols for representing different amounts of a variable. The fundamental meaning of numbers being that of magnitude, differences in the meaning of numbers represent differences in magnitude. Variations in amount of any event characteristic can be represented by numbers varying in size. In this way a closer degree of correspondence is achieved between the event characteristic and the conceptual descriptive symbol than can ever be attained by the use of nonnumerical word descriptions.

High levels of precision are obtainable with numbers because of the fine gradations of magnitude possible with numbers. Gradations in magnitude in the number series can be as large or as small as the needs of the event demand. Whether the amount of the event gets progressively smaller or progressively larger, we can find a number that has a corresponding meaning of magnitude.

Universal Application. Lastly, the abstract nature of numbers gives them universal application. As adjectives, they can be used to modify any measuring unit. They can be used to modify units of length, units of weight, units of speed, units of accuracy, units of test performance; in short, any kind of unit of measurement.

Assigning Number Meanings to Psychological Variables. As we learned earlier, there are several conditions that must be met before we can assign quantitative meanings. Number meanings can be assigned to a variable only when the characteristic of the variable under consideration exists in differing amounts and when these different amounts can be readily identified. Accurate description also requires measuring procedures by which the amounts of the characteristic can be estimated. Lastly, only when there is some meaningful correspondence between the number meanings being applied and the meanings of the characteristic being described can we claim that valid measurement has been achieved

It is worthwhile for us to examine ways of interpreting the correspondence required between the meanings of the number symbols and the meanings of the observed psychological variable.

Ignoring the Meanings of the Psychological Variable. According to this point of view, number meanings are assigned to the scores or measures of a variable without due regard for the empirical meanings of the variable. Following the assignment of the number meanings to the scores, the mathematical manipulations then proceed without further reference to the empirical meanings. To illustrate this interpretation, let us consider an imaginary set of scores. Suppose that we have collected performance measures on the following variables: mental age, height, reaction time, reasoning ability, and memory for names. We correlate the scores of each variable with mental age and get fairly low relationships. Then we continue trying out many different combinations of the scores until we find that if we add height scores to memory for names and divide by the reaction time we get a measure that correlates rather highly with mental age. We then proceed to compute such measures and use them for predicting the mental ages of children. It should be apparent that the empirical meanings of the several test scores are lost sight of in the processes of analyzing and combining in order to get a composite score that correlates significantly with mental age. Adding height to memory for names and dividing by reaction time does not appear to have a corresponding meaning in the psychological world.

It is difficult to conceive of any scientist endorsing this point of view. Even the theoretical physicist, who has developed the application of mathematics to scientific subject matter to the highest degree yet achieved, implies in his discourse that he is talking about nature. He is not merely referring to the abstract meanings that he has developed through rational manipulation of mathematical symbols.

Requiring Meanings That Are Mathematically Manipulable. This interpretation states that we should apply number meanings to only those characteristics of a variable that can be sensibly manipulated as required by the particular mathematical process to be applied. Certainly, meanings obtained through the application of a mathematical equation may or may not be applicable to the empirical characteristics of the variables from which the function and the equation were developed. Symbols in an equation can be manipulated in ways that cannot conceivably be applied to the original psychological data.

Suppose we have scores on two psychological variables to which we wish to apply the arithmetic process of addition. The two variables should have a common meaning that can be subjected to this arithmetic manipulation, or the final outcome may be either erroneous or absurd in meaning, or both. Let us consider an illustration. John's spelling ability is measured by his response in correctly spelling 90 words out of 95. His arithmetic ability is measured by his correct solving of 80 problems in 85. We now average his two scores and conclude that his average performance in the two subjects is 85, i.e., $(90 + 80)/2 = 85$.

Obviously the figure 85 does not apply either to arithmetic or to spelling, but to some new meaning that is found common to both of these factors. It is not apparent just what this new meaning is. It is difficult to say what is done when spelling ability is added to arithmetic ability and an average computed. To say that 85 is an average of the two abilities is absurd. Eighty-five is merely the average of the numbers 90 and 80, and does not tell us anything about the nature of the magnitude in the two variables presumably being assessed in the number 85.

Using Predictive Propositions for Discovering Meanings. One way of applying number meanings is to form propositions stating functional relationships between psychological variables, and to use these fundamental relationships in interpreting new situations. Such a proposition may contain conceptual elements, but these elements stem directly from the empirical facts. The proposition describes a probable functional relationship, and is expressed by means of numerical symbols. The function, in the form of some numerical equation, is then applied to a new situation. The meanings of the terms of the predictive proposition, however, must in some sensible way be applicable to the variables. If this is not so the predictions cannot be verified, and therefore they serve no purpose.

Success in verifying predictive propositions leads us to believe that they do express meanings that are useful in interpreting and controlling psychological variables. This is not to say that every meaning applicable to the numerical symbols in a functional equation is also applicable to the behavior being analyzed. Some meanings of symbols cannot be directly applied to psychological variables.

Let us consider an example. Suppose again that we have the scores of persons on several mental-abilities tests. We cannot actually add the abilities of any given person. We can, however, add his ability scores, combining them in some statistical way in order to obtain one measure for all abilities. The importance of this new meaning, which cannot be directly observed in the psychological variables being described, derives from the fact that it enables us to discover further meanings that are useful. The averaging of the scores from the several ability tests given an individual provides us with a new meaning that we can call the individual's general ability. We are unable to find behavior processes that correspond to this general ability. Despite this, however, we can make predictive use of the individual's general-ability score. It can be used to improve our understanding and control of the individual's activities. Thus we gain from the information provided by the general-ability score even though we have not found any empirical processes in the individual to which it can be directly referred or with which it closely corresponds.

Limitations in Assigning Number Meanings to Psychological Variables. Psychological variables are difficult to measure. Human behavior has stubbornly resisted measurement. The quantitative aspects of complex behaviors are not readily identified, and procedures of measurement applicable to global types of behavior are difficult to devise. Most psychological measuring instruments now available are sensitive to changes coming from without the variable being measured, such as changes in the sample studied, in the person doing the measurement, or in the mode of applying the measuring instrument. Psychological measurement procedures often lack the stability that characterizes physical measurement procedures. These limitations are serious handicaps in applying mathematical equations to functional relationships in behavior. Not all psychologists are aware of them, and some of those who are aware of them still continue to apply their measuring techniques uncritically.

Particularly must the psychologist be on guard against committing the error of assigning inapplicable number meanings to his variables. Unless he knows from the empirical evidence what the behavior processes are to which his numerical symbols refer, the value of his mathematical equations is to be questioned. Under these circumstances, statistical manipulations applied to his data are suspect. One caution he can observe is to place less confidence in meanings that are abstracted so far from natural behavior processes that he cannot readily return to empirical situations to check them. A second caution he can observe is to refrain from using new meanings derived from mathematical equations until he can conduct empirical tests to verify them. Demonstration of the applicability of the new meanings to behavior processes is a necessary condition of their acceptance.

CONDITIONS NECESSARY FOR ACCURATE MEASUREMENT

To measure an object, we apply some unit of measurement against the object and determine how many times the unit is contained in the object. The point at which we start applying the measuring unit is at "no amount," and the point at which we discontinue applying the unit is at "all amount." The amount of the object is represented as the number of units needed to go from the one point to the other. The two necessary conditions for measurement, then, are a unit of measurement and a zero point.

Units of Measurement. *Units in "The Thing Itself."* In many common measuring situations, the unit of measurement consists of a small amount of the thing that is to be measured. For example, to measure length we use a small amount of length, such as the inch, or the foot, or the yard. To measure time we use a small amount of time, such as the second, or the minute, or the hour. In these situations, measurement is accurate because the amount of the thing being estimated is expressed in terms of identically the same kind of phenomenon as itself.

Units in a Functionally Related Variable. Measurement is possible and can be done very accurately by using a unit of measurement that is not a small amount of the characteristic being measured but a small amount of some other variable which bears a functional relationship with this characteristic.

In the measurement of weight we have an example that will make this clear. Weight can be measured either by a unit that is a small amount of the thing itself or by a unit in another variable bearing a constant functional relationship with the weight variable. When a balance scale is used, the object to be weighed is placed in a pan at one end of a lever and small weights are placed in a pan at the opposite end. Here the unit is a small amount of weight. In a spring scale, the weighing pan is connected through a lever to a spring. Placing the object to be weighed in the pan stretches the spring, and a pointer that is fastened to the spring is made to move along a printed scale of numbers indicating differences in the amount of weight. In the spring scale, the unit of measurement is a unit of length. A functional relationship is established between the amount of weight and the linear extension or "stretch" of the spring.

Thus, to measure weight it is not necessary to have a unit of weight. The fact is that a very large proportion of the weighing of goods in the commercial world is not done by the use of units of weight.

The Equality of Units of Measurement. Equality of the unit of measurement refers to the constancy of the size of the unit as it is applied in the process of measurement. For example, a foot of length is always the same; it remains constant in amount during the process of measurement. Suppose we made a foot rule from some kind of rubberlike substance, so it would readily change its length while being manipulated. Obviously, the units on the rule would change in size as we changed our tension on the rule in the process of using it. Measurements made at different times with this rule would not be equal but would vary slightly according to the changes in tension applied to it.

Physical measuring units are sufficiently constant for most purposes of measurement. Although a steel rule will change in length with changes in temperature, these changes are usually so small as to be of no consequence in most situations in which steel rules are used. If we were concerned with measuring to an accuracy of a millionth of an inch, we would need to control temperature variations. The amount of change in the size of the unit of measurement that can be tolerated is, then, a function of the purpose for which the measurement is being made.

Zero Points. *The Need of Stable Zero Points.* Measurement involves comparisons. For accurate comparisons we must have some point to which we can refer our measurements. These comparisons may be between different measures on the same individual or group, or between different individuals or groups in terms of the same measures.

We are not justified in comparing two objects or processes if they are not measured from the same stable beginning point. Suppose we have two tape rulers, one of which is worn away on the zero end so it begins at the ½-inch mark. If we were to use the two rulers in measuring respectively the heights of two persons, these height measurements would not be referred to the same zero point. Again, if in measuring the height of two people we were to allow one to wear shoes and the other to stand in bare feet, we would not be measuring from the same point in the height dimension and our comparison would be in error.

We are not justified in making comparisons of measures taken at two different times if the reference point changes its position between the two measurements. Suppose we introduce some change in an experimental variable between two measurements, and at the same time there occurs a shift in the zero point of the measurements. Any difference obtained between the measures taken on the two occasions could not then be attributed solely to the change in the experimental variable because, in part, it would be due to this shift in position of the reference point. What is needed in all measurement is a stable zero point.

Zero as "No Amount of the Thing." In everyday trade situations, measurement of objects usually begins at a point that represents no amount of the characteristic being measured. In such items as 2 pounds of meat, an 8-foot table, a charge of $20, etc., the measuring process is begun at a point of no amount of the characteristic involved. This type of zero is often called the absolute zero because there is no possibility of getting a value smaller. It should go without saying that the value of any given absolute zero is a constant, and therefore all measurements involving such a zero will be started from exactly the same reference point.

Zero as a Defined Stable Point. Situations frequently arise in which we wish to measure the amount of a characteristic but do not have an absolute zero from which to begin the measurement. The scale of hardness, which consists of 10 minerals varying in their hardness, does not have an absolute zero. The least hard mineral is talc, with a value of 1, and the mineral of greatest hardness is diamond, with a value of 10. Talc can be used as the point from which to begin measurement because under a given set of conditions its hardness remains constant. As a reference point, the hardness of talc is a stable zero point.

Consider the measurement of the psychological characteristic called intelligence. No usable absolute zero has been found for this characteristic. Although we can define an absolute zero as no amount of intelligence, we cannot devise a practical situation wherein measurement will begin from this zero. In this type of situation we can resort to a statistically defined relative zero, such as the mean of a set of scores. It is important that such a relative zero be stable if the ensuing measurements are to be accurate enough for comparative purposes.

Measurement with a Functionally Related Unit of Measurement and a Relative Zero. Accurate measurement is possible without units that are a small amount of the characteristic being measured and without zeros that represent no amount of this characteristic. We can overcome the first difficulty if we find another characteristic with measurable variations that bear a constant functional relationship with the magnitudinal changes in the characteristic to be measured. We can overcome the second difficulty by using a stable relative zero in place of an absolute zero. Let us consider the example of the measurement of temperature.

In measuring the temperature of a room, we cannot find a unit of temperature that is a small amount of the characteristic itself. There is no unit of hotness or coldness that can be divided into the room temperature in such a way as to give us the number of temperature units in the room. It is known, however, that mercury and other liquids change in volume with changes in temperature. Furthermore, when the liquid is forced to expand and contract in a calibrated enclosure like a glass tube, the change in the liquid can be measured in the dimension of length. The change as measured in the linear dimension is functionally related to the change in temperature, and therefore measurement of temperature is made possible.

To compare changes in temperature we need a unit of measurement and a zero point. We can define the unit arbitrarily, just as was done in the case of length in selecting the inch, or in the case of weight in selecting the pound. The zero point can be any point so long as it is constant or varies within very narrow limits.

Temperature measurements are made from a stable relative zero. When thermometers were first devised, the absolute zero of temperature was not known. An arbitrary set of conditions was adopted for defining a relative zero. On the centigrade scale, zero temperature is represented as that temperature at which pure ice melts at sea level. It will be noted that three special prescriptions are made, namely, melting point, pure ice, and sea level. Constancy or stability of the zero point is achieved by meeting these three prescriptions.

The unit of temperature measurement, the degree, is also arbitrarily defined. In the centigrade scale, a second point on the scale was established as that temperature at which pure water boils at sea level. This temperature was given the value of 100. The degree was then defined as $\frac{1}{100}$ of the distance between this point and zero temperature.

Measurement of temperature, then, is obtained by starting the measuring process from a relative zero and by using a unit in a wholly different characteristic than temperature itself.

UNITS OF MEASUREMENT IN PSYCHOLOGICAL ANALYSES

Kinds of Units. *Physical Units.* Physical units are those that have been developed in connection with the description of physical phenomena. Many of these units are essential to the work of the psychologist, such for example as units of time, length, weight, voltage, force, etc. Because most behavior expressions have a durational characteristic, the unit of the time dimension particularly proves of inestimable value.

Psychological Units. Psychological units consist of small amounts or divisions of behavior or performance, and reflect either positive and effective or negative and ineffective response. The following are some examples: completing a trial in a maze, typing a page of text, failing to work a mathematical problem, constructing some object such as a picture puzzle, misspelling a word, failing to accomplish a given task in the allotted time, and the like.

Psychological Units as a Small Amount of "The Thing Itself." It is sometimes possible to utilize as the unit of measurement a small amount of the psychological characteristic being assessed. In measuring the ability to add, the unit used is a problem in addition. In measuring the ability to spell, the unit used is a word spelled. Here we are defining the abilities to add and to spell in terms of the characteristics elicited in the performance of individuals when they are solving problems and spelling words.

It may be argued that by the phrase "ability to add" we mean more than merely the characteristics manifest in working problems; that there is something over and above the performance that we wish to call "the ability." This is more clearly seen in the measuring of the variable of intelligence. In the measurement of intelligence, we use such items as analogies, arithmetic problems, identification of objects, detection of relations, number completion, interpretation of proverbs, arithmetic reasoning, and others. The argument is made that intelligence is reflected in every one of these types of items and therefore should not be identified with the psychological processes involved in the solution of any one of them. Obviously, the units differ from one type of item to another, so there is really no single unit of measurement. It cannot be construed that these units are small amounts of the ability called intelligence. When the characteristic is defined in terms of the objective manifestations of performance, however, it is possible to interpret the problems or exercises used as small amounts of the characteristic being measured and to use the problems or exercises as units of measurement.

Units of a Functionally Related Variable. When no unit in the characteristic can be found, it is sometimes possible to devise a unit in another characteristic related to the characteristic that we wish to measure. A functional relationship is then the basis of measurement, and it is important that there be a known and close correspondence between the changes in magnitude of the original variable to be described and the changes in the values of the adopted variable through which measurement is achieved.

Suppose the problem is to measure the ability of students to do the work required for graduation from college. Having decided that ability to work arithmetic problems and knowledge of vocabulary might reveal ability to do college work, we could construct a test utilizing problems in addition, subtraction, multiplication, etc., and another test utilizing the definition, meaning, and use of words. We would assume that the number of arithmetic problems correctly worked and the number of items passed on the vocabulary test would be indicative of a person's ability to do college work. We would then set up an experiment to determine empirically the relationship between performance on the tests and performance in college. If the correlation between the two were found to be high, it would be possible to use the tests as measures of ability to do college work. The unit of the test would be an item—a problem or question—and increasing numbers of items correctly answered would be considered to measure increasing amounts of the ability necessary to work successfully at the college level. Obviously, the all-important task would be to devise test situations that correlate highly with college success.

The following are some examples of this type of measurement in psychology: measuring the racial antagonism of a group by the number of items on a racial tolerance scale that the group is willing to endorse; measuring the attention-holding power of a stimulus by the amount of time the individual's eyes are fixed upon it; and measuring forgetting by the amount of relearning necessary to bring a person back to his original level of proficiency. In none of these instances is the variable in which we are interested being measured directly. Rather, we measure changes in the variable in terms of differing amounts of another variable the values of which are positively related with those of the first variable.

The Problem of Equality of Units. *Physical Units.* When we use physical units for measuring psychological variables, we often escape the problem of inequality of units. Obviously, this is true when we measure physical characteristics of individuals such as height and weight. It may also be true when the characteristic being measured is psychological in nature. In the latter case, the ability is defined in terms of concepts for which we have objective counterparts. The measurement of reaction time will be used as an illustration.

Reaction time is defined as an ability possessed by the individual. Its primary meaning is that of duration. This meaning is also the most important meaning of the time dimension, and we have invented many measuring instruments for assessing differences in duration. In a situation in which the individual, through his performance, can objectively express his reaction-time ability, we can utilize one of the time instruments and accurately assess this durational meaning of his reaction time. For example, the braking-reaction time of an automobile driver is measured by the time required in removing the foot from the accelerator pedal and applying it to the brake pedal.

Psychological Units. In the measurement of psychological variables, quantitative description at low levels of precision can be attained without equal units of measurement. Ordering by means of frequency and ranking can be achieved without equality of the units. If the ranks can be accepted as being approximately equivalent, more exact descriptions are made possible.

When we use such units as a problem worked, a word spelled, an error committed, and the like, the tacit assumption is made that within a given instrument any unit is equal to every other unit. Obviously, this assumption is not true. For example, in arithmetic tests, differences between problems will be smaller when we use a large number of simple problems than when we use a small number of complex problems. In other words, equality of units is approached as the problems are made simple in nature. This is one of the common procedures used in obtaining equal units. It is severely restricted in application, however, being usable with only very simple psychological processes.

Another procedure suggested for achieving equality of units in psychological tests is to determine empirically the difficulty of all the items and then use only those items that are known to be equally difficult. Thus, for an arithmetic test, the items would be given to a large group of individuals comparable to those for whom the test is being devised. The difficulty of each item would be determined in terms of the proportion answering it correctly. The test would then be constructed of items of approximately the same difficulty.

The foregoing procedures for achieving equal units of measurement are not applicable to many important psychological variables, particularly to global or molar behaviors. To overcome this deficiency, the psychologist utilizes statistical procedures for achieving equal units. Brief consideration will be given here to one of these statistical procedures. A more complete discussion of the mathematical aspects of the procedure will be found in Chap. 10.

The Standard Deviation as a Unit of Measurement. One of the recurrent problems in psychology is the measurement of differences in performance both within individuals and between individuals within a group. The standard deviation serves as an accurate index for measuring these differences, and so it serves as a unit of measurement for evaluating performance. The measurement of the performance of persons within a group will be used to illustrate the serviceability of this unit.

When many persons are measured by means of some test or other instrument, the performance scores vary in value, there being a striking tendency for scores of medium value to occur more frequently and scores of low value or high value to occur less frequently. A definite relationship is found between the frequency of occurrence and the size of the score, a mathematical function occurring that is similar to the one diagrammed in Fig. 1 of Chap. 5. There is a mathematical formula available for expressing this relationship, and the standard deviation, which is part of this formula, is used to measure the amount of dispersion or spread occurring among the scores. It is possible to determine the distance that separates any score from any other score and to express this distance in terms of the number of standard-deviation units. It is also possible to express in standard-deviation units the distance separating any given score from the mean of the scores.

For any given group of scores the standard deviation has only one value, and therefore its value as a unit is constant in all of the comparisons in which it is used. We have already learned that one of the important characteristics of a unit of measurement is that it have a constant value. We have, then, in the standard-deviation unit a constant unit of measurement.

The standard-deviation unit can be computed for any variable for which there is a distribution of scores. It is expressed in terms of the scores or measures themselves; therefore, it is a small amount of the "thing" being measured, when this is interpreted as referring to performance only. Because of its almost universal applicability, the standard-deviation unit has proved the most useful unit of measurement yet devised for evaluating human behavior.

ZERO POINTS IN PSYCHOLOGICAL MEASUREMENTS

It will be remembered that accurate measurement is made possible when we have equal units of measurement and stable zero points. When we meet these two requirements we can order either individuals or groups on a continuum representing the characteristic being measured. We have the basis for making accurate comparisons among individuals or among groups.

Psychology's Need for Zero Points. In the science of psychology we need stable relative zero points. Our primary concern is with comparing the performances of different individuals and groups, or with comparing two or more different performances of the same individual or group. In each of these tasks we are concerned with the quantity of a given performance in relation to the quantity of another performance. We are not concerned with the quantity of a given performance in relation to "no performance at all," i.e., absolute zero. This is to say that, in the main, the needs of psychological measurements are satisfied when the two performances are comparable.

The two conditions that must be realized to make two or more measurements comparable are those already mentioned, namely, equal units of measurement and common stable zero points. Given equal units, relative zeros—if common and stable—are then sufficient to accomplish the majority of comparisons involved in the quantitative evaluation of human behavior.

The Need for Common Zero Points. By "the need for a common zero point" we mean that the point must have the same meaning for measurement purposes for the two or more variables being described. No problem arises when the measures to be compared are from the same instrument, as when two groups of persons are tested on the same psychomotor test apparatus. Here we really have two manifestations of the same variable, so the measurements are made from the same zero point.

When comparisons are made between different variables, it is necessary to devise a common zero point. Suppose we desire to compare the relative superiority of a group of college sophomores in two subjects such as physiology and psychology. Comparable zero points in the two subjects are required. We must be assured that the zero point in the measuring instrument for physiology is at a point on the physiology-ability continuum that is comparable to the point occupied on the psychology-ability continuum by the zero point in the measuring instrument for psychology.

If we gave the group a difficult physiology test and an easy psychology test, we would not be justified in assuming that the zero points on the two tests were comparable.

In this problematic situation the psychologist has appealed to statistical procedures for achieving a solution. A stable zero point in each subject is statistically feasible. The mean score is most frequently utilized. We must be assured, however, that the mean scores are not subject to large sampling errors and that they are comparable in the sense of being at approximately identical points on the continua of the two abilities. This comparability is attained by randomly selecting the subjects from appropriately defined populations and by utilizing large numbers of subjects. In our example, if the group is representative of college sophomores in so far as their knowledge of physiology is concerned and if, similarly, they are representative of college sophomores in so far as their knowledge of psychology is concerned, then with a large number of cases entering the computations we should obtain mean scores that are equivalent on the two continua.

Characteristics of Relative Zeros. A relative zero should have the characteristic of stability mentioned in previous discussions. Furthermore, if comparisons of two or more variables are to be made, then the relative zeros in the several variables should have a common meaning pertinent to the purpose of measurement as described in the foregoing section.

Two additional characteristics of a relative zero are important. It should be rigorously defined, and it should be relatively easy to determine. By being rigorously defined we mean that the zero point should be so described that different investigators are able independently to arrive at its value. This can be accomplished if the zero point is stated algebraically in terms of a mathematical formula. Ease of determination is recommended as a characteristic in order that the zero point will receive wide use in scientific investigations.

The mean score, when determined from a large number of cases that have been representatively selected according to the purposes of the comparisons to be made, fulfills all of the conditions suggested for an acceptable relative zero point.

Absolute Zero Points in Psychological Measurement. Having an absolute zero allows us to apply the higher-order meanings of multiplication and division to our measures. For example, if there are two measures having the values of 20 and 40, we can say that 40 is twice 20, or that 20 is one-half 40. It should be apparent that in such physical dimensions as length, weight, time, and the like, we have succeeded in devising practicable and useful absolute zeros.

In the measurement of complex psychological variables, we do not have absolute zeros. For some psychological variables it is possible to conceptualize an absolute zero, as was previously pointed out in regard to the ability called intelligence. But for such variables no practical situations have been discovered by which such conceptualized zeros can be empirically demonstrated in performance situations. In the case of some psychological variables, absolute zeros cannot even be sensibly conceptualized. What would be the meaning of an absolute zero in personality or of an absolute zero in social behavior? It is difficult to conceive of a person without personality or of one who does not manifest social behavior either adjustive or unadjustive in nature.

In most measurement situations in psychology we can evolve meanings that are restricted to the objective performance that provides the measures, or we can rationalize beyond these meanings to conceptualized characteristics that we assume underlie the performance. If we restrict ourselves to a consideration of performance per se, we can apply an absolute zero, defining it as no performance or zero performance on the particular measuring instrument being used. In this instance we can say that a performance of 40 is twice as great as a performance of 20.

In many problems, the nature of the conceptualized ability is the goal that is sought. We then utilize the performance scores to represent the conceptualized ability considered basic to the performance. In this instance there is no absolute zero. If we wish to compare differences in absolute amounts of this ability by means of differences found in the empirical scores, we are not justified in making comparative statements that involve the number meanings of multiplication or division. We must conclude that in so far as human abilities are concerned we are not justified in our comparisons of individuals or of groups to say that one score represents a given number of times the amount of ability represented by another score.

Measurement of psychological variables is handicapped very little, however, by the absence of absolute zero points. As noted in earlier sections, accurate measurement can be accomplished with stable relative zeros. Common stable zeros as points of reference are sufficient for achieving precise quantitative comparisons.

THE QUANTIFICATION OF CONCEPTUALIZED ABILITIES

Several times we have had occasion to refer to the abilities or capacities underlying human behavior. Conceptual abilities are postulated by which we can explain the objective performance. When these conceptual abilities are supported by sufficient evidence we accept them as facts and proceed to work out their individual characteristics.

The Basis for Postulating Conceptual Abilities. The logic of postulating abilities underlying behavior is not difficult to understand. We observe wide variations in the quality and quantity of performance in different individuals under the same or very similar sets of stimulating conditions. Inasmuch as the environmental stimuli eliciting the behavior are approximately constant for different individuals, we conclude that the observed variations are to be ascribed to differences in the psychological make-up of the individuals.

Facts point to the existence of stable characteristics in the make-up of every individual. If we repeatedly observe the behavior of a given individual we discover that certain qualities and combinations of qualities are frequently manifest in his performance. We therefore postulate one or more abilities as being responsible for these stable characteristics. We then devise names by which we can distinguish these abilities.

The Logic of Measuring Conceptualized Abilities. The logic of measuring conceptualized abilities is straightforward and simple. The qualitative and quantitative characteristics of different individuals are stable and occur frequently in the form of overt response patterns. To describe these responses accurately, we devise stimulating situations that will consistently elicit these stable performance patterns from the individual at different times. To introduce quantity into our descriptions, we select those aspects of the performances that are amenable to the assignation of number meanings. If, when tried out empirically, such stimulating situations consistently elicit the same quantitative and qualitative characteristics in performance, we infer that we have measured that stable characteristic in the individual that we have called his ability.

The Nature of the Relationship between Performance and Ability. The interpretation of the nature of the relationship between the performance and the postulated ability is one fraught with difficulty and misunderstanding. What we know are the facts characterizing the objective performances of the individual. What we want to know is the nature of the abilities that lie behind the performances. We must infer the latter from the former.

Various interpretations of the relationship between the performance and the ability are possible. We can assume a one-to-one relationship between the objective response and the postulated counterpart, regardless of how we define it. In this case we can assign identically the same number meanings to the ability as we are able to justify for the performance. Another interpretation is to apply the number meanings to the objective expression, but assume that the quantitative relationship between the performance and the ability is less than perfect and that, therefore, the number meanings apply only in a rough way to the postulated ability. A third interpretation is to apply the quantitative meanings to the performance and make no attempt to apply any of them to the ability.

Which of these interpretations, or some other, will be championed in the quantitative description of a given ability will depend upon several factors. Important among these are the amount of evidence favoring the existence of the postulated ability, the precision with which the objective performance can be quantitatively described, and the extent of the empirical evidence justifying the assignation of number meanings to the ability. The scientific psychologist cannot afford to remain strictly on an operational level and define all factors and relationships in terms of only the situation in which they are found. With this approach, psychological theorizing is severely restricted, a situation that science can ill afford to tolerate. On the other hand, error can be committed in assigning a reality to the postulated ability before the facts justify it. In this instance, the scientist, in terms of certain performance measures, may interpret the ability as a fact when in reality it is not. He may then make predictions about the abilities of individuals that lead to errors of serious consequence.

SELECTED READINGS

Cohen, M. R., and E. Nagel: "An Introduction to Logic and Scientific Method," chap. 15, Harcourt, Brace and Company, Inc., 1934. The authors present the logic underlying some of the tasks of measurement. The following topics are considered: the purpose of measurement, the nature of counting, the measurement of intensive qualities, the measurement of extensive qualities, the formal conditions of measurement, and numerical laws and derived measurement.

Guilford, J. P., and A. L. Comrey: Measurement in Psychology, in H. Helson (ed.), "Theoretical Foundations of Psychology," chap. 11, D. Van Nostrand Company, Inc., 1951. This chapter gives a brief chronicle of the development of psychological measurements, then reviews some of the problems faced by the psychologist in quantifying behavioral characteristics. Among the topics considered are the following: measurement and mathematics, applications of numbers to data, types of measurement scales, psychophysical measurement, scaling methods, and mental testing.

Jahoda, M., M. Deutsch, and S. W. Cook: "Research Methods in Social Relations," vol. 1, chap. 4, The Dryden Press, Inc., 1951. In the discussions of this chapter, the student is introduced to some general problems in psychological measurement. The particular topics considered are: variations in scores on measuring instruments, the reliability of measurements, the validity of measurements, and precision as reflected in scales of measurement.

PART TWO

Steps of the Scientific Method

The scientific method does not consist of a single set of steps followed in some invariable chronological order. To a large extent, the chronology of a scientific experiment is tied to the ups and downs of the scientist's motivations. At some time in the early training of a student of science, however, there is need for a systematic treatment of those steps that are fundamental to any scientific attack upon a problem. In presenting such a treatment, no claim should be made that the steps are well delineated one from another or that the order of the steps is established regardless of the nature of the scientist's progress. The chronology of the steps given herein is to be interpreted as a serviceable one and as a frequently used one, but not as an invariable one.

The definition and delimitation of a scientific problem are discussed in Chap. 7. It is accepted as a fact that we can get a solution faster and the solution is likely to be a better one if we understand all of the elements and implications of the problem to be attacked. The time spent in the early phases of a project learning about the nature of the variables involved is amply repaid in later stages in the form of a more precise and dependable experimental design.

A very frequently used procedure of the scientist is to set up his problem in the framework of a hypothesis. The value of this approach is pointed out in Chap. 8. A systematic account is given of the steps used in deductively elaborating a hypothesis and in evolving theorems and testing situations for collecting facts about the hypothesis. In systematizing these steps, fairly precise definitions are given to the concepts presented. It is not intended that the treatment reflect the variety of interpretations given these concepts by other scientists. The object is to give the reader a clear exposition of the logical processes involved so he can see both the means and the ends of hypothesis formulation. Once the logic is understood, the reader should have no difficulty deciding upon the meanings he personally wishes to assign the concepts.

When the problem has been formulated, the next step is to collect facts that are pertinent to the hypothesis. Chapter 9 describes how the scientist must devise an empirical testing situation in which the variables he wishes to study will be allowed to operate, freed from the influence of other interfering variables. The problem of control is a central one, as is also the problem of measurement. These problems are difficult to solve, especially when global types of behavior are under study. It must be recognized, however, that it is only through using adequate control and measurement procedures that trustworthy evidence can be obtained.

The full import of the facts collected on a problem cannot be obtained from a cursory examination of the data. Chapter 10 presents some of the common problems faced by the scientific psychologist in the organization, analysis, and interpretation of his facts. The facts must be ordered in a way that will give answers to the questions that initiated the study. Certain characteristics of human behavior, such as the mean and variability of performance, should be quantitatively analyzed and evaluated. When several variables have operated in an experiment, the nature and amounts of the relationships existing among them should be stated quantitatively.

The final step taken by the scientist is to formulate generalizations about the meanings that are revealed in the data. As described in Chap. 11, this is a hazardous and difficult task. It is the step wherein the scientist points out the value that his results may have. He suggests how his findings contain the solutions to the specific problems he is studying. He also projects his findings into yet unchartered areas and suggests implications that they have for yet unsolved problems. The rational deductions he makes must be based on sound logical relationships between his own findings and the elements and characteristics of the situations to which he refers his generalizations.

CHAPTER 7

The Definition and Delimitation
of a Scientific Problem

What starts the scientist on his quest? How do the problems arise which later he so intently studies? What does he do in order to discover the potential solutions that he undertakes to investigate? These are questions that long have troubled the scientifically untrained person and the scientifically immature individual who has yet to grapple at close hand with an original problem.

THE CENTRAL POSITION OF THE PROBLEMATIC SITUATION

Inquiry begins when some past belief is questioned, when a familiar solution fails, or when we do not understand some fact. The resulting uncertainty leads us to a consideration of the underlying factors and conditions and eventually to the recognition of a problem. Analysis of the problem then leads us to trial hypotheses and possible solutions.

An Inquiry Starts from a Problem. At the beginning, every scientific investigation arises from some problematic situation. The mere collecting of facts, regardless of how precise the procedures and techniques that are utilized, does not constitute a scientific investigation. It is idle to collect facts unless they are referred to some problem or question.

Sometimes a student of science becomes enamored of a method or technique and then looks about for a problematic situation in which to use it. For the most part this approach is unproductive except as it serves to develop the student's skill in the techniques employed. The primary concern is to define a problem, not to look for a method. So much is known about methodology that the solution of many new problems seldom demands a radical change in method. Even research findings of "world-shaking" proportions have arisen from only slight alterations in already well-established and familiar methods.

One of our first tasks is to develop an accurate and comprehensive description of our problem. We shall find this task much more difficult than we at first suppose. It is not easy to put our finger on the particular crucial points that are giving rise to our doubt and uncertainty. In fact, it is a mark of scientific genius to discover immediately the key sources of a problem and to know at what points to apply scientific procedures to discover a satisfactory solution.

The Problem Sets the Direction of the Study. The initiation and direction of all phases of an investigation are influenced by the problem. As already mentioned, a scientific investigation is not aimless fact gathering. It is directed toward the attainment of specific aims, and the facts which are collected gain significance in direct proportion to their contribution in attaining these specific aims. To understand the problem means to learn the location of the key points of difficulty. Knowing these points enables us to direct our efforts insightfully. We avoid running after intriguing but false notions. We are better able to relate the subproblems in the most meaningful relationships. We know which phases merit first consideration. If we know the nature of the problem we know what to look for, where to look for it, and when it can be expected to occur.

The Problem Reveals Methods and Procedures. The nature of the problem directly conditions the methods. Frequently, the problem implies or designates the particular methods to be used. Different types of problems raise different types of questions requiring different types of answers. These answers must be discovered through the use of different types of procedures. The kinds of answers needed, then, determine the approach we make to the problem. As soon as we have gained an adequate knowledge of the problem, we can expect to discover some kind of method for attacking it.

Occasionally a scientist gets so wrapped up in a particular procedure that he uses it on nearly every type of problem. His conviction is so strong that he will not wait for the analysis of the problem to give him needed knowledge concerning the nature of the most appropriate procedures. In his cocksureness he modifies the problem to adjust it to the procedure, rather than modifying the procedure to adjust it to the problem. When he has completed his study he may, no doubt, have arrived at a solution, but certainly the solution will not be for the problem that originally stimulated his interests. Knowledge of the problem not only precedes the application of methods; it determines what methods are appropriate.

Knowledge about the Problem Aids in the Control of Bias. A thorough knowledge of the problem lessens the opportunity for the introduction of the biases of the investigator. Every investigation will reflect the qualifications and points of view of the investigator because he directly or indirectly enters into every phase of the study. There are, then, many opportunities for the entrance of bias. The initial phases of a study are particularly likely to reflect the peculiar notions of the investigator. Here he first encounters the unknowns with which he must deal, and he will employ every conceivable scientific "trick" at his command to understand them. He is likely to be a little less critical at this stage, when the "going is tough."

A thorough analysis of the problem will reveal the many ramifications that it has and will enable the scientist to track down its many implications. Such an analysis will tend to point up neglected phases and to reveal any twists resulting from personal bias. There is no guarantee against the introduction of bias into a scientific investigation, but a comprehensive knowledge of the problem will greatly reduce the likelihood of its occurrence.

EVOLVING A CONCEPTUAL FRAMEWORK FOR THE PROBLEM

Our knowledge about any problem can be roughly divided into what are called facts and what are called explanations. The former are empirically substantiated. The latter are the best guesses and reasons we devise to enlarge our understanding of the problem. It is quite impossible to separate the two in our thinking while we are attacking a given problem. For purposes of discussion, however, we shall want to treat them as if they were so separated.

The steps involved in framing a problem for scientific investigation will be more easily understood if we parallel our discussion with the description of an actual problem. Suppose we select a problem in highway-accident prevention, an area in which most everyone will have some background knowledge. To begin with, we should start with a very vague and general notion of the problem, that is, we should make believe that we are as naive as we would be with a problem about which we knew very little. As each step is presented we can then develop the problem little by little toward a more specific and workable problem for investigation. Let us start with the general question: How can automobile accidents be reduced?

The Meaning of a Conceptual Framework. The evolution of a conceptual framework for a problem means organizing our knowledge into a meaningful set of relations which will enable us to get a clear perspective of the variables at work and which will reveal modes of attack for collecting additional information. In gaining an understanding of the nature of a problem we study it from every possible angle. We collect both facts and explanations and try to piece them together into some kind of unitary picture that will encompass all phases of the problem. We seek out relations among the facts, relations among the explanations, and relations between the facts and the explanations. In this way we extract as much meaning as we can from our present knowledge, and using this as a base we then evolve possible solutions to the problem which can be tested under empirical conditions.

The Listing of all Possible Constituents. *The Problem.* Our first step is to list all possible constituents of the problem. A constituent is any item of information, either factual or theoretical, that we consider relevant to the problem. For most problems with which we would be concerned we would have some items of information. We would know about some of the factors, elements, aspects, characteristics, conditions, etc., that contribute to it. At this point we should not be too ready to discard items of information that seem to have little meaning for our problem, for we are not prepared to make sound judgments about the pertinence of the relationships involved. We should include the questionable items and make the listing of constituents as complete as possible.

Our list should include all explanatory postulates that in any way bear on the problem. The phrase "explanatory postulates" sounds somewhat formidable, and may cause us to wonder why at this early stage—a stage bordering on complete ignorance—we should attempt to deal with elusive conceptions instead of concrete down-to-earth facts. The logic of justifying this course of action is simple. What is needed for solving any problem is a solution. At the beginning, a solution consists primarily of an explanation. If we discover the explanation of a problem, we usually solve the problem. The elements or relationships that we conceive as a solution of the problem are then to be listed as constituents.

Even though the task is a difficult one, it cannot be overemphasized that we must thoroughly examine the theoretical constituents of the problem. As we learned earlier, explanation projects beyond the known into the unknown. Explanatory postulates serve as bridges by which we cross from the known constituents to the unknown solutions. Through them we are able to set up possible solutions that can be tested empirically.

An Illustration. Let us list some of the constituents of the problem of how to prevent automobile accidents. Remember these are ideas that come to mind as we think about the problem, ideas that we think somehow belong to the problem. Let us phrase them just as they come to mind.

The degree of traffic congestion.
The time of day of accidents.
Glare blindness.
The condition of the roadway.
People who drink should have their driver's license permanently revoked.
Divided highways.
Make of car.
Poor eyesight causes most automobile accidents.

Most drivers are accident prone.

Violating the right of way.

Reckless drivers cannot be improved.

Good roads will eliminate accidents.

Sex and age of the driver.

Type of accident.

Highway markers.

Some of these constituents concern situational factors, others concern personal or driver factors. Some are specific in nature, others are rather general. Some are factual and concrete, others are explanatory and abstract. The interrelations among some are close, among others remote. Obviously, with further thought many more constituents could be listed.

We should note that some of the explanatory postulations suggest determiners to be investigated. For example, visual acuity as a determiner of automobile accidents can be developed readily from the rather extreme statement that poor eyesight causes most accidents. Here, then, is a bridge from a known theoretical constituent on the one hand to an unknown but possible solution on the other. Furthermore, this suggested functional relationship is one that can be studied empirically.

In connection with this same suggestion, the reader is invited to demonstrate for himself how the nature of the problem contributes to the determination of the method. No mention will be made here of a possible method to study visual acuity in relation to accidents in order that the reader can devise one by himself and in so doing become aware of how the understanding of a problem readily leads to a possible method for its investigation.

Determining the Theoretical Security of the Constituents. *The Problem.* Having listed as many constituents as we can, the next step is to examine the theoretical basis for each constituent. The expression *theoretically secured* means that there is an acceptable explanation indicating that the constituent bears a relation to the problem. We assume that there is a theoretical structure (explanation) for each constituent. We must discover it, trace it, and describe it. We do this by determining the nature of the relationship existing between the constituent and all other constituents, both factual and explanatory. We should not be concerned at this point if we find no obvious relation between a given known and theoretically secured constituent and a constituent that is only guessed and is theoretically unsecured. Although we should be on the lookout for such relationships, we should not despair if they are not observable at this early stage of our analysis.

Many of the constituents can be placed in one of three general classes: (1) constituents that are determinate and theoretically secured, (2) constituents that are indeterminate but theoretically secured, and (3) constituents that are indeterminate and not theoretically secured. By determinate is meant that facts are available to support the contention that the constituent can be examined empirically. In our illustration, the make of the car, the time of day, and the condition of the roadway are examples of determinate constituents. Indeterminate refers to the lack of evidence to justify at the time the belief that the constituent can be examined empirically. An example is the constituent of accident proneness. This constituent has yet to be sufficiently clearly defined to be subjected to empirical testing.

Some of the constituents will be difficult to classify and evaluate at the beginning of our analysis. Their theoretical significance may be unknown and revealed only after much further study. Also, with additional study we may have to revise some of our evaluations. A constituent might be judged to be secured theoretically, but after further empirical evidence is obtained it might be demonstrated that the factor has little significance for our problem.

An Illustration. Let us consider the theoretical security of two of the accident constituents. First let us examine the factor of time of day. What we want to do is to show logically that time of day might have some pertinent relation to automobile accidents. There is considerable evidence that the effectiveness of man's responses varies with the hour of the day. Studies made with factory workers doing various psychomotor tasks amply justify this conclusion. It would be expected that the psychomotor task of driving an automobile would be subject to similar diurnal fluctuations. If this is so, then the driver's effectiveness would vary and he would be more likely to have accidents at some hours than at others. We can engage in a little naturalistic observation here and suggest that the driver is not wide-awake early in the morning and is tired at the end of the working day, so his effectiveness at the wheel might be less at these hours. We can, then, probably safely assume that the time of day is related with accidents and deserves investigation.

A little more thought might lead us to think of density of traffic as also varying at different hours of the day. There is the morning rush to work and the evening rush to return home. We now have the time-of-day constituent coming into relation with the constituent of degree of traffic congestion. Further consideration might lead us to suspect that time of day may not be as important as we at first thought, that what we are calling time of day is not an accident determiner at all but merely an objective sign that helps us to discover and localize factors about the driver (sleepiness and tiredness) and factors about the roadway (congestion) that merit further study.

Accident proneness can be suggested as another concept frequently used in explaining accidents. It should be said, however, that the concept has been applied uncritically as a determiner of accidents. Presumably, according to this concept, if we could discover the accident-prone drivers and rule them off the highways, we would greatly reduce the number of accidents. It might come as a surprise to the reader to learn that accident proneness has not yet been shown empirically to be a useful concept in the prevention of automobile accidents. The concept is not as well secured theoretically as its proponents lead us to believe.

Forming a Theoretical Framework for the Problem. *The Functions Served by a Theoretical Framework.* At this point in our study we are in need of discovering some unifying principles that will bring all the factors into an integrated whole. We have presumably completed a listing of all of the factual and explanatory constituents we can discover. The picture is somewhat chaotic because there are so many individual and apparently unrelated factors. We need to formulate a theoretical framework.

The task is to go as far as we can to round out and strengthen the explanation of all constituents, and particularly to strengthen the weakly secured constituents and to discover explanations for the unsecured ones. It should be obvious that there will be differences in the degree of effectiveness of the explanations of the various constituents. Not all theory is equally sound. We find ourselves confronted with theoretically secured constituents, weakly secured constituents, and theoretically unsecured constituents. These latter may turn out to hold key positions in the eventual solution of our problem. Regardless of the theoretical security of the individual constituents, we must tie all constituents together into a theoretical system of interrelated structures, paying particular attention to the theoretical trends that extend from the center of the determinate and theoretically secured elements to the periphery of the indeterminate and unsecured elements.

The formation of an over-all theoretical framework gives us a very essential theoretical perspective, a perspective of the problem in its larger aspects. No longer will the constituents appear as unrelated elements. We shall see that the problem has ramifications in a variety of directions and thus can be studied from a variety of angles. The weakly secured and unsecured constituents are accentuated and brought into relief by their relations or lack of relations with the theoretically secured constituents. Within our framework we can realign, shift, reinterpret, and manipulate in many ways the meanings and emphases by which tentative solutions can be evolved. It should be remembered that a theory must be discovered that will encompass the unexplained constituents, and in all likelihood this will be accomplished by extending to them the explanations of the determinate elements.

With this theoretical framework we can better determine the main dimensions of our problem. Up until now we have not been able to distinguish the heart of our problem from any other part of its anatomy. With a theoretical framework we can detect the more important determinate variables. We shall then be less likely to overlook the factors that hold the key to the correct solution. We can better detect false, though intriguing, leads and shall be less likely to proceed in directions tangential to the main issues of the problem.

Another contribution of our framework of theory is that it furnishes a solid base of operations for attack upon the unknown factors. It furnishes bridges of theory by which we can go from the determinate elements to the indeterminate elements—from the known to the unknown. This is the crux of our task. When knowledge is lacking, explanation through theory must fill the gap. For our problem, which at this point is largely unknown, explanation through theory is not only necessary, it is the only way open to us. In tracing the nexus of relations existing between the constituents of our problem and in attempting to explain the unsecured constituents, we have an opportunity of bridging the gap between the known and the unknown. In the theoretical perspective of the totality of constituents the position occupied by the theoretically unsecured constituents offers clues by which potential explanation of these constituents can be evolved. Tracing out the theoretical relationships among the constituents is, then, a powerful lever for breaking loose "chunks of the unknown."

An Illustration. Let us make a beginning toward formulating a theoretical framework of our accident-prevention problem. In our brief examination of the constituents we saw that some were more closely related to our problem than were others. We also saw wide variation in the interrelations among the constituents. Even with such a brief examination there began to emerge some broad characteristics that might lead us to an integrated picture of the constituents. We observed that some of the constituents were to be found in the driver, e.g., visual acuity, sleepiness, accident proneness. Other constituents were characteristic of the driving situation, e.g., condition of the road, divided highways, highway markers. Probably most accident constituents could be placed in these two categories—the personal and the situational.

Let us further examine the constituents for other general characteristics. Condition of the highway breaks down into many more specific factors like slipperiness due to snow and rain, rock slides, hairpin turns, blind intersections, narrow and soft shoulders, etc. If we examine these factors more closely, we find that they vary in their permanence. Rock slides are usually temporary or transitory hazards. Rain and snow are variable in their duration, depending upon geographic location and season of the year. Hairpin turns and blind intersections are likely to be more permanent hazards. Situational factors can then be described in terms of their degree of permanence.

Can we now find this character of degree of permanence in the personal constituents? Fatigue and tiredness are probably to be classed as transitory. Depending upon the nature of the disorder, eye defects vary from very transitory, such as a little dust in the eyes, to permanent defects, such as a cataract. Some motor defects of the driver are transitory, as a sprained ankle; others are permanent, as loss of an arm.

We now have the beginning of a theoretical framework. Constituents can be classified as either personal or situational, and under each category they can be further classified as transitory, semipermanent, or permanent. Only by considerably more analysis can we learn whether or not this particular framework will be a productive one.

The task of formulating a theoretical framework for the accident-prevention problem should be interpreted as a continuous one. Further study will reveal other dimensions along which meaningful relations between constituents can be developed. Theory will expand and become more and more intricate as we continue to study the problem. From time to time within the total framework definitive explanatory postulates will crystallize. These will merit further analysis and eventual empirical testing.

Discovering New Constituents. *Procedures to Use.* In tracing the theoretical structure of a constituent, we shall eventually find ourselves being concerned with new constituents and their theoretical security. The discovery of new constituents necessarily follows from the essential nature of phenomena. As we found in earlier chapters, natural events, as we experience them, have the characteristics of orderliness and interrelatedness. We shall find this orderliness and interrelatedness among the constituents as we continue our search.

At this stage the picture is not complete; it contains some voids. We are only beginning to create a meaningful picture of all constituents known to us. In continuing we must locate the indeterminate factors in the picture as best we can. We must try to discover new constituents in the voids and then develop satisfactory explanations for them. The framework affords us a means of moving in theory towards these voids, extending and elaborating known theory toward unknown constituents. Here we are treading the narrow line between the known and the unknown. With the filling of each void we achieve a step toward the solution of our problem.

There are several little tricks we can use in hunting for new constituents. One procedure is to work on the assumption that points whose explanation seems obvious and complete often need further study. Another idea to explore is that commonplace elements, which by snap judgment are considered irrelevant, may contain some significant meanings. Ideas that we may have tried and discarded in times past may deserve to be "resurrected" and given another examination. Much too frequently, as beginning scientists, we overlook the obvious elements because we have the notion that complex problems must have complicated solutions. Sometimes we can expect to find our solution in the simple relationships to be found among factors that are already familiar to us.

An Illustration. Referring to the problem of accident prevention let us note how new constituents can be developed. Although the ideas to be presented are not now being developed for the first time, some process akin to the associations to be mentioned occurs when we begin to trace out factors in the development of a new problem. Let us state the over-all theory we developed: Accidents are caused by personal and situational factors, some of which are transitory while others are semipermanent or permanent in nature.

When we considered the factor of time of day in our analysis, we were led to think about two other factors: sleepiness and fatigue. We also mentioned the characteristic of poor eyesight, which led to the constituent of visual acuity. We could have raised the further question of whether other eye deficiencies might condition accidents, for example, color blindness, side vision, or vertical and horizontal imbalance.

Inasmuch as one of the general categories is that of personal factors, we could comprehensively examine all manner of human responses that are related to driving behavior. As a result we might think of diseases, such as epilepsy; of habits, such as starting late for appointments; of attitudes, such as the obsession of having to pass all other cars; of the practice of driving after drinking alcoholic beverages, etc.

One of the constituents we listed was the type of the accident. This would be a fruitful lead to other factors. Study of head-on collisions might lead to the factor of three-lane highways and to the need for laws to regulate improper passing. Study of intersectional accidents might lead to an examination of street lights and signs, of one-way streets, of laws governing parking along main arteries during peak periods.

It is apparent that we should take advantage of any association between constituents that will lead us to new ideas. At this stage we should not be overly critical of the relevance of these ideas but rather adopt the philosophy that the more constituents we can discover, the greater the chances will be that we shall hit upon constituents that will lead us to a solution of the problem.

TESTING THE THEORETICAL FRAMEWORK AGAINST FACTS

In evolving a theoretical framework for our problem, we made use of any facts that came to mind. We did not systematically review the known facts in support of our constituents. Now, with the conceptual meanings of our theoretical framework before us, we can collect our facts more intelligently because our theories will suggest the directions we should take in our excursions into facts.

The General Nature of the Factual Analysis. Current facts are to be brought to bear on the entire theoretical system. Seldom will adequate explanations be derived from a study restricted to the theoretical phases of a problem. The exposure of known theory to factual tests usually results in the improvement and extension of the theory. The factual study now being suggested revolves around the theoretical framework with the intention of correcting its deficiencies and extending its coverage.

This factual study is not intended to be an intensive empirical testing of any specific postulate. Actually we have not yet evolved a particular problem. We are still working with the over-all picture, which includes all of the constituents. We are not ready to delimit some specific explanatory postulate for intensive study. Inasmuch as our main objective is to understand the over-all problem, the factual study is oriented toward this objective, which means, then, that theory and explanation are central to the factual analysis.

In our accident-prevention problem the theoretical framework is barely begun. It lacks coverage and detail. We are certainly not ready to plan any experimental investigation. There is a world of facts available that we must incorporate in our system. These facts will help strengthen the weak spots and will furnish support for many of the interrelations that we perceive developing in our framework of theory.

Starting Factual Analyses with Simple Situations. In beginning our factual study, we should start with simple manifestations of our constituents. In our state of relative ignorance we would do well to begin our analysis with simple constituents and leave the more complex and involved ones for later examination. The implications of the simpler elements will be easier to trace than the implications of the more complex ones. This does not mean that we should neglect the complex, but merely postpone their consideration in the hope that the earlier study of the simpler elements will give us a better preparation for tackling the more complex variables.

In our accident problem, the constituents of "reckless drivers cannot be changed," "people who drink should have their driver's license permanently revoked," "most drivers are accident prone," are constituents that should prove very difficult to analyze. "Type of accident," "time of day of accident," "sex and age of driver," are constituents that should prove less difficult of analysis.

Increasing the Theoretical Security of Constituents. *The Problem.* One step to keep continually in mind during the factual analysis is to relate the facts to the explanations of our theoretical framework. In reference to theory, facts can be utilized in two ways; namely, facts can be used in the discovery of theory, or facts can be used in the testing of theory already discovered. We are suggesting the use of facts in both ways, but we are primarily concerned with the discovery of theory. The theoretical framework that we devise for any problem must be filled in, its weak points strengthened, its boundaries enlarged. When we have completed this task, we are then on the way to evolve a specific problem. The theory underlying the specific problem will then need to be subjected to an empirical test.

By exposing the theoretically secured constituents to factual study we not only obtain further evidence of their validity but we widen our knowledge of the theoretical relations that these constituents have to others. As we noted earlier, in a theoretical analysis of a problem constituents will vary in their theoretical security, some being adequately explained, others having no satisfactory explanation. We will gain greater precision in our explanation of weakly secured constituents if they are brought into theoretical proximity with those that are adequately secured. We may be fortunate in finding factual situations in which secured and unsecured constituents are present and interacting. Such situations should be highly prized and they should be carefully examined for all characteristics and interrelationships. If there is linkage between the theoretically secured and unsecured elements, we may immediately gain an important leverage over the explanation of the unsecured constituents.

An Illustration. In our accident problem, we suggested poor visual acuity as a probable determiner of accidents. We should seek facts on this factor. We are certain that blind people should not drive—although occasionally one is found driving, depending upon another person to direct his driving activities. We ought to find out what level of acuity is necessary for driving. Is it necessary to have the same keenness of vision for driving a car as is required for reading a book? Is driving a problem of near vision or of far vision? Can a person have good near vision and poor far vision? Is the opposite of this possible? If a driver cannot see very effectively without glasses, does the wearing of glasses, which gives him normal vision, satisfy the visual-acuity demands of safe driving? These are questions that point up some of the aspects of visual acuity for driving. They are questions about which facts can be collected. There may be empirical studies available that will enable us to evaluate better the place of this constituent in our theoretical system.

Analyzing Indeterminate Constituents. *The Problem.* Factors may be classified as indeterminate constituents because we have insufficient knowledge about empirical situations in which they might be manifest. An examination of the available facts may reveal ways by which a formerly indeterminate constituent is seen as determinate. Factual studies should increase our knowledge of situations where an indeterminate constituent might be found or of situations where other constituents possibly related to it are manifest. As stated before, it is through investigating the possible relationships of a constituent with other constituents that its determinateness and theoretical security are revealed.

An Illustration. The concept of accident proneness is one of the least understood of any of the variables suggested as determiners of accidents. The question arises as to whether or not it is really a determinate constituent. When we inquire into the meaning of accident proneness, the most frequent answer we receive is that it refers to proneness to have accidents. This is a very unsatisfactory definition; it is defining a concept by merely repeating the term itself. Of course, statistics are presented to show that a large percentage of accidents can be attributed to a small percentage of drivers. But when such questions are asked as: What is it that makes the driver accident prone? Is it his hearing? or his vision? or his motor coordination? there are no replies.

What is needed is a search for facts about accident proneness, however it is defined. Before we can attribute accidents to some enduring process or deficiency of an individual, we must show that the so-called accident-prone drivers continue to have high accident records for a considerable length of time. One factual source of information might be the records of the frequency of accidents of a group of individuals which extend over a fairly long period of time. We could determine if the accident rate remains approximately constant for a certain proportion of the drivers. It would be interesting to know if those drivers who are known at a given time to be responsible for a large proportion of accidents continue month after month and year after year to remain in the high accident group. If they do, this fact would point to the possibility of some enduring process or deficiency of the driver. It would not tell us what the condition of the driver was, and we would still need to seek additional facts to learn the exact nature of this enduring condition which masquerades under the term accident proneness.

Discovering Unknown Constituents. *The Problem.* In the theoretical framework of all problems there is the need of discovering additional constituents. There are unknowns to explore. We are not always certain of where the gaps in our knowledge are, and do not always understand the nature of these gaps. The more we can use the theoretical framework to estimate what the probable qualities and characteristics of the unknown constituents are, the sooner we shall be able to find factual situations in which we might discover them. The interrelations worked out in our theoretical system provide much information about unknown constituents, but this information needs to be checked against fact. Exposing our ideas about the projected unknown constituents in factual situations where determinate constituents are operating often results in improving our understanding of the unknowns. It provides new implications for theory that apply to the unknown constituents. At all times in our analysis, this building of theoretical bridges to the unknown constituents must be kept constantly in our thinking.

An Illustration. We have listed glare blindness and traffic congestion as two constituents in the accident picture. Statistical studies indicate that accidents occur more frequently at night than is warranted by the amount of night driving. Facts also indicate that although the preponderance of traffic is in the urban areas, about half the accidents occur on the open highways. We do not have an adequate theoretical framework to understand fully these two factual results. There are probably several unknown constituents in each situation, and these should be objects of discovery. Glare blindness provides us a start on night accidents, but it is wholly inadequate to explain the high frequency of these accidents. Traffic congestion is readily accepted as a very important source of accidents, the thought being that high accident rates are to be found where congested traffic conditions are prevalent. This determiner must be reexamined in the light of the fact that about half the accidents occur in noncongested areas. The study of night accidents and of open-road accidents should be further pursued in order to discover any additional constituents that may underlie the high proportion of night accidents on the open highway.

Three Standard-type Situations to Look for in the Factual Analysis. The scientist has developed several ways of organizing the variables of his problem in order to get the best revelation of the relationships he wishes to investigate. Although these organizations characterize the experimental designs of laboratory research, arrangements somewhat similar to them can be found in nonlaboratory situations. Three types of arrangements are presented in the following discussions.

Factual Situations with and without a Given Constituent. A standard experimental situation often used by the psychologist involves two groups of subjects. One group is exposed to the experimental variable, the other is not. In all respects but this one the two groups are supposed to be equivalent. If positive results are obtained from the experiment, they are then attributed to the factor in which the two groups differed.

In searching for facts about our constituents we should be alerted to those accident situations that are comparable in all respects related to accidents except in reference to the presence of the constituent that is to be examined. There should be situations in which the constituent is operative and others in which it is not found. Such comparable situations, although not easy to find, offer a tremendous leverage for uncovering knowledge about a constituent because of the sharpness with which the constituent is brought into focus.

A case in point in our accident problem can be suggested. Suppose that we are in search of information about the constituent of restricted side vision. The theory is that people whose vision is peripherally restricted will have more accidents than those without restriction, because the restriction will prevent them from always seeing cars coming in from the side. We can ask: In what practical situations would the handicap of restricted side vision be likely to interfere with safe driving? Certainly cutting in on the highway would be one. Driving behavior at intersections would probably be an even better situation to study because of the greater frequency with which safety problems arise in this situation. The procedure would be to examine the accident statistics for two groups of drivers, one group with restricted side vision and the other with no restriction. Accidents at intersections would be selected in which factors other than side vision restriction could be ruled out. Any differences in the frequency of accidents between the two groups would then be largely attributable to the factor of restricted side vision.

Factual Situations with a Constituent Varying in Amount. Another standard experimental procedure in psychology requires that several situations containing the experimental variable be created that are equivalent in all relevant respects except in the amount of the expression of the experimental variable. It is expected that if the experimental variable is related to some end effect, this effect will vary in some consistent way with the differences in amount of the experimental variable. Suppose we wish to measure in a crude way the intensity level of hearing of a group of individuals. We use electrical devices that will enable us to keep the pitch of the tone constant while varying the intensity through measurable levels. We ask the individuals in the group to raise their hands when they hear the sound. A few hands will be raised at the low intensities, and as the intensity is increased the number of hands that are raised will increase. A functional relationship can be found between the intensity of the sound and the number of individuals who are able to hear it.

Certainly the accident constituent of speed of driving is associated with frequency of accidents. We should be able to find accident situations in which the rate of speed varied. Our principal problem in such a factual study would be to achieve equivalence between the situations in all relevant factors other than that of speed of driving. In situations in which equivalence was achieved we could make an accurate analysis of the relationship between speed of driving and frequency of accidents.

Factual Situations Involving Interaction. Interactions might be found under a variety of conditions. Interactions among different theoretically secured constituents might be found. Such situations would supply us with information concerning the relative importance of the several constituents. Constituents that are theoretically secured might be found interacting with weakly secured or unsecured constituents. Here we would find a means for extending our theories toward those constituents needing further explanation. Occasionally we might find highly complex forms of interaction among the constituents. In one situation an unsecured constituent might take on a very significant meaning on one occasion because of its apparent relationship with a theoretically secured constituent, but on another and similar occasion this meaning might not apply. A search usually would reveal that the presence or absence of the particular meaning is a function of the nature of the interaction between the constituents. Such complex types of interrelations are not easily analyzed, but when found and understood they usually contribute a tremendous amount of information about the problem under study.

In accident situations we encounter enormous complexity, interaction being the rule rather than the exception. For example, interaction occurs between the constituent of speed of driving and such other constituents as driver-reaction time, traffic congestion, ability to recover from glare stimulation, mechanical condition of the brakes, divided highways, slides on the highway, and many others. Obviously, in many accident situations several of these variables are interacting with one another.

The problem of determining the relative importance of interacting accident variables is one of the most difficult tasks confronting us. One generalization can be expressed now. The relative importance for accidents of any given constituent is likely to be a function of the specific characteristics of the accident situation. Because of our limited knowledge we are not justified in indiscriminately applying a generalization about the importance of a certain constituent to situations in which many other constituents are involved until we understand the effects of their interactions.

THE DEVELOPMENT OF A SPECIFIC PROBLEM

The General Evolution of a Problem. The evolution of a specific problem usually extends from rather vague notions and hunches about a subject to a word picture of a particular problem which has precise theoretical boundaries and is amenable to empirical study. The translation—really transformation—from vagueness and abstractness to preciseness and concreteness frequently runs a protracted and uncertain course. One of the "facts of scientific life" that we should learn early is that solutions to significant problems do not come easily.

The nature of the specific problem will be a function of our interests, ability, and background. Certain phases of the theoretical framework will have more appeal than others because we understand them better, because they hold out more promise for immediate testing, because they are more closely related to some earlier studies, or for any one of many other reasons. From such factors our thinking takes shape and is channelized in reference to some particular phase. Gradually there emerges a framework for a specific study.

The Value of Asking Specific Questions. The framing of specific questions serves the very useful purpose of forcing our attention to the detailed meanings from which a particular problem can be evolved. The general theoretical framework that we have formulated serves as a backdrop against which many individual issues and hypotheses can be developed. Eventually we want to develop a particular problem for intensive study. We can ask ourselves many specific questions which concern special and detailed aspects of our original problem and which therefore will aid in accentuating the particular issues out of which a special problem can emerge.

Many questions will arise during the interchange between theory and fact. Theoretical notions will be questioned. Items of fact will be questioned. The relations between theory and fact will be questioned. These questions serve to bring into relief those parts of our theoretical framework that are still weak and incomplete. They keep our thinking directed toward the unsecured and indeterminate constituents. They tend to fix the trouble spots in our thinking, and as a result we are alerted to possible answers and solutions which otherwise might escape notice.

Setting Limits to the Problem. In developing a specific problem, we should set such limits to it that make it reasonable of attainment. Regardless of the nature of the area in which we are working or the ultimate purpose of our work, we must set limits that are reasonable in terms of our abilities, facilities, time, energy, and similar factors. Setting what we might judge to be narrow limits to an inquiry does not necessarily mean we must lose sight of the "forest" because our attention is focused on the "trees." Nothing prevents us from organizing a topic which will contain many individual problems and which will therefore be realized piecemeal by many separate inquiries.

The possibility may arise of restricting the scope of our problem to such narrow limits that we do not get satisfactory answers to the questions that we have evolved. Here the trees are obstructing part of the forest that is essential to our purposes. We should be particularly concerned with any restriction that so severely limits the theoretical development of the special problem that it is difficult for us to move out in theory toward other problems in the larger theoretical framework.

Describing the Specific Problem. The description of any problem requires that the relationships among the concepts and facts be represented in understandable symbols that carry meanings that are unambiguous both to the scientist himself and to others who are capable of learning about them. This step of framing the problem in verbal terms deserves careful attention. It is a most difficult task.

The Contents of the Description. In the process of tracing the theoretical structure of the constituents of a special problem, many meanings are evolved. These must be incorporated in the description of the problem. There should be a description of the determinate, indeterminate, and unknown elements. There should be a description of the theoretical security of all of the relevant constituents, whether determinate or indeterminate. There should be an accurate tracing of all lines of relation as they extend between secured and unsecured elements, and between determinate, indeterminate, and unknown constituents. When possible, all constituents should be described within one framework of theory.

We should describe all explanatory concepts that bear on the problem. Rather exact explanations of some of the constituents should be possible. The unknowns can be only alluded to. By tracing the theoretical lines from a known to an unknown, however, it may be possible to describe the expected characteristics and relationships of unsecured and unknown constituents.

In our description we should include all factual information. We should support our lines of theoretical relation with whatever evidence is available. Our predictions of the characteristics of the unknowns must be related to whatever facts are known.

The Accuracy of the Description. Our statements should be as accurate as we can make them. Word symbols are not single-meaning symbols. We are confronted with the task of forming patterns of words for the purpose of transmitting certain precise meanings to individuals who do not have the relevant background and experience that we presumably possess. Singleness of meaning is a primary objective.

No vaguely described inquiry is possible of solution. If we do not describe the problem accurately, we cannot expect to discover an adequate solution. When the problem is stated precisely and accurately, the nature of the observations required for investigating it are implied in the description. If we know the nature of the observations demanded by our problem, it is then but a short step—albeit sometimes a difficult one—to devise the procedures through which these observations can be made.

The Comprehensiveness of the Description. The theoretical and factual analyses are conducted to detect and describe all of the angles, phases, aspects, conditions, factors, variables, and the like in any way thought to be associated with our problem. Somehow we must get all of these incorporated into the description of the problem. Obviously the procedure is not one of enumerating them but rather one of placing them in relation one with another in terms of the theoretical framework.

We cannot overemphasize the fact that scientific genius in solving any problem is not the result of lucky inspiration, nor is it born from exposing the problem to a brilliant but vacuous mind. It depends upon a rich store of conceptual and factual knowledge arranged comprehensively in terms of an over-all theoretical framework. It is this which must be transformed into verbal symbols and preserved for future study and testing.

A CONTINUAL INTERCHANGE DEMANDED BETWEEN THEORY AND FACT

We have suggested two very significant phases connected with the framing and formulation of a problem: first, the establishment of a theoretical framework, and second, the testing of this framework against available fact. The suggestion to start the theoretical phase first was made in order to establish conceptual meanings that could be used to direct us in the search for facts. Following this it was suggested that a thorough search of current knowledge should be made to increase our understanding of the factual bases of the theoretical framework and to discover ways of completing and extending this framework.

The two phases were kept apart primarily for purposes of discussion. Actually, in any given problem it is difficult in our own thinking to learn whether some explanatory notion or some item of fact came first. A systematic treatment of theory should be started first, but facts should follow immediately. After we are well embarked on the consideration of a problem, theory and fact become inextricably interwoven. They support each other and are to be developed interdependently. During any factual study, theory should be introduced at any time we are intelligent enough

—or fortunate enough—to have ideas about the determinants underlying our problem. There is a continual interchange between theory and fact as our knowledge about the problem expands and takes form. We should then proceed to get all of the facts we can and to apply these facts continually as a means of developing sound theory.

As pointed out before, in defining a problem we are working at the hazy, indefinite, and indistinct border between the known and the unknown. Ideas for bridging the gap between the two regions seldom will appear crystal clear when first recognized. Notions that show no promise when first evolved may later prove highly significant. Ideas that seem so obvious that they *must* work very frequently turn out to be "duds." These are common occurrences encountered while seeking to evolve a problem. In embarking on our search we are better off if we adjust ourselves early for a protracted study, one punctuated here and there with false clues, but one which, if we are willing to keep going, will eventually furnish the information needed to crystallize a particular problem worthy of thorough study.

SELECTED READINGS

Anderson, J. E.: Methods of Child Psychology, in L. Carmichael (ed.), "Manual of Child Psychology," 2d ed., chap. 1, John Wiley & Sons, Inc., 1954. Although specifically oriented toward research with children the problems, methods, and techniques discussed are in the main applicable to all levels of human development. A very thorough but brief account is given of many factors that a scientist must consider in setting out to study behavior systematically.

Jahoda, M., M. Deutsch, and S. W. Cook: "Research Methods in Social Relations," vol. 1, chap. 2, The Dryden Press, Inc., 1951. The discussion deals with the topic of selecting and formulating a research problem, with illustrations given from the field of social science.

Northrop, F. S. C.: "The Logic of the Sciences and Humanities," chaps. 1 and 2, The Macmillan Company, 1947. The initiation of an inquiry is discussed in chap. 1. A critical evaluation is made of suggested procedures for initiating a study as given by Bacon, Descartes, Cohen, and Dewey. Chapter 2 emphasizes the importance of a thorough analysis and definition of a problem before proceeding with any collection of data.

CHAPTER 8

The Use of Hypotheses in Formulating a Problem

One of the most productive verbal forms to be used in expressing a problem is that of the hypothesis. Stating the problem as a hypothesis minimizes exposition and leaves the essential elements framed in a brief statement. A hypothesis describes a possible future event or condition to be discovered. Thus, the problem is not framed in terms of its antecedents but rather in terms of its implications for future knowledge. In the present chapter we shall discuss the use of hypotheses in formulating a problem. We shall consider the nature and functions of hypotheses and the logic and method used in subjecting them to empirical testing.

THE NATURE OF HYPOTHESES

A Definition. A hypothesis is a proposition about factual and conceptual elements and their relationships that projects beyond known facts and experiences for the purpose of furthering understanding. It is a conjecture or best guess which involves a condition that has not yet been demonstrated in fact but that merits exploration. It may be framed as a potential solution to a problem, or as an explanation of some unknown fact. It may describe an element or a relationship which, if found true, would by logical inference offer support to some explanation or theory.

This definition restricts the meaning of the term hypothesis. Not just any kind of statement of a problem is to be interpreted as meeting this definition. Let us consider an example. If we were interested in the underlying nature of color vision, we could phrase our ideas in the following statement: Color responses are inherited reactions. This statement is not a hypothesis. It does not express a specific condition, relation, or element to be explored; it does not state a solution to be tested; it does not juxtapose factual and conceptual objects in some definite relationship.

Suppose we state the problem as: Color responses result from the activity of different types of cones in the retina. This is a more precise

153

statement; it suggests specific conditions that can be explored. It is based on the fact that there are retinal cones, and it conceptualizes about the functions which these organs might possess. As a best guess it states that seeing different colors might be the result of the activity of different kinds of retinal cones.

The Conceptual Nature of Hypotheses. An important characteristic of a hypothesis is that it is developed by reasoning and so contains conceptual elements. Starting from known events and relations we think of new possibilities. These may include possible new objects, possible new functions, possible new relations—literally, the possible existence of any kind of aspect that is known to us or can be imagined by us. It is apparent that reasoning may know no bounds when it is being applied in the formulation of a hypothesis.

The new aspects of any hypothesis are conceptual in nature. In some problems the elements of the hypothesis are perceptual in nature, the postulated relation between the elements being conceptual. In other problems the elements themselves are conceptualized. The point is that every hypothesis contains some element or relation that has never been perceptually experienced. To be sure, the conceptualized aspect has been formed out of the experiences of the past, but it may vary so radically from known objects or relations as to bear little similarity to them. In fact, the conceptualized aspect may never exist in the sense of being experienced perceptually. Its acceptance, then, is based on relevant facts from which the existence of the conceptual aspect is inferred.

In our example from the field of color vision, there are two known or "perceptualizable" elements: the fact of seeing different colors, which lies within the capacity of almost all individuals, and the existence of retinal cones, which is accepted as a characteristic of the retinas of all but a few individuals. The conceptualized aspect is the postulation of different cones for different colors. Through reasoning we formed the notion that different color sensations result from the functioning of more than one type of cone. We did not specify the number of types of cones to be expected. Actually, of course, this hypothesis has been the subject of study, and several sound empirical tests have been made of it.

Let us consider another hypothesis. It is an accepted fact that the rods of the retina mediate colorless sensations—the black-gray-white sequence of sensations. It is known that the rods are activated by chemical changes produced by light in a substance called rhodopsin or visual purple. This substance completely surrounds the rods. Suppose we are interested in knowing how the cones are activated. Reason would dictate that we assume the existence of a substance surrounding the cones comparable to rhodopsin. Our hypothesis might be: The cones are activated by chemical changes in a substance that surrounds them. Here we are conceptualizing the nature of the processes that produce cone activity. We postulate a substance surrounding the cones. We further postulate that it is this substance that is changed by light and that in turn activates the cones. Again, several studies have been made exploring this hypothesis. To date, however, the evidence is not as complete as the evidence available on rod functions, and therefore additional studies are in order.

Verbalization of Hypotheses. Hypotheses vary in the extent to which their elements and relations can be accurately depicted. The accuracy of the description depends upon the degree to which the postulated aspects can be traced to relevant existing facts.

Sometimes we may entertain implicit, nonverbalized hypotheses, that is, hypotheses that we have not thoroughly developed and therefore cannot accurately express. If we attempt any experimentation with such a hypothesis, however, we shall be working in the dark. The anticipation of obtaining significant results from our efforts is predicated more upon hope than upon knowledge. A hunch is not a hypothesis. It is the subjective beginning of an idea, and must undergo considerable analysis and development before it can be called a hypothesis. Through theoretical and factual analyses we must objectify the hunch. We must determine its constituents and associate these constituents with all facts known to be relevant to them. This process of objectification enables us to separate those elements or relations that can now be accepted as factual and those that, being largely conceptual, must be further studied and tested.

Sometimes we may devise a hypothesis prematurely, that is, we may verbalize our hunch before completing our analysis of the problematic situation. This undue haste results in error. As a consequence of our premature verbalization we may restrict too greatly the range of our investigation. We may develop a biased interpretation and attack. We may fail to detect and control all of the determinant variables. We may waste time and effort in following false leads and collecting data of little consequence to the primary issues of our problem.

The accuracy of verbalization of hypotheses directly depends upon the accuracy with which we objectify the elements and relations of the problematic situation. Obviously, as the elements and relations of our problem become more and more objectified, they lose their indefiniteness and ambiguity. Gradually the hypotheses needing study crystallize in a form that can be accurately verbalized. Eventually, if we persevere in our analysis, we reach a point where our understanding is sufficient to enable us to describe hypotheses that contain testable theorems.

Let us refer to our example on color vision. Suppose we formulate a hypothesis about the function of the cones before we collect all available pertinent facts. We have learned that the rods and cones differ in certain anatomical features. They differ in shape, size, distribution in the retina, and in the nature of their neurological connections with the cortical visual centers. With only these facts before us, suppose we prematurely formulate a hypothesis as follows: The function of the cones is different from the function of the rods. Very likely this statement is true, because of the anatomical differences just noted, but we framed the hypothesis before we were aware of all of the factual and conceptual elements and relations. The hypothesis as stated is ambiguous and indefinite. It does not specify some condition that can be empirically explored.

We now continue our search for facts. We learn that the retinas of nocturnal animals contain mainly rods, few cones. From this we reason that because we do not see colors in dim illumination, for example, at night, probably these animals do not see colors at all. Their visual experience might be restricted to brightness vision. Continuing our search we learn that occasionally a human being is found who is completely color-blind. This individual experiences pain in bright illumination; he has what might be called "daylight blindness." At night, however, his vision is good. We now recall one of our first learned facts, that cones are found in large numbers in only the central portion of the retina. To this we add a related fact that through reflex action the pupil of the eye is restricted in bright illumination so the light rays tend to reach only the central region of the retina. At this point in our thinking we reintroduce the facts that we learned about the vision of nocturnal animals. From all of these facts we now reason that the totally color-blind individual must have a peculiarly constructed retina, probably mainly rods, because his visual reactions resemble those of the cone-free nocturnal animals.

With the addition of the few facts given above we are now in a position to improve our hypothesis. We could set up the hypothesis that cones are the retinal organs for seeing color. We could then set up theorems to collect facts relevant to this hypothesis. One theorem would be that animals like the owl cannot discriminate colored objects. Another theorem would be that totally color-blind humans have a cone-free retina. The new hypothesis is tied to more facts than our original hypothesis. It is more highly objectified and less ambiguous than our original hypothesis. It specifies conditions that can be formed into empirically testable theorems.

The Forward Reference of Hypotheses. A hypothesis has a forward reference in the sense that it contains a conceptual element or relation that requires further examination. It is necessarily a rational leap beyond known facts and experiences.

In everyday life we carry knowledge forward and apply it to situations similar in nature to those in which the knowledge was discovered and developed. Much of the time we do this without verbalizing about it and without explicitly framing any hypotheses. As the new situations vary more and more from familiar past situations, a given application is less likely to succeed. We then become more and more aware of the need for further analyses by which we can determine the nature of the situations in which we can reasonably expect the application to succeed and the limits beyond which we can expect it to fail. At this point we are in need of a hypothesis. Through a hypothesis we can set up a situation for empirically establishing the limits within which we can expect success.

A hypothesis, then, anticipates nature and proposes certain conditions that might be found to exist, but that do not now exist so far as we know. It is a guess that needs to be explored. It must be demonstrated that the conceptual aspects of the hypothesis are supported by empirically derived facts. We set up an investigation to test the implications of the hypothesis and thus to collect evidence concerning these conceptual aspects.

THE FUNCTIONS SERVED BY HYPOTHESES

In the following discussion we should keep in mind the fact that there are inadequately formulated, overgeneralized, and logically unsound hypotheses which do not fulfill the accepted functions of a hypothesis. The statements which follow apply to hypotheses that have evolved from a thorough and comprehensive analysis of the problem; an analysis similar to that which was described in the preceding chapter.

Hypotheses as Explanations. One of the most important functions served by a hypothesis is that of explanation. The effectiveness of a hypothesis as an explanation is judged in terms of the significance of the meanings that it introduces into the situation containing the unknown factors.

Let us consider this explanatory function. The resolution of a problem requires postulation of conceptual elements and relationships. Examination of the observable data has shown them to be ambiguous and incomplete. There are elements that appear unordered and unrelated to any other elements that are known. There are unknowns for which there are no satisfactory meanings or interpretations. The tasks needing to be done, then, are to complete the data, to detect the potential meanings and relationships, and to order the phenomena. These are the explanatory functions served by hypotheses.

Hypothetical explanatory elements and relations are the principal means for setting up trial solutions for a problem. Conceptualizing makes possible the introduction of elements and relations not directly observable, thus enabling us to proceed beyond the known data. A hypothesis may contain conceptual elements that complete the observable phenomena, conceptual relationships that organize the unordered elements, or conceptual meanings and interpretations that are applicable to the unknown factors.

Hypotheses as Stimuli to Research. Another general purpose served by the hypothesis-making function concerns the origination of problems for research study. Hypothesis making literally becomes a mental characteristic of the scientist—a kind of habit of thought. It serves as a generalized frame into which he can thrust all of his uncertainties and difficulties, and he does just that. We must grant that scientific method is primarily in the hands of specialists. In serving the specialist in science, the hypothesis-making function is a device for creating and crystallizing problems for investigation. As a type of mental set it makes him receptive to problematic situations. His habitual use of the function then enables him to see problems that otherwise would escape his notice.

Hypotheses as Sources of Methodology. In the formulation of a hypothesis, procedures are often suggested that can be used in the empirical testing of the postulated solution. Frequently the hypothesis is phrased as a conditional sentence the consequences of which are pertinent to the solution. In phrasing the conditional statement we are led to examine the pertinent variables. We are also led to methods for empirically testing the points at issue. These methods are usually revealed by simply following the implications that arise from the hypothesis.

Let us do some reasoning about the accident-prevention problem and see how methods are suggested by the hypotheses we develop. It was suggested earlier that fatigue might be a determiner of accidents. If this were true, then more accidents should occur when drivers are fatigued. In considering this idea we are led to the possibility of collecting accident statistics at the times drivers are fatigued. We would probably conclude that for most drivers the greatest fatigue comes at the end of the working day. This suggests getting accident statistics between the hours of 4:30 and 6:30 P.M. After a little thinking about this idea we would realize that there might be factors in addition to fatigue that would cause accidents during this period, such as congestion due to workers returning to their homes, or lowered visibility in the wintertime during these hours. In formulating the empirical testing situations, we would also want to collect accident statistics when traffic was congested at hours other than between 4:30 and 6:30 P.M., and we would control visibility by not using accident cases that could be attributed to this factor. If we did find more accidents during the hours from 4:30 to 6:30 P.M. than during any other 2-hour period of the day, we would want to be assured that the greater frequency during the evening hours was caused by fatigue of the drivers and not by congestion or lowered visibility. With these ideas in mind we might continue our thinking and turn up other factors that would differentially affect the driving picture at these hours.

Following this, we would seek means for eliminating or controlling these factors in the study we anticipated making. It should be noted that in this brief period of reasoning, various methodological suggestions have appeared as "part and parcel" of our thinking.

Hypotheses as Criteria for Evaluating Experimental Techniques. A hypothesis often sets conditions against which we can judge the appropriateness and adequacy of the instrumental or statistical procedures of our empirical test. When the solving of a problem requires the use of apparatus, we must have some means of determining when the apparatus is adequate for the solution. We really have only one criterion and that is the hypothesis we are going to study. If the apparatus enables us to collect data in the form required for checking the implications of the hypothesis, then it is to be considered adequate. This logic is not restricted to evaluating apparatus but is applicable to all procedures and operations, including any statistical designs we may need to employ. Any procedure is declared appropriate and sufficient when the ends served by it satisfy the conditions of the hypothesis.

Let us consider an example. One of the hypotheses suggested in the accident problem concerned glare blindness. Inability to recover rapidly from bright light stimulation might contribute to accidents. It is only a short logical step from this notion to the idea of examining the glare-recovery times of all drivers who have accidents at night. This, of course, presumes that we can obtain or devise an apparatus for measuring the glare-recovery time. The hypothesis requires that we be able to measure reliably individual differences in time of recovery from glare stimulation. An apparatus that does this will meet this particular condition of the hypothesis.

Hypotheses as Organizing Principles. A hypothesis serves as an organizing principle around which all pertinent knowledge can be related. Thus it aids in establishing the relative emphases to be place on different aspects of the problem. It contributes to the determination of the temporal direction that any effort toward a solution will take.

The hypothesis, as an organizing principle, aids in determining the needed coverage of the several phases of a problem. The scientist, like all other workers, needs some principle to follow that will enable him to tell when his task is finished; that is, to tell when he has collected a sufficient number of facts to test the solution adequately. He might stop his experiment prematurely or he might continue it longer than necessary. If the hypothesis is stated too generally and indefinitely, the scientist never knows when he has collected a sufficient amount of data for empirically testing its implications. When the hypothesis is so stated that its implications are amenable to statistical evaluation, then the scientist can determine rather precisely when he has enough data collected.

In the example in which we postulated fatigue as a determiner of auto-mobile accidents, it was suggested that other factors would have to be brought under control. Accepting fatigue as the experimental variable establishes an organizing principle through which the importance of these other factors can be determined. To a very significant degree it deter-mines what action should be taken in reference to time of day, conges-tion, speeding, and similar factors.

If we make our fatigue hypothesis more explicit, we can take advantage of statistical procedures devised for quantitatively evaluating hypotheses. This requires that we derive a theorem that can be quantitatively tested. Such a theorem might be stated as follows: More accidents will occur at the intersection of F and K streets between the hours of 4:30 and 6:30 than between the hours of 11:30 and 1:30, when the volume of traffic is approximately equivalent. This theorem can be accurately evaluated by conducting an empirical test and statistically evaluating the results. It will be noted that in deriving a theorem amenable to measurement we substituted accidents at stated hourly periods for the concept of "fatigue" as the object of immediate concern. Should the findings support the theorem, it would still be necessary for us to establish as fact the rela-tionship that the greater accident frequency during the afternoon period arose from the greater fatigue of the drivers.

HYPOTHESIS IN RELATION TO FACT, THEORY, AND LAW

Hypothesis and Fact. Knowledge in the form of description comes from studying the facts; knowledge in the form of explanation comes from the substantiation of hypotheses involving conceptual elements and relationships. Although this statement expresses the relationship between facts and hypotheses as knowledge-gaining mechanisms, it fails to point out that at times it is difficult to distinguish the one from the other. There are times when the content of a hypothesis approaches the status of a fact, and times when the substance of a fact approaches the status of a hypothesis.

In the beginning, a hypothesis contains unobservable conceptualized elements and relationships. In this form it serves as an explanatory mechanism. Empirical evidence supporting the hypothesis may reveal the actual existence of the elements and relationships that are postu-lated, and thus they are accepted as facts. This transition from hypothesis to fact usually is not accomplished in any single study, and it may require a large number of investigations and take place over the span of many years.

At any time, however, these conceptualized elements and relationships now accepted as facts can be brought into question, if new evidence serves to discredit them. Thus, what once was considered fact may no longer be accorded this status. The former facts, however, may continue to be accepted as the most likely hypothetical explanations currently available.

It is obvious that with facts changing to hypotheses and hypotheses changing to facts there is not always a clear distinction between the two.

One of the suggested hypotheses concerning color vision was that there is a substance surrounding the cones that activates them when it is chemically changed by light rays. The existence of this chemical substance was purely hypothetical when the idea was first enunciated. Since then, considerable evidence has been collected that supports the contention. Today, many workers in the field of color vision maintain that the cone substance should now be accepted as fact.

Hypothesis and Theory. A distinction can be made between the two terms hypothesis and theory even though they are often used interchangeably. A hypothesis and a theory are alike in that they both are conceptual in nature and have as their primary function the explanation of natural events. The difference between the two concerns the extent or complexity of the area encompassed. Hypotheses are more restricted in their coverage. Theories are more general in nature. A theory may contain several hypotheses. When there are several interrelated areas of phenomena to be explained, more than one hypothesis may be necessary to account for all of the varied phenomena. The several hypotheses are usually mutually compatible and supplementary and can be fitted together into a more inclusive and comprehensive conceptual scheme of a theory.

Hering's theory of color vision contains a number of hypotheses. He postulated the existence of three retinal processes underlying visual experience, one process for red and green, one for blue and yellow, and one for black and white. He postulated two chemical phases in the processes; one he called anabolism (building up), and the other he called katabolism (tearing down). He postulated that the anabolic phase gave rise to green, blue, and black, and that the katabolic phase gave rise to red, yellow, and white. He postulated further that color mixtures and blends resulted from the simultaneous activity of two or of all three of the processes, either in the anabolic or katabolic phases. Further hypotheses concerning the retinal processes were suggested to account for the phenomena of color blindness, peripheral color sensitivity, negative and positive afterimages, and other visual experiences.

Hypothesis, Theory, and Scientific Law. Scientific law differs from both hypothesis and theory in that it has received sufficient verification and confirmation in fact to be accepted with little question. Like hypothesis and theory, law retains the explanatory function. In backward reference, it is used as a means of accounting for the occurrence of phe-nomena. In forward reference it is used as a means of predicting what is to occur.

Before attaining its current status, a law was either a hypothesis or a theory. Its continued acceptance as a law is predicated upon its continued success in accounting for the events that it is designed to encompass. It may be called into question when new findings are found not to con-form to its tenets. It may then revert to the status of a hypothesis or theory, and its acceptance will be continued in terms of its usefulness as a hypothetical explanation. If sufficient negative evidence arises to demon-strate the law to be false, it may be completely abandoned.

FACTORS CONTRIBUTING TO THE ORIGINATION OF HYPOTHESES

Originating a hypothesis is one phase of the scientific method that must be learned through hard work and the application of trial-and-error procedures. We can be dogmatic to the extent of saying that there are no prescriptions which, if meticulously followed, will guarantee success to the uninitiated. We can state arbitrarily that a hypothesis cannot be "conjured up" in a vacuum.

Generalizing beyond Results of Previous Investigations. Sometimes hypotheses are readily formulated by generalizing beyond the findings of previous studies. The procedure may consist in applying the logic of simi-larities and inferring that because some principle X worked for condition A it therefore should work for condition B, which has many of the char-acteristics of condition A. For example, rhodopsin having been found surrounding the retinal rods, we could postulate that there should be a similar substance surrounding the retinal cones.

The procedure of generalizing beyond previous findings may consist in applying the logic of differences. We infer that principle X, which worked successfully for condition A, must be modified before it will work for condition B, because condition B differs from condition A in certain important respects. For example, it has been found that the cortical brain in rats is undifferentiated in respect to the problem of maze learn-ing. That is, no part of the cortex is more important for the maze-running habit than is any other part. The cortex is equipotential for this habit. For the problem of brightness discrimination, we probably should not think of all parts of the cortex as equipotential because there is a specific visual area in the cortex of most mammals. The hypothesis could be re-stricted to the cortical visual area instead of the whole cortex. The hy-pothesis then would state that within the cortical visual area the brain is undifferentiated in respect to the habit of brightness discrimination. This hypothesis has been confirmed by several experimental studies.

Analyzing Factual Conditions Needing to Be Explained. Hypotheses may often be formulated from thinking about possible determiners of some factual condition for which there is no satisfactory explanation. In any area in which we desire to construct hypotheses we must be aware of both the gaps that exist in our knowledge and the theoretical security and boundaries of our facts. Thorough acquaintance with the gaps and with the relevant theoretical background makes more probable the discovery of possible explanations. We cannot expect conceptual discoveries from vacuous minds.

In the accident problem, we do not have a satisfactory explanation for the fact that about 50 per cent of automobile accidents occur at night, although only one-third of automobile traffic occurs after daylight hours. Examining the problem further, we might be led to such factors as sleepiness, lowered visibility, fatigue, glare blindness, faster speeds, etc., as possible explanations. Any one of these factors could be stated in the form of a hypothesis and set up as a potential explanation for the high frequency of night accidents.

The Intellectual Equipment of the Scientist. The hypothesis-making function depends for success upon the personal qualifications of the investigator. Keenness of observation, ability to detect potential relationships, breadth and intensity of imagination, facility for manipulating concepts, etc., are aspects of intellectual equipment that every scientist must cultivate as essential to his profession. When appropriately applied, these intellectual qualifications result in greater numbers of hypotheses and in more fruitful hypotheses.

Inspiration as a Source of Hypotheses. Little credit should be given to this method as a means of evolving hypotheses. If we acquaint ourselves with the methods of the great scientists who have claimed the sudden appearance of hypotheses in dreams during sleep or in flashes of insight at some seemingly inappropriate moment, we shall find that they advocate much the same procedure we have suggested in the theoretical and factual analyses of the problem as described in the preceding chapter. One fact, of which we can be fairly certain, is that the wild guesses of the unsophisticated are not the high-quality hypotheses that mature men of science have claimed they have received suddenly, as by some inspiration. The insightful flashes of the immature and uninitiated have no claim for immediate verification. Their empirical testing should wait upon thorough theoretical and factual analyses of the problem.

THE DEDUCTIVE ELABORATION OF A HYPOTHESIS

There are five stages in the development and the confirmation or dis-confirmation of a hypothesis. (1) We start with empirical facts, with data that are in need of explanation and further understanding. (2) From these data, through a procedure of rationalizing, we derive a hypothesis, a conceptual explanation that helps us to understand the data. (3) We then evolve from the hypothesis implications that show promise of being amenable to empirical study and that can be stated as theorems having certain consequences. (4) Next, we devise factual situations that will test the theorems. (5) Lastly, we conduct the empirical tests, collect the relevant facts, and confirm or disconfirm the hypothesis in terms of these facts. In these several stages we complete a cycle from the initial facts through the theoretical development of the hypothesis to the collec-tion and evaluation of additional facts. The deductive elaboration of the hypothesis is begun in stage 2. It is the primary task of stage 3.

Separating the development and confirmation-disconfirmation of a hy-pothesis into five stages assists in gaining an understanding of what goes on in the scientist's thinking when he evolves a hypothesis. It is to be understood that these stages are not always clearly recognizable. Further, there is not full agreement in the use of the terms we have adopted for representing these stages. Many scientists do not restrict the word hy-pothesis to stage 2 but use it loosely to stand for the implications and theorems, stage 3, and sometimes to stand for the empirical testing situa-tion, stage 4. The authors believe that a more rigorous use of the term is needed, and that not just any kind of problem that proves amenable to study should be dignified by the word hypothesis.

The Meaning of Deductive Elaboration. This is the step in which, by realistic and incisive thinking, we discover the bridges between the known and the unknown. It is both one of the most important and one of the most difficult individual procedures in the execution of the scien-tific method.

In deductive elaboration we endeavor to detect and develop as many implications as we can logically evolve from the hypothesis, and to frame them in the form of theorems. Every hypothesis is based upon certain postulates and assumptions which we should examine carefully for im-plications. The assumptions and postulates will imply certain elements and relationships that presumably must exist if the hypothesis is valid. These elements and relationships issue logically from the hypothesis. They can be stated in the form of theorems having certain consequences. We bring evidence to bear on the hypothesis through a study of these theorems.

A simple formalized procedure that can be utilized is as follows: If postulate A is true, then under condition M certain X consequences will occur. The phrase "if postulate A is true" refers to an assumption of the hypothesis. The phrase "under condition M certain X consequences will occur" is a theorem.

The significance of any hypothesis is to be found in its implications. It is through its implications that the hypothesis "reaches out" toward the unknown. The theorems and their consequences, which are logically deduced from the implications, serve to force the implications into a form that can be empirically examined. The hypothesis itself is not directly tested, rather, it is attacked indirectly through a study of its theorems. We can use the facts collected about the theorems as evidence for evaluating the hypothesis only if the relationship between the theorems and the implications and the relationship between the implications and the hypothesis are logically sound.

Let us consider the factor of glare vision in our problem of reducing automobile accidents. Some of the facts from which we could initiate further studies are that a large proportion of automobile accidents occur at night, that at night the driver is temporarily blinded by the bright headlights of oncoming cars, and that people differ markedly in their rates of recovery from bright light stimulation. From these facts we might evolve the hypothesis that slow recovery from glare stimulation is a determiner of night accidents. From this hypothesis we can derive the implication that drivers with slow rates of recovery might be responsible for a disproportionate number of night accidents. We can phrase this implication as a theorem as follows: A study of night accidents would reveal that a disproportionate number of drivers would report that they did not see distinctly just preceding their accident because of the glare from the headlights of oncoming cars. Whether or not we could substantiate this theorem would depend upon the results obtained in subsequent factual studies.

The Conceptual Nature of the Deductions. How much it is necessary to postulate nonobservable elements and relationships in a hypothesis depends upon the nature of the problem and the kind of solution that is desired.

Sometimes the solution may be obtainable with little conceptualization. Some implications developed from a hypothesis may be confirmed from a reconsideration of past observed events or by new evidence readily obtainable. Thus, the implications may issue in consequences that can be quickly and directly studied. The new elements or relationships required are revealed in immediate experience. In such instances the new postulated elements and relations required by the hypothesis are closely associated with factual and theoretical elements and relations that are known.

When immediate empirical evidence is found to support a hypothesis, our grasp of the problem is greatly strengthened. Such evidence may even provide the solution to the problem. In such a case, the hypothesis does not attain a high level of abstraction and the conceptual elements are not far removed from empirical phenomena. In the example dealing with glare recovery as a cause of accidents, the conceptual elements were not far removed from available facts.

The more difficult problems of deductive elaboration occur when the postulates and assumptions of the hypothesis involve elements and relationships that are not directly observable with any known techniques, and, in fact, may never become directly observable. The postulated concepts of the hypothesis then have meanings that are several steps removed from empirical phenomena. Despite the difficulty of the task, we must deduce theorems from these implications that will issue in empirical testing situations. Hering's hypothesis concerning the anabolic and katabolic processes yielding the various colors has so far not proved amenable to experimental attack.

Sometimes when a scientist is working on a large research program he will introduce highly abstract and conceptualized constructs into the deductive elaboration of a hypothesis when the solution in terms of immediately observable events is "begging" for his recognition. There is justification for this behavior. For most of us, the solution of the immediate problem consumes all of our attention. For the theoretician, the problem is one of intellectual curiosity. There is no urge for an immediate factual type of solution. The individual hypothesis is not his only concern. The hypothesis may be just one part of a larger theoretical scheme. The contribution to his over-all theory of a highly conceptualized solution of a single hypothesis may far outweigh an immediate factual solution. In other words, the scientist may postulate an elaborate system of conceptual entities and relations for the immediate problem because they are appropriate for other problems in his larger theoretical system. The immediate problem gives him an opportunity to get empirical evidence for this larger scheme.

The Duration of the Deductive Elaboration. In our deductive analysis it is a good policy to continue the elaboration as long as we are evolving what seem to be testable ideas about the problem. We should deduce as many implications as we can. Even what appears to be a rather remote implication may, through further knowledge, lead to significant results. Let us be reminded again that we are working in the region between the known and the unknown, and if we are fortunate enough to have numerous ideas about the implied consequences of the hypothesis, we certainly should describe as many of them as we can. A comprehensive deductive elaboration in which some of the theorems prove to be untestable is to be preferred to the procedure of immediately setting up an empirical test for the first theorem that is evolved.

The deductive elaboration of a highly significant hypothesis is a process that may go on for years, occupying the attention of one and then another investigator. Seldom does one individual achieve a comprehensive elaboration and justification of all the implications of such a hypothesis.

The Need for Thorough Theoretical and Factual Analysis. It should be obvious that before we begin the deductive elaboration of a hypothesis, we should make careful analyses of the theoretical and factual backgrounds of the problem. The framing of the hypothesis depends upon these analyses. Very likely the hypothesis we decide to investigate is the last of a succession of trial hypotheses that we have evaluated. The procedure is mainly one of trial-and-error reasoning, and trial hypotheses should be evaluated in terms of logical consistency and logical pertinence before they are considered acceptable for further study. At this stage, trial hypotheses may be discarded because they are not logically consistent with the theory of the determinate factors of the problem, or because they are not very pertinent to the questions needing to be answered, or because they offer little in the way of implications that can be incisively tested. Success in correctly choosing a significant hypothesis and in adequately elaborating the hypothesis chosen directly depends upon the thoroughness with which we have developed the theoretical and factual backgrounds of the problem.

THE EMPIRICAL TESTING OF THE THEOREMS

After completing the deductive elaboration of his hypothesis, an investigator will sometimes proceed to use the hypothesis as an explanatory device before he has found factual substantiation for the relevant theorems. Such premature application is frequently made by the nonscientific person and occasionally by the scientist. It is not to be condoned.

The Need for Empirical Testing. A hypothesis is not valid until there has been an opportunity to test the theorems against facts. It retains the characteristics of a guess until factual support is forthcoming. Its use may give the investigator satisfaction, because it purportedly accounts for bothersome unknowns—thus giving some relief from uncertainty. Or its use may prove satisfying because it completes an explanatory system, taking care of certain annoying loose ends. It should be realized, however, that "satisfyingness" is a matter of feeling and not a matter of fact. Logical completeness or logical consistency do not produce facts; therefore, these processes cannot confirm hypotheses. Only an exposure of the theorems of the hypothesis to empirical testing will confirm or disconfirm the hypothesis.

The use of the concept of accident proneness as a cause of automobile accidents is a good example of the utilization of an explanatory hypothesis before it has been adequately confirmed. Many workers in the field of accident prevention get great satisfaction from this concept because it comes in so handily in their discussions on why accidents happen. Its widespread use is not justified, however, because little succsess has been achieved in subjecting the concept to empirical verification.

The Nature of the Empirical Test. Formal logic plays an important role in the testing of theorems. In the deductive elaboration of the hypothesis we found that the implications must follow logically from the assumptions and postulations of the hypothesis and that the theorems must follow logically from the implications. In the present step we must be certain that the empirical test we organize logically satisfies the conditions of the theorem. It must relate the elements in the manner stipulated by the theorem. Of course, the test should measure the particular theorem under consideration and not some other theorem. In evaluating a hypothesis, we say that if we can demonstrate the truth of the theorem through empirical testing and the theorem is logically derived from the implications of the hypothesis, then we have evidence that supports the hypothesis. This appears to be the only possible approach when the assumptions and postulates of the hypothesis are conceptually removed from empirical observation.

A check can be carried out on a theorem regardless of the state of our knowledge regarding the postulates and assumptions from which the theorem is derived. The postulates may be wild guesses, but as long as they issue in implications that eventually can be stated as theorems and subjected to empirical study, they may be productive and deserve empirical study.

The empirical test can be of almost any variety, provided it furnishes factual material bearing on the theorem. The most important features of the testing situation are those that determine whether it accurately and adequately represents the variables, conditions, relationships, etc., of the theorem being tested. Only if this is true is the test a valid one for the particular theorem. Representativeness can be achieved by many different kinds of empirical situations. The experimental laboratory approach is one procedure. Other methods, such as controlled observation of naturalistic situations and procedures involving psychological tests, inventories, interviews, surveys, and case histories, will also serve the purposes of an empirical test, provided they adequately represent the conditions of the theorem.

The Procedure for Devising an Empirical Test. In order to devise a test, we search for an empirical situation in which we can demonstrate the theorem. The theorem is a statement of a relationship presumed to hold between two orders or kinds of phenomena. We ask ourselves the question: What are some examples of these two orders in which the conditions of the theorem can be demonstrated? When a factual situation is found in which phenomena of the two orders can be made to agree with the conditions of the theorem, we have devised an empirical test. If we are not able to find an empirical situation encompassing the conditions of the theorem, we probably have an untestable theorem. If so, we must return to a further deductive elaboration of the hypothesis in order to evolve a theorem that can be subjected to empirical examination.

In the example of glare blindness and night accidents, we developed the theorem that in a study of night accidents a disproportionate number of drivers would report that they did not see well just preceding the accident because of the glare from the headlights of oncoming cars. At first thought, it might be considered relatively easy to set up a factual test of this theorem. For instance, we could just ask individuals having night accidents if the glare of headlights affected their car control just preceding their accidents. This study, however, would be difficult to execute. We would not be able to observe the accident conditions first hand and so would have to rely on accident records for much of our data. Accident records are notorious for their deficiencies. We would have to have some assurance that factors other than glare blindness were not operating in the accidents in which glare blindness was reported. We would have to be sure to get an adequate sampling of night accidents, because the theorem involves a relative percentage (disproportionate number) of drivers, that is, the number of drivers experiencing glare blindness in relation to the number not so reporting. To encounter such difficulties in setting up an adequate factual test for a hypothesis is not unusual. We can expect success only after considerable trial and error.

The Verification of a Theorem by Empirical Testing. Verification of a theorem is dependent upon two conditions. First, we must be sure that the testing situation meets the demands of the theorem. The variables, elements, relations, etc., comprising the theorem must have adequate representation and must be allowed to function in a representative manner in the testing situation. Secondly, the facts collected must correspond with the consequences stated in the theorem. That is, the facts must favor the theorem. The testing situation may or may not be an adequate test of the theorem. The factual evidence collected may be either favorable or unfavorable to the theorem.

Whether the facts collected in a test are favorable or unfavorable to a theorem is not to be found just in the facts themselves but also in the relation of the facts to the conditions of the theorem. The facts collected in a test are seldom to be gainsaid. But even though we are seldom justified in challenging the facts, we most certainly are justified at any time in challenging the logic by which the facts are related to the theorem.

In a test of the theorem developed for the glare-blindness hypothesis, the principal conditions would be: that the test involve accidents occurring under night-driving conditions, that accident cases be found in which the driver had to report that he was or was not glare-blinded from the glare of headlights just preceding the accident, and that an adequate sample of night accidents be studied. For the results to favor the theorem, we would have to find that a disproportionate number of drivers reported being glare-blinded just preceding their accident. It should be obvious that it would not be an easy task to find empirical situations that would satisfy all of these conditions.

We may be inclined to think that facts favorable to a theorem are the only desirable or useful kind. If the test is adequate and the theorem pertinent to the hypothesis, negative results are as significant as positive results. They may not be as pleasing to an investigator who is greatly enamored of his hypothesis, but they will be scientifically important—indeed, they may be more important than positive findings.

Let us refer to a hypothetical illustration. Suppose that in the studying of some disease such as infantile paralysis, there had been developed a hypothesis that a certain X form of organism was the primary determiner, and that millions of dollars had been spent trying to identify the organism. Now, suppose we hit upon a theorem the consequences of which, if positive, would strongly indicate that this X organism was the primary determiner. We conduct a test which authorities in the field believe soundly represents the theorem, and get negative results. Such negative findings would have a powerful effect upon any subsequent research on the disease.

THE PROBLEM OF CONFIRMING A HYPOTHESIS

In the previous discussion, it was pointed out that we do not directly test a hypothesis, but rather we test theorems that evolve from the implications of a hypothesis. The substantiation of a hypothesis, therefore, is not accomplished directly. It is achieved indirectly through its theorems. It is therefore important that we understand the process of confirming a hypothesis.

The Meaning of Confirming a Hypothesis. *Logical Considerations.* There are several steps of logical relationships involved between the facts obtained in an empirical test of a theorem and the hypothesis to be confirmed. Stated briefly they are as follows: (1) The implications should follow logically from the assumptions and postulates of the hypothesis.

They should, of course, involve the significant constituents of the problem. (2) The conditions, elements, relationships, etc., of the implications should be contained in the theorem. (3) These same conditions, elements, and relationships should function in a representative manner in the testing situation. (4) The facts collected in the empirical study should be favorable to the theorem. If any one of these relationships is not realized, then the evidence cannot be accepted as substantiating the hypothesis. To repeat, a hypothesis is not confirmed if the results of the test do not correspond to the consequences stated in the theorem, or if the test situation does not adequately represent the significant aspects of the theorem, or if the theorem does not include the conditions, elements, and relationships of the implications, or if the implications do not logically issue from the important constituents of the hypothesis.

These several logical relationships are the essential elements of the indirect attack upon the hypothesis. Only through such a series of relationships can we transfer the factual evidence of the test to the problem of validity of the hypothesis. A failure at any point of the series invalidates the transfer of the facts from the test to the hypothesis.

"Confirming" Compared with "Proving" a Hypothesis. Up to this moment we have not found it necessary to define the term *confirm*. Its meaning should now be made clear so we will not confuse it with the more popular term *prove*.

Confirm means to make firm or firmer, to strengthen, to substantiate, to make valid. These meanings are relative in nature—they signify a sliding scale to which we can ascribe the characteristic of more-or-less. Thus, for example, the validity of a test is a more-or-less type of characteristic—a continuum, the lower end of which reaches to zero and the upper end of which approaches certainty.

Hypotheses are never proved. The term prove carries the notion of "certainty," of "always" or "absolutely true." That is, if a proposition is proved, then there is no further question about its truth characteristic; it is established for all time. In this sense we can never prove a hypothesis. We must remember that a hypothesis is an explanation; that it contains conceptual elements and relationships that are only purported to exist. We are required to accept these elements and relationships if we are to understand the event that we are including within the framework of the hypothesis. As long as the elements and relationships remain conceptual, so long is there a possibility that the hypothesis is false. Never should we consider that because a hypothesis is confirmed by verification of its theorems, it is therefore established for all time. There is nothing sacred about a hypothesis.

Choosing a Hypothesis from Several Rival Hypotheses. Almost any problem in human behavior invites the use of more than one explanation. There is ample justification for this state of affairs. For any complex behavior there are usually many different sets of relevant factual data, all of which need to be explained. Sometimes these data may be construed to favor each of several rival hypotheses. There is then need to select one of these for further study.

The Basis for More than One Hypothesis. The conceptual nature of hypotheses is what makes possible the devising of more than one hypothesis to explain a given set of events. A particular hypothesis is composed of conceptual elements and relationships that are thought necessary for explaining some given phenomenon. When positive results are obtained in empirically testing a theorem of this hypothesis, it is said that the hypothesis is confirmed. A different way of stating this is to say that the results obtained in the empirical test are to be attributed to the conceptual elements and relationships of the hypothesis. This latter interpretation, however, is not necessarily true. There is nothing to prevent us from imagining several hypotheses, containing a variety of conceptual elements and relationships, each hypothesis being framed to explain the same set of events. Some other hypothesis than the one that concerns us may explain the findings as well as or better than the one we are championing. By this is meant that the facts are more compatible with the postulates and assumptions of another hypothesis, or are better ordered by another hypothesis than by our own.

One of these other possible hypotheses, and one that is potentially present in every study, is the hypothesis of chance—attributing the findings to the operation of chance factors. Sometimes the results obtained in a study cannot be attributed to any known set of conceptual factors but seem to be attributable to an unknown set of factors that are operating in a random or hit-or-miss way. These are chance factors.

The Hypothesis of Chance in the Study of Behavior. In past discussions we learned that in all scientific studies of behavior chance factors should be examined as a primary source of determination. The determiners of man's responses are legion in number. They are complexly interconnected and are interacting with one another in many diverse ways. We are only able to identify a few of these determiners. We can verbalize about many of them in a very general way, but we do not actually understand fully the individual contribution of any of them. In this welter of factors there are determiners that contribute to our experimental results without our knowledge. Sometimes they contribute positively, sometimes negatively. Because we cannot identify them, we are unable to provide controls for them. Actually, we do not understand the particular factors which produce chance variations in the results of an experiment. We merely have suspicions about their nature and function, which we frame in the form of assumptions.

Knowing that these chance factors may contribute to the results, we should always examine the hypothesis of chance. Tests should be made to determine statistically the significance of the hypothesis. If chance can be used to account for the results, we are then not justified in concluding that the results confirm our hypothesis, even though they seem positively to support it.

We are fortunate in having statistical procedures for measuring the expected contribution of chance factors in our findings. Appropriate mathematical formulas are available by which we can estimate the extent to which our results may have occurred from chance determiners. This knowledge greatly assists us in evaluating any hypothesis we may be investigating. These statistical procedures can be found in most books on statistical methods.

Criteria for Evaluating Rival Hypotheses. Before we proceed to an evaluation of our own or another conceptual hypothesis, chance factors should be evaluated as possible determiners of the results. Once the hypothesis of chance has been ruled out, we can then use the following criteria for evaluating the several conceptual hypotheses.

First, we should mention the stimulating effect any hypothesis has on subsequent scientific research. Some hypotheses yield more significant implications than do others and thus they supply the bases for more empirical investigations of the resulting theorems. Through its implications, a hypothesis usually gives rise to more problems than it solves, some of which may be only remotely related to the problem for which the hypothesis is designed. The criterion of productivity of new ideas is a very important one.

The number of facts that are brought into a system or order by the hypothesis is another criterion. The purpose of a hypothesis being to explain consequences, the hypothesis that explains the most consequences is to be preferred, other things being equal. This is a function of the ease with which inferences and implications can be formed from the hypothesis. Of course, evidence for and against every hypothesis is continually changing, so that the relative explanatory merits and power of any hypothesis can be expected to undergo change as progress is made in performing empirical tests. It is, then, possible for rival hypotheses to change in their relative explanatory power with reference to the same set of events.

The degree of complexity of rival hypotheses must be considered before we make our choice. Complexity refers to the number of assumptions and postulates required in the framing of the hypothesis. This criterion suggests the use of the most simple of several competing hypotheses. The choice, however, should not be made solely on the basis of the simplicity of the theoretical foundations; the amount of factual support of the assumptions should also be considered. A complex assumption well substantiated factually and logically is probably less precarious than a simpler assumption deficient in theoretical and factual support.

A criterion that is in use, but one that should be discouraged, is the amount of satisfaction that the application of the hypothesis gives to the investigator. This refers to the fact that a scientist may experience considerable satisfaction when his hypothesis enables him to bring together several bothersome loose ends that have plagued him over a long period of time. As stated elsewhere, facts substantiate hypotheses; feelings are not a source of evidence for confirming hypotheses. Choosing from several hypotheses the one that is personally satisfying should be done only when that hypothesis measures up to the other criteria mentioned above.

Determining When a Hypothesis Is Confirmed. *The Problem.* As we have indicated elsewhere, confirming a hypothesis does not require the removal of all doubt. We are not required to attain certainty in the predictions based on the hypothesis. Rather, we determine in terms of the evidence how well the hypothesis is substantiated. If there are many different kinds of data pertinent to the hypothesis and favorable to it, we conclude that the hypothesis is well confirmed. With few positive data, we conclude that the hypothesis is poorly confirmed or unconfirmed. The concept confirm is to be interpreted as a continuum along which there are varying degrees of sustantiation justified by varying amounts of favorable and unfavorable evidence. The question: When is a hypothesis confirmed? is a very difficult one to answer.

The Evaluation of Chance Factors. As previously stated, the first steps to be taken in establishing our confidence in a hypothesis is to evaluate, and if possible dispose of, the hypothesis of chance. We determine the extent to which chance contributes to the positive results that we would like to credit to our hypothesis. Similarly, in fairness to ourselves as scientists, if we obtain results that are contrary to our hypothesis, we must also learn to what extent these results can be attributed to chance factors. Although it is not possible to rule out completely the operation of these factors, it is possible to get a fairly accurate quantitative statement of the extent to which they might be contributing. If it turns out that the contribution is negligible, we can ignore the chance hypothesis and proceed with some confidence to a positive justification of a conceptual hypothesis.

The Level of Confidence Acceptable to Scientists. The confirmation of a hypothesis is related to the confidence that the scientist places in it. Level of confidence has to do with how much evidence must favor a hypothesis to justify its widespread use. As we have seen, hypotheses are never proved, and they vary widely in the degree to which they are supported through empirical studies. Evidently we should not wait until we are certain of the truth of a hypothesis, for this would be an *eternally* long time. Neither should we begin applying it before it has been subjected to empirical examination. Somewhere in between these two points we shall have to establish confidence in our hypothesis and be willing to recommend its use to other investigators.

By using certain statistical procedures for evaluating the empirical evidence supporting his hypothesis, the scientist can compute what are called confidence limits. These limits are mathematical statements of the probability that chance might have accounted for the results. By choosing limits within which the contribution of chance is small, the scientist has confidence that his own hypothesis might be an adequate explanation of the results.

The point at which a hypothesis is found acceptable is conditioned, in part, upon certain personality characteristics of the individual scientist. If he is willing to be found wrong occasionally he will be willing to advocate the utilization of the hypothesis with less evidence available than if he is conservative in nature and wants to make doubly sure before he advocates its use.

The Explanatory Power of a Hypothesis. The confirmation of a hypothesis is related to its effectiveness as an explanatory device. This refers to the number and importance of the facts, conditions, relationships, etc., that are encompassed by the hypothesis. It refers to the extent to which the hypothesis enables us to reach toward unknown variables and incorporate them through theory with the known variables. The effectiveness of the explanatory function is closely related to the amount of factual evidence. A good gauge of this amount is the number of empirical tests that have favored the hypothesis. Another characteristic to be evaluated is the pertinence of the evidence. This is determined by the importance of the implications that have been examined and the degree to which the theorems and the empirical tests have represented and evaluated these implications.

The Predictive Power of a Hypothesis. Another factor conditioning the degree to which a hypothesis is confirmed is the power and significance of the predictions that issue from it. If the hypothesis enables us to make successful predictions about the constituents of our problem, we have another source of evidence favoring the hypothesis. When evaluating our hypothesis, we must carefully consider the following: the number of predictions that are successful, the degree of effectiveness of the predictions, and the variable nature of the situations in which predictions are successful.

The Effectiveness of Rival Hypotheses. An additional factor that should be considered in confirming a hypothesis is the effectiveness of rival hypotheses. Although the evaluation of one hypothesis can be made independently of the existence of any other hypothesis, the scientist finds greatest confidence in that hypothesis that is supported by the largest amount of evidence. Having been able to show from empirical tests that one hypothesis is superior to all other hypotheses, he will be able to apply this one with greater confidence. To demonstrate the superiority of any one hypothesis, however, involves a comparison of all of the hypotheses in terms of the various characteristics that we have considered in previous sections. This is no mean task, but its accomplishment amply repays the investigator in terms of greater insight into the meanings, implications, limitations, and validity of the hypothesis that he finally selects for further study.

SELECTED READINGS

Cohen, M. R., and E. Nagel: "An Introduction to Logic and Scientific Method," chap. 11, Harcourt, Brace and Company, Inc., 1934. In this chapter on Hypotheses and Scientific Method the authors discuss the role of hypothesis making in the development and solution of scientific problems. Some of the topics considered are: the development of hypotheses, the formal conditions for hypotheses, and the role of analogy in the formation of hypotheses.

Copi, I. M.: "Introduction to Logic," chap. 13, The Macmillan Company, 1953. The nature, use, and importance of hypotheses in scientific investigations are discussed. A description is given of the steps involved in formulating and testing a hypothesis. Several excellent examples are included.

Hull, C. L.: The Hypothetico-deductive Method, in M. H. Marx (ed.), "Psychological Theory: Contemporary Readings," pp. 218–232, The Macmillan Company, 1951. This selection provides a discussion of the applicability of the hypothetico-deductive method in psychological science. The need and importance of definitions, postulates, and theorems are explained.

CHAPTER 9

Collecting the Facts

In the immediately preceding chapters, steps were described for developing a problem for empirical study. Starting with rather vague notions about the problem, we learned how to delimit its boundaries by theoretical and factual analyses and to reduce it to concrete and precise empirical conditions. It was shown that some advantage accrues from stating our problem in the form of a hypothesis and deriving from this hypothesis one or more theorems that can be empirically tested. In this deductive elaboration of a hypothesis, suggestions are often obtained concerning the nature of the empirical testing situation and the procedures to be used in objectively testing the theorem.

In the present chapter, we shall be concerned with problems associated with setting up and conducting the empirical test. An adequate test of a theorem requires that the empirical situation contain the conditions or factors that are stated or implied in the theorem. Through the testing situation, facts are collected that bear upon the variables and relationships contained in the theorem. The situation must, then, provide for the presentation of the particular stimuli that will initiate or force the expression of the relevant behavior variables. Procedures should be used that will make possible an accurate description of all the variables operating in the situation. Furthermore, the observations of the scientist should be accurately recorded, and should be sufficient in number to provide reliable answers to the various questions raised by the theorem.

DESIGNING THE EMPIRICAL TESTING SITUATION

Basic Conditions to Be Met. *Designing the Test to Fit the Problem.* The organization of the particular procedures, materials, apparatuses, and subjects selected to form an empirical testing situation is called the design of the study. The central thesis in terms of which this selection and organization is accomplished is the specific theorem to be tested. The theorem expresses the potential relationships among the variables that are judged pertinent to a given hypothesis. The testing situation is designed to get an empirical expression of these variables under the specific conditions set by these relationships.

The theorem is the standard against which we evaluate our methods, apparatuses, and operations. The phenomena encompassed by a theorem usually are restricted to some particular class of objects and relationships that are described in terms of their nature, frequency of occurrence, probable extent, etc. These characteristics of the theorem serve as checks against which to evaluate the testing situation. We can inquire if the specific phenomena that we have chosen for a test situation are representative of the class of phenomena stipulated in the theorem; if the situation that we have selected affords ample opportunity for the expression of the phenomena under the conditions of the theorem; and if the relationships that are expressed among the phenomena in the concrete situation that we have selected are the relationships demanded by the theorem. Thus we can logically evaluate the test for consistency and pertinency before we actually put it into operation. The theorem then determines the appropriateness of the techniques, methods, apparatuses, etc., previous to their being utilized.

Let us consider a problem dealing with the functioning of the cerebral cortex of the brain. Suppose that we start with the hypothesis that the mass of the intact cortical tissue determines the effectiveness of behavior. From this we deduce the theorem: Increasing amounts of destruction in the frontal lobes of the cortex produce increasing amounts of deterioration in intellectual-type functions. Let us see how the design of the study will be conditioned by the variables and relationships expressed in the theorem. We must select subjects that have well-developed frontal lobes, to be sure that cortical tissues are present. We must obtain individuals (human or animal) with varying amounts of loss of frontal-lobe cortex. This, then, means that if we use human subjects we must depend upon head-injury cases and the rather infrequently occurring cases with surgical lesion. With animal subjects we can produce the lesions through surgical means. We must select or devise procedures for measuring varying amounts of destruction of the brain tissue. We must study the performance of the subjects in problems that reflect intellectual behavior. We must organize objective situations in which variations in quality or effectiveness of behavior can be expressed and measured. We must establish controls over variables other than the variable of destruction of frontal cortex which might produce deterioration in the intellectual type of behavior selected for study. We must select statistical or other procedures by which we can detect the nature and extent of any relationship that might occur between deterioration in behavior and cortical destruction. These are a few ways in which the design of the experiment must be tailored to the specifications set down in the theorem.

Eliciting Expressions in the Experimental Variable. A problem delimited for the purpose of scientific study usually consists of one variable—or at the most a few variables—which logically is directly related to the conditions or elements of the theorem. As noted earlier, such a variable is known as the experimental variable. It is so called because it is through this variable that the theorem is experimentally represented in the empirical testing situation. Although the term experimental variable is usually used to refer to the variable that is purposely changed, it should be noted that we are interested in the changes in some other variable that follow this purposeful variation; that is, we are interested in the functional relationship between the two variables.

One of our problems is to set up the experimental variable in such a way and in such amounts that the conditions of the theorem will be adequately represented in the objective situation. The characteristic of representativeness is neither easy to describe nor easy to realize in a given experimental study. The theorem will state or imply the characteristics that the experimental variable should have. These will include the nature of the variable and the amount or frequency of its occurrence. The variable selected for our test must be the kind demanded by the theorem, and we must elicit expressions of the variable in the amounts or frequencies that will test the relationships pertinent to the theorem. Usually, it is necessary to have expressed at least two values or amounts of the variable—but preferably more than two—in order to determine precisely any functional relationship that might be present.

Let us continue with the theorem that concerns the relationship between deterioration in behavior and the amount of loss of cortical tissue. Suppose that we select rats as our subjects. We can do this if we have assured ourselves that rats have a well-developed frontal cortex and are capable of behavior that can be described as intellectual in nature. To continue with the development of the testing situation: we must be able to produce variable amounts of cortical destruction in the frontal lobes of the rat. There are, of course, several ways this can be done through the use of cauterizing electric currents. We must also be able to determine the relative amounts of destruction of cortex in the different operative rats. Again, there are several methods available by which the amount of destruction can be estimated after the brain is removed from the skull. It is, then, possible to produce variable amounts of expression of the experimental variable—amount of cortex destroyed—and to estimate the amount of destruction in each of the operated rats.

In our empirical test, we also need to have a means for measuring the rat's intellectual behavior. Learning a complex maze would be appropriate. Maze learning requires the use of several sensory capacities of the animal and requires him to perform rather complicated behavior in response to a complex stimulating situation. The maze behavior of the rat can be quantitatively described so that reliable estimates can be made of the amount of any loss that might occur after a cortical lesion.

Controlling Related Variables. When working with complex global behaviors, we usually discover many variables that are functionally associated with the behavior we wish to study. Having chosen one—or a few —of these as the experimental variable, it is imperative that the effects of other associated variables be prevented from influencing the behavior during the experimental testing period. These other variables might elicit changes in the behavior similar to those expected from the experimental variable. Obviously, upon completion of a study we shall want to ascribe the results to the variations instituted in the experimental variable. We cannot do this, however, if one or more other variables have been present to which the results can be ascribed. It is possible that these other relevant variables might produce an effect opposite to that expected of the experimental variable. Under such a condition, the effect of the experimental variable would be canceled out. Our findings would then indicate that the experimental variable was not related to the behavior under study, whereas in fact it was positively related to this behavior.

In our experiment on the cortex of the frontal lobes, we would purposely produce variation in the amount of tissue destroyed but try to eliminate the effects of any other variables which might cause a deterioration in the performance of the animals. It has frequently been found that rats with brain operations are more susceptible than nonoperated rats to respiratory infections such as colds. If the colony of rats we were studying became afflicted with colds, this variable would tend to produce a change in behavior similar to that associated with loss of brain tissue. That is, the colds would be expected to cause a deterioration in performance, and the deterioration would be greater for the rats with the most severe or most prevalent colds. These, of course, would be the operated rats.

Evaluating Chance Factors. Even after the experimental and relevant systematic variables have been brought under control, there will remain other variables affecting the behavior under study. These are the unsystematic variables discussed in Chap. 5. They operate both to facilitate and to inhibit the behavior. Although in the long run the expressions of behavior associated with the experimental variable will not be influenced in a constant direction, at times these chance factors may operate strongly enough in one direction to account for the changes observed in the data of a given experiment. When this occurs we are not justified in ascribing the changes to our experimental variable.

In designing an experiment, we must devise the data-collecting procedures in a way that will provide a basis for estimating the importance of chance factors. This is accomplished when all factors but the experimental variable are forced to operate in an unsystematic manner. In the discussion on Control of Psychological Variables we noted some of the methods by which this can be done. In later chapters we shall have occasion to consider the problem again. The designing of a study to make possible an evaluation of chance factors is sometimes a very difficult matter, and it is not possible here to describe the variety of problems that may arise and the procedures available for solving them. It is important for us to know that the evaluation of chance factors depends upon the nature of the design of the data-collecting procedures, and that there are experimental and statistical methods appropriate for most of the problems that arise.

To illustrate how chance factors may enter into the design of an experiment, let us consider our study on the function of the frontal lobes. Suppose we perform operations involving three amounts of destruction, say 10 per cent, 20 per cent, and 40 per cent, and include only two rats in each of these conditions, or a total of six rats. Experience has shown that there are large individual differences in the learning performance of rats on mazes. Furthermore, it has been demonstrated that a given amount of cortical destruction will not have exactly the same effect on the behavior of different rats. By chance alone, we might assign the two fastest learners to the 40 per cent condition and the two slowest learners to the 10 per cent condition. Thus chance distribution of this factor of learning ability would tend to cancel out any differential effects of the various amounts of cortical destruction. Increasing the number of rats and careful random assignment of the animals to the different lesion groups would mitigate against chance factors contributing significantly to our results.

Exploratory, Confirmatory, and Crucial Experiments. *Exploratory Experiments.* In the development of a problem for scientific study, questions often arise concerning details of the procedures that cannot be answered satisfactorily from the then current knowledge. Information can be collected on these questions by conducting pilot or exploratory experiments. Questions may arise in connection with the effectiveness of a piece of apparatus, the feasibility of a procedure, the difficulty of a set of instructions to be given the subjects, etc. It is preferable to conduct exploratory studies to collect factual information about the apparatus or procedure or instructions than to put complete trust in a subjective judgment of their effectiveness. For example, pilot studies are often made in order to evolve accurate procedures for destroying brain tissues. The amount of destruction of cortical tissue from the use of an electric cautery is a function of several variables among which are the size of the electrodes, the amount of current, the duration of the current, the pressure applied to the electrodes, and the amount of fluid surrounding the area to be destroyed. It is not likely that we could determine through reasoning the exact combination of these factors that would give us the particular amounts of destruction that we have planned for the study. Furthermore, for such a complex problem, even experiments similar to our own, previously conducted by others, would seldom provide the exact data necessary to set up and calibrate our own apparatus and procedure without the aid of exploratory studies.

Exploratory experiments are not limited to problems of procedure but may be conducted on nearly any question that concerns the reduction of the theorem to an objective test. Sometimes certain characteristics of the individuals to be used as subjects are sought in exploratory studies. Sometimes items of theory may need preliminary investigation. The purpose of exploratory experiments is to perfect all of the rational and empirical phases of the test situation so that the objective of devising an adequate empirical check of our theorem will not be defeated.

Confirmatory Experiments. As the name implies, this kind of experiment is conducted to confirm or disconfirm a hypothesis. It is set up to test a theorem of that hypothesis. As already stated, any empirical study of a hypothesis must be established on a series of sound, logically developed relations between the hypothesis and its theorem and between the theorem and the empirical test. If these relations are logically substantiated and if positive results are obtained in the experiment, then the findings confirm the hypothesis.

An experimental study may be very efficiently conducted and still not either confirm or disconfirm the hypothesis under examination because of failure to develop sound deductive relationships between the hypothesis and the test. At times, however, such a failure may actually prove beneficial, because of the corrective effects it will have on any subsequent deductive elaboration of the hypothesis. The experiment has then served an exploratory function.

Crucial Experiments. This kind of experiment is one that presumably settles the fate of the hypothesis being studied. It is a rare occurrence in science. The highest probability of its occurring is when the hypothesis is extremely simple in structure, when the hypothesis can be adequately represented in a single theorem, and when, in turn, the theorem can be given a thorough check in an empirical situation involving a few well-controlled, accurately measurable variables. When the hypothesis involves highly conceptualized elements, or complexly structured variables, the probability is almost nil that a single theorem can be devised that will encompass all of its conditions. If such a theorem were devised, the probability again is almost nil that it could be represented in a single objective experimental situation in which the measurement of the variables and relationships would be unassailable in respect to their reliability and validity.

It is possible, of course, to formulate hypotheses of simple structure and deduce theorems that can be adequately checked in a single experiment. For example, we could champion the idea that there is a positive relation between the amount of pigment in the eye and intelligence. The theorem could be stated: All blue-eyed babies develop into dull-witted children. Obviously, by discovering one intelligent blue-eyed child we could disconfirm the hypothesis.

A problem simple enough to be reduced to a crucial experiment usually will not add greatly to our knowledge because it will involve a highly restricted theorem and a very narrow type of test situation. In our effort to improve our understanding of such a complex organism as man, we need not worry ourselves about crucial experiments—they have been and will continue to be extremely rare in occurrence.

Choosing from among Several Testing Situations. *The Problem.* Sometimes more than one testing situation will come to mind in connection with a given theorem, and we may be compelled to make a choice among them. It is not presumed that each testing situation will represent equally well all of the conditions implied in the theorem. Probably the theorem would have to be modified somewhat to justify the use of all of the situations. Modification of a theorem, however, does not necessarily weaken it. Once we are under way in planning a test we may be willing to modify the theorem in terms of some new development that arises out of our effort to devise a testing situation. Whether the theorem is strengthened or weakened will depend upon the soundness with which the changed theorem represents the conditions of the hypothesis.

Other factors that may strongly influence our selection of a given testing situation are the relative ease with which the test can be conducted, the relative cost of the test, our ability to execute the test, the availability of apparatus or subjects, and the like. The final choice, however, should rest primarily on whether the test selected will adequately check the theorem we have decided to examine.

An Example. The following example will illustrate how different testing situations can be evolved for studying the same hypothesis. A little reflection will show that the several situations would not all be checking exactly the same theorem even though logically relevant to the same hypothesis. Suppose, as a personnel psychologist in a factory, we set up the following hypothesis: Emotional upsets result in lowered production. Facts could be collected by conducting an experiment in a psychological laboratory where subjects would be given work to do and then exposed to social stimuli that were upsetting in nature. Or an experiment could be conducted with workers at a factory bench while they were doing their regular work tasks. Or a special room at the factory could be used for an experiment where only certain selected types of work were presented. Or records could be kept of the workers' production at the bench and examined periodically, and when a worker's output showed a tendency to decline he could be given a special interview to determine whether or not any emotional difficulties were present. Or workers could be asked to keep diaries in which they would describe their current emotional difficulties, and then these difficulties could be checked against their record of output. Not all of the facts collected through these different methods would be comparable. It would not be expected that an answer based on the findings of any one study would necessarily be supported by those from any other study.

SOME CHARACTERISTICS OF THE PHYSICAL TESTING SITUATION

In any science, the fundamental problem exists of producing the conditions necessary to test the theorem under consideration. In psychology, it is through the production of the appropriate stimulus conditions that we elicit the particular elements in behavior that are related to the theorem we have under study. The facts required for testing the theorem are facts about response characteristics.

The Stimulus Situation. *Focal and Contextual Stimuli.* As we have pointed out several times, any given situation contains many different stimulating features. For the purpose of creating a particular type of effect upon a subject, a given stimulus characteristic is singled out for manipulation. The subject is directed to pay special attention to this aspect of the situation. Because the characteristic is the center of attention, it is called the focal stimulus. For example, if the subject were required to discriminate two red lights differing in brightness, the intensity of the lights is the focal stimulus and would be varied. The wave lengths and composition of the lights would be held constant.

Other aspects not part of the center of attention are referred to as contextual stimuli. They also may be the object of experimental study and may be varied in much the same way as focal stimuli. Usually the subject is not made aware of this variation, since the investigator is interested in the effect of the stimulus when it functions as context. To make the subject aware of any variation introduced in the context would likely change the stimulus from contextual to focal. For example, in studying the effect of masking noises upon pitch discrimination, various levels of noise as contextual stimuli are introduced coincident with the tones to be discriminated. If the subject attends to the changes in noise level rather than to the changes in tone, the object of the investigation is defeated.

Stimulus Categories. The psychologist has been concerned with manipulating many varieties of sensory stimuli, and in so doing he has devised several workable schemes for classifying them. One of these—the familiar sensory modalities—will serve our purpose. The categories are the familiar ones of visual, auditory, cutaneous, olfactory, gustatory, kinesthetic, static, and organic. These categories originated from the differences in activity of the several special kinds of sensory tissues in the body.

We need to add symbolic stimuli to the sensory modalities in order to achieve a comprehensive classification of the many kinds of stimulation used in psychological research. By symbols it is possible to present problems requiring the use of the higher mental responses. Through these stimuli the more complex global types of behavior can be elicited. Although symbolic stimuli are primarily visual and auditory in sensory character, to place these symbolic stimuli in one or the other of these sensory categories does not classify the stimuli in terms of their primary stimulating effect, namely as word or sign meanings. The stimulating effect of symbols comes from the meanings that are aroused by the visual or auditory cues and not from the sensory characteristics peculiar to visual and auditory objects.

Kinds of symbolic stimuli are many and varied. They include word stimuli, both seen and heard. They include natural objects of all kinds, such as plants, animals, human beings, and the like. These are capable of wide variations in their stimulating effects. Symbolic stimuli literally include all stimuli that are capable of eliciting meanings not directly reducible to the sensory experiences of the moment.

The Production of Stimuli. One problem confronting us is the production of a stimulus of the right kind, in the appropriate amount, at the most opportune time. In simple laboratory-type discrimination problems, such as distinguishing between lights of different color or brightness, or sounds of different pitch or loudness, the nature of the stimulus can be very accurately controlled. It can be varied with great precision by means of simple electrical devices inserted in the light- or sound-producing circuits. Sometimes producing the right kind of stimulus in the laboratory situation may prove a difficult problem. For example, the generation of a stimulus tone that can be varied from a half-cycle duration to several cycles and produced at different frequency and intensity levels requires an expert knowledge of the physics of sound.

The nature of the stimulating effect is a critical characteristic in most testing situations involving symbolic stimuli. The particular meanings aroused will depend upon the interpretations placed upon the symbols by the individual subjects. In simple memory and perception experiments, adequate control of meanings can usually be achieved. In memory experiments, for instance, careful selection of the material to be learned enables us to reduce the possible variation in meanings and at the same time to achieve some control over the difficulty of the task to be presented to the subject.

In social-type situations, where several individuals are interacting, very little control may be attained over the meanings aroused. Suppose the problem requires the study of a child's social behavior in response to the stimulating influence of several persons of his own age. This can be done in the play-school situation. Some control over the stimulus situation can be achieved by a careful selection of the stimulus children to whom the subject is to respond, by the types and number of toys that are provided to all of the children, by the instructions given to the stimulus-children on what they are to do under certain conditions, and so on. But even the most elaborate planning of the stimulus situation does not guarantee that the exact stimulus-meanings that are planned to be presented to the child will actually occur. The particular meanings that the child will ascribe to the situations presented are in large measure dependent upon his own past experience and his mood of the moment, neither of which is brought under control.

Producing the stimulus at the most opportune time can readily be achieved in laboratory experimentation. In the laboratory, the subject can be stimulated to respond more or less at the convenience of the scientist. In a complex social situation, the scientist must seek out the particular occasions when the behavior he wishes to examine occurs under the least interference possible from unwanted disturbing variables. Suppose that the hypothesis he wishes to investigate is concerned with human relations, and that the conditions of the theorem selected for study could be found in representative expressions in the labor-management type of conference. It would then be necessary to delay the investigation until an issue arose for which a conference between labor and management was called. Conditions of the theorem very likely would not function in a representative fashion if a conference were especially arranged to conduct the study when no bona fide difference between labor and management existed.

Subjective stimuli are far less easily manipulated than objective stimuli, and the timing of their occurrence is usually very difficult. For example, in studying the influence of some drug, such as Benzedrine, on a given type of learning behavior, it is difficult to select that moment for commencing the learning that will coincide with some particular moment in the absorption of the drug, such as that moment at which the drug is producing its greatest effect on the individual.

The Quantification of the Stimuli. The problem of producing the stimulus in certain desired amounts occurs in every experiment. The nature and amount of the behavior elicited by a stimulus very frequently is a function of the amount of the stimulus presented. In sensory experiments involving simple stimuli such as brightness of lights, pitch of sounds, intensity of pressures, the amount of the physical stimulus can be accurately determined.

Symbolic stimuli vary in the amount-intensity characteristic, but there is no simple unambiguous meaning of magnitude that can be applied to every form of symbolic stimulus. Frequently, the meaning of amount is referred to the number of stimulus units presented, for example, the number of words to be memorized in a learning experiment, or the number of problems to be solved in a reasoning experiment, or the number of trials to be completed on a psychomotor coordination test. Sometimes the amount meaning is referred to the level of difficulty of the stimulus material or task. Words to be learned, problems to be solved, and psychomotor tasks to be completed can be devised that vary in the ease with which the person can perform the required response. It is then possible to present symbolic stimuli that vary in the level of difficulty with which they can be understood and responded to by the subject.

In many studies it is necessary that the experimental variable be expressed at several predetermined levels of amount, and that any one of these magnitudes be produced at the convenience of the experimenter. This objective can usually be obtained for the simple forms of stimuli involved in the study of sensory processes. It is more difficult to achieve for the stimuli utilized in the studying of learning, memory, and thinking. It is very difficult to achieve in the study of responses expressive of emotion and personality.

The production and control of a stimulus variable at any level of effectiveness is greatly improved by the use of measuring devices. These devices are not restricted to apparatus of the brass-instrument variety. Measurement and control of symbolic stimuli can be obtained through the use of lists of verbal material, test items and problems, pictures and diagrams, and oral and written instructions.

The Representativeness of Stimuli. One of the difficulties associated with stimulus manipulation is related to the problem of representativeness. Testing a theorem requires the functioning of a certain variable or combination of variables in a representative fashion. This means that the stimuli eliciting the variables must be controlled in a way that will achieve the desired representative functioning. The exact meaning of representativeness is difficult to state except in reference to the specific variables involved and the relationship between the functioning of these variables and the conditions demanded by the particular theorem.

The problem of representativeness can be illustrated by a hypothetical experiment requiring that we obtain the mean performance of high school graduates on a college entrance examination in geometry. Although the problem merely demands the mean performance of a specified group on a certain type of test, it is a very complex one to solve in terms of the factor of representativeness. There are three aspects to representativeness in this particular example, namely, getting a set of geometry problems that are representative of those used in college entrance tests, getting a representative sample of high school graduates, and getting the sample of subjects to perform in a representative fashion on the geometry examination. The first and third aspects are directly concerned with the representative nature of stimuli. The choice of the test and its items forms one aspect of the stimulus variable. A second aspect includes the associated stimuli by which high school graduates are encouraged to respond representatively to the test conditions. Failure to achieve representativeness in any one of the three ways mentioned would prevent a solution to the problem.

Representativeness and Interaction among Variables. Interactive effects among variables make it difficult to obtain representative expression. We have learned that the testing of a theorem may require the production of combinations of stimuli. In psychology, the simultaneous functioning of several variables is the rule rather than the exception. When several determiners function simultaneously they interact with one another. This interaction is to be conceived as being itself a variable of considerable complexity. It also must be interpreted as a determinant variable, for the influence that a factor will have on some end result is determined in part by the presence or absence of some other factors that facilitate or inhibit its expression. When the picture is complicated by having many factors operating simultaneously, the problem of interaction becomes undeniably difficult to unravel.

It is apparent that to obtain representative performance in a given variable we must have considerable knowledge about its functional relationships with other variables. These other variables must be forced to function in the particular ways and in the particular amounts that will produce a representative performance in the variable under study. The various aspects of the stimulating situation must be balanced in such a way as to achieve this objective.

The problem of interaction is often avoided by setting up a test situation in which only one variable is allowed to change in value, all other variables being eliminated or held constant in value. It should be obvious that under these conditions the variable under study is restricted in its function, and its expressions are not representative of those that would be obtained if other variables were free to change in value. This problem is illustrated in the early attempts to study multivariate determiners of a given response. In these early studies, the logical step was taken of forcing the multivariate problem into the form of the single-variable experiment. For example, if there were four factors contributing to the determination of a response, then four experiments were conducted. In each experiment one of the four factors was allowed to vary while the others were held constant. It should be apparent that as long as interaction is a possible variable, the contribution of any factor to a total situation cannot be discovered by multiple application of the single-variable experiment. Although there now are several procedures especially designed for isolating and measuring interaction, they are not universally applicable to the diverse situations encountered in studying behavior.

The Registration of Stimuli. Registration of the characteristics of the stimulus is necessary in order that the stimulating conditions can be kept constant over time and constant among the different individuals serving as subjects. If an apparatus is used for generating the stimuli, it is usually a simple problem to calibrate the adjustments or settings of the dials or other controls so that the same stimuli can be reproduced whenever desired. Registration of the nature, the intensity, or the duration of the stimulus is then not difficult.

With symbolic stimuli, the problem of registration may be simple if the symbols elicit uniformly the same meaning on different occasions and from different subjects. The registration becomes extremely complicated when the interactions of several subjects are part of the stimulus situation, for then the meanings and interpretations of the stimuli are constantly changing. In this type of situation, a complete record can be taken of the verbalized stimuli by means of a wire or tape recorder. So much of the stimulus situation as is transmittable through auditory symbols can then be studied. This procedure does not make possible a measurement of all of the characteristics of the situation, but it provides a great deal of important information about certain aspects of the stimuli, some of which can be put into numerical form. For example, transcripts of the deliberations in conferences between representatives of labor and management have made it possible for investigators to quantify as to frequency of occurrence certain attitudes displayed by management toward labor and certain attitudes displayed by labor toward management.

The Response Situation. *Response—Process or Product.* In studying behavior, we can consider the activity in progress, which involves a study of the psychological processes occurring during the response, or we can direct our attention to the changes resulting from the response, in which case we analyze the end activity or the product created by the activity. Both types of procedure discover fundamental facts by which the nature of behavior can be unraveled. When only one attack is possible, the facts revealed by this one usually make possible inferences concerning the facts that would otherwise be gained from using the other procedure.

That is, we can make inferences about products from knowledge of processes, and we can make inferences about processes from knowledge of products.

Response Categories. When the words response, reaction, or activity are used, we should not think only of the overt changes observable in the movements of an individual. Behavior consists of many forms of response; these can be subsumed under one of the following five categories: sensory and perceptual experience, higher mental activities, skeletal muscular response, visceral and glandular reactions, and sense-organ and nervous-system changes. These categories are not mutually exclusive. For example, responses of the first two categories are mediated through the changes in sense organs, nervous system, and muscles, which comprise the other three categories.

The immediate response to most stimuli is sensory or perceptual experience. Sensory experience is distinguished from perceptual experience primarily in terms of the direction of attention of the subject. In studying sensory experience he attends to the subjective impressions elicited by the stimuli. His attention is focused upon the sensory experience itself. In perception, the subject attends to the stimulus objects and their relationships. The problem is to determine how accurately these objects and relationships are observed. The attention is on the objective facts rather than on the subjective experience.

Stimuli in the form of symbols arouse conceptual meanings. Through these symbols the subject may be required to utilize the higher mental responses such as memory, reasoning, imagination, judgment, and the like.

Skeletal muscular responses are executed by the surface muscles of the body. These responses are either phasic or postural in nature. The first refers to rapid periodic changes in the muscles by which certain end adjustments are accomplished, as, for example, movements of the leg, arm, eyes, vocal cords, etc. Postural responses involve the tonic contraction of skeletal muscles which effects the long-enduring substratum of tension upon which the phasic movements are superimposed.

Visceral and glandular reactions include all of the vital functions of the body. Heart action, vascular changes, respiration, digestion, and endocrine-gland secretion are examples. At times these internal responses become important conditioning factors of other forms of response, as in the case of emotional reactions. For example, all of us have had the experience of being unable to recall a familiar name (mental activity) because of feelings of anxiety (emotional activity) which result from the increased visceral activity engendered by the importance of the general situation.

Sense-organ and nervous-system responses refer to the actual tissue changes that occur when sense organs and nervous tissues are excited to activity. The psychologist at times turns physiologist and delves into the mechanics of tissue change that underlie both sensory experience, as mediated by the sense organs, and various mental activities, as mediated by the central nervous system.

The Detection of Response. We must be able to detect in the subject all of the changes that are pertinent to the stimulus conditions we present to him. Some behavior components are readily detected, such as movements in the surface muscles of the body. The expressions of the face, the clenched fist, the eye-hand coordinations in typewriting, are all easily observed.

Subjective responses are difficult to detect, especially when the nature of the response process rather than the result of the response is being studied. A perennial problem that still baffles the psychologist after many years of research is the exact nature of the feelings of pleasantness and unpleasantness. These feelings are familiar reactions. All of us know when we feel pleasant or unpleasant. Difficulty arises when we try to detect the behavior changes that underlie these affective experiences. We seem not to be able to describe accurately what goes on when we feel pleasant or unpleasant.

Similar difficulties arise when we study higher mental responses like learning or thinking. We can detect part of the response in terms of the product resulting from the activity. For example, we can discover some facts about learning from the length of time required to learn or from the amount of material recalled after an elapse of time. It is more difficult to find out exactly what happens in the individual when he learns. One approach to this problem is to study stimulating situations that vary in some prescribed way intended to evoke different mental processes. The differences among the stimulus conditions are constructed so as to require the subject to use different mental procedures in evolving the solutions. If the results obtained differ for the several situations, the chances are high that they have resulted from differences in the mental processes of the subject. Some information about the subject's mental processes can then be inferred from the differences in the nature of the stimulus conditions presented to him.

The experiments comparing logical and verbatim learning illustrate this approach. In logical learning, the subject is encouraged to form associations among the meanings of the material to be learned and between these meanings and his past experiences. In verbatim learning, the subject memorizes by merely repeating over and over each meaning, with little or no effort being made to discover or form relationships among the meanings. The relative effectiveness of these two procedures is tested in the subsequent recall of the material learned. Logical learning always proves to be markedly superior to verbatim learning in terms of the accuracy and amount of the material recalled. This result would be construed to mean that the mental processes in logical learning, which involves associations among varied types of experience, issue in more effective retention than the mental processes occurring in verbatim learning, which involves associations among more restricted types of experiences.

Verbal Reporting by the Subject. This procedure is basic to a large amount of laboratory experimentation. For the psychologist interested in the nature of the process of response, as in the higher mental functions, it is indispensable; and for the study of products, it may at times prove very valuable. Verbal report is used to refer to all communications of a subject during an experiment that in any way are related to the execution of the experiment. It is not to be considered synonymous with the word introspection. Introspection is restricted to the subject's description of the experiences aroused by the stimulating situation. Verbal report includes these descriptions. In addition, it includes descriptions of the objective phases of response and of any aspects of the total stimulus-response sequence under study.

The accuracy of the findings of a study very often rests directly on the accuracy of the subject's report. For example, in an investigation concerning the effects of continuous work upon feelings of tiredness, the subject would be called upon to report the extent of his feelings of tiredness. If the task is quite simple he would very likely lose interest in it, and, rather than reporting his feelings of tiredness, he would describe the extent to which he is bored. In this instance, the subject would introduce an error into the experiment by describing the wrong mental state, that is, boredom instead of tiredness. In making his report to the experimenter, however, he would utilize words that would lead the investigator to believe that the mental state of feeling tired was being described.

The Registration of Response. This problem involves getting a record of the changes in behavior. For registering overt changes, a wide range of procedures are available, from an accurate sound-motion picture record of the event to the inaccurate recall by the experimenter of what he observed.

For subjective reactions, we are occasionally able to use mechanical registration, as in measuring blood pressure, stomach contractions, or the psycho-galvanic response. Most subjective reactions, however, especially the higher mental responses, must be registered crudely, through the introspective report of the subject. Here is a situation peculiar to the science of psychology. In other sciences, the object of study can be produced externally to and separately from the devices used to register the changes. In studying the processes that go on in such an activity as reasoning, the object of study and the registering instrument are one and the same, namely, the individual acting as the subject-observer.

The registration of social behavior is proving a very difficult problem to solve. The situation to be observed is increased in complexity because there are several rather than one individual to observe. The interpersonal responses among the different subjects are more than any one experimenter can accurately observe. The addition of sound recorders and motion-picture cameras increases the accuracy. Even with these, however, it is impossible to capture all of the changes occurring in behavior.

The Quantification of Response. Quantification of the subject's reactions is closely associated with registration of response. Devices which record muscular reactions can often be made to register the amount or frequency of the changes. Writing levers registering reactions on "endless" paper tapes may provide records of the general form of the responses as well as their durations, extensities, and frequencies.

Mental activities can be quantified through their products. The number of problems worked in a given time, or the amount of time required to work a given number of problems, provide bases for expressing the responses in numerical form. Performance in motor skills, learning of mazes, memorizing of verbal materials, solving problems through reasoning, etc., can be quantified in terms of units of work accomplished. Accuracy of the performance can also be measured by counting the number of mistakes or errors made either in a given amount of time or in a given amount of work.

Measurement of attitudes, interests, and personality traits can be accomplished through the use of questionnaires, inventories, tests, or ratings. The development of procedures for quantifying these complex behaviors has been a slow process, and the best measures now available still lack the precision necessary for accurate prediction of individual performance.

CONDUCTING THE OBSERVATIONS

The Nature of the Observing Process. *Mechanisms Involved in Observing.* Observation of an event means being aware of the event; that is, the observer experiences the event. Environmental changes, both internal and external, stimulate the sense organs, which in turn elicit changes in the sensory nerves. When these sensory-nerve changes reach the brain, we have an experience of the event. These experiences are given names and their familiar aspects are carefully symbolized.

Observation of an event is not merely the arousal of a sense organ and the consequent elicitation of activity in a sensory nerve or the brain. It also includes an attentive adjustment of the individual to the event and the rearousal of past experiences in the form of meanings associated with the event. Recognition of some aspect or feature of the event is conditioned upon a rearousal of past experience, as is also the naming or symbolizing of the experience.

The Active Nature of Observing. Scientific observation of phenomena is not a passive but an active response. As scientists we do not sit in a grandstand and watch a parade of unit experiences go by, like observing the horses at a race track. On the contrary, we question nature; we go out and prod nature and then note what happens. The problem that the scientist selects for study and the testing situation he establishes for attacking the problem in a large measure determine the particular variables and relationships that will be examined. Nature, then, is not only what takes place, but what is allowed or forced to take place.

"Mental Sets" in Observing. Observation is not an idle collecting of facts. Scientific observation is characterized by mental sets. By the nature of the problem we have chosen to investigate, we are set to become aware of certain facts and to ignore other facts. Other mental sets which influence our observation are traceable to biases stemming from our over-anxiety to establish a hypothesis, or to prejudice stemming from too strict an adherence to a point of view or a school of thought.

An additional mental set, which sometimes hinders us from getting all of the experience or facts that a testing situation affords, is the set to observe sameness or similarity. We should convince ourselves that the observation of differences is just as important as the observation of similarities. Progress in science comes from observing differences. They are the points of take-off on the way to new discoveries. We should remember that the "same thing" can be either the same or different, depending upon how we are set to observe it.

The Scientist as Observer. *Distinguishing Fact and Inference.* With the scientist playing a major role as an observer, it is necessary that safeguards be established to minimize the contribution of subjective bias and maximize the objective nature of his experiences. Facts of sensation are observable. They should be recorded and described in the forms and relationships in which they are observed. Inferences about the meanings of these facts are important and necessary. These inferences may also be facts, but they should be recognized as inferential responses. They should not be confused with the sensory facts. There are safeguards we can take to reduce the error of confusing sensory facts with inferential facts and to prevent subjective interpretations from being substituted for objective observations. These safeguards are bona fide and essential parts of the scientific method. They are directed primarily at controlling the scientist's observational behavior, as he is the major source of subjectivity in the scientific method.

Safeguards in Attitude. Let us begin with the factor of attitude. The scientist must disclaim infallibility. This admission of the possibility of error has two salutary effects; namely, it keeps him on the alert during the making of his observations, and it makes him critical of his interpretations of these observations. The scientist must acknowledge the need for the elimination of bias and take positive steps to control it. There is much truth in the statement that a "pet theory makes for prejudiced observation." To counteract his own preconceptions, the scientist should deliberately search for the exceptions. His attitude is not one of proving his notions but one of testing them.

Adequate Training in Observational Techniques. Accurate collecting of the facts demands a thorough background in the field of the problem to be investigated and acquaintance with the observational techniques that are applicable in this field. Accurate observation results from practice in observing the kind of phenomena to be studied. A mere intention to observe accurately does not guarantee accuracy. If, in the field selected for research, special procedures have been developed through which the phenomena can be made to occur under conditions that will enhance accuracy of observation, then these procedures should be learned and used by the scientist. Adequate training will prepare the scientist, not only to know what he is looking for, but to know where and when to look. Knowing where to expect an event and approximately when it will occur goes far toward guaranteeing that when the event actually takes place it will not escape observation.

Mechanical Supplements to Observation. Frequently, the sensory mechanisms of observation can be aided by mechanical means. If the scientist is required to observe a visual object, he has many optical devices to aid him. Depending on the problem, use can be made of telescopes, magnifying glasses, microscopes, cameras, polygraphs, recording oscillographs, and similar gadgets. In the modality of hearing, there are sound detectors, amplifying tubes, recording machines, and the like.

The Temporal Course of the Observations. *The Necessity for Constant Conditions of Observation.* Nearly all research studies occupy an appreciable period of time, the observations extending over days or months or even years. If the observations made at different times are to be comparable, it is necessary that the conditions of observations be held constant. In psychology, this fact is of prime importance because of the possibility of change occurring in the powers of observation of the experimenter, of the subject, or of both, during the course of an investigation.

Temporal Variations in Subjects. When persons are to be used as subjects, as in experimentation on sensation, perception, imagination, thinking, and similar mental activities, it is often necessary that they develop and maintain a particular set or point of view toward the stimuli presented to them. They must have sufficient background experience so that they can correctly understand the particular psychological concepts being utilized. Much controversy has occurred in experimental work on sensation because descriptive terms were not well understood, with the result that during the course of the experiment, variation occurred in the subject's attitude or set toward the tasks given him.

The stimulus-error experiment supplies an illustration of this point. Many studies have been conducted in an attempt to learn the nature of sensory experience. Frequently, the experiments included reactions to visual stimuli because of the fact that more precise control over the stimulus situation could be achieved in vision than in other sense modalities. The subject would be presented with a visual stimulus and asked to describe his experience of it. Sometimes the subject described characteristics of the stimulus object, and sometimes he described characteristics of the sensory experience. The stimulus-error was committed when the subject paid attention to the stimulus object and described it instead of attending to and describing the experience aroused by the stimulus. The vacillation of the subject between the two points of reference in his descriptions produced uncontrollable variations in the course of the experimentation, which made it impossible to interpret the results correctly.

Constancy of certain characteristics in the subject is necessary even though he is not acting as an observer. The tasks a subject is given to do are to be carried out in the particular way specified by the experimental procedures. Deviating from these procedures produces noncomparable conditions and thus noncomparable results. For example, if, in a study involving the computation of arithmetic problems, the subject is told to work every problem in order, that procedure should be rigorously held to by every subject throughout the testing period. If a subject ignores the instructions at a given point in the test and skips some problems to get to others which he feels are easier, his performance is invalidated. Again, in a psychomotor pursuit task the subject may be told to work as fast as he can. If he chooses to work for accuracy instead of speed his performance is invalidated.

The subject's cooperation in correctly following the experimental procedures depends upon two factors; namely, his correct understanding of the particular procedures he is to follow and his willingness to maintain full cooperation until the test is completed. The first is usually not difficult to obtain. A pilot study can be conducted after the instructions or procedures are readied and the findings used for perfecting their clarity and ease of understanding. It is more difficult to be assured that the subject is cooperating fully throughout the test. This is particularly true when the subject is called upon to perform a routine task over an extended time, such as adding 1-place numbers for a 3-hour period. Sometimes, having the subject report his feelings about the task or about his achievement in the work assigned him may provide clues concerning his attitude. However, such information is not always reliable.

In the case of animal subjects, it is often necessary to give preliminary training in the testing situation to familiarize the animal with its general physical features. In experiments on learning, the animal may be required to manipulate objects, such as opening gates, pulling strings, or pushing levers. The animal's ability to operate such devices is usually not the probem being studied. It may be necessary for him to operate a device, however, in order that his ability to learn some other task can be observed. For example, one-way gates are used in mazes to prevent retracing. The rat must learn to open the gates, but the problem under study concerns the rat's ability to learn the pattern of the maze. The rat must be taught to operate the gates before practice on the maze is begun, in order that the learning of the maze pattern will not be affected in a systematic way by a delayed learning of the gate-operating procedures.

Temporal Variations in Apparatus. We have already noted the usefulness of apparatus in presenting and registering stimuli, in controlling and registering responses, and in supplementing the observational powers of the experimenter. Continued use of a piece of apparatus requires periodic maintenance and calibration. Even the best-constructed apparatus will show variations in precision with continued operation. The performance of different subjects cannot be considered comparable if the precision of the machine registering the stimuli or responses varies during their performances.

Before an experiment is actually begun, trial runs can be made to determine the likelihood of instrumental variation and to set standards of precision to be maintained throughout the experiment. Periodic calibration checks can then be instituted and the apparatus maintained at an approximately constant level of precision during the testing.

The Number of Observations. *Variability of Behavior.* The number of observations required in a scientific study is a function of the variability of the behavior being examined. We have emphasized several times the intricate nature of the orders underlying behavior. It should be apparent that an understanding of any functional relationship—even the most simple—develops from many observations of it. A single observation, although true as an existential fact, adds little to our knowledge of a phenomenon unless we relate it to other facts about that phenomenon. An observation in isolation has little meaning. It takes on meaning as it is related to other observations, both those that agree with it and those that are in disagreement.

Consider the very commonly occurring fact of variation in the performance of an individual reacting several times under a given set of conditions. A runner in a track meet does the 100-yard dash in 9.6 seconds. Under similar conditions last week his time was 10.1, and for the week before it was 9.8. A tackle on the varsity football squad gains the plaudits of the crowd in one game by applying a key block on the opposing quarterback who appeared to be on his way to making the tying touchdown. The next Saturday he misses his tackle under much the same conditions, and the resulting touchdown becomes the margin of victory of the opponents. If we were given the task of characterizing this tackle's ability as a prospect for all-American honors, we would want to observe his playing over many games of the season so there would be opportunity for us to learn what he would be expected to do most of the time.

This variation in performance is found in all animal and human subjects studied in psychological experiments. Their performance varies from one sitting to another. If only one performance is obtained, it is not possible to learn how closely this one is equivalent to the average performance, or to learn if it is above or below the expected average. Only by observing many performances can we be assured of having enough data for computing a value that is near to or equivalent to what would be expected "on the average."

A similar problem of variability in performance exists when our task is to characterize the behavior of a group, or when it is to characterize the nature of a given psychological process. The study of two or three or even eight or nine members of a football squad would not be enough to establish the team's national rating. The study of the test performance of only a few members of a psychology class would not furnish enough information to characterize the average ability of the class. The performance of a few subjects in a memory experiment on poetry would not furnish the factual basis for describing the psychological processes involved in memorizing a poem. In all such problems, reliable conclusions must wait upon the pooling of many observations. Any human performance is just too variable to be encompassed within one or a few observations.

Replication of Observations to Achieve Representativeness. An important reason for making many observations is to get a representative expression of the variables. In a previous section we described the need for selecting variables that adequately represent the theorem to be tested and for eliciting performances in our testing situation that are representative of the variables. As we have seen, a variable may have many expressions. We need to learn what its characteristic expression is under the specific conditions of our testing situation. When several variables are interacting we need to learn how they interact "on the average" under the conditions of our experimental situation.

In our previous example of the football player, we would need to observe him many times to learn how he would perform "on the average." To determine if he were deserving of all-American mention we should observe him performing the characteristic tasks of a tackle, such as blocking, tackling, and running interference. We should watch him do all of these tasks many times. If we see him perform only part of the tackle responses, or observe him only once or twice performing any tackle response, we really lack the information necessary to determine if we have observed a representative performance. It should be obvious that to learn how our tackle would behave "on the average" in the various tackle responses we must observe him on many occasions.

Getting the variables expressed in representative ways and making many observations of these representative performances give us stability in our statistics. In psychological research we want to achieve stability in our measurements. We want measures that will "stay put" any time they are used. A measure of a group's performance, such as the mean, is not a very useful statistic if it varies widely in value each time the group is measured.

Statistical Compared with Practical Significance. The number of observations bears an important relation to the concept of "significance." If a scientific finding cannot be accounted for by the operation of chance factors it is declared "statistically significant." Sometimes a finding is of little "practical significance" even though it is statistically significant. The greatest contribution is made when the finding is both statistically and practically significant.

Consideration of an example will make these two concepts clearer. Suppose that in a program of educational guidance it is important to know whether the scholastic ability of upper classmen is higher than that of lower classmen. We administer a scholastic ability test to 1,000 freshmen and sophomores and to 1,000 juniors and seniors to learn if there is a significant difference between their mean performances. The difference is found to favor the upper classes by 5 points, the mean of the lower classes being 175 and the mean of the upper classes being 180. Is this a real difference? If we mean by "real" that the difference is large enough to be useful in deciding what kinds of courses should be placed in the several college years, then the answer is no. A difference this small has no practical significance. If by "real" we mean that the difference cannot be accounted for by chance factors and therefore that the upper classes are scholastically superior to the lower classes, then the answer is likely to be yes. If the groups are fairly homogeneous, then the large number of cases tested would result in stable means and the difference probably would be found to be statistically significant.

Designing the Study in Order to Increase the Number of Observations. We should design an experiment so that observations can be added to those completed if the latter are insufficient in number to give us stable measures of our variables. We are unable to predict the number of observations we shall need to get significant results. We may design an experiment for 30 cases and find at the end that our results are not statistically reliable. If an additional 20 or 30 subjects are likely to produce significant results, we may want to continue the experiment. In such a situation it is necessary that the subjects added later be comparable in terms of our variables with those used in the first part of the study. If this condition is not realized, then the expression of the variables is not representative throughout the entire investigation. We are then not justified in pooling the two sets of measures in order to gain more stable statistics.

Suppose there are two groups of subjects available to us for an experiment, 35 eighth-graders and 35 ninth-graders. We use the eighth-graders because it is more convenient. After collecting the data we find that we need additional subjects, and now use the ninth-graders. Suppose the interest and ability of the two groups are different and are related to our problem. The differences between the two groups introduce systematic differences into the two parts of the experiment. A better design would have been to randomly select half the subjects from the eighth grade and half from the ninth grade at the beginning. The same procedure could then be followed when additional subjects were needed. The characteristics of the subjects would then remain comparable throughout the entire study.

Recording the Observations. *The Need of Records.* Analysis and interpretation of the variables in an experiment become possible only when records are made of their expressions. An experience lasts but a brief moment. Most performances occupy but a short period of time. Without some permanent representation of these transitory events, which can be leisurely examined following their occurrence, we can make little progress toward understanding the variables.

Records Should Be Comprehensive. It should be obvious that the accuracy and thoroughness of the analyses will be conditioned by the comprehensiveness of the records. The nature of the problem, of course, will also determine the kind and amount of the records. The records should be complete enough to afford an accurate appraisal of the variables related to the theorem under test. Inasmuch as we usually are unable to foretell the exact kind and amount of information we shall need, it is better to err on the side of recording more data than are needed than to find after the collection of facts is completed that the data are insufficient for our purposes.

The Accuracy of Records Varies with the Degree of Conceptualization. The accuracy of the records depends upon the degree to which the symbols used correspond with the empirical changes being represented. A natural event perceived through one of the exteroceptors arouses a less variable experience than an event that stimulates us through an internal sensory mechanism. When symbols such as words are assigned to experiences, then the less the variability of the experience, the more uniform will be the understanding of the meanings assigned the words, and therefore the closer the correspondence between the words and the experiences of the natural event. As we proceed from this sensory level of fact to levels involving abstraction and conceptualization, where rational processes enter into the determination of the fact, the agreement obtained between different observers decreases, resulting in a lower degree of correspondence between symbol and fact. In general, then, the highest correspondence between symbol and fact is attained in what we call sensory meanings, with the correspondence becoming less as more conceptualized meanings are introduced into the description.

Incorrect symbolization results in incorrect meanings. Later analyses and interpretations made of the recorded data are then in error. In turn, this means inaccuracy in our conclusions and generalizations.

Limitations of Apparatus Recording. A distorted and incomplete picture of the variables in an experiment may result if instrumental recording is not supplemented by the observations of the scientist. A testing situation is never so perfected that the scientist can absent himself until the facts are collected. No apparatus has yet been invented that will record all of the changes in the stimuli and responses occurring during a psychological experiment. Certainly, some characteristics of the stimulus-response relationships can be accurately registered by writing levers, photographic film, and other means. In simple experimental situations, such recording has reached a high level of precision. When complex combinations of stimuli are involved and the subject's reactions require coordinated changes in many muscle groups, the automatically recorded picture may even be a distortion of the true characteristics of the behavior. It requires the observations of the scientist to detect and correct this distortion. When global behavior is under investigation the components of response in the form of attitudinal and motivational changes are not even directly detectable by instrumental recording.

The argument being advanced here is that we cannot dispense with the observations of the scientist. No instrument has been invented that has the observational powers of the human being. The scientist, therefore, should not conclude that a record of his personal observations is unnecessary because he has devised a fancy brass recorder. Apparatus recording is highly desirable, but one of the very important reasons for justifying such recording is that it gives the scientist greater freedom in directing his observations upon those features that are not reducible to instrumental registration.

An example of possible overdependence upon apparatus recording is found in some of the time-and-motion studies of worker performance. Very accurate registration has been made of the manual responses of bench workers, such as assemblers. Stereoscopic motion cameras made it possible to trace accurately the motion of the arms and hands in the performance of very complicated kinds of tasks. Registration on the film of a time record made it possible to estimate the time of each of the different motions. With such accurate depicting of the time-and-space characteristics of the minute changes in the arms and hands during a task, it was possible rationally to combine part responses in such a way as to produce, conceptually speaking, a "best" way of performing the assembly. In their enthusiasm for analyzing the response records of the workers, the investigators lost sight of the psychological principle of individual differences. According to this principle it is psychologically improbable that one "best" way can be found that will allow every worker to produce at his individual best. This ignoring of the principle of individual differences would probably not have occurred if more time of the investigator had been spent in noting to what degree and for what reasons one worker performed a given task in a different way from that of his fellows.

Keeping a Daily Record. A daily record of events transpiring during the conduct of an experiment often proves of great value in the analyses and interpretations of the data. The scientist should not trust to memory all of the little details of procedure—and changes in procedure—that must be recalled later during the analysis and interpretation of the experimental results. One good practice to follow is to record the date of occurrence and additional pertinent information concerning any subject's performance on the card, sheet, film, or tape on which the performance itself is registered. Another good practice is to keep a daily log or notebook. This record should include comments about preliminary experiments or trial runs, descriptions of unpromising procedures or techniques tried out, diagrams of apparatus or equipment designed, descriptions of breakdowns or changes in procedure in the confirmatory studies, suggestive explanations for failing to achieve the desired controls, pertinent incidental comments of subjects, time periods required for certain processes such as the developing and printing of film or the preservation and staining of tissues, and similar items of information. The daily log should contain any fact arising during the collecting of the data that at a later time might prove useful in the interpreting of the performance records of the subjects.

SELECTED READINGS

Davis, R. C.: Methods of Measuring and Recording Action, in T. G. Andrews (ed.), "Methods of Psychology," chap. 14, John Wiley & Sons, 1948. The author's purpose is to acquaint the reader with some of the problems encountered in recording behavioral changes and with representative procedures and recording systems for solving these problems. He discusses the following topics: the purposes and principles of measurement, characteristics of recording systems, some common recording systems, measuring work and energy, and measuring electrical changes.

Jahoda, M., M. Deutsch, and S. W. Cook: "Research Methods in Social Relations," vol. 1, chap. 5, The Dryden Press, Inc., 1951. This selection presents problems and techniques associated with conducting scientific observation in social-type situations. Particular attention is given to participant observation, systematic observation, and observation in standardized experimental or test situations.

Postman, L., and J. P. Egan: "Experimental Psychology: An Introduction," chaps. 7, 8, and 9, Harper & Brothers, 1949. These chapters are selected to give the student a brief survey of content and methods in a particular area, that of visual perception. Two model experiments are presented in each chapter. Chapter 7 deals with the perception of color, chap. 8 with the perception of form, and chap. 9 with the perception of space.

CHAPTER 10

The Organization, Analysis, and Interpretation of Facts

The general purpose of the organization and analysis of data is to derive meanings by which the results of an investigation can be correctly interpreted. The data as collected in an experiment, survey, interview, or other type of study are often not organized or arranged with particular reference to the problem in hand. The initial organization is frequently dictated by convenience. Furthermore, the meanings inherent in the data are not obtainable from a cursory examination. Many logical and statistical analyses are required to extricate these meanings. What then is needed is a reorganization of the data in terms of the purpose for which the study is being made and the execution of such analyses as will reveal all meanings relevant to this purpose.

Organization, analysis, and interpretation are not postponed until all the facts are collected but are begun as soon as the first facts are in. Few studies are so perfect in design that no questions or problems arise during the period of collecting the facts. Frequently, the knowledge of how the variables are interacting, which is gained in the early phases of a study, provides the basis for adjustments in procedures that greatly increase the precision achievable in the later phases of the study.

GENERAL OBJECTIVES OF ORGANIZATION AND ANALYSIS

Working over the facts that are collected serves many purposes, not all of which may have been in mind when the study was begun. We try primarily to learn if the facts confirm the hypothesis around which the study was evolved. Regardless of whether the findings are favorable or unfavorable to the hypothesis, we must determine if the results are reliable. If they are reliable, we then proceed to determine the explanatory and predictive value of our findings through the process of generalization. While going through these three phases of our examination, unanticipated events may happen. We may encounter problems that lead us off into new areas of research. We may evolve ideas for changing our hypothesis. We may get "bogged down" trying to determine the meaning of some unique relationship that we discover in the data. Because of the uncertainties and surprises involved, extracting meanings from our experimental results is one of the most fascinating and exciting phases of the scientific method.

Relating the Facts to the Hypothesis. *The Use of Simple Classification.* Usually the first step in organizing the data is to classify them in respect to some characteristic that is significant for the theorem under study. The theorem has stated or implied certain consequences which presumably would follow from the conditions of the experiment. Classification arranges the data to determine if the consequences obtained are the same as those stated or implied at the beginning. If they are the same, the evidence is accepted as confirming the hypothesis.

Suppose we conduct a survey in which we select the subjects from several nationality groups. This study might be concerned with the effect of nationality background on opinion toward the use of war. Our hypothesis might be that the degree of tolerance for war as a national instrument is a function of nationality. We decide to investigate the theorem that Nordic, Alpine, and Mediterranean nations differ significantly in their opinions concerning the conditions under which a nation should resort to war. We construct a questionnaire for sampling opinions of these three national groups with respect to their tolerance toward the use of war. We collect the opinions from our respondents as convenience and feasibility dictate, and the responses are arranged simply in the order in which they are obtained. The first variable to serve as a basis for classification and one that is basic to the problem is that of nationality. The records are then rearranged in terms of the nationality of the respondents. With the responses so classified it now becomes possible to apply various descriptive techniques, such as computing an average tolerance score for each respondent based on the number of his responses favoring or disfavoring the use of war. An average tolerance score can then be computed for each of the nationality groups. These averages are new meanings being extracted from the data. They add more precise information about a variable basic to the hypothesis.

The Use of Multiple Classification. In most experiments there will be several variables functioning. It is, then, possible to classify the data several different ways. These classifications are not equally significant for the theorem, but contribute important information about the variables on which the test of the theorem is based.

In the example cited we could collect information on the sex and age of the respondents. Then we could classify the subjects on either of these two variables independently of the other variable and independently of the variable of nationality. We could use simple classification to do this. On the other hand, we could use multiple classification procedures. We could first classify according to nationality, then within nationality classify according to sex, and then within sex classify according to age. Such multiple classification makes possible many new meanings and greatly facilitates our interpretation of the results. For example, having computed a tolerance score for each age group within each sex within each nationality, we could proceed to evaluate the contribution of these three variables of nationality, sex, and age. We could compare age groups within sexes within nationalities, or age groups between sexes within nationalities, or age groups between sexes between nationalities. We could compare sexes within nationalities, or sexes between nationalities. We could compare nationalities within sexes or nationalities within age groups. Of course, these comparisons are not equally meaningful or relevant to the hypothesis. It should be apparent, however, that some of these comparisons would shed considerable light on the nature of the variables underlying the facts that we have collected.

The Relevance of Classification to the Purpose. It should be emphasized at this point that the value of classificatory categories depends upon how closely they are related to the purpose of our study. As seen above, any data can be arranged or organized in many different ways. Only those ways relevant to the theorem being tested will result in meanings that will serve our purposes. Making all possible comparisons afforded by every possible classification usually is to be considered busy work. Occasionally in such byplay a scientist will chance upon a significant finding which was not in any preconceived way related to his problem. Such findings, however, are indeed rare.

The Need for Evaluating Variability of Performance. When dealing with human behavior, we can expect wide variation in the performance records of the subjects. This variation must be evaluated in our attempt to justify the hypothesis. Performance variation is a function of three factors, namely, the generality of the hypothesis and the theorem developed from it, the precision of our testing situation, and the psychological nature of the variables.

Variability in performance may be decreased, but it cannot be entirely removed. Removing from a testing situation any factor affecting the performance of the subjects will usually result in a decrease in the variability of the measures. For instance, narrowing the base of the hypothesis has the effect of reducing the number of variables that will condition performance. Furthermore, increasing the precision of the testing situation by removing the effects of variables not directly related to the theorem also reduces the variability in performance. Regardless of how narrow the hypothesis or how high a precision is attained in the test situation, there will continue to be variation in the performance of subjects because of the inherent variability of psychological abilities. This variability must be evaluated in our effort to confirm the hypothesis. We shall return to this problem in a later section.

The Consequences of Negative Results. If the findings do not verify our theorem, the hypothesis is not confirmed. When this occurs, either one of two alternative actions may be taken. The hypothesis may be adjusted to conform to the new evidence and further tests then made. Or the hypothesis may be abandoned and others sought. The first procedure is followed when other lines of evidence support the hypothesis or when the hypothesis seems to be working successfully in terms of its predictive effectiveness. The second alternative is followed when the evidence is overwhelmingly against the hypothesis, and especially when other hypotheses of more promise remain to be evaluated.

Evidence from a test may be sound and still not increase our knowledge about the hypothesis. This is because the theorem tested is not pertinent. It may be found that the results favor another hypothesis more than the one that is being examined. This is not likely to occur when the steps involved in the deductive elaboration of the hypothesis have been correctly executed.

Determining the Reliability of the Meanings. *Some Logical Aspects of Reliability.* The confirmation or disconfirmation of a hypothesis is based on the pertinence of the evidence, the amount of the evidence, and the relation which the evidence bears to alternative hypotheses.

Verification of any hypothesis can only be approximate, regardless of the relevance or amount of the evidence. The results of a test situation are examined in terms of the number of facts favoring the hypothesis and the degree of favorableness of these facts. The results of the test are compatible with the hypothesis only in terms of degree and not in any all-or-none sense. Variation in evidence means variation in degree of compatibility. The acceptance or rejection of a hypothesis is then never final in any absolute sense.

The favorableness of the facts for a given hypothesis is a relative matter. It depends, in part, upon the extent to which the results also favor one or more other hypotheses. The facts are then examined in reference to alternative hypotheses. In the logical development of our hypothesis we attempt to devise theorems and test situations that issue directly from the hypothesis. We also attempt to model the theorems and test situations so they will be either unrelated or opposed to rival hypotheses. This objective is easy to state but difficult to accomplish. Therefore, in the analysis of the results we must determine if and to what degree the findings are related to rival hypotheses.

The significance of the results for any hypothesis also rests upon the degree to which other factors than those purposely varied by the investigator have operated in the test situation. The presence of these factors may vitiate the relationship that the results bear to the favored hypothesis. They may also be very pertinent to competing hypotheses. If in an experiment the theorem required the determination of the correlation between reading ability and college success and we failed to evaluate such factors as high school preparation, scholastic aptitude, and study habits, we would not obtain a reliable measure of the relationship that we sought. One of the tasks in organizing and analyzing the results is to determine the method of operation of any vitiating factors and to remove their effects from the results during the process of relating the results to the hypothesis under study. There are statistical procedures by which this can be done, providing the study was originally designed to encompass these factors. The methods of partial and multiple correlation and of analysis of variance and covariance are powerful tools for accomplishing this purpose.

The Statistical Reliability of the Results. The reliability of performance of a subject refers to the extent to which his performance can be attributed to the functioning of systematic variables. We know that the measurements of psychological characteristics are subject to many variable factors and we can expect errors of measurement even under the best-designed testing situation possible. Even after carefully standardizing all of the experimental procedures, we cannot be sure that the performance obtained from a subject is representative of his ability, that is, that the performance we obtained would closely approximate what he would do on the average if we tested him a large number of times. Actually, what we would get in repeating the measurements would be a variation in his performance (see Fig. 1, Chap. 5). We would like to obtain what is called his representative or "true" performance for the set of conditions under which we require him to perform. A given measurement is reliable to the extent that it approximates the value of this true performance.

The statistical meaning of unreliability deals with the degree to which variables that do not operate systematically are determining the results. Interest is centered on the factors that result in unsystematic or variable errors, that is, variations in the subject's performance that occur in both positive and negative directions to about the same amount and in about the same frequencies. We increase reliability by reducing these factors giving rise to variable errors. In previous discussions we have referred to these factors as chance factors. Regardless of how well we think we have prevented these chance factors from operating, it is still necessary in analyzing our results to evaluate their contribution to the subjects' performance.

The Evaluation of Chance Variation. From the arguments on the meaning of reliability it is seen that one of the important objectives of organization and analysis is the evaluation of chance factors. We assume that these chance factors affect the performance of subjects in a random fashion, so that the values of the experimental variable will be increased and decreased equally. Furthermore, we assume that small effects upon the experimental variable will occur more frequently than large effects, and that very large effects will occur very infrequently.

As noted in Chap. 5, for most psychological variables chance variation will follow a definite function called the law of error. The law of error is very important in that it enables us to evaluate the contribution of chance error in our results. When we perform an experiment only once, we do not have the opportunity to learn exactly how chance actually operates on the performance of our subjects. We therefore estimate that for our results the law of error found characteristic of most other psychological factors would be applicable to our variables. It then becomes a problem of estimating the amount of the chance error and taking it into account when we are working with the variation attributable to the changes introduced in the experimental conditions. If we know the total amount of change reflected in the experimental results and can estimate the amount of change that could have resulted from the operation of chance factors, we have a basis for deciding whether or not significant variation can be attributed to the experimental variables. Said another way: we obtain information about the significance of our experimental variation by estimating the probable amount of variation due to chance factors. If the error variation is so small as to be insignificant we have confidence that the experimental variation is significant. This is one of our most important procedures for evaluating our experimental results.

In a study by the authors on the effect of vitamin deficiency on the rat's general activity level, the mean activity scores of the deficient rats on each day were higher than the mean scores of the normal rats. Furthermore, the two activity curves based on the means became more and more divergent as the experiment progressed.[1] A more thorough examination of the data, however, showed that the difference between the two curves was not significant. Chance factors operated to produce wide fluctuations in the performance of both deficient and normal rats, vitiating the comparison based on the diet variable.

Facilitating Generalization and Prediction. *The Objective of Generalization and Prediction.* The objective of both generalization and prediction is to go beyond the immediate facts and meanings established in the testing situation. As we have seen, a hypothesis is never actually "proved." Rather, it is confirmed in those aspects that have been set to empirical test

[1] See Chap. 11, p. 255, Fig. 10.

by some form of experimental or other kind of study. Not only should a hypothesis be consonant with the facts collected in the testing of its theorems, but it should be compatible with the facts of many other situations and conditions. No single study of a hypothesis provides us with knowledge of all of its many ramifications and implications. Generalization functions to apply the hypothesis as broadly as possible. It carries its implications into new areas where the variables and factors operate somewhat differently than they did in the situations already studied. Generalization actually points the way to additional studies that need to be done.

Generalization also forms the basis for making predictions about the consequences that would be expected to occur when the hypothesis is applied to a situation containing components not yet examined. This predictive function is very important in science. It is the procedure used in justifying the generalizations with which science is concerned. The success of any prediction will be conditioned upon the degree to which the predicted situation agrees with the predictor situation. Organization and analysis aid us in determining the characteristics that are essential to the hypothesis. This information then enables us to discover new situations in which we can make effective predictions.

Establishing Meanings to Be Used in Generalization and Prediction. Organization and analysis are the means for establishing the nature of the generalizations and predictions justified by the data and also of determining in large measure the accuracy with which these generalizations and predictions can be applied. The meanings basic to generalization and prediction are the meanings evolved in the organization and analysis conducted to confirm the hypothesis. Organization and analysis enable us to set limits to the meanings by describing and measuring the determinant variables and their interactions.

The future situations to which the generalizations and predictions are referred must possess some of the determinant characteristics. We must learn which of these characteristics are important and necessary for the hypothesis. We must further abstract these characteristics from their concrete reference points and extrapolate them to the new situations. In organization and analysis the meanings are freed from as many of the concrete ties found in the testing situation as is possible; such ties as refer the meanings to persons, places, times, conditions, and the like. Obviously, the more carefully the abstraction is performed and the more accurately the meanings are delimited, the more accurate will be any projection of these meanings in the form of generalizations or predictions.

SOME COMMON CHARACTERSTICS NEEDING DESCRIPTION

Whether we are studying humans or animals, groups or individuals, complexes of behavior determiners or relatively simple reflex actions, there are certain characteristics of response that past research has demonstrated are important and that should be described quantitatively when possible. Actually these common characteristics are very fundamental meanings which are extremely useful in understanding many different kinds of data. A thorough familiarity with them as general concepts is expected of any scientific psychologist. The three most important of these characteristics can be stated in general form as follows: the level of achievement, the variability of performance, and the relationships among performances that are alike in one or more characteristics.

The Level of Achievement. *Meaning of the Concept.* Interpreted broadly, level of achievement refers to "goodness" of performance. It is assigned a more exact meaning according to the nature of the particular response being evaluated and the purpose of the evaluation. Regardless of the way a performance is described, to assign the meaning of level of achievement is to assign some value to the performance.

Some examples will show the wide variety of situations in which the meaning of level of achievement can be utilized. One of the most familiar situations is the classroom, where the teacher represents students' performances in terms of grades. Evaluation of level of achievement helps to answer such questions as the following: How is Jack doing in school? Does he have the ability to graduate from high school? Does he show a particular aptitude for certain school subjects and an ineptitude for others?

Evaluations of achievement are constantly made in business and industry. Management needs to know the relative effectiveness of workers on the job. It asks such questions as: Are Smith's sales up to par? Is Jones' production still suffering from his recent illness? Are the lathe operators turning out enough units of work?

In the areas of personal and social adjustment, information on achievement is of importance in evaluating the individual's success in getting along with his fellows. We desire to know if Bill gets along well with his older brothers, if he has a high regard for his parents, if he approves of the efforts of his family in helping him to meet his college expenses. Evaluations of adjustment are needed in such social situations as are provided by the school, the fraternity, the club, the gang, etc. Answers are needed to such questions as: Does Bill have many male friends? Is he popular with the girls? Is he invited to parties and dances? Has he been bid to a fraternity? What interest does he show in school activities?

It should be apparent that many different special meanings can be given to the term level of achievement. These meanings vary with the nature of the response situation and the purpose for which the meaning is needed. It should also be apparent that different evaluation procedures will be required to measure level of achievement as it is given these different special meanings.

Ways of Representing Goodness of Performance. Level of achievement may be represented symbolically in three different ways, namely, by word descriptions, by assigning one of several large quantitative categories, or by assigning a numerical score.

Description by numerical scores is considered the most accurate kind if the assignment of the number meanings can be justified. As we noted in Chap. 6, counting is a number process readily applied to behavior when the behavior is manifest in the form of unit responses. For example, the number of items assembled by a bench worker in a specified period of time is a numerical description of the amount of his performance. The number of pages completed by a typist is a similar score. Quality or accuracy of performance is also represented through counting. The number of items spoiled by the bench worker, or the number of errors made in the copy by the typist, are quantitative scores representing inaccuracy of response. Numerical description of level of achievement is then possible when the performance is divisible into small comparable units. Numerical scores offer a very adequate symbolic representation.

Whenever the behavior is not readily divisible into comparable small units, large quantitative categories of description are used. It is difficult to represent degrees of prejudice or strength of political conviction by counting up units of prejudice or units of conviction. We then resort to large categories in the given variable. These categories are located on one continuum representing various values of a single magnitude. For example, the degree of prejudice can be measured by means of a rating scale in which the range of prejudice from very prejudiced to very tolerant is divided into five, seven, or some other number of categories. A person's prejudice, say toward a given race, can be rated by acquaintance judges and assigned one of the categories. Frequently the categories are represented by letters, as in the case of letter grades assigned students' performance in the classroom.

The use of numerical scores and larger quantitative categories has not supplanted the use of word descriptions. Levels of achievement in more global or molar types of behavior are not accurately represented solely by means of scores or large categories. Of course, a limited characterization of such behavior can be so represented, and different scores can be used for describing different aspects of the behavior. The meanings of several separate scores become less accurately applicable, however, as the nature of the behavior being represented becomes more general. Separate scores then do not represent or describe the unitary nature of the behavior. They must be supplemented by word descriptions.

The need for word descriptions is readily observed in the area of personal adjustment. Certainly there is no question but that some individuals are better adjusted than others. The better adjusted persons can be considered to have reached a higher level of achievement in behavior. We can devise several large quantitative categories by which the different levels of achievement can be represented. To depend upon a single category to describe the level of adjustment of a given individual, however, is to ignore further refinements in evaluation that can be realized through word descriptions. Whether these word descriptions are called quantitative or qualitative in nature is not of great consequence as long as they contribute to a better understanding of the level of achievement. Suppose we are concerned with the social adjustment of a male college student. One area in which the effectiveness of his adjustment would be reflected is his association with members of the opposite sex. We could obtain a rating of the individual as to whether during the past year he had had a large number, a few, or hardly any girl friends. A rating that he had a large number of girl friends fails to give us an accurate description. He may be genuinely popular, and so finds it easy to associate with girls. Or he may find it difficult to remain very long on good terms with a girl and thus has to change his girl friends often. In either case he might receive the same rating. In this type of situation a description in broad categories or in numerical scores is not sufficient because the goodness of behavior cannot readily be represented in a single-type value.

Evaluating Goodness of Performance in Terms of a Standard. Whether words, large quantitative categories, or numerical scores are used, the evaluation requires a comparison of the performance of the individual or the group with some standard. The behavior being evaluated is referred to some norm, and meanings about the behavior arise from comparing the behavior with the norm.

If, in a word description, we say that Bill is getting along very well socially, there are social norms against which his behavior is being evaluated. "Getting along well" means agreement with the social norms. These norms will not be the same in different societies nor within different strata of the same society. Furthermore, there will be local, neighborhood, or gang ways of behavior that will be used as standards. There may be differences between the local ways and the more general society ways. As a consequence, different evaluations of the same behavior may be in disagreement when gauged by norms of different kinds. For example, a delinquent act of a teen-ager may be appraised differently by a judge in court than by the fellow members of his gang.

Evaluation of performance by means of large categories is also normative in nature. The goodness of an A grade in school arises from the fact that this descriptive category is applied to a certain select few from among a large group, the remainder of whom are assigned other letter grades denoting lesser achievement.

The meanings of a numerical score are gained from a knowledge of the frequency of that score as compared with the frequency of other scores and from a knowledge of the characteristics of the group of individuals in question. Knowledge of the group's characteristics is needed although seldom brought to our attention. Its importance will be seen if we consider the evaluation of a child who has been held back a year in school. Suppose that according to chronological age a child belongs in the fifth grade but actually is only in the fourth grade. Superior performance of the child measured in terms of the performance of fourth-grade children would be considered less than superior when measured in terms of the behavior of children of his own age.

Meanings of an individual's performance can be gained by comparing his score with other scores of a group to which he belongs, provided he possesses characteristics common to the others in the group, such as age, educational achievement, physical growth, conditions of health, etc. The common characteristics, of course, should be relevant to the performance being evaluated. Suppose that Bill's score is 25. If the lowest score in the class is zero, this knowledge adds meaning to Bill's score. Further meaning results if we know that many of the class got scores between zero and 25. A more precise meaning is gained when we know that 75% of the class scored below 25.

We see, then, that meanings of an individual's level of achievement are extracted from relationships, namely, relations between the performance of the individual and the standard or norm of performance. The norm or standard may be set up as a law, as a social value, or as the specific performances of individuals in a group to which the individual is conceived to belong.

The Variability of Performance. *Meaning of the Concept.* Whether we speak of group performance or of individual performance, it can be characterized as variable in nature. The determiners of a given act are not identical for different individuals. Performance of the act will, then, not be the same for different persons. Also, within the individual the large number of factors conditioning any performance are constantly fluctuating in value. These fluctuations produce changes in the various components of response and thus produce variations in the level **of**

achievement in any given activity measured on different occasions in the same person. When one performance is obtained from each of many subjects, we must deal with interindividual variations, usually referred to simply as individual differences. When many performances on one task are obtained from one subject, we must deal with intra-individual variations. When several performances on a given task are obtained from several subjects, we must deal with both kinds of variation.

Individual Differences. The study of variation in level of achievement among individuals forms a very important chapter in psychology. Recognition of this concept is of prime importance in the schoolroom, at the factory bench, in the business office, in the training of children within the home, in fact, in every situation where the behavior of more than one person is involved. Individuals differ in response under conditions which physically appear to be alike. Knowing the extent of these differences enables us to know to what extent we should vary the training, the discipline, the treatments, the recognitions, the awards, etc., by which each individual is encouraged and enabled to attain the highest level of adjustment.

Variations within the Individual. To understand a person and to make successful predictions about his behavior, it is necessary to study intra-individual differences. When an individual performs an act many times, instead of being the same on all trials, his scores vary in amount and form a distribution around his average performance. The accuracy of our prediction about any future performance of the individual rests upon the extent of these variations in his performance. If he fluctuates wildly our prediction will be less accurate than if he performs consistently within narrow limits. It is then important that we be able to measure or estimate intra-individual variations.

Suppose that in the manufacture of mechanical toys a machine requires the close attention of a machine tender. The machine is set to operate within a narrow range of speeds that will result in the greatest number of acceptable toys in an 8-hour period when operated by the average worker. It is then important that the variability of the machine tender comes within the tolerance limits of the machine. If his performance varies to the extent that he gets behind the machine, then the toys produced will be defective, the machine might get clogged, and the waste in materials and labor could be considerable. The tender might even try to operate the machine faster than it is set for. Again, the chances would be high for jamming the machine and for producing defective toys.

Measures of the consistency of performance under distraction are often required. Some individuals seem unable to readily adjust to distracting stimuli, and their behavior fluctuates wildly when such stimuli are encountered. Consistent behavior under fire is desired in the operator of a phone exchange during an emergency, such as an earthquake, in the aircraft gunner during an air raid, in the surgeon during an emergency operation, or in the chairman of a political body during a heated debate.

Another form of variation within the individual concerns the consistency of response in different areas of behavior. No individual is equally variable in all of his activities. A measure of his response consistency in important kinds of activities greatly improves our understanding of the individual and his potentialities. For example, it is important to know the variability of an individual in respect to various traits of personality. When we ask the question: Can Mr. Jones be trusted to do the job? we are inquiring about several kinds of behavior. We might have in mind consistency of response in respect to his ability to organize the different components of the job, his facility for working with people, his available drive and motivation, his tolerance for routine work, or other such behaviors connected with the job to be done.

The Analytical Use of Measures of Variation. Brief mention should be made of the fact that the characteristic of variation can be used in evaluating the contribution of each of several variables determining a complex act. Simply stated, the variation of a given complex form of behavior stems from the variation in the many factors underlying it. These factors will not vary equally among themselves. Some knowledge about the importance of the different factors can be gained from the relative proportion of the total variation contributed by each of the factors. A statistical procedure, called the analysis of variance, has been devised by which this apportioning of the variation among the determinants can be achieved. It is beyond the scope of the present text to explain this procedure, but the reader should be aware of the fact that through the evaluation of the characteristic of variation it is often possible to discover the relative importance of the several determiners of a given complex event.

Relational Meanings among Variables. *Relational Meanings Arising from Comparisons of Variables.* We have noted earlier that our knowledge about a variable is evolved by comparing it with other variables. Facts are relational in nature. Facts about a variable include the ways in which it relates to other variables. Meanings, as descriptions of the relationships among variables, reveal characteristics of the variables themselves.

One way of relating variables is to note the presence or absence of common characteristics. Variables are described as similar in nature if they possess common characteristics. They differ in nature if each possesses characteristics that are unique. We noted earlier that this type of relational meaning is utilized in interpreting level of achievement by comparing a given performance with some standard or norm.

A more precise statement of a relationship is made possible when quantitative categories or numerical scores are used to describe the variables. Differences in magnitude of one variable may be related to differences in magnitude of a second variable. For example, for eighth-grade students it might be found that the higher the score on a reading test, the more likely the success of the individual in mastering high school subjects. Mastery of high school subjects could be indicated by averaging the grades at the end of some stated time, such as at the end of the freshman year. The average grade category of each student could then be compared with his score on the reading test. It might be found, in general, that the higher the reading score, the higher the average high school grade. Such a relationship could be quantified by means of correlation.

Analyzing the Composition of a Complex Variable. A frequently occurring research objective in psychology is the determination of the nature of the composition of a given complex act. The determinants of complex behavior often function simultaneously in very involved interrelationships. Through the process of analyzing the act into its parts and seeking the nature of the relationships among the parts, significant impetus is given to our understanding of the act as a whole.

To illustrate the compositional analysis of a complex variable, let us consider the important characteristic called ability, which has been under scientific study for many years. Numerous attacks have been directed toward learning about its nature. All of these attacks start from two fundamental bases that can be considered as necessary assumptions. First, regardless of our definition of ability, we agree that it is expressed or manifest in the objective behavior of the individual. Secondly, the individual differences in performance so readily observed objectively among individuals are considered to reflect these differences in ability. The type of ability that has been studied most often is that reflected in performance on mental and motor tests. Performance on the different kinds of tests is considered to be the expression of one or more abilities. The differences in test performance of different individuals are considered to reflect differences in these abilities. As a result of many research studies, the general conclusion is being formed that the variations in performance obtained on a large variety of tests can be referred to a small number of abilities. Research is now being directed to determine just what these primary or necessary abilities are and how many must be postulated to account for all the performances observed in a situation involving a large number of tests.

Another compositional analysis might be concerned with the determination of the various components of a group's attitude toward political freedom. Certainly, the psychological factors conditioning any group's stand on a given social issue are large in number and contribute in varying ways and amounts to the expression of opinion by its members. One of our objectives is to discover the picture of the components. We could study them as simultaneously functioning contributors to the current expression of the group. Our control and prediction of the group's performances would be improved through such a compositional analysis.

The industrial psychologist also is faced with a problem requiring compositional analysis when he endeavors to define successful performance on a given job. He must learn how ability, training, job experience, incentives, home conditions, vacations, procedures for advancement and promotion, union membership, overtime pay, management's supervisory policies, and other similar factors function and interact with one another to condition the job performance of the workers.

Relationships Ordered in Time. Determinants of behavior can be studied as they are related in time, one preceding, another following. This type of relationship has been mentioned as one of the important orders sought by the scientist in nearly every project he undertakes. It differs from the compositional type of relationship described above only in the greater emphasis placed upon the temporal character of the relationship.

One type of temporal relationship presents a unidirectional connection between the variables. In some kinds of behavior there is an irreversibility between the factors in that one variable seems always to come before another. For example, eating food results in the alleviation of hunger. The reverse of this, that the alleviation of hunger precedes the eating of food, does not seem to be empirically justified. In the investigation of thresholds of sensitivity, with increase in the intensity of the objective stimulus the subject notes a difference in experience. The stimulus change always precedes the change in experience.

The temporal aspect of relations is an important element in genetic studies of behavior. The determinants of present behavior are traced back in time by being related with earlier behavior conditioners. A child's adjustments today are certainly better understood after we have learned the conditions surrounding his earlier training. The study of religious tolerance, mentioned earlier, could include an investigation of genetic factors. We could study the following hypothesis: Attitude toward religious freedom becomes increasingly less bigoted and more tolerant with increasing chronological age.

USEFUL PROCEDURES FOR ORGANIZING, ANALYZING, AND INTERPRETING DATA

For convenience of exposition, the various methods available for discovering and assigning meanings to the original performance records of a study can be subsumed under the following three headings: tabular procedures, graphical procedures, and numerical procedures. Although certain tabular procedures often are utilized first, there is no particular order in which these three types of methods should be applied. In fact, they are to be considered closely related rather than distinctly separate procedures. For example, we may use a graph for purposes of analysis and get from it ideas for applying numerical procedures. Or, after performing certain numerical analyses, we may make a graph of the results and get a better conception of what the numerical computations have accomplished.

A very large number of tabular, graphical, and numerical procedures are now available to the research worker. It will be possible here to present only the broad outlines of the purposes served by a few of these procedures. In addition to the procedures described there are many others with which every scientist should be familiar.

Some Tabular Procedures. *Uses of Tabular Procedures.* The two primary purposes served by tables are those of organizing the data and of facilitating numerical computations. As we learned earlier, the arrangement of scores or other measures recorded during the conduct of an experiment is usually based upon convenience. For example, if we were running subjects in a study on learning we would very likely arrange our data chronologically, that is, according to the days of the month on which the subjects were tested. If the purpose of the experiment were to determine if auditory presentation of the material were less effective than visual presentation, the data must then be rearranged in order to provide a basis for comparing the results obtained from the two modes of presentation. Tables enable us to organize the data in ways suitable for extracting information about the theorem under investigation.

Tabular arrangement of data often facilitates the computation of statistical constants. In later sections, mention will be made of certain constants used in measuring average performance, variability of performance, and correlation between variables. When records are being analyzed from a large number of subjects, there is considerable labor involved in computing any statistical constant. By arranging the data in tabular form, certain short-cut methods of computation can be used, and much time and labor is then saved.

Tables of Classification. Tables are basic to the ordering of facts through classification. Facts must be organized in reference to the experimental variables. In the example of a survey on tolerance toward war, several possible ways of classifying the data were mentioned. In Table 2, a multiple classification is made of fictitious tolerance scores

Table 2. Comparison of Fictitious Average Tolerance Scores by Age, Nationality, and Sex

Age groups	Nordic nations			Alpine nations			Mediterranean nations		
	Male	Female	Both	Male	Female	Both	Male	Female	Both
	A	B	C	D	E	F	G	H	I
15–24	10	8	9	11	11	11	14	15	14
25–34	12	15	14	14	14	14	16	17	17
35–44	15	16	15	17	16	17	17	18	17
45–54	16	18	17	19	19	19	18	18	18
55–64	17	17	17	21	20	20	19	20	19
65–74	20	19	19	22	22	22	19	19	19

with the variables of age, nationality, and sex as the axes of organization. Each entry would be the average of the scores of several respondents. Letters have been inserted in some of the columns for reference purposes.

An examination of Table 2 will show the ease with which various comparisons can be made. Comparison of nationalities by age groups can be done by studying the columns labeled C, F, and I. The tolerance scores of males can be compared between nationalities by age groups by using columns A, D, and G. Similarly, females can be compared between nationalities through columns B, E, and H. Comparison by age groups of the tolerance scores of male and female within each nationality can be accomplished through columns A and B, D and E, and G and H for the three nationality groups.

The Frequency Distribution. One of the most frequently used kinds of tables is the frequency distribution illustrated in Table 3. The data tabled consist of 200 scores ranging in value from 0 to 130. Obviously, great difficulty would be encountered if we tried to extract meaning from a single column of scores 200 numbers in length. We would do better to order the scores from low to high, and to combine them into larger units called class intervals. The interval used in Table 3 has the value of 10. In preparing the table we would use some form of tally mark, as indicated, which enables us in one step to translate the scores from any heterogeneous arrangement in which we find them to the ordered ar-

Table 3. Frequency Distribution of Scores of 200 College
Students on an Intelligence Test

Class interval	Tally	Simple frequency
0–9	//	2
10–19	///	3
20–29	ﬀ//	7
30–39	ﬀﬀ/	11
40–49	ﬀﬀﬀﬀ//	22
50–59	ﬀﬀﬀﬀﬀﬀ////	34
60–69	ﬀﬀﬀﬀﬀﬀﬀﬀ///	43
70–79	ﬀﬀﬀﬀﬀﬀ///	33
80–89	ﬀﬀﬀﬀ/	21
90–99	ﬀﬀ//	12
100–109	ﬀ//	7
110–119	////	4
120–129	/	1
Total......	....	200

rangement of the frequency distribution. The frequency of scores within
each interval is determined from a count of the appropriate tally marks.
The table in its final form consists of only two columns, the class intervals
and the frequencies.

Many meanings are obtainable from examining the frequency distribution. We can learn the approximate value of the lowest and highest
scores. The greatest concentration of scores is revealed by the interval
having the highest frequency. The changes in the frequencies from one
end of the distribution to the other enable us to form a notion of the
shape of the distribution of scores.

If the scores of two or more groups are to be compared, the frequencies
of scores for the several groups can be arranged in parallel columns in
the table. The meanings noted above can be extracted for each group
and comparisons across groups can readily be made.

The Per Cent Frequency Distribution. This type of distribution is used
when groups are to be compared that contain different numbers of cases.
The name per cent frequency distribution is given to this type of distribution because the frequencies are translated into fractions of 100 and
thus expressed as percentages.

Suppose we have the test scores on a scholastic-ability test of a sopho-
more group of 155 cases and a junior group of 310 cases. The distributions

Table 4. Comparison of College Sophomores and Juniors on Fictitious
Scholastic-ability Test Using Original Frequencies and
Per Cent Frequencies

Score values	Frequencies		Per cent frequencies	
	Sophomores	Juniors	Sophomores	Juniors
0	5	10	3	3
1	7	15	5	5
2	10	19	6	6
3	15	31	10	10
4	24	48	15	15
5	33	65	21	21
6	24	49	15	16
7	16	31	10	10
8	10	21	6	7
9	7	13	5	4
10	4	8	3	3
Total....	155	310		

for these two groups are provided in Table 4. Comparison of the groups
on any given score value is difficult because of the difference in total
number. For example, for a score value 2 there are 10 sophomores and
19 juniors. If we considered these frequencies alone we might conclude
that a greater proportion of juniors obtained this score than did sophomores. This difficulty is readily overcome by expressing the frequencies
as percentages. This is done in columns 4 and 5 of the table. In the sopho-
more group the total number of cases is 155. In order to change the frequencies to per cent frequencies it is necessary to divide each frequency
by 155 and multiply the result by 100. The frequency of 10 for score 2
now becomes 6 per cent. In the junior group with 310 cases, each frequency must be divided by 310 and multiplied by 100. The frequency of
19 for score 2 now becomes 6 per cent. The same percentage of cases in
the two groups obtained the score of 2, therefore no difference between
the groups can be claimed for this particular score value.

Some Graphical Procedures. *Uses of Graphical Procedures.* As with
tables, graphs are useful in organizing research data. They are particularly serviceable in discovering trends of relationship between variables
and in communicating relational meanings to other investigators.

To represent the relationship between two variables we arrange the variables on a two-dimensional graph using rectangular coordinates. One variable is placed on the abscissa (horizontal axis) and the other on the ordinate (vertical axis). The score values or score intervals of the two variables are recorded on the respective axes. Paired values are then plotted, a dot being placed at the point of coincidence of the values of a given pair. For example, in Fig. 2 the relationship is plotted between the height and weight of 20-year-old boys. For simplicity, only five pairs

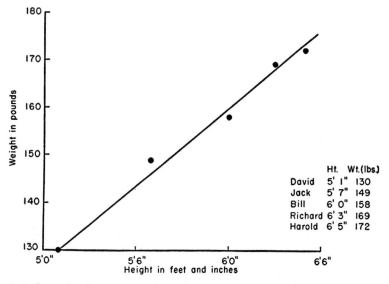

	Ht.	Wt.(lbs.)
David	5' 1"	130
Jack	5' 7"	149
Bill	6' 0"	158
Richard	6' 3"	169
Harold	6' 5"	172

Fig. 2. Relationship between weight and height of 20-year-old boys (measures are fictitious).

of measures are used. Within the figure are the paired values for five boys. Consider the height and weight of Richard. We locate his height of 6 feet 3 inches on the abscissa and his weight of 169 pounds on the ordinate. We then extend imaginary lines on to the graph from these values and where the lines intersect we place a dot. Thus there is one dot for each pair of values, that is, one for each boy. A line is drawn through the plot of points in such a way as to leave the least amount of deviation of the points away from the line on either side.

Examination of the graph reveals a pronounced positive relationship between height and weight. As height increases, weight increases. The plot of points is represented better by a straight line than by a curve. This then is a rectilinear relationship. Although such relational meanings can also be detected in the corresponding pairs of numbers, they are much more difficult to extricate from the numbers than from the graph.

Graphs are very popular as a means for communicating relational meanings because of the inherent ease of visual perception. Far less effort is required to examine and analyze relationships portrayed graphically than when they are represented by columns of numbers. In a graph, the essential nature of the meaning is abstracted and symbolized by lines. The reader is then not required to examine the many original numbers from which the relation stems. If a meaning can be represented in two-dimensional space it can readily be communicated to other investigators by means of simple rectangular coordinate graphs.

Graphing Functional Relationships. A functional relationship between two variables is readily depicted in a two-dimensional graph. Usually, rectangular coordinates are used as in Fig. 2. In a functional relationship one variable of the pair is considered independent because in some respect it has priority over the other variable. This priority may be determined by the time of occurrence of the variables, the variable coming first being considered the independent one and the other the dependent variable. Priority may be determined by the degree of control we exert over the variables. In research, the experimental variable that is systematically manipulated is the independent variable. In graphing a functional relationship it is customary to place the independent variable on the abscissa and the dependent variable on the ordinate.

A very familiar functional relationship in psychology is the learning function. Here we have the amount of progress associated with the amount of practice. Obviously, the more an individual practices, the better will be his performance. The nature of the rate of improvement with continued practice—whether the rate of improvement is the same throughout the several practice periods or is faster at one time than at another—should be decided only by an appeal to empirical facts. The learning curve of Fig. 3 was made up to represent improvement that might be manifested by a group of 10 subjects doing simple multiplication problems. The number of correct problems is a function of the number of practice sessions of 1-minute duration.

Several meanings are revealed from an inspection of the learning curve. Most apparent is the sharp decrease in the increments of improvement from the earlier to the later practice periods. This reduction in rate of learning—called negative acceleration—is quite characteristic of most forms of learning. The flattening of the curve at the terminal end is quite revealing of another characteristic, that of reaching a limit beyond which improvement is difficult to achieve. Sometimes this is called the physiological limit, especially if the performance is such as to involve the speed and coordination of muscle groups, such as in typewriting. In explaining the physiological limit, one argument states that the bodily mechanisms involved are working at their maximum.

Another meaning to be obtained from most learning curves comes from the irregularity of the achievements associated with increasing practice. It will be noted that the curve does not pass through all of the points. Although each point is the average of 10 performances, the points form a jagged or irregular line. The curve is smoothed by drawing the line through the plot of points rather than through every point. It is argued that through smoothing we obtain the form of improvement that would most likely occur under ideal conditions.

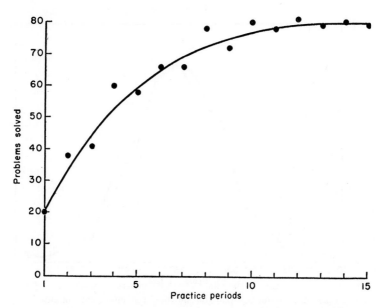

Fig. 3. Learning curve for working simple multiplication problems.

The Frequency Polygon. One of the simplest and most significant types of graphs in psychological research is the frequency polygon. This is a graph of the relationship between frequency of occurrence and score value, the same relationship as is represented in the frequency distribution table. In the frequency polygon the scores are known first and are thought to condition the frequency of occurrence. They are therefore placed on the abscissa. The frequencies are considered a function of the size of the scores and are placed on the ordinate. The word polygon means many sides. The solid line in Fig. 4 is a polygon; the many sides are formed by drawing the trend line through every point. When the line is smoothed it is then referred to as a curve. The broken line in Fig. 4 is the frequency curve, and geometrically speaking it is considered to have an infinite number of sides.

An inspection of either line in the graph will give most of the meanings obtained from the frequency-distribution table and will give these meanings with less search and with greater clarity. In addition, the general contour of the frequencies and the symmetricality of the frequencies on either side of the mid-point are much easier to detect in the graph than in the tabular distribution. The relative variation of the frequencies for different score units is an especially important characteristic. For example, if greater frequencies occur at either end of the range of scores than in the midrange, it usually is indicative of the operation of impor-

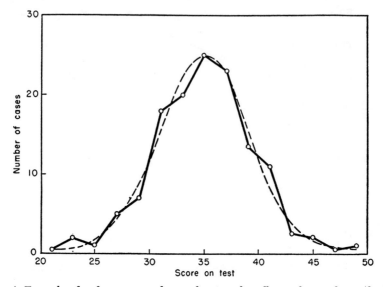

FIG. 4. Example of a frequency polygon showing the effects of smoothing (broken line).

tant factors, and it is a sign that further analyses are in order. When there are two regions of high frequencies, the curve is called bimodal.

The Normal Frequency Curve and the Normal Probability Curve. The normal frequency curve has several special characteristics. It is like that of Fig. 4 in being a symmetrical bell-shaped curve with the frequencies decreasing from the middle to each extreme. It is not just any bell-shaped curve, however, but one in which the frequencies decrease according to a particular mathematical law. The curve of Fig. 4 actually was drawn to approximate closely a normal frequency curve.

The theoretical curve obtained from the mathematical formula is called the normal probability curve. The particular formula of this curve was developed by the mathematician to represent the expected occurrence of events having certain mathematical probabilities. A good empirical example would be that of predicting the fall of 100 pennies tossed 10,000 times. The events would be the different combinations of heads in the 100 pennies, namely 100 heads, 99 heads, . . . , 1 head, and 0 heads. The formula enables us to predict how frequently each of these combinations of heads would occur in 10,000 tosses. If we actually performed the experiment we would obtain a frequency distribution that would closely approach the form of Fig. 4.

A most significant finding in psychology is the fact that the distribution of occurrence of values for a very large number of psychological characteristics closely approximates the normal probability curve. This is often referred to as the "normal law." Thousands of times the psychologist has had the occasion to study the frequency of occurrence of the various values of his variables. In a very large proportion of these studies the variables have been found to be distributed according to the normal law. We then have the following two facts: (1) the mathematician has developed a formula which accurately describes a particular type of distribution function, and (2) the psychologist has empirically demonstrated that a large proportion of his variables follow this distribution function. On the basis of these two findings the psychologist then uses the mathematical characteristics of the normal probability function to analyze and describe his empirically derived normal frequency distributions.

The decision as to whether or not a given frequency distribution is normal need not be left to subjective judgment. A statistical test is available for determining in a quantitative way if the empirical data distribute themselves according to the law of normal probability. If the frequency curve approaches sufficiently closely the mathematical curve, then we are justified in utilizing the characteristics of this curve in the analysis of the data.

Bar Charts. Although the graphs previously described are often used for displaying and communicating meanings, there are some graphs specifically developed for this purpose. The bar chart and the column diagram are popularly used for this purpose. Bars or columns are used on one axis to represent amounts in the dependent variable, while the independent variable is arranged along the opposite axis. The dependent variable is placed on the vertical axis in the column diagram and on the horizontal axis in the bar chart. Comparisons among a wide variety of variables are possible with these graphs.

Suppose, on a bar chart, we wish to depict the relationship between performance on an intelligence test and college graduation. Figure 5 illustrates this type of relationship. The performance scores on the test are placed on the vertical axis and the proportions of individuals graduating from school are placed on the horizontal axis. The lengths of the bars are made to correspond to the per cents of graduating students falling in the several score intervals. We can see from a glance at the chart that, in spite of some reversals in the increments from one score interval to the next higher one, there is a definite relationship between size of score and per cent of graduates: the higher the score, the greater the proportion of students succeeding. It will be noted that the relationship is not rectilinear but curvilinear, which can be demonstrated by passing a smooth line through the ends of the bars. From this curve we can note that what is being measured in the first few lower steps in the

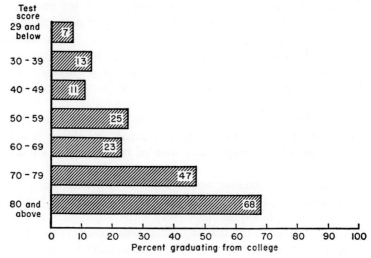

Fig. 5. Per cent of students graduating from college as predicted by an intelligence test.

test continuum is more significant in terms of accounting for failure to graduate than what is measured at the higher levels of test score. The type of information depicted in this chart would be very valuable to persons concerned with the educational guidance of college students.

Some Numerical Procedures. In earlier chapters, the importance of using number meanings was discussed. Being symbols, numbers can be manipulated rationally. Furthermore, being relatively free from ambiguity of meaning, they become symbolic vehicles that enable us to attain high levels of accuracy and precision in quantitative descriptions. It is necessary, of course, that the variable we are describing be capable of manipulation in the ways required by the number meanings that we desire to assign to it. In the present section we shall briefly consider numerical procedures for describing the three characteristics of level of achievement, variation in response, and relationships between variables. The emphasis will be upon the meanings and purposes of certain numerical constants and not upon methods for computing them.

The Mean as a Measure of Level of Achievement. In previous sections, we reviewed the use of numerical scores and large quantitative categories as means of describing the level of achievement. The present discussion will concern the mean as a measure of achievement. It can be used to represent an individual's performances or the performances of a group of individuals. The mean is the familiar statistical constant we compute by adding the amounts of several given items and dividing this total by the number of items. Suppose a student obtains the following scores in six examinations: 20, 21, 24, 22, 20, and 19. We decide that the mean will provide us with a reliable estimate of his average achievement. Adding the scores we obtain the total of 126. Dividing this sum by 6 results in a mean of 21. We have reduced six performance scores to a number that can be used to represent all of them.

One characteristic we desire the mean to have is that of representativeness. Its function is to stand for and take the place of all of the items. It can be said that the mean represents each of the items of a group because the value of every item enters into its computation. In the above example every score contributed according to its value, e.g., the score 24 contributed 24, which is 5 more points than was contributed by the score 19. Logically speaking, if we have no reason for thinking that the score 24 is unduly large because of the operation of chance factors or other factors not concerned with the knowledge of the subject matter being tested, we shall not want to reject it or add it in at some other value, but shall want it to contribute according to its own amount. We have here an exemplification of one of the fundamental rules of statistics, namely, that the investigator is not justified in rejecting any values of his variable unless there are sound empirical reasons—not personally biased reasons—for excluding them.

Another characteristic desirable in any statistical constant is stability. By this is meant that its value will not be greatly sensitive to chance or sampling fluctuations. The mean is a stable measure. For example, if we tested a given group three times in some ability that was known to remain constant and the three testings were conducted under approximately the same conditions, then the three means obtained from the three administrations would have nearly the same value.

The mean has several other characteristics that recommend its wide adoption. It has the mathematical property of being algebraically manipulable. We can add, subtract, divide, and multiply means as we do other numbers. This is one of its most important properties but need not

be developed further in our discussions. The mean is also easily computed and is readily understood, two additional characteristics that make
it a very serviceable constant to use.

The Standard Deviation as a Measure of Variation. As noted in Chap.
6, the standard deviation is a statistical constant that can be used to
measure variation either in individuals or in groups of individuals. When
we examine a distribution of scores depicting repeated performances of
one individual or the single performance of each of many individuals,
it is apparent that to measure the variability of the scores we must have

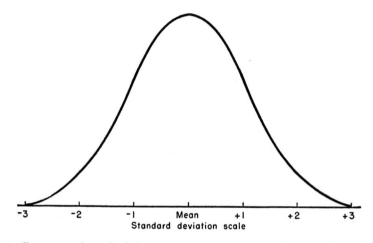

FIG. 6. Illustration of standard deviation units in relation to the normal distribution.

some central point from which the scores deviate. This is to say that a
score can vary only in relation to some point set up as a reference point
from which the extent of variation or deviation can be measured. In the
use of the standard deviation the distance of each score from the mean
is the prime consideration. The square root of the mean of the squares of
these deviations is the value given the standard deviation. The constant
is then rigorously defined by a mathematical formula. It further has the
significant property of being algebraically manipulable. Like the mean,
we can use the standard deviation in the computation of other statistical
measures. The standard deviation is abbreviated SD and is sometimes
represented by the Greek letter sigma (σ).

The standard deviation contributes its most significant meanings when
applied to a normal frequency distribution. These meanings are readily
obtained from a graphic illustration of such a distribution as is given in
Fig. 6. In the figure the unit of 1 standard deviation is marked off along
the base line of the curve. The unit is expressed in terms of the particular
score units of the instrument of measurement, e.g., if the score unit is the

number of problems worked, then SD is expressed as a given number of problems worked. The actual value of the standard deviation is obtained from the data by applying a formula. A careful inspection of the curve will reveal that the inflection points—those points in the curve where the slope changes in direction—fall at -1σ and $+1\sigma$ from the mean. The distance between the points -1σ and $+1\sigma$ from the mean includes 68 per cent of the scores. When laid off in both directions from the mean a value of 3σ approximates the ends of the distribution. This is to say that ap-

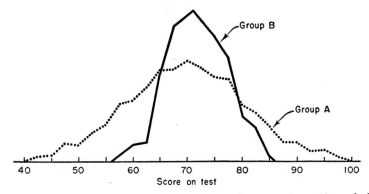

Fig. 7. Distribution of scores of two groups with similar means but with marked differences in variability.

proximately 100 per cent of the scores are included in the distance between -3σ and $+3\sigma$.

A further characteristic of the standard deviation is that it is a constant unit of measurement. One sigma distance is the same along the base line of the normal curve regardless of the particular point in the range at which it is applied. That is, 1 sigma distance is the same number of score units at the low end, in the middle, and at the high end of the distribution of scores, because for a given group of scores the standard deviation is constant in value.

Another characteristic of the standard deviation is its representativeness. In computing sigma the value of every score is used.

The importance of the standard deviation as a means of characterizing groups of individuals can be pointed out by considering the problem of comparing two groups in terms of their scores on a common examination. Such a comparison is presented in Fig. 7. It will be noted that the two groups do not differ significantly in mean score, group A obtaining a mean of 70 and group B a mean of 71. If we had only the means as a basis for comparing the two groups we would have to conclude that they were almost identical. From the graph we can see that the groups are very different except for their means. Group A is much more variable than group B. The standard deviation of group A is 10, and that of group B is 5. We can say that group A is twice as variable as group B in its performance on the examination. This difference is clearly portrayed in the curves of Fig. 7.

The Measurement of Relationship by Correlational Methods. Co-relation or correlation refers to the fact that variables "go together." Another way of expressing it is that there is a concomitant variation between the variables, or more simply "varying togetherness." A coefficient of correlation is a single number that expresses the extent or amount of the relation between two variables. It measures the extent to which variation in one variable is associated with variation in another variable.

Correlation in its broader aspects includes many kinds of relationships. Many specific adaptations of the concept have been made and corresponding mathematical constants have been derived for quantifying the particular types of relationships that have been studied. We shall be concerned primarily with the correlation coefficient between two continuous variables that are rectilinearly related. A continuous variable is one in which the units or scores are divisible into any size required, that is, the variable being measured changes in magnitude by infinitesimal amounts, as in the case of intelligence. This is the type most widely found in the study of psychological variables. Correlation between two continuous variables will illustrate characteristics that are applicable in varying degrees to the correlation between discrete variables, dichotomized variables, and variables related curvilinearly.

An effective measure of relationship should reflect the amount or degree of relationship between the variables. Some variables are closely related with each other, others are only moderately related, and still others are remotely related or unrelated. We need a procedure for expressing in quantitative terms this variation in amount of relationship which extends from no relation on the one hand to perfect relation on the other. For pairs of continuous variables we have such a procedure in the product-moment coefficient of correlation, also called the Pearsonian coefficient after the mathematician who derived the formula. It is symbolized by the letter "r."

Figure 8 will help us reach an understanding of this concept of the amount of correlation. Using rectangular coordinates we represent the correlation between two variables by placing one on the horizontal axis and one on the vertical axis. As we learned earlier, in a functional relationship the dependent variable is placed on the ordinate. When no functional relationship is involved, either variable can be placed on either axis. The score values of the two variables are recorded on the respective axes, the low values usually being placed at the bottom of the vertical axis and at the left of the horizontal axis. The data to be represented usually consist of two sets of measures on the same group of individuals. A point is plotted on the diagram for each individual by placing a dot at the intersection of imaginary lines extending vertically and horizontally from his scores in the two variables.

Different amounts of relationship are represented in the three plots. For the sake of simplicity only a few points have been plotted in each diagram. In Fig. 8A we have what is termed a perfect relationship. The points all fall on a straight line and the change in one variable is directly proportional to the change in the other. When the values of two variables so related are inserted in the formula for computing the coefficient of correlation, the resulting coefficient will have the value of 1.00. In Fig. 8B

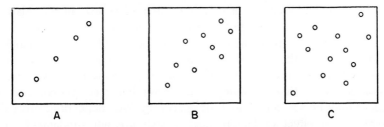

FIG. 8. Illustration of three degrees of correlation.

the relation is less than perfect but there is discernible a definite trend of relation. Coefficients of correlation of relationships of the order diagrammed in this figure have values in the neighborhood of .60. Figure 8C demonstrates a very low correlation. It will be noted that the divergence of the points from the trend line is much greater than in the other diagrams, but there is still a slight indication of a relationship between the variables. Coefficients of correlation of relationships of this order have values around .10.

It can be seen from these diagrams that the amount of relation is represented by the extent to which the points deviate from the best-fitting straight line. This line is known as the line of relation. It is further noted that the meaning of amount of relation varies continuously as the relationship varies from the point of no relation to the point of perfect relation. The product-moment coefficient of correlation is sensitive to this continuous change, and its value varies continuously from 0 to 1.00.

Negative values of the correlation coefficient are obtained when the trend of relationship is opposite to that illustrated in the diagrams. When high scores in one variable are associated with low scores in the other, the trend will be from upper left to lower right, and the coefficient will be a negative number. In the study of psychological variables we usually are interested in knowing if effective behavior in one variable is associated with effective behavior in another; that is, that "goodness" of performance in factor A goes with "goodness" of performance in factor B. If in all of our variables we represent goodness of performance by high values and poorness of performance by low values, then genuine negative relationships between psychological variables are seldom found. For instance, relationships among human abilities are nearly always found to be positive in nature.

The amount of relationship indicated by a coefficient may be in error relative to the "true" amount of relationship existing between the variables correlated. In interpreting the meaning of a coefficient of correlation we must remember that the coefficient that we compute measures the amount of relationship existing between the scores that are inserted into the formula. We are primarily interested, of course, in the relationship between the psychological variables underlying the scores. Therefore, the scores must be reliable measures of the variables if the meanings obtained through the coefficient are to be justifiably applied to the variables. At times we are ignorant of the nature of many of the systematic determiners operating to influence the scores being correlated. The coefficient may be spuriously high or spuriously low, depending upon the nature of the effect of factors present that are not fundamental determiners of the psychological variables underlying the performance scores. Unless we possess sound knowledge of the determiners underlying the performance scores we should not extend our generalizations very far from the particular relational meanings for which there is supporting empirical evidence.

It should be clear from the foregoing discussions that the concept of correlation gives us a tremendous advantage in understanding relationships, whether they are functional or nonfunctional. In functional relationships, the coefficient of correlation adds information about the determinant relationship existing between the variables. In nonfunctional relationships, the coefficient may furnish leads by which we can trace the determiners of the variables correlated in terms of the nature of the relationships these variables have with other variables. A simple example of a nonfunctional relationship is the correlation of height and weight. Neither of these variables can be interpreted as the determiner of the other, but the high correlation between them is indicative of the fact that common determiners of the two variables may be found in the fundamental growth processes of the body.

SELECTED READINGS

Cartwright, D. P.: Analysis of Qualitative Material, in L. Festinger and D. Katz (eds.), "Research Methods in the Behavioral Sciences," chap. 10, The

Dryden Press, Inc., 1953. A major problem faced by social psychologists is the adaptation of qualitative types of facts for purposes of research. This selection treats the analysis of qualitative material, pointing out the importance of this kind of material for scientific study and describing procedures and techniques for achieving its quantification.

Hyman, H. H., and P. B. Sheatsley: The Authoritarian Personality—A Methodological Critique, in R. Christie and M. Jahoda (eds.), "Studies in the Scope and Method of the Authoritarian Personality," pp. 50–122, Free Press, 1954. In this selection the authors critically evaluate the methodology of a research study published in book form as "The Authoritarian Personality." In the section entitled *Analysis,* errors committed in the selection and use of analytical procedures are pointed up.

Walker, H. M.: "Elementary Statistical Methods," chaps. 3, 4, 5, 7, 8, 11, and 12, Henry Holt and Company, Inc., 1943. In browsing through these chapters the student will be able to understand much of the logic underlying the statistical treatment of data without having to work out the computations underlying the concepts presented. Topics covered in the discussions include the frequency distribution, tabular methods, measures of relative position, averages, measures of variability, the normal distribution, and the concepts of regression and correlation.

CHAPTER 11

Generalizing from Scientific Data

Generalizing is the last step in the conduct of a scientific study, the step wherein we evaluate and apply the experimental findings obtained from our investigation. Our interest is in learning what significance these findings have for the hypothesis we are studying and for other purposes and problems which differ from those of our study. This process of discovering and stating the implications of the results for our hypothesis leads us to conceptual elements and characteristics that are logical extensions of the empirical facts of our investigation. Forecasting to other situations by extending the empirical findings contributes valuable solutions to problems of both practical and theoretical significance.

As the value of scientific research is a direct function of the range of accurate generalization that is achieved, we shall profit greatly from a consideration of the types of errors that must be avoided if sound generalizations are to be formulated.

THE PURPOSES SERVED BY GENERALIZATION

Knowledge grows because the legacy of understanding left from the past is insufficient to solve all of our present-day problems. Growth in knowledge comes about by the addition of small increments of fact to what is already known. We effect this growth by studying hypotheses and generalizing about new facts collected to confirm or disconfirm these hypotheses.

Generalization as a Means of Attacking Unsolved Problems. In addition to containing the solution of the problem for which it was organized, each completed investigation puts forward tentative solutions of related problems and raises additional questions that need to be studied.

One of the criteria used in the evaluation of a research project concerns the extent to which the findings of that study can be applied in situations that differ from the one in which the findings were discovered. Most investigators want their experimental results to serve many purposes, so they direct their generalizations to the solution of other problems than their own. If a study has no meanings that can be extended beyond its immediate results in order to solve related problems, it must be judged as of little worth.

Any research study should be evaluated in terms of the number of significant questions it raises as well as the number of problems that it solves. Seldom are the data discovered in an experiment so comprehensive in nature that they describe all aspects of the problem and provide answers to all questions relevant to the problem. In fact, scientists consider projects to have great value when they are pregnant with new problems and new questions. Questions raised by a study actually extend the findings of the study and lead to their application in new situations. An important function that the scientist can perform for his fellows is to point his generalizations toward unanswered questions and develop the generalizations with such clarity and detail that other scientists will be encouraged to embark on a search for the answers.

An illustration will clarify the foregoing points. A situation in psychology in which generalization might be severely restricted is one in which the conclusions merely list the characteristics of the sample of subjects studied. For example, we could set up the problem of determining the intelligence, reading ability. spelling ability, and social adaptability of the students in Miss X's eighth-grade class in school Y. With the data collected, our conclusions could simply be a description of these characteristics of this particular sample. Obviously, we have solved the problem but we have not extricated all of the meanings inherent in the data.

We could use the information for making various decisions about this particular group. If the class were deficient in reading ability, we could look to the intelligence test scores for a possible answer. If the class contained a group of mischievous students who were doing well in their lessons but who, nevertheless, were responsible for most of the classroom disturbances, we could determine if they were exceptionally bright and if they scored low on the social adaptability test. Thus, relationships among these several attributes might provide leads to the explanation of some of the behavior of the group or of individual members of it. The findings would thus be extended as trial solutions to other related problems.

Questions of some importance might arise if we carefully analyzed the results. For example, questions could be raised concerning the nature and extent of the relationship between intelligence and each of the other attributes, the nature and extent of the relationship between the social-adaptability scores and the frequency of classroom misconduct, and similar relationships. These questions would issue in problems requiring further research.

Similarly, we could use the information for generalizing about the behavior of other groups of eighth-grade students, and probably for generalizing about the behavior of students in grades other than the eighth. Questions similar to those mentioned in the preceding paragraphs could be asked about these other groups.

Generalizing as a Means of Advancing the Application of Knowledge. Generalizations setting forth problems yet to be solved can be directed toward applications in practice or applications in theory. We should not think of these two phases as unrelated but rather as mutually interrelated and interdependent. Growth in practical applications arises from previous accomplishments in theory. In turn, practical applications reflect upon theory to reveal additional needs for theoretical development.

Advancing Practical Applications. Findings of the theoretical scientist arouse the interest of the practical scientist and lead him to make generalizations that eventually result in some technological convenience. Obviously, if no one had ever thought beyond the findings of the theoretical scientist, and pondered over what practical use could be made of these findings, we would not now have the many applications of science that are enriching all phases of physical and psychological living. Each time a new technological convenience has been provided, there previously has been an insightful generalization from preexisting theory. If theory should stagnate, practical applications would shortly cease.

Many theoretically bent scientists refuse to consider the practicality of their research findings. This would appear to be an extremely short-sighted policy. For instance, in psychology there seems to be no sound reason why insight into the control and prediction of behavior in daily-life situations should be considered as something to be avoided by the theoretician. In his analyses a theoretically bent psychologist frequently will see possible practical applications of his findings. He should transmit such insights to others even though he himself is not interested in following up any practical applications.

Advancing Theoretical Applications. A steady growth and enrichment of theory is one of the most important needs served by generalization. The full understanding of any phenomenon can come only from the use of theory. With his experimental findings in hand the scientist can return to the theoretical framework of his problem. He can determine those constituents that will be made more secure by reason of his results. He can discover those directions in theory that are implied in these results. He may even be led to valuable explanatory postulates concerning the nature of the unknown constituents.

Generalizing for theoretical purposes gains from practical application. The practical applications made possible by theory usually reveal new problems requiring solution. Obtaining the solution may have to wait upon the further development of theory. Thus in many instances the practical situation provides important problems for the development of theory.

For the good of both future theory and future practice, present theory should be maintained in a vigorous state.

THE PROCESS OF GENERALIZATION

Through statistical and logical analyses and interpretations, we discover the meanings inherent in the data we have collected. Through generalization, we extend these meanings to situations differing in some significant aspect from the situation in which we evolved them. The accuracy of the generalization will depend upon our correctly extracting the meanings from the data and upon our discovering in the new situations an adequate number of the determinants underlying these meanings.

The Probabilistic Nature of Generalization. By this is meant that there is no certainty that a given generalization will hold true. On the basis of the available evidence we decide whether or not we are willing to make the generalization, realizing, of course, that we can be found in error. The meanings available to us have been obtained from evidence that is formally incomplete. That is, the meanings have not been obtained under exactly the same set of conditions required by the generalization we are making. For example, we may have based our evidence on a sample of subjects and wish to generalize to the population. Or we may have studied one or two kinds of expression of a psychological process—e.g., learning—and wish to generalize about all forms or manifestations of this process. Or we may have studied a part of a certain complex work procedure—e.g., assembling a radio chassis—and wish to generalize about the procedure of assembling the entire radio. In each of these instances there are unknowns not covered by our evidence. Our inferences must be the most likely ones, the ones best substantiated in the data already collected. But they will always contain some uncertainty; there will always be a guessed portion that can never be completely removed. By careful organization and analysis of the data we reduce the amount of the uncertainty and form an estimate of the probability that our generalization will be correct.

The Nature of the To-Be-Generalized-To Situation. *The Problem.* In order for the meanings discovered in one situation to hold true for another situation, it is necessary for the two situations to have in common the determinants of these meanings. Suppose we have developed an aptitude test which successfully predicts graduation from a liberal arts college, and we generalize that it would be equally effective if used in a college of engineering. We assume that the to-be-generalized-to situation (graduation from engineering college) will be determined in much the same way as the situation that we have studied (graduation from a liberal arts college). Without this assumption there would be no basis for generalizing. We cannot generalize in a universe "ruled by caprice."

We must juxtapose the pattern of determinants of the experimental and the to-be-generalized-to situations and make judgments about the correspondence between the two in terms of the meanings to be generalized. This is difficult because the new situation to which the generalization is to be applied is not a known situation in the sense of occurring at the time. It is a postulated future situation. It must be patterned on the past, but it must have certain new characteristics demanded by the generalization. Uncertainty is introduced in endeavoring to describe a future situation containing the essential characteristics required by the generalization and also having a high likelihood of occurring. In our example the new and uncertain element is whether the aptitudes needed for completing the work required by engineering colleges are those measured in our test.

There is the further problem of clearly describing the point of reference in the to-be-generalized-to situation, that is, the reference point to which the generalized meanings are to be applied. Points of reference to which generalizations may be directed are of many varieties, but for purposes of description they can be subsumed under three kinds, namely, persons, facts, and principles.

Generalizing about Persons. The purpose of many generalizations is to predict the characteristics and behavior of particular persons or groups of persons. Having studied the attributes of a group of individuals and formulated generalizations that contain the characteristics of the group as a whole, we may then proceed to apply the generalizations to the subsequent behavior of the group or of any individual within the group. Or again, we may apply the generalization to similar individuals or to similar groups of individuals. In these latter instances the generalization can be accurate only if the determinants underlying the generalization as found in the population studied also operate similarly in these other individuals or groups. In evolving the to-be-generalized-to situation we must describe the characteristics of the persons studied and the persons to whom the generalization is being referred.

Generalizing about Facts. Generalization may serve the useful purpose of deducing a fact that is not directly observable. In a given study, after we have marshaled and organized all the facts we possess, we may find that there is still a missing element, that there is a blank that must be filled before we can solve the problem. Generalizing about the nature of this fact may enable us to complete the picture. This function of generalization is illustrated in the reading of detective stories. The reader often has to generalize about missing factual aspects of the story before he can reach a conclusion concerning the identity of the person who commits the crime.

Generalizing about Principles. The common goal of all scientific psychology is to discover fundamental principles underlying behavior. One of the primary purposes of generalizations is to develop and expand explanations of behavior. When a generalization involves principles, it is often difficult to evolve an accurate and comprehensive description of the to-be-generalized-to situation.

A generalization about explanatory principles may be made without regard to any specific population to which it might apply. The generalization is directed toward an understanding of the psychological processes involved in the behavior under study, and there is little concern given to the characteristics of the subjects used in obtaining the facts. For example, suppose we wish to study the rate of forgetting as a function of time since learning, and we use volunteer subjects for the experiment. We are selecting the subjects with no particular to-be-generalized-to population in mind. After we collect and analyze the facts, our generalizations are referred to principles and not to persons. That is to say, our conclusions are about the rate of forgetting irrespective of the particular persons who volunteered as subjects. Certainly one of the primary purposes of scientific psychology is to discover laws of behavior without in any important sense referring these laws to particular kinds of persons. This kind of reference point is very frequently used by the investigator in theoretical psychology.

Evolving the Meanings to Be Generalized. *The Problem.* From a very complex array of interrelated conditions we must evolve the pattern of determinants that underlie the meanings to be generalized. In any study of behavior, many determinant factors will be operating. Some of these factors will be understood, others only partially understood, and still others wholly unknown. Some of the factors will be relevant to our problem while others will be irrelevant. Some of the factors will be under adequate control, others partially controlled, and still others uncontrolled. Despite this complexity we must learn what the determinants are, whether they have operated in a characteristic or representative manner, and what the relative importance of each is. We must also make sure that our description of the determinants is accurate and represents the objective situation with a high degree of fidelity.

Abstracting the Meanings. As we learned in Chap. 10, the meanings that underlie generalizations are extracted from the data by dint of many logical and statistical analyses. These meanings tend to be abstract in nature. They are derived from the facts obtained in our investigation coupled with whatever other relevant knowledge we have. Primarily they are abstracted and conceptualized from the meanings that are readily observed in our data or can be readily traced to the data. Meanings that are immediately available from superficial inspection of the data are seldom of great significance except as starting points from which to generate more highly conceptualized meanings.

Success in applying a meaning to a subsequent situation rests in part upon freeing the meaning from much of the particular immediate context of the experiment in which it was discovered. If we find that an essential determiner of the meaning cannot be freed from the particular context of the experiment, generalization is impossible. By this is meant that if the meaning to be generalized results from some determiner unique to the investigation in which it was discovered, that is, a determiner that cannot be reproduced in a different situation, we lack the basis for making a generalization. A few characterologists have achieved some success in diagnosing personality because of their personal understanding of people. A false generalization is made when they attribute this success to some system they have devised, e.g., phrenology. The system in the hands of another does not bring success because the essential determiner, the knowledge of the characterologist himself, is not transferable with the system. To be successful, a meaning to be generalized should stem from those empirical conditions that we suppose can be duplicated in subsequent situations.

It is incumbent upon the scientist to abstract the meanings. He is the person most able to determine the particular conditions from which the meanings can be safely abstracted. He is the one most familiar with all of the conditions and findings of the investigation, and presumably he is well acquainted with the pertinent current knowledge. He, then, is the one best prepared to determine the extent to which any given meaning can be reproduced under changed and untried conditions.

The Essential Determinants of the Meaning. One of the objectives of the generalizing process is to find the conditions essential for the meaning. We are here faced with problems similar to those we encounter in defining and delimiting a problem, as discussed in Chap. 7. It will be remembered that in analyzing the determiners of automobile accidents it was a difficult task to discover the importance of any given factor.

In every psychological study there will be conditions that are of little significance for a given meaning and others that are essential. Among the latter there will be determinants that are sufficiently well known that they can be reproduced under a large variety of contexts. There will be others that are limited in the extent to which they can be duplicated under changed contexts. There may be still others that are peculiar to the original investigation and cannot be reproduced unless the original procedures are adhered to in a very rigorous manner.

It is the scientist's task to discover and describe the essential determinants—those determinants that can be reasonably assumed to underlie the meanings to be generalized. Furthermore, he should point out any conditions that prima facie appear likely to elicit the meaning and yet will not. Obviously, when there is a patent error possible in generalizing, the scientist must warn others of it. This he does when describing the essential determiners of the meanings.

The Need for Unambiguous Description of the Meanings. A very important task is to describe the origin and development of the meaning to be generalized in order that other investigators may learn just how much abstraction and conceptualization were needed to obtain it from the available facts. Any given meaning may remain closely associated with the empirical facts from which it was derived, or it may be found removed from these facts by several steps of logical abstraction. If another investigator is to adopt the meaning in a changed context, it is necessary that he learn in detail how the meaning was evolved. A thorough description of the facts upon which the meaning depends will go far toward enabling him to utilize it correctly under a changed context. An example of a failure to give an unambiguous description occurs when a scientist derives a meaning through certain mathematical formulations but fails to describe these formulations accurately when he presents the meaning.

The Mechanics of Generalizing. *The Problem.* To generalize a meaning accurately we must show that its essential determinants can be reproduced in the to-be-generalized-to situation. This we may be able to do if we have an accurate knowledge of the characteristic meanings occurring under the new set of conditions. Our problem is to match the determinants of the abstracted meanings with factors in the new situation.

Not all of the variables of the experimental situation should be reproduced in the to-be-generalized-to situation. Actually, the value of a generalization is a function of the extent to which differences are introduced between the two situations. That is to say, the greater the difference between the two situations, the further the generalization reaches into the unknown. It is also true that the greater the difference between the two situations, the fewer the common determinants underlying the generalization. It is, then, very necessary to determine the relative importance of the common factors.

Similarity of Determinants as the Basis for Generalization. Similarity of determinants is basic to the formulation of a generalization. We are referring to the similarities between the known situation and the to-be-generalized-to situation. Our task is to study the similarities or likenesses of the two situations and frame the generalization in terms of the kind, number, and amount of the common determinants. Which determinants must be the same and which can be different will be a function of the nature of the generalization that is formulated. Similarity of determinants merely refers to the fact that some of the determinants must be the same.

Other things being equal, the greater the number of common determinants, the more likely is the generalization to be found valid. Of course other things are not equal, and the number of common determinants needed for realizing a given generalization will then be a function of the relative importance of the common determinants underlying the meaning to be generalized.

The amount of the contribution of any determinant must also be assessed. Some determinants will contribute more than others, and some determinants will contribute more under one set of conditions than under another set. When we compare the experimental and the to-be-generalized-to situations, merely learning the presence or absence of common determinants is not a sufficient goal.

It should be obvious that the two situations can be alike in respect to characteristics that are not determinant in nature. There may be similar aspects that are not part of the nexus of determiners basic to our generalization. Errors will result if we base our generalization on these nondeterminant similarities. An error of this type is described on p. 256.

Analyzing for Common Determinants. This task is central to generalization, and is not an easy one to perform. We must thoroughly familiarize ourselves with the determinant constituents of the experimental study in which we are engaged. We must also thoroughly familiarize ourselves with the potentially functional determinants of the postulated to-be-generalized-to situation. We must then make judgments about the determinants of the particular meaning we wish to generalize. Lastly, we must make comparative judgments about the two situations in terms of the determinants that are considered essential for the generalization.

The task of analyzing the determinants has both positive and negative aspects. They will merely be enumerated here. We should describe those characteristics that must be reproduced without change in the new context before the generalization can be expected to be valid. We should describe those characteristics that can be dispensed with in the new context without changing the meanings to be generalized. We should describe those variables of the experimental situation that can be expected to function under changed conditions without radical difference in their contribution. We should describe those determinants that are not part of the meaning but that if allowed to function in the new situation will introduce changes in the meaning and therefore make accurate generalization impossible. Lastly, we should identify the factors found only in the new situation the functioning of which appears to be related to the generalization but in fact is not.

The Process of Generalizing for Practical Purposes. *The Problem.* In this type of generalization we are usually concerned with a to-be-generalized-to situation that can be devised by making changes in present situations. We can therefore obtain an immediate check on our generalization. The new situation is of a practical nature, and the generalization is concerned with meanings that can be readily introduced into this situation.

Suppose that a practical problem arises for which an immediate solution is needed. Our task is to devise an experiment in the hope of finding a solution. Because of the practical nature of the problem, we can obtain suggestions from the empirical situations in which the problem is found. We can find aspects of our problem in these situations, and from them we can get hints about the characteristics of the solution. In fact, some of the important features of the solution are stipulated by the demands of these situations. The generalizations from any study we complete can be referred back to these empirical situations to determine their validity.

An Example. Suppose we are approached by the manager of a factory with a request to develop a battery of tests for selecting workers for operating bench lathes. Our task is to devise psychological tests by which we can predict the abilities required for the operation of these lathes. At the end of our study the major generalization would be that applicants having the particular combinations of abilities we had evolved would be successful bench-lathe operators.

The generalization is directed to a future practical situation much like an existing situation. The to-be-generalized-to situation involves the operation of bench lathes as it is practiced in this particular factory. This situation is knowable for our purposes because it can be considered to be the present situation of operating bench lathes in the factory. Before devising any tests we are able to conduct analyses that reveal the determinants of lathe operation under present factory conditions. By gaining knowledge of these determinants we thereby gain knowledge of the determinants of the new situation to which we wish to generalize.

Our generalization can be rigorously tested because we are generalizing back to a factual or a to-be-factual situation. Predictions can be made of the success in operating bench lathes of the applicants we test, and these predictions can be checked in terms of the subsequent success of the employees on the job.

We do not wish to give the impression that this task is an easy one because there is an actual objective situation in which many of the psychological determinants can be found. Actually, this situation comprises a complex global type of behavior which is difficult to analyze and describe but which we must understand to a significant degree before we can proceed with the construction of the tests. Once the determinants are known and the tests constructed, however, the remaining procedures are straightforward and require no departure from well-established empirical methods.

The Process of Generalizing for Theoretical Purposes. *The Problem.* This type of generalizing is the one used by the scientist interested in theoretical problems. He is primarily concerned with the advancement of knowledge in terms of explanatory concepts. There is usually no current practical situation conforming to the characteristics of the to-be-generalized-to situation. Inasmuch as his purpose is to generalize beyond the experimental situation from which he obtained his facts, he sets up hypothetical conditions that form the to-be-generalized-to situation. Of course, this situation may at some later time be reduced to empirical form for the purpose of testing the generalization.

The to-be-generalized-to situation is created wholly or in major part for the specific purpose of testing the generalizability of the experimental findings. The factors operating in the hypothesized situation must then be representative of those responsible for the experimental findings. In addition, however, the new situation must differ from the experimental situation in the ways and amounts stated in the generalization. Significance for theory is realized only when the determinants of the hypothetical situation are varied from those of the experimental situation. The characteristics in which the two situations differ are deliberately planned differences set up to advance theory. They are either explicitly expressed or clearly implied in the statement of the generalization. The generalization is then formed on the assumption that the findings will hold true for a new situation that is not an exact duplication of the experiment in which they were obtained. The to-be-generalized-to situation is created to show how the propositions evolved in the experiment can be applied under a stipulated set of changed conditions.

The differences between the two situations will be the source of any errors in the generalization. If we are not shrewd enough to keep in the to-be-generalized-to situation the significant determinants of the meanings, our generalization will not be valid.

Equally important is the fact that in these same differences lies any contribution that the experiment is going to make. It is in terms of the extent by which the to-be-generalized-to situation differs from the experimental situation that we advance theoretical knowledge. If we are successful in discovering determinants that are significant in some respects and that can be adapted to conditions differing from those of our experiment, then we shall be able to phrase a valid generalization. The nature and extent of the differences will be determined by the nature of the hypothesis or theory that we are advancing.

An Example. This type of generalizing is illustrated by generalizations in which the findings from one research area of behavior are extended to explain behavior in another area. An example is the adaptation of conditioned-response learning theory to the phenomenon of serial learning of nonsense syllables.

One generalization made from conditioning experiments using animal subjects is to the effect that if an indifferent or neutral stimulus is presented together with an adequate stimulus to which the animal is making an appropriate response, the indifferent stimulus will become effective in eliciting much the same kind of response. Thus, in the conditioning experiments using the hunger drive, the bell stimulus becomes an adequate stimulus for arousing the salivation response which normally is associated with the meat stimulus.

Let us apply this idea to the serial learning of a list of nonsense syllables.[1] Suppose the human subject is presented with a list of syllables to learn. On the first trial he is shown the list, one syllable at a time, and is asked to pronounce each syllable. On subsequent trials he is shown the first syllable and asked to recall the second. Whether he recalls it or not, the second syllable is shown and he is asked to recall the third. This procedure is continued until the subject can anticipate every syllable, that is, he can pronounce it before it is actually shown.

The question now arises: What stimulus is operating to evoke the recall of a syllable by the subject before the syllable is actually presented to him? One explanation is based on the conditioned-response theory of learning. The first response of vocalizing a syllable after it is shown (trial 1) can be explained as dependent upon old well-established language habits. Vocalizing the syllable before it is presented (trials following trial 1) is dependent upon the auditory and kinesthetic sensory experiences that arise from the preceding vocalized response. This is to say that the vocalizing response itself elicits auditory sensory stimuli (the heard syllable) and kinesthetic sensory stimuli (the muscular feel of the throat mechanisms in pronouncing the syllable). These sensory experiences occurring at the same time as the actual visual experience of the next syllable will eventually function as stimuli to elicit the next vocalized response.

Clarification of this extension of the conditioned-response theory can be obtained by reference to Fig. 9. The first visually presented syllable, S_1, arouses the first vocalized response, VR_1. This VR_1 response gives rise to auditory and kinesthetic sensations indicated as aks_1. These aks_1 ex-

---

[1] This example is adapted from W. M. Lepley, Serial Reactions Considered as Conditioned Reactions, *Psychological Monographs*, vol. 46, no. 205, 1934.

periences continue active up to and probably beyond the time that the second visual stimulus S_2 is presented. Thus aks_1 and S_1 are paired together preceding the arousal of the second vocalized response, VR_2. This contiguity of the two stimuli is similar to the pairing of the conditioned and unconditioned stimuli in the animal experiments. After several pair-

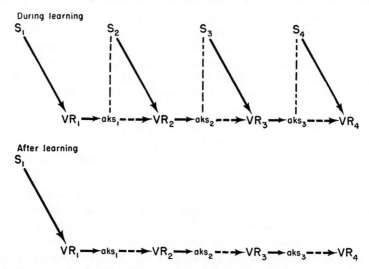

Fig. 9. Diagram of substitution of secondary auditory-kinesthetic stimuli for original visual stimuli, according to conditioned-response learning theory, as applied to serial learning of nonsense syllables.

ings, aks_1 by itself is sufficient to elicit VR_2. Conditioned-response theory thus supplies an explanation of why a given response is made before its own adequate stimulus is presented. Further extensions of the theory can be made to explain the linkage between S_1 and more delayed responses, such as VR_3, VR_4, and VR_5, which are often subsumed under the term of remote excitatory tendencies.

Many problems in human learning have been attacked in terms of leads arising out of conditioned-response experiments with animals. In fact many of the most productive theorems for research on human learning have stemmed from experiments on conditioned-response learning.

SOME SOURCES OF ERROR IN GENERALIZATION

The remainder of the chapter will be devoted to a discussion of sources of error in generalization. It is believed that much can be learned about the process of generalizing by studying the ways in which inaccurate generalizations arise. For purposes of discussion, errors in the scientific method that may result in inaccurate generalization can be classified in three broad categories roughly corresponding to three stages in the conduct of a scientific investigation. These stages are the deductive elaboration of the hypothesis that is to be studied, the execution of the experimental procedures of the empirical testing situation, and the extension of the meanings to similar behavior situations.

Examples of different types of errors from these three stages will be described in the following sections. A given inaccuracy in generalizing may be attributable to more than one type of error. The particular errors that are discussed are not then to be considered completely independent of one another.

ERRORS ARISING IN THE LOGIC OF DEVELOPING THE HYPOTHESIS

We shall be concerned here with errors of logic that occur during the developmental phases of our problem. We cannot expect to make valid generalizations if in devising and elaborating our hypothesis we fail to introduce the significant determinants of our problem and to establish these determinants in such logical relationships as will reveal meanings essential to a solution.

Errors Due to Selecting Unimportant Implications. *The Nature of the Error.* For a hypothesis to be confirmed, we must discover evidence for the existence of the elements, relationships, or conditions that we postulate in the underlying implications. In a previous chapter it was pointed out that hypotheses are based on certain assumptions or presuppositions. These assumptions form the starting point for the implications we derive from the hypothesis.

We can expect that most hypotheses will have several implications and that these implications will vary in respect to the significance of the relationships that they bear to the hypothesis. Some implications will involve only a few aspects of a hypothesis, while others will embrace many aspects. We may just happen to choose an implication that readily develops into a testable theorem but that adds evidence of no great significance for the hypothesis. We are not then justified in generalizing that the hypothesis has been confirmed.

It is not to be expected that we shall always be aware of the relative importance of the different implications issuing from a hypothesis. Scientists of repute have committed errors of generalization by not discovering and developing the more significant implications of their hypotheses. It is to be emphasized, however, that the error is minimized when we perform thorough theoretical and factual analyses of our problem.

An Example. To illustrate this type of error, let us refer to a rather general hypothesis that underlies much of our thinking about human behavior, the hypothesis: Personality is a function of bodily mechanisms. Let us accept this phrasing of the hypothesis as a first statement, but without the intention of defining it more precisely. We can derive many implications from this hypothesis. For example, personality is a function of:

The complexity of organization of the bodily mechanisms
The speed of reaction of the bodily mechanisms
The physiological integrity of the bodily mechanisms
The size of the bodily mechanisms
The shape of the bodily mechanisms
The chemistry of the bodily mechanisms
The electropotential characteristics of the bodily mechanisms

A common generalization underlies all of these implications, namely, that behavior is the functioning of organic tissue, and thus personality behavior is a function of various characteristics of organic mechanisms.

A close examination of the implications should make it clear that although they are all related to personality responses, they are not of equal importance in the study of personality. It is not possible here to present reasons for and against the use of each implication. In the light of present knowledge, however, certain implications seem more productive for personality theory than do others. For example, the physiological integrity of the bodily mechanisms has proved more fruitful than the electropotential characteristics of the bodily mechanisms.

Errors Due to Using an Inadequate Theorem. *The Nature of the Error.* By the phrase "inadequate theorem" is meant that the theorem selected for testing is not closely related logically to the implication from which it presumably was developed. We are here assuming that we have selected a significant implication to develop but that the theorem we decide to test is not significantly related to this implication. The theorem does not adequately represent the conditions of the implication. Testing such a theorem may result in facts that are positively related to the hypothesis, but the relationship is not sufficiently close to substantiate the hypothesis. Any generalization to the effect that the hypothesis is confirmed would then be fallacious.

An Example. Let us develop further the implication that personality is a function of the physiological integrity of the bodily mechanisms. The phrase "physiological integrity" refers to the physiological health of the tissues. From this implication we infer that when bodily tissues become pathological, changes in personality responses will occur. To assume an extreme position, suppose we decide to test the theorem: Traits of excitability are a function of decayed teeth. Obviously, this theorem would not represent the conditions of the implication as adequately as would a theorem involving one of the glands, such as the adrenals, thyroid, or pituitary. Decayed teeth, although affecting personality responses, are not as basically related to these responses as are pathological conditions in the endocrine glands.

Errors Due to Using a Testing Situation That Does Not Logically Represent the Theorem. *The Nature of the Error.* Errors of generalization occur when the experimental or other situation that we devise does not logically develop from the theorem. We are presuming that a significant implication has been found and that a theorem has been developed that adequately represents the basic elements of the implication. We must then plan such conditions for the empirical situation as will logically allow the elements and relationships of the theorem to function in this situation in the manner required by the theorem. If they do not so function we cannot accept the test as a comprehensive check of the theorem. The test may contribute some useful information, but the objective of confirming the hypothesis is not achieved. We are then not justified in generalizing that a hypothesis is confirmed when the conditions demanded by the theorem are not adequately reproduced in the test.

An Example. Suppose we decide to devise an empirical testing situation for the theorem: Traits of excitability are functionally related to excessive secretion of the thyroid gland. "Traits of excitability" are now a more restricted and definitive expression of what in the hypothesis we called "personality." "Excessive secretion of the thyroid gland" is a more restricted and definitive expression of what in the hypothesis we called "bodily mechanisms." We can err by not introducing into the testing situation representative measures of "traits of excitability" or representative measures of "excessive secretion of the thyroid glands." For example, if we used a pencil-and-paper test of introversion-extroversion we would not adequately measure traits of excitability. The argument could be advanced that we would still be measuring personality traits, but this is beside the point. We have selected a definite theorem to test, which involves traits of excitability, and a measure of introversion-extroversion does not adequately represent this personality phase of the theorem.

ERRORS ASSOCIATED WITH THE REPRESENTATIVE FUNCTIONING OF THE VARIABLES

Assuming that we have accurately and comprehensively elaborated our hypothesis and have made no mistakes in logic in devising an empirical testing situation, we may still make errors in the actual execution of the test. These errors are not errors of logic. They are concerned with our failure to achieve in the empirical situation the expression of the variables that the logical development of our hypothesis has shown to be necessary.

Errors Resulting from Distortion Introduced by Extraneous Variables. *The Nature of the Error.* In order to investigate a hypothesis, we must devise conditions that will force the experimental variable to function according to a prearranged plan which conforms to the demands of the theorem. The theorem contains the elements and relationships by which the hypothesis is translated from conceptual events to empirical events. Any distortion in the experimental variable means a failure to represent correctly these elements and relationships.

The functioning of the experimental variables is frequently distorted by the presence of unwanted interfering variables interacting with it. These interfering variables may either facilitate or inhibit the expressions of the experimental variables, and the effect, whether facilitory or inhibitory, may vary in terms of amount. A failure to prevent or remove the effects of these interacting variables results in their contributing to the empirical findings as determinant factors. It is then impossible to separate the contribution of these factors from the contribution of the experimental factors under study.

The presence of interfering variables may prevent us from accurately detecting and measuring the effects of the experimental variables. Suppose that an experiment containing unwanted interacting variables is conducted, with the results showing no positive evidence in favor of the hypothesis. These results can be explained by (1) supposing that the experimental variable had no effect, (2) supposing that the experimental variable was inhibited from functioning by stronger opposing variables, or (3) supposing that the experimental variable had an effect opposite to that intended but that this effect was canceled out by the positive effect of the other variables. It should be apparent that if interacting variables prevent the experimental variable from functioning in the manner prescribed by the theorem, then any generalizations based on the distorted expressions will be invalid.

An Example. In an unpublished study by the authors on the effect of vitamin B deficiency on maze behavior of rats, interacting motivation and motor-incoordination factors interfered with the functioning of the experimental variable. The theorem under test was that deficiency in a certain vitamin B complex, by having a deleterious effect upon mental ability, would increase the time and errors in learning a maze. Inasmuch as the diet variable was directly related to food consumption, the use of food as an incentive for learning the ordinary alley maze was considered inappropriate. Instead, a water maze was used. The rat was lowered into the water and was required to swim through the maze in order to get out of the water. From the beginning of the maze running, the experimenter observed a great reluctance on the part of the diet-deficient rats to enter the water and considerable trouble by many of these rats to swim the course of the maze. The control rats manifested these characteristics to only a minor degree. These observations led to the conclusion that the behavior of the deficient rats in the water maze was reflecting motivational factors and motor strength and coordination factors in addition to possible mental-deterioration factors. It was impossible to isolate and control the motivational and motor-coordination factors, so the experiment was discontinued.

Errors Due to Generalizing from Insufficient Data. *The Nature of the Error.* Let us assume that the development of the theorem is logically sound and that an adequate test has been devised. Errors due to insufficient data may arise if we do not collect enough facts to give our theorem a fair empirical testing. We prematurely stop the test before collecting enough facts to make possible a statistically sound evaluation of the theorem. Any generalization will then be formulated prematurely. It may be correct or it may be incorrect; there will not be enough data to determine which it is. When the data are insufficient, generalization should be held in abeyance until further facts can be collected.

An Example. Generalizations based on insufficient data are sometimes found in investigations in which traits of personality are associated with anatomical features of the body. Types of criminality have been linked with head shape, personality traits with body proportions, psychological temperament with body chemistry, etc., with little statistically sound supporting evidence.

Suppose we study a sample of 36 criminals and discover a positive association between head shape and type of crime committed, as indicated in the left half of Table 5. It is seen that extortioners tend to have

Table 5. Hypothetical Distribution of Head Shapes in Six Hypothesized Subsamples of Persons

Head shape	Type of crime			Randomly selected subsamples		
	Extortion	Theft	Embezzlement	I	II	III
Round........	6	3	3	5	2	4
Square........	3	6	4	2	7	3
Egg-shaped....	1	3	7	3	3	7

round heads, thieves square heads, and embezzlers egg-shaped heads. With such a few cases, however, we cannot be assured that these distributions are not artifacts of our sampling method. Now suppose we have a noncriminal sample of the same racial stocks, ages, sex, etc., as the criminal sample. We randomly draw three subsamples of the same number of cases as we have in the criminal subsamples and obtain the results given in the right half of Table 5. Again we see a tendency for each head shape to be concentrated in a given subsample. If the subsamples really were randomly selected, results like these would offer sound evidence for rejecting any functional relationship between head shape and type of crime. Actually, we would want to study hundreds of criminals and hundreds of noncriminals before we would have a statistically sound basis for either accepting or rejecting any hypothesis purporting to link criminal behavior with head shape.

Errors Due to Ignoring Large Chance or Sampling Variations. *The Nature of the Error.* Sampling or chance variations may be sufficiently large to account completely for the results of any experiment. When this is true, the investigator is not justified in attributing his findings to the variables that he purposely manipulated. Of course, he still may do so because for one reason or another he does not recognize the importance of these errors. He may be ignorant of the procedures now available for statistically evaluating the errors, or he may have a personal bias against utilizing statistical methods of evaluation. Regardless of the reason, his ignoring of chance or sampling errors and his failure to evaluate them as possible explanations of his results cannot be excused. The scientist makes a very worthwhile contribution if he shows that chance and sampling factors play an insignificant role in the determination of the meanings about which he wishes to generalize. He runs the risk of making invalid generalizations if he does not evaluate these factors.

An Example. In an unpublished investigation of the effects of vitamin B deficiency on the activity level of rats, the authors obtained the results shown in Fig. 10. It is apparent that the mean activity scores by days were larger for the deficient group and that as the experiment progressed the difference between the deficient and nondeficient groups became increasingly greater. The day-to-day variability in the error scores, however, was very large, especially for the deficient group. So great was the daily variation in performance of the individual rats that the differences between mean scores of the two groups were not statistically significant. Here is an instance in which, without a statistical test of the reliability of the results, the generalization might readily be made that vitamin B deficiency produces a significant increase in the general activity level of the rat.

Errors Due to Failure to Exploit the Data. *The Nature of the Error.* This can be described as an error of undergeneralization. The investigator is too conservative in extracting meanings from the data. He errs in not drawing a positive generalization when such a generalization is supported by the findings. He is unwilling to credit the results to his hypothesis unless he can do so at a very high level of confidence. But in doing this he may declare a hypothesis unconfirmed when actually it is

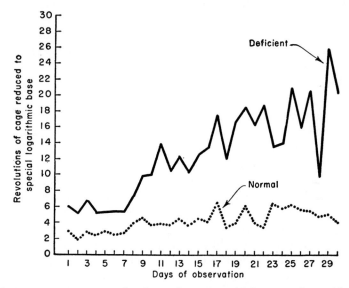

Fig. 10. Mean activity scores by days of vitamin-B-deficient and normal rats as measured in activity cages.

confirmed. Sometimes this overconservatism is interpreted to mean that an error is being made on the "safe side." Certainly, declaring that a hypothesis is not substantiated when actually the data confirm it is not erring on the safe side.

To clarify the foregoing arguments it will prove profitable to review briefly the probabilistic nature of generalization. In earlier sections it was explained that with the accumulation of favorable evidence hypotheses change into laws; that laws are not to be accepted as certainties; and that with the accumulation of sufficient negative evidence laws may revert to the status of hypotheses. If we accept these interpretations, then the point at which a given hypothesis is considered confirmed rests upon the subjective judgment of the scientist.

Scientists have arbitrarily decided to utilize two confidence levels in describing their findings, the 1 per cent level and the 5 per cent level. These levels refer to the probability of their results arising from the operation of chance or unsystematic factors. Frequently these levels of confidence are included in the statement of a generalization. This is to say that an experimenter will often state that "at the 5 per cent level of confidence we are assured that under M conditions X consequences will not occur from the operation of unsystematic factors."

The question may be asked: What level of confidence should be reached before a generalization is made? The answer depends upon the purpose or objective of the scientist. In a preliminary study, a 10 per cent level of confidence often proves sufficient. If the generalization involves a matter of life and death, then a very conservative attitude is justified, such as accepting a generalization only if it is accounted for by chance at the .1 per cent level. For most scientific problems, the 5 per cent level is acceptable.

An Example. There are conservative scientific psychologists who hesitate to generalize unless they can do so at the 1 per cent level of confidence. Suppose that in a study of racial differences in emotional traits we use many measures from which we compute a large number of differences, together with their statistical significance. Suppose further that only 4 differences are significant at the 5 per cent level or better, 20 significant between the 10 per cent level and the 5 per cent level, and only 4 differences significant below the 10 per cent level. Here is an instance in which holding to the 1 per cent level of confidence would result in generalizing that there is very little evidence that real differences in emotional traits exist between the races. In fact, the evidence as presented strongly favors positive but small differences. The results would support a generalization to the effect that there were small differences in emotional traits between the racial groups which could not be accounted for by the operation of chance factors.

ERRORS ASSOCIATED WITH THE CORRESPONDENCE BETWEEN THE EXPERIMENTAL AND THE TO-BE-GENERALIZED-TO SITUATIONS

As indicated earlier in the present chapter, for any generalization to be valid there must be a certain amount of correspondence in the determinant factors between the known and postulated situations. It is not an easy task to discover which determinants between the two situations can be varied and which must remain the same for a given generalization to be valid. Errors in generalizing occur because we make mistakes of judgment concerning the nature and significance of the similarities between the experimental and the to-be-generalized-to situations.

Errors Due to the Use of Nondeterminant Similarities. *The Nature of the Error.* The results of any study are to be attributed to certain factors functioning as determinants. In addition to these factors there will be others which, although functionally present, do not bear directly on the determination of the results. It is possible for an investigator to confuse these two types of factors. It is possible for him to attribute the results to the nondeterminant factors, which he, of course, believes are functioning as determinants. When this mistake has been made, errors in generalization are likely to occur. Obviously, if the to-be-generalized-to situation contains these factors but does not contain the factors that actually functioned as determiners in the original experiment, the generalization cannot be valid.

An Example. To illustrate this error, let us refer to certain generalizations of those who call themselves characterologists. Among the implications stemming from the relationship between personality and bodily mechanisms, which were listed earlier, body chemistry was mentioned as a possible determinant of personality responses. In one system of characterology the relation between body chemistry and personality is reduced to what is called the law of color. This law refers to the difference in skin pigmentation of persons of the same race, such as the difference between blonds and brunets. The law holds that the more pigment possessed by a given person, the more markedly will he possess the characteristics of the brunet in his physical and mental constitutions. The fundamental assumption is made that there are distinct personality differences between blonds and brunets. However, the results of several experimental studies show this assumption to be false.

The error with which we are here concerned is that of treating the pigment factor as a determinant of personality. Granting the false assumption that there are significant differences in personality traits between these two groups, we are still faced with the problem of finding the possible determinants of such differences. The fact that our stereotyped thinking associates certain traits with blond-complexioned persons and certain other traits with brunet-complexioned persons is not in itself evidence that pigment plays a determinant role. This kind of fallacious reasoning underlies the logic of all of the systems of characterology in which anatomical signs are first associated with personality responses and then thereafter are considered the determinants of these responses.

Errors Due to Noncorrespondence in the Characteristics of Populations. *The Nature of the Error.* Error may result when a generalization based on a hypothetical population is extended to a particular real population. It was pointed out earlier that when a scientific psychologist is interested in learning about the nature of some psychological process as a phenomenon distinct from the individuals manifesting it, he may not concern himself with the nature or characteristics of the sample of subjects he uses. This procedure is justified and is scientifically sound. The subjects are considered a sample of some hypothetical population. If the findings from studying these subjects are favorable, then the hypothesis is considered substantiated. Any generalization made is concerned with the nature of the psychological process investigated rather than with the nature of the individuals used as subjects. It is to be understood, of course, that the characteristics of the particular individuals studied may have contributed in some way to the findings obtained. Error becomes possible when the generalization is applied to some particular group of persons differing from the experimental subjects.

Sometimes it is important to apply a generalization evolved in this way to a particular group of individuals. It may happen that the psychological process investigated is an important characteristic of certain classes of persons and that the findings concerning the psychological process would be very significant to these individuals if they were applicable. Here the generalization must be broadened to include the nature of the subjects as well as the nature of the psychological process investigated. But the generalization will be valid only if applied to samples or populations possessing the determinant characteristics that were found important for the process in the subjects studied.

Certainly, findings about every psychological process probably should be applied eventually to particular groups of individuals. It is important to generalize about real populations, such as college sophomores, factory bench workers, clerk typists, juvenile delinquents, hospital patients with mental defects, and many others. But such generalizations are not justified unless correspondence in determinants is found between the group studied and the to-be-generalized-to group.

An Example. Suppose we are interested in learning about the most effective length of a student's study period. We are teachers in a boys' military academy, and use as subjects the 10- to 12-year-old students in our classes. Let us presume that we find that the most effective time period is between 40 and 50 minutes, longer and shorter times being less effectively used. Obviously, this is an important finding and can be generalized beyond the confines of our own experimental classes.

We must remember that any generalization involving a group of persons is restricted by the sampling and selective methods that were utilized in the experimental conditions. In earlier discussions we learned that sampling and selective procedures are used to effect control over variables that cannot be directly physically manipulated. Whether special methods of selection are purposely used by us or not, the characteristics of our subjects, regardless of how we select them, will contribute to the experimental results. To the extent that this is true, our methods of selection establish the nature of the population to which we can refer our generalizations. In our study, we would not be justified in generalizing our findings to girl students, high school students, college students, students in nonmilitary schools, or other groups until we were assured that the new population probably had the characteristics that were essential to the results obtained in our experiment.

Errors Due to Noncorrespondence between Groups and Individuals. *The Nature of the Error.* Generalizations about psychological processes based on a study of a group are not applicable in every detail to new individuals. When psychological processes are being studied, it is almost impossible to form a group in which every individual possesses every determinant underlying the psychological process under investigation. Describing a psychological process of a group, of course, is done by studying the individuals comprising the group, but the generalizations formulated encompass those aspects that are found to characterize the group as a unit. For a generalization based on a group to hold for an individual it is necessary that the individual possess a minimum number of the determinant characteristics discovered in the group. Just what these characteristics must be will depend upon the nature of the generalization that is made.

Generalizations about specific behaviors to be expected in any new individual are subject to gross errors. Generalizations that are restricted to expectations of probable tendencies in the new individual have a higher likelihood of being valid.

An Example. This error is often made when we make predictions about students' performances in college from a knowledge of their intelligence-test scores. It has been amply demonstrated in studies of groups that there is a high correlation between intelligence-test scores and college success. The average success in college has been computed for various levels of intelligence, and it has always been found that the level of success increases with increase in the level of intelligence. This is merely a problem in statistical computation. Knowing a given student's intelligence level, however, does not enable us to make a precise prediction about his future success in college. This is to say that we cannot ascribe to him any precise level of college achievement. We must state our generalization in terms of probability. We can say that he has a high chance of making a certain achievement level or a low chance of making some other achievement level, but we cannot stipulate the precise level he will achieve. This is because we are uncertain of the extent to which the determinants of college success operating in the group originally studied will be operating in the given individual. Our generalizations must then be probabilistic in nature.

Errors Due to Generalizing about Elements or Relationships Not Empirically Tested. *The Nature of the Error.* This is a form of overgeneralization. Having verified a theorem and thus obtained evidence substantiating his hypothesis, the investigator may be inclined to broaden his generalization to include elements and relationships that were not included in the test. This usually leads to error.

No experiment ever confirms all of the elements and relationships of a hypothesis. The breadth of any hypothesis is reduced as we logically develop its implications and theorems and devise situations that can supply empirical knowledge. Seldom can a theorem be formulated that will encompass all of the implications of a hypothesis, because restriction of the hypothesis is necessary to bring it within the limits of a testable theorem. There are, then, elements and relationships of the hypothesis that are removed from consideration in this process of evolving an empirical test. Of course, if these omitted elements and relationships are closely related to those that are tested, a generalization can be made about them, provided that it is presented as a tentative suggestion with the full expectation of checking it empirically with additional tests. If such a generalization involves a practical application to individual behavior, it is seldom justified, especially if the new elements and relationships are very different from those originally investigated. Additional factual tests should be made to justify the use of the generalization under the more widely divergent conditions.

An Example. Generalizations extended from the psychological laboratory to the field of practice are subject to this type of error. The error was made in some of the early laboratory studies on the power of advertisements to attract potential buyers. The psychologist worked with college students in his laboratory, utilizing made-up booklets of advertisements and testing the attentive and memory value of advertisements which were varied in different dimensional characteristics. Advertisements lend themselves to objective and quantitative manipulation. They can be varied in size, color, amount of copy, illustrative material, amount of filled space, kind of type, nature of message, etc. The psychologist then studied the effect of variations in these different characteristics on the attentive and memory value of advertisements. Some investigators became overly enthusiastic about their findings and generalized beyond their data to the practical sales situation. Some of them—albeit not the most reputable investigators—even advised business and advertising firms on how to construct advertisements to achieve the greatest attraction power and thus the greatest return in sales.

Any specific generalization about the make-up of advertisements extended from the experimental laboratory to the field situation would be subject to error. Clearly, there would be many determinants functioning in the practical situation that would not be operating in the experimental study and that therefore would not be subjected to examination in the laboratory. Several of these factors are pointed up in the following contrasts: the casual examination of advertisements by the layman as contrasted with the specific mental set of the experimental student in attending to the advertisements; the appearance of advertisements among other reading material in the layman's experience as contrasted with the presentation to the students of made-up booklets composed solely of advertising matter; the many variable ways in which the layman is exposed to advertising as contrasted with the artificial and restricted exposure given the students; the buying interests of the lay public as contrasted with the students' interest in following the instructions of the experimenter; the many ways in which the potential buying public differs in personal characteristics from a group of college students engaging in an experiment in psychology. It should be apparent that many of the factors that operate to determine a lay buyer's reaction to an advertisement cannot be duplicated in the experimental laboratory. Any generalization from a laboratory experiment to a practical advertising situation would then be extended to elements and relationships that actually could not have been empirically tested in the experimental study.

SELECTED READINGS

Black, M.: "Critical Thinking," 2d ed., chaps. 15 and 16, Prentice-Hall, Inc., 1952. These two chapters deal with inductive procedures and present several methods by which generalizations are established. Statistical generalizations evolved from functional relationships are included in the discussion. Reasons are given for the superiority of scientific generalizations.

Cohen, M. R., and E. Nagel: "An Introduction to Logic and the Scientific Method," chap. 14, Harcourt, Brace and Company, Inc., 1934. The subject considered is *Probability and Induction.* The following topics are discussed: the nature of inductive reasoning, the role of fair samples in induction, the mechanism of sampling, and reasoning from analogy.

Hyman, H. H., and P. B. Sheatsley: The Authoritarian Personality—A Methodological Critique, in R. Christie and M. Jahoda (eds.), "Studies in the Scope and Method of the Authoritarian Personality," pp. 50–122, Free Press, 1954. In criticizing the methods used in a research study entitled "The Authoritarian Personality," the authors discuss many factors that restrict the generalizations that are justified by the data collected. They point up the restrictions placed on the generalizations about attitudinal relationships by the method of sampling used, by the effect of sampling biases, by biases arising from the study of extreme groups, by failure to use national norms for evaluative purposes, by failure to take account of the similarities of functions measured by presumably different instruments, by biases in the coding of the data, by formulating causal inferences solely on correlational relationships, and by other methodological deficiencies.

PART THREE

Some Individual Scientific Procedures

In Part Two the separate steps involved in conducting a scientific study were discussed. We learned that the scientist first develops a problem, framing it in the form of a hypothesis. Next he derives a theorem that represents the elements of the hypothesis and sets up an empirical situation in which the theorem can be tested. In the empirical test, he uses procedures that will provide facts that are pertinent to the theorem and that can be subjected to logical and statistical analyses. Lastly, he draws inferences in the form of conclusions or generalizations which project beyond the limited boundaries of his own study but which are directly supported by the facts he has collected. These are the major steps of the scientific method.

We are now ready to consider some of the more specialized procedures that the psychologist uses in his research studies. Some of these procedures can be subsumed under the term experimental because they are primarily concerned with the production, arrangement, ordering, and recording of the expressions of the variables being studied. Some of them can be classified as measurement procedures because they are primarily concerned with the quantifying of these expressions. A hard-and-fast line should not be drawn between these two categories. Experimental and measurement procedures are complementary in function, and in nearly every study they must be used together in order to accomplish the desired ends. A very large number of specialized experimental and measurement procedures have been devised. Only a few of the major ones can be considered.

In Chap. 12, some of the procedures devised to control factors in the physical stimulus situation are described. A very common problem in psychological experimentation concerns the relationships existing between the characteristics of the physical stimulus and the nature of the ensuing psychological experience. Many specialized procedures have been developed to control and manipulate physical stimulus factors in order that accurate comparisons between stimuli can be made. To this

263

end, much attention has had to be given to ways by which equality among stimuli can be achieved and maintained. Another recurring problem in psychological research is that of controlling interfering variables arising within the experimental procedures themselves. Not only does a subject react to the particular stimuli the experimenter presents, but he is also affected by the timing, ordering, spatial arranging, etc., of the stimuli. These factors must be kept constant unless they are part of the experimental variable under investigation.

Experimental procedures connected with factors in the responding subject are discussed in Chap. 13. The behavior of a subject can be interpreted as reflecting fundamental psychological predispositions. These predispositions are defined broadly as tendencies to respond in certain ways, and can be classified as interests, attitudes, abilities, and past experiences. Predispositions function not only as experimental variables to be investigated but also as unwanted interfering variables. Controlling them demands the use of many specialized procedures.

Because of the complexity of human behavior, a large number of procedures are needed for quantifying the different characteristics of response. In Chap. 14, the following major methods used for measuring psychological variables are described: frequency of occurrence, highly structured tests, inventories and questionnaires, unstructured stimulus situations, ratings, and interview procedures.

Coincident with the development of valid experimental and measurement procedures the psychologist has broadened his interests to include the investigation of behavior phenomena not found in highly controlled laboratory situations. Examples of several different kinds of field-type studies are presented in Chap. 15.

CHAPTER 12

Physical Variables in Psychological Experiments

The problems to be discussed in this and the next chapter are not restricted to those that might occur only in a psychological laboratory. A scientific experiment contains essentially the requirements we have discussed in preceding chapters, namely, a working theorem, a procedure for collecting data, logical and statistical analyses of the data, and generalizations evolved from these analyses. These requirements can be met in many situations outside of the so-called experimental laboratory. In the following discussions of experimental procedures no attempt is made to distinguish them in terms of their being used either in or out of the psychological laboratory.

In the present chapter, we shall discuss methodology as it is conditioned by factors associated with the physical stimulating situation. By manipulating physical factors in the experimental test the scientist can achieve control over many of the variables he wishes to study. In the following chapter, we shall consider methodology as it is conditioned by factors residing in the responding subject.

VARIABLES OF AN EXPERIMENT

Before discussing some of the special procedures used by the psychologist for experimenting with behavior, we should have in mind a generalized picture of the variables that are likely to be functioning in any experimental study.

The Logic of an Experiment. The primary purpose of an experiment is to collect factual evidence pertinent to a theorem. Obviously, this evidence is going to be found in some form of human or animal behavior. It is then necessary that there be an empirical situation in which behavior can be observed and, when possible, registered in some form of permanent record.

In order to be useful the behavior must supply evidence that is related to the theorem. In any situation in which humans or animals are responding, behavior determiners that are not a necessary part of the theorem-testing situation will always be found; that is, there will be behavior that is not required as evidence for the theorem. Some of this behavior will be pertinent to the theorem, however, and therefore it must be considered in the experimental planning. Some of the behavior will have no significance for the theorem. The investigator must distinguish among these several kinds of behavior in order that he can evolve the best possible case for his theorem.

These different kinds of behavior usually can be distinguished by tracing the responses to the several sources of stimuli that are operating. Some stimulus conditions are purposely established by the investigator to elicit expressions of the variables that are selected for testing the theorem. Usually there are other stimulus conditions present that are pertinent to the theorem but are not part of the variables selected for the empirical test. It is important that the effects of these latter conditions are not overlooked in the evaluation.

Objectives of the Experimental Design. If an empirical test is to furnish evidence pertinent to a theorem, it is necessary that the experimental conditions be designed to meet the logical relationships that are demanded. This is accomplished through several general objectives.

The experimental procedures must be designed to elicit and control the expression of the variables through which the conditions of the theorem are represented. We have called these the experimental variables.

The experimental procedures must be designed to control the expression of all other variables that are operative in the empirical situation. We have called these variables unwanted systematic variables and unsystematic variables.

The experimental procedures must be designed to register all behavior that may either directly or indirectly pertain to the testing of the theorem. This requires that procedures be used that make a faithful and permanent record of any changes reflected in behavior that result from variables operating during the empirical test.

The experimental procedures must be designed to separate the behavior changes pertinent to the theorem from all other behavior changes. It is necessary that the behavior changes that can be used as evidence be in a form that can be analyzed independently of other behavior changes.

The experimental procedures must be designed to enable the investigator to evaluate the amount of evidence and the degree of pertinence of the evidence in relation to the theorem being tested. This is best accomplished by quantitative description of the variables and quantitative analysis of the relationships existing among the variables.

The foregoing statements express the ideal experimental situation toward which we should strive. We may not always be able fully to attain each of the objectives outlined, but to the extent that we are successful, to that extent will we accumulate sound experimental evidence that can be applied to the hypothesis we are studying.

Major Classes of Determinants in a Psychological Experiment. The determinant variables of an experiment can be distinguished in terms of their pertinence or nonpertinence to the theorem, as described in the preceding sections. They can also be distinguished as being in the physical world or being within the behaving organism. Determinants in the organism can be further distinguished as being primarily physiological or being primarily psychological in nature. We here need merely to mention these distinctions, leaving further clarification for later sections.

Let us briefly consider the classes of variables that can be manipulated in order to elicit the behavior pertinent to a theorem. One way we can purposely elicit a desired change in behavior is by manipulating the physical-stimulus situation. By changing the quality, intensity, amount, location, etc., of objective stimuli, we can elicit change in the experience and overt behavior of the subject being stimulated. Similarly, by changing the stimulus situation internal to the organism we can elicit variations in the reacting subject. Much less precision is usually attained in controlling this type of stimulation than in controlling external physical stimuli. Behavior change pertinent to a theorem may also be produced by manipulation of the physical mechanisms of response. In general, all behavior can be referred to changes in sense organs, nervous system, endocrine glands, and muscles. By purposely changing the functioning condition of one or more of these mechanisms, it is possible to produce variations in behavior. Finally, there are many psychological determiners of behavior, such as attitudes, abilities, skills, past experiences, and the like, that can be manipulated as experimental variables in the testing of theorems. Changes in these variables cannot be accomplished with the directness possible in the manipulation of physical-stimulus objects, but controlled variation can be achieved with sufficient precision to make these psychological predispositions a very fertile area for studying behavior change.

As already stated, we must design procedures to control and record variables operating coincidentally with those purposely associated with the theorem being tested. Although these coincident variables are not expected to produce differential effects, nevertheless they may do so. Inasmuch as they are either real or potential sources of behavior change, they must be treated with the same thoroughness as is applied to the experimental variables. Control of these coincident variables must be achieved in the same ways as were described for the experimental variables; namely, by manipulation of the external stimulating situation, the internal stimulating situation, the physiological mechanisms of response, and the predisposing factors of a psychological nature. In dealing with these coincident variables, the general purpose is either to remove them entirely from the empirical testing situation or to keep their effects constant in all phases of the experiment.

THE CORRESPONDENCE BETWEEN PHYSICAL-STIMULUS FACTORS AND PSYCHOLOGICAL-RESPONSE FACTORS

We should not interpret the relationship between the objective stimulus and the subjective experience or response as necessarily being simple in nature. Rather, this relationship varies through a very wide range, from the simple relations found in some experiments on sensory phenomena to the very complex and relatively little understood relations encountered in experiments on the higher mental processes.

Simple Relationships in the Area of Sensory Phenomena. By restricting the change in the physical stimulus to one attribute and registering behavior change in terms only of the changes in the experience of the subject, a simple relation between the stimulus and the response is often encountered. Experiments in vision, audition, touch, and kinesthesis have yielded such simple relationships.

The relationship between the intensity of light and the experience of brightness is a case in point. When the intensity of the stimulus light is low, we experience a low degree of brightness. With increasing intensity we experience an increasing brightness, until a dazzling brightness is experienced which we refuse to endure for any great length of time.

Similarly, in the field of hearing, an increase in the amplitude of vibration in the stimulating object results in an increase in the experience of loudness until we reach a level that we refer to as deafening.

In the foregoing examples the experience is not restricted, respectively, to brightness and to loudness. In each instance, at the high intensities of the stimulus an experience of pain is aroused. This indicates that even when the change introduced in the physical stimulus is restricted to one attribute, the corresponding sensory experience may be altered radically by changes within this attribute.

Relationships in Simple Space-perception Situations. When the subject is called upon to make a judgment about certain spatial characteristics of environmental objects, there may be a very low degree of correspondence between the physical stimulus change and the subject's responses.

This can be illustrated with judgments of distance in visual space. It is a well-known physiological fact that the size of the retinal image of an object becomes smaller as the distance of the object from the eye is increased. A given object located far away produces a small retinal image; this object located close by produces a large retinal image. We would expect, then, that our experience of the distance of objects would follow closely this relationship and that in judging distance we would always see the object with the larger retinal image closer than the object with the smaller retinal image. Another factor enters, however, which is our knowledge of the "natural" sizes of objects—the average sizes of objects when they are perceived equally distant away. We know that a horse is larger than a man, so the retinal image of a horse is *on the average* larger than the retinal image of a man. When we estimate the relative distance away of a horse and a man, this knowledge somehow influences our judgment. A horse located only a small distance farther away than a man will produce a larger retinal image than the man. If we were using simply the relative sizes of the retinal images, the horse would be judged closer than the man, but in spite of the fact that the retinal image of the man is smaller than that of the horse, the man is judged to be closer.

In the area of visual illusions we find many examples of lack of correspondence between the subject's experience and the variation in the physical-stimulus object. For example, when we look down a railroad track we observe the rails coming together at a point near the horizon. Here is an instance in which the form of the object as experienced differs from that which we know to be true in the objective world. The experimental psychologist has subjected various kinds of illusory figures to analysis in an attempt to find out what aspects of the stimulus are responsible for arousing the illusory experience. The pattern of the lines comprising the figure has been found important in many cases, but the direction of the observer's attention, his eye movements, and his mental sets and attitudes also play determining roles in the response.

"New" Sensory Experiences without Counterparts in the Physical Stimulus. Sometimes when we continue changing the physical stimulus in what appears to be a simple progression, an experience may occur that does not have a counterpart in any physical characteristic of the stimulus. This can best be illustrated in the area of hearing, with what are called intertones and difference tones.

If two pure tone stimuli, equal in intensity, are varied in vibration rate, several changes in experience may occur. When the vibration rates of the two sounds differ by only a few cycles per second, only one tone is heard. It is the intertone, and it corresponds to a tone that in terms of physical characteristics would have a vibration rate intermediate between the vibration rates of the two sounds. As the difference between the vibration **rates** increases, the intertone gradually fades out and the two primary tones are heard.

When the two sound stimuli vary in frequency by more than about 40 or 50 cycles per second, a third tone is heard which has a pitch corresponding in vibration rate to the difference between the rates of the primary vibrations. This is the first difference tone. A difference tone is a subjective tone arising from mechanisms within the ear. It has no counterpart in the vibrations of the stimulating objects. If the subject is provided with a tone variator, which enables him to change the pitch of tones, he can produce a tone from a physical source that matches the difference tone in pitch. This tone has a vibration rate that equals the difference between the rates of the two stimuli from which the difference tone originates. Several difference tones can be made audible through the use of a resonator or amplifier.

Relationships in More Complex Behavior Situations. The relationship between the physical stimulus and the consequent behavior of the subject becomes increasingly complex as the stimulus becomes more symbolic in function and as the number of responses potentially associated with the stimulus becomes greater. As the symbolic function of the stimulus increases in importance, there is a greater variety of ways in which the experiences, attitudes, interests, abilities, etc., unique to an individual can contribute to the response that he makes to the stimulus. The effect a stimulus will have is then less accurately predicted from a knowledge of the physical dimensions through which it might be varied.

The free word-association test, although a rather simple form of symbolic stimulus, presents a situation that results in a wide variation in the responses elicited from different subjects. In this test the experimenter pronounces a word and the subject replies with the first word that comes to mind. The stimulus words are usually nouns, selected to represent a wide variety of situations, and presented to the subject under standardized conditions. Some of the variations in the responses to the stimulus word *white* will serve to illustrate the point. Over 130 words were obtained in examining a group of 1,000 subjects. Following are some of the response words with their frequencies of occurrence:

black	308	cloth	17	almost	1	lie	1
color	170	paper	17	body	1	lovely	1
snow	91	colorless	11	cherries	1	napkin	1
light	51	clean	10	day	1	pretty	1
dark	35	blue	9	good	1	rightness	1
dress	34	milk	9	hard	1	soul	1
pure	20	red	7	innocence	1	swan	1
purity	19	green	6	lady	1	trousers	1

STIMULUS COMPARISON

The Problem. One of the first problems investigated by experimental psychologists concerned the functional relationship existing between various aspects of the physical stimulus object and the resulting experiences reported by the subject. A wide range of stimulus characteristics in the several modalities of sense was studied.

The primary problem was to quantify the relationship existing between a given stimulus characteristic, e.g., intensity of vibration of a sound stimulus, and the resulting reported attribute of experience, e.g., loudness of the sound. This presented a problem of measurement in respect to both the stimulus and the response. Quantification of the stimulus characteristic was readily attained for most sensory stimuli, especially in vision and hearing, because of the ease with which the characteristics of objective stimuli could be represented in terms of physical measuring units. There was no obvious corresponding way to measure changes in experience, and so the establishment of some scale of measurement for the sensory experience occupied the attention of many of the early investigators.

From the work of these investigators were developed several important experimental procedures, particularly those that are known as the psychophysical methods. These were evolved in the study of problems in sensation and perception, such as the absolute threshold (the minimal amount of a stimulus that can be detected) and the difference threshold (the minimal stimulus difference that can be detected). Here there are two series of values, that of the physical stimuli and that of the subject's judgments. Additional procedures were evolved in areas in which there is no quantitative scale of physical stimuli, as in measuring the subject's preferences. It is obvious that judgments of the subject can be obtained in which he indicates that he prefers one stimulus rather than another, e.g., one color rather than another, or one painting rather than another. There is no way of arranging the stimuli on a common physical scale, but it is possible through the judgments of the subject to arrange the stimuli on a scale according to his preferences. These procedures are called psychological scaling methods.

Space does not permit describing all of the psychophysical and psychological scaling methods. Certain of the standard and frequently used procedures will be briefly described and illustrated.

The Method of Constant Stimulus Differences. As the name implies, this method is used to measure differences between stimuli. A limited number of stimuli are used, one standard and usually from four to seven comparison stimuli. Pairs of stimuli (the standard and one comparison stimulus) are presented to the subject, usually in a random order. The subject makes a judgment each time a pair is presented, reporting whether one stimulus is either greater than, equal to, or less than the other.

Suppose we are interested in measuring the difference threshold for linear extension, that is, the amount that must be added or subtracted from a given length in order for it to be seen as different in length. A simple device for presenting the problem to the subject is to use black lines on strips of white cardboard. A standard stimulus card is prepared with a line of a given length, say 12 inches. Other comparison cards are prepared, say seven, one of which is equal to the standard, while the others differ from it, three in which the length is longer and three in which the length is shorter than the standard. The lengths of these longer or shorter lines are not simply guessed but are worked out in preliminary experiments. They must differ from the standard without any given line being of such a length that the subject will judge it as always longer or always shorter than the standard line.

The experimental procedure requires the standard card to be paired with each of the comparison cards and these pairs presented to the subject a large number of times in a random order. The subject is asked to state whether the standard stimulus is longer than, equal to, or shorter than the comparison stimulus. The per cent of times the standard is judged longer (or shorter) than each variable is determined. The thresholds are then statistically computed. The upper threshold is that difference in length that yields a judgment of *longer than* 50 per cent of the time. Similarly, the lower threshold is that difference that yields a judgment *shorter than* 50 per cent of the time.

The Method of Minimal Changes. This is also known as the method of limits. In this method, a series of stimuli is presented to the subject, each stimulus differing by a slight amount from the preceding one, the series being continued until a critical change occurs in the subject's judgment. The experimenter manipulates the stimulus. Sometimes in the series the stimuli ascend (increase) in value, and sometimes they descend (decrease) in value.

This method is admirably suited for determining the absolute threshold. Suppose the absolute threshold for intensity of sound is desired. A tone of simple frequency is selected and the necessary electrical control circuits devised so the tone can be gradually increased and gradually decreased in intensity. In the ascending series the tone is set at an intensity well below the threshold and gradually increased over successive trials until the subject detects the tone. In the descending series the tone is set at an intensity well above the threshold and decreased through a series of trials until the subject says he can no longer hear the tone. A threshold value can be computed for each series. The best estimate of the general threshold value is computed by averaging the threshold values of all of the individual series.

The Method of Average Error. This method is also called the method of reproduction, because the subject manipulates the comparison stimulus. He is presented with a fixed standard and an adjustable comparison stimulus. His task is to manipulate the comparison stimulus until it appears equal to the standard. Sometimes the comparison is set at a value below that of the standard and the subject has to increase it to reach the

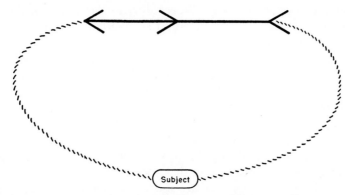

Fig. 11. Diagram of subject's control adjustment in Müller-Lyer Illusion Experiment.

point of equality. At other times the value of the comparison stimulus is greater than that of the standard and the adjustment is in the direction of decreasing the size of the comparison stimulus.

This method can be used to measure the influence of extraneous factors upon human judgment in those situations in which a judgment of subjective equality can be made. An example is a study of the Müller-Lyer illusion, as seen in Fig. 11. The apparatus is constructed so the line lengths between the points of the arrows can be adjusted both by the experimenter and by the subject. If only one-half the illusion is to be adjusted in size by the subject, the other half of the figure is stabilized. It will be noted in Fig. 11 that the adjusting rope is made in the form of a complete loop, enabling the subject to move the adjustable portion of the arrow either to the left or to the right. For a given trial the experimenter makes the length of the adjustable arrow different from the stationary one and directs the subject to manipulate the adjustable line until he judges the two parts of the illusion as equal. Some of the factors that may be investigated in regard to their relation to the judgment of equality are the length of the arrows, the length of the arrow tips, the angle of the arrow tips, the space error (adjustment made only on the right or only on the left), the movement error (adjustment in only a decreasing direction or in only an increasing direction), time error (variation in the time given for making the adjustment).

The Method of Equal-appearing Intervals. Instead of asking the subject to give a judgment of present or absent (absolute-threshold experiments), or of same or different (difference-threshold experiments), we may wish him to judge the distances between stimuli. We can ask him to bisect a tonal interval, e.g., find a stimulus tone the loudness of which falls midway between that of two others; or to bisect the distance between two gray values, e.g., select a gray that falls midway between two other grays. The method varies in detail according to the nature of the problem; e.g., the experimenter manipulates the stimuli in some problems, the subject in others.

An adaptation of this method has been successfully applied in the scaling of propositions that are designed to reflect differences in attitude toward some social problem. Statements of opinion are collected on some fundamental issue, e.g., attitude toward war. They vary in all degrees from being extremely favorable to extremely unfavorable to the issue. About a hundred statements representing points along the whole continuum are selected for scaling. These statements are given to a hundred or so judges to sort into categories that appear equally separated along a scale. Usually eleven categories are used. The middle neutral category and the extreme favorable and the extreme unfavorable categories serve as standards or anchor points. Several statistical procedures are applied for selecting statements that have high discriminating power and fall at approximately equal points along the continuum from one extreme to the other. Such statements can be formed into an attitude scale for measuring either individual or group attitudes towards the social issue involved. Below are several statements from an attitude scale on war devised according to the method of equal-appearing intervals.

Compulsory military training in all countries should be reduced but not eliminated.
The benefits of war outweigh its attendant evils.
He who refuses to fight is a true hero.
An organization of all nations is imperative to establish peace.
War in the modern world is as needless as it is suicidal.

The Method of Pair Comparisons. This is one of the psychological scaling methods. It can be used for scaling items or specimens, such as specimens in a handwriting scale, but it is more frequently used in the measurement of esthetic judgments, such as in making color preferences, or in the evaluation of feeling tone, such as in judging the pleasantness of tones. The individual stimuli to be judged are arranged in all possible pairs. Each pair is presented separately to the subject who designates the member of the pair that he prefers. The number of pairs is much larger than the number of individual stimuli (number $= n(n-1)/2$). The amount of work required of the subject becomes excessive when about 15 or more stimuli are to be judged, and special short-cut procedures have been devised for reducing it. Various statistical formulas are available for determining the scale separations of the stimuli forming the continuum.

One study in which the method of pair comparison was used was in determining preferences for national groups. The name of each of nine national groups was paired with that of every other group. The subjects were shown each of the 36 pairs of names and asked to state a preference. By the pooling of the responses of a large number of subjects, proportions were computed indicating how frequently each national group was preferred to each other group. Statistical procedures were used to place the several groups on a common continuum of preference as determined from the judgments of these particular subjects. In this study the national groups, as ranked from the most preferred to the least preferred, were scaled in the following order: English, Scotch, French, Swedish, Italian, Russian, Greek, Mexican, Turkish.

STIMULUS EQUALITY

The Problem. In psychological experimentation there are several major problems connected with the equivalence of stimuli. It is frequently necessary to produce stimulus conditions that will have the same stimulating effect upon the subject whenever they are presented to him. A closely related problem is the need to be able to repeat exactly for each subject the changes introduced in a stimulus during the various conditions of an experiment. A further problem is to maintain constancy in those aspects of the stimulus that are not part of the experimental variable under study.

The difficulties encountered in solving these and related problems of the stimulus situation vary greatly with differences in the nature of the stimulus. In the areas of behavior in which there is a fairly close correlation between the characteristics of the physical stimulus and the characteristics of the response elicited, the problems are usually readily solved. Most of the experiments on sensory thresholds support this statement. The loudness, pitch, and in some respects the timbre of sounds are closely associated with physical aspects of the vibrating body. Loudness is associated primarily with the amplitude of vibration, pitch is associated primarily with the frequency of the vibration, and timbre can be made to undergo systematic variation by manipulating the intensity of the several vibratory frequencies composing a complex wave. A similar correlation is found in vision, with color being associated with the wave length, brightness with the amplitude, and saturation with the relative amount of the several wave lengths composing the stimulus.

Problems of stimulus equivalence are more difficult to solve when the subject's response is less closely correlated with the physical characteristics of the stimulus and is more closely associated with the symbolic or representative functions of the stimulus. The meaning that any perceptual, memorial, imaginal, or reasoning stimulus item has for a given subject determines in large part the response he makes to it. The problem of equating stimuli in these areas is then more difficult because equivalence is no longer a simple function of the physical characteristics of the stimulus but is a complex function of the psychological characteristics of the responding subject. To make certain verbal materials equivalent, as, for example, the words to be used in a learning experiment, the investigator must study the meanings that these verbal materials have for the subjects on whom they are to be used. To make problems involving simple arithmetical processes equivalent as materials for an experiment in mental work, the investigator must know the arithmetic background of the subjects.

Another area in which stimulus equivalence is a function of the subject's characteristics has to do with the complexity of the physiological response required in executing some particular behavior. For example, coordination of response and speed of response are not the same function although they are closely related. A subject may be able to perform a certain psychomotor coordination with 100 per cent accuracy if he is allowed to pace himself; whereas if he is forced to work faster than his normal speed he may perform very badly. The effectiveness of his response is not a simple function of his ability to do the complex response, but is also a function of his ability to vary his rate of work.

The Equivalence of Sensory Stimuli. This topic needs little additional comment. It was noted in preceding discussions that equivalence in most instances can be achieved by making the physical characteristics of the stimulus equal. An explanation of how this is done, as in the field of hearing by means of electrical circuits or in vision by means of prisms or filters, would lead us too far afield. Suffice it to say that if we understand the physical nature of a stimulus, and if there is a close relationship between the physical characteristics and the psychological experiences, a high degree of precision in manipulating and controlling the stimulating effects can usually be attained.

Stimulus Equality as a Function of Familiarity. Familiarity with the stimulus characteristic being studied conditions the response that the subject will make. Whenever the stimulus characteristic of importance for testing a theorem does not touch upon experiences common to all of the subjects, or touches upon the experiences of various subjects in a differential manner, it will not then serve as an equivalent stimulus. If variation in response due to differences in familiarity with the stimulus is not the experimental variable under consideration, then any behavior change resulting from this factor must be considered as experimental error.

The factor of familiarity with stimulus characteristics is encountered in most experiments in which symbolic materials are utilized. The problem of task familiarity arose early in experiments in learning and memory in which verbal materials were used. Nonsense syllables were devised as a means of creating memory material equally familiar to most persons. In this instance, the equivalence of stimuli was achieved by making the material equally *unfamiliar* to most persons.

Equality as a Function of the Abstractness of the Stimulus. In many experiments on the higher mental processes, the purpose is to measure the subject's power to behave independently of the nature of the stimulus materials he is called upon to manipulate. The more abstract and general the stimulus material can be made, the more independent the test becomes of the particular nature of the stimulus. A positive relationship is usually found between the abstractness of the material and the amount of ability required to manipulate it; that is, the more abstract the stimulus characteristics, the greater the ability demanded. For example, in problem solving, the more abstract the characteristics and relationships involved in a problem, the more difficult is its solution.

In this as in other experimental situations, there are the two problems of keeping the stimulus at a constant value during a given condition and producing the stimulus at different amount levels in different experimental conditions. In regard to verbal or symbolic stimulus materials, this means devising individual stimulus units, such as items which are equally abstract in nature for all the subjects. Further, it means that items or units must be devised that differ in some magnitudinal way in the degree of abstraction involved. Several levels of abstraction may be required, with the items within any level being equally abstract in nature.

One method frequently used to achieve equally abstract stimuli is to reduce greatly the meaningfulness of the material by using nonlanguage or simple language stimuli. One example in which this was done is an experiment on concept formation in which Chinese characters were paired with simple English words. It will be remembered that a concept is a meaning that has been found common to many otherwise diverse situations and that has been abstracted from these experiences to the degree that it can be reacted to independently of them. In the experiment referred to there were 12 lists of pairs, each containing 12 Chinese-type characters. Each of the characters in a list was built around a certain radical—a particular pattern of lines—and this radical was repeated in one of the characters in each of the lists. Thus there were 12 radicals in a list and each radical appeared once in each of the 12 lists. An English syllable was assigned to each of the radicals. The task of the subject was to learn to associate the English syllable with its corresponding radical. The subject, of course, did not know about the radicals, and the problem was to determine if he would learn the common feature or radical that was associated with a given syllable.

Equivalence of Stimuli and the Problem of Difficulty of Task. Differences among stimuli often result in differences in difficulty. Difficulty as here used does not refer to difficulty experienced in sensing the material—although in some experiments in sensation this may be a problem—but difficulty experienced in the learning, or memorizing, or reasoning associated with the material. Several procedures are available for minimizing differences in difficulty among the tasks presented to the subject. These will not only effect an increased comparability among the stimuli in terms of the factor of familiarity but will accomplish the same result in regard to the factor of abstractness.

One procedure to obtain equality of difficulty is to use the judgments of experts. This should be considered as only preliminary, to precede a more exact empirical determination.

The most scientifically sound procedure is to base the determination of the equality of difficulty on results obtained from using the material under conditions similar to those to be included in the experimental study. For example, if nonsense syllables are to be used with college students in experiments on learning, then a large number of representative lists of syllables should be given to a large number of representative college students, thus providing the necessary empirical data for evaluating the difficulty and learnability of the syllables. With such findings on hand, we can prepare lists that are equal in difficulty and lists varying in difficulty by some empirically stated amount to form a graded series. If such a study is done with representative subjects under representative conditions, the results can be used by many investigators. Similarly, empirical procedures can be used in determining the difficulty of arithmetic problems, rational learning problems, and the like.

With some materials, a procedure of combining all the available stimulus elements in all possible ways can be used. For example, if simple addition problems of 1-place numbers are to comprise the unit, it is possible to construct problems involving all possible combinations of the numbers from 0 through 9. Usually, certain modifications are introduced in this procedure. Investigations of children's difficulties in arithmetic processes have revealed certain combinations of numbers to be more difficult than others. It is obvious that combinations using the number 0, 1, and 2 are less difficult than combinations using other numbers. It is possible in terms of such information for the experimenter to select certain combinations that are likely to be more nearly equal than other combinations. Of course, if there are significant doubts concerning the equivalence of different combinations, the appeal to an empirical evaluation of the combinations is indicated.

Stimulus Equality as a Function of Time of Exposure. It should be apparent that when the difficulty of the stimulus, the physiological adaptation to the stimulus, or the nature of the relationship between unwanted systematic variables and the experimental variable change rapidly in time, constancy of the time of exposure becomes an important objective. For example, in an experiment requiring the reading of a passage of prose and the answering of questions on the passage, the length of exposure to the selection must be constant for all subjects. The questions become easier to answer, the longer the time given for reading the passage.

In learning and memory experiments, several procedures for controlling the length of exposure of the material have been devised. One frequently used way of accomplishing this is to utilize material that can be easily divided into units, such as individual words or other symbols, arrange these units in a list, and then present each word by itself through a small aperture in front of the subject. The time of the exposure of each unit can be kept constant by an electrically controlled shutter device for covering the aperture periodically.

In experiments on olfactory and skin sensitivity, the exposure time of the stimulus is important because the rate of adaptation of the sense organs is rather rapid and the recovery following adaptation is often very slow. When a series of stimuli are to be presented, the adaptation and recovery phase following one stimulus may interfere with the appreciation of the next following stimulus. This is particularly true in experiments on olfactory sensitivity. It is necessary that the exposure time to the stimulus be carefully determined to minimize this interference.

In the glare recovery experiment described in an earlier chapter, the subject was exposed to a very brilliant light. The rate of recovery is in part a function of the length of the exposure to the bright light. It will be remembered that this function was not the one under investigation, and so variation in exposure had to be removed as a possible systematic determiner by maintaining a constant exposure time.

Stimulus Equality as a Function of Motor-skill Factors. Sometimes a subject is required to manipulate the stimulus or part of it. We must then make sure that the effect of the stimulus on the subject is not differentially influenced by this manipulatory response. It will be remembered that in the psychophysical method of average error the subject adjusts the comparison stimulus. If this motor adjustment is not part of the experimental variable, then it should be a response which in itself does not affect the appreciation of the stimulus; in other words, it should play a completely neutral role. Very often this is realized if the response is a very simple one in terms of motor adjustment.

Difficulty in performing a response required in a learning experiment can change the effect that the stimulus situation has on the subject. This sometimes occurs in experiments involving the learning of the multiple-T alley maze by rat subjects. In running this maze, the rat must not only learn to traverse the alleys but also to open one-way gates placed between the consecutive units to prevent retracing. One type of one-way gate is operated by having the rat push himself under the gate, the gate falling closed behind him. If the rat gets only his head under the gate and decides to withdraw, there is the likelihood of his head being momentarily caught under the gate as he backs away. This experience of getting caught under the gate sometimes is intense enough to condition the rat negatively to the gate. The gate stimulus now is an object to be avoided rather than one to be manipulated. Thus the stimulating effect of the maze is differentially affected because of the rat's unpleasant experience with the manipulation of the gates.

As described earlier, the subject is often given preliminary practice in the responses he must make in manipulating the stimulus. Thus in the maze experiment the rat is gradually trained to manipulate the gates. At first the gate is left open when the rat goes under it. Then with each successive trial the gate is lowered by a small amount until eventually the rat moves the gate up with his head without any difficulty. This training, of course, is not given in the maze itself but in a single unit located apart from the maze.

In a later section the procedure of giving preliminary training will be discussed in reference to controlling the subject's ability and experience.

MINIMIZING THE CONTRIBUTION OF INTRAPROCEDURAL FACTORS

In experimental studies of behavior, determinant factors sometimes arise within the experimental procedures themselves, with the consequence that the results cannot be attributed solely to changes in the experimental variable but must be attributed in part, and sometimes almost entirely, to these intraprocedural factors. In such investigations, steps should be taken to control these potentially systematic factors, and we find several well-formulated procedures used as standard practice for this purpose.

The Problem. In research studies in psychology, the experimental design requires that a constant routine be followed in applying the procedures that affect the control and manipulation of the variables. We shall be concerned here with physical-stimulus factors. We shall be interested in characteristics of the physical stimulus that are associated with the manipulation and control of the experimental variable and of potentially disturbing associated variables. In particular, we shall be concerned with experimental procedural factors associated with unwanted systematic variables and unsystematic variables. Obviously, these factors may function to disturb the systematic functioning of the experimental variable. Effecting control over potentially disturbing intraprocedural factors will improve the manipulation of the variables associated with the testing of the theorem under study.

Equal Exposure of the Subject to the Experimental Conditions. In an earlier section we discussed the need for keeping constant the exposure time of the experimental stimulus. The present section is related to this, but covers a somewhat broader area. It is concerned with the equality of exposure of the subjects to all phases of the experiment.

It is difficult to find a satisfactory definition of the phrase "equality of exposure." An acceptable working definition is equality of opportunity for the subject to perform in a representative manner. More specifically, it means equal opportunity for the subject to be influenced by any experimental variables that are functioning and equal protection from the influence of any unwanted interfering variables. Stated as a question, the problem is: Do the experimental procedures afford every subject an equal opportunity for manifesting his characteristic behavior under the conditions of the experiment? There are several standard procedures for solving this problem.

One very frequently used procedure is called the time-limit method. The logic underlying this procedure is that equal time to work means equal opportunity to achieve a representative performance. The evaluation of the performance is in terms of the quality and/or quantity of the product. Quality is measured in terms of accuracy; e.g., the kinds and numbers of errors. Quantity is measured in terms of the total number of units of work completed, or the number of acceptable units of work completed.

In connection with this procedure, a question may be raised concerning differences between individuals in their pace of work. Certainly, it is true that some individuals work faster than others. When the experimental design requires each subject to participate in every phase of the experiment, then presumably the factor of individual pace does not contribute a differential effect. But when the experimental design requires the utilization of two or more groups of individuals and assigns a given individual to only one phase of the study, then the investigator must equate the groups in terms of the factor of pace of work.

A second common procedure is called the amount-limit method. In this procedure the subject is presented with a certain amount of work to do, and his performance is evaluated in terms of the time required to complete the task and the nature and number of errors committed. In some experiments the task is repeated several times, and performance is evaluated in terms of the number of trials required to achieve a certain level of proficiency, e.g., two successive errorless trials in learning a maze.

In this procedure the subject usually is allowed time to complete the task, and so his pace of work is reflected in his performance. In fact, it contributes in a major way to the score that is assigned his performance. The logic underlying the use of this procedure in the measurement of some fundamental attribute of the individual is that his rate of work is an accurate index of the amount of the attribute that he possesses. When different groups of subjects are to be assigned to the different experimental conditions, it is necessary that the groups be equated in this rate of work factor before the experiment is begun.

The use of time scores to measure performance has not always been found to be a reliable procedure. Number of trials and time required for mastering a problem have proved to be unreliable indices in the case of problem boxes and problems in which insightful behavior is possible. Consider the measure of time per trial to reach a solution in the problem-box situation. In a hypothetical setup, one subject might work for an hour or so during the first two or three trials before he hits upon the correct solution, then in later trials he may need only 5 seconds to solve the problem. Another subject might get the solution in 5 minutes or less during the first few trials and then in later trials use from 20 to 30 seconds per trial, but never less than 20 seconds. It would not be sound to compare the performance of these two subjects in terms of their trial times. The experimenter might note that the first subject spent much of the time of the first few trials in what looked like aimless behavior. He also might note that the second subject in the later trials did not appear as highly motivated as he appeared at the beginning of the learning. Here are two subjective judgments of an experimenter that might be more valuable in arriving at a correct evaluation of the two performances than would be the record of the trial time scores, especially if the latter were being considered without recourse to other information about the ways in which the subjects attacked the problem.

Minimizing the Contribution of the Spatial Arrangement of Procedural Factors. It has long been known that errors may result from the particular spatial arrangement of the experimental apparatus or materials. The space error in psychophysical experiments arises from the relation of the position of the apparatus to the position of the subject. Removal of these errors requires a counterbalancing of the spatial relationships among stimulus characteristics as these are presented in the experimental conditions. The space error is encountered in the threshold experiments on length of lines using the method of average error. In this method the subject is shown a standard stimulus line and is instructed to change the length of a comparison line until he judges it to be equal to that of the standard. The comparison line can be presented either on the right or on the left of the standard. If the comparison line is placed always on one side of the standard, a space error is likely to occur.

Another factor associated with the position of the apparatus is the direction of the manipulatory response required of the subject. This factor can readily be illustrated in the same psychophysical experiment described above. In manipulating the comparison stimulus to produce a line approximating that of the standard, the subject can move the line from the right to the left or from the left to the right. A movement-direction error may result if all adjustments are made in only one direction.

Control of these two factors, the spatial relation of the apparatus to the subject and the direction of the adjustive movement, in order to avoid procedural errors, is accomplished by the method of counterbalanced order. In this method the factors are ordered in such a way that there is an equating of the right-left position factor and the right-left movement factor. The procedure is to compute the various possible combinations of positions and movements and then order them in a random arrangement. The combinations of these factors arranged in random order in the length-of-line experiment are as follows:

Standard line on right and change in comparison line by inward movement

Standard line on left and change in comparison line by outward movement

Standard line on left and change in comparison line by inward movement

Standard line on right and change in comparison line by outward movement

Brief mention should be made of the serial arrangement of the units of material used in memory experiments. This factor is a combination time-and-location factor. Learning experiments often require the memorizing in serial order of units of material like words or nonsense syllables. Words at the beginning and end of a series are learned more quickly than those in the middle of the series, demonstrating that the position within the series is contributing to the rate of learning. In most learning studies this is not a crucial factor because it presumably operates equally in all experimental conditions being used. If serial order is suspected of having a differential effect upon the results, it can be controlled by arranging the units in all possible orders and randomly selecting for use as many of these orders as can be appropriately organized into the experimental conditions.

Minimizing the Contribution of Temporal Factors within an Experimental Sitting. The time that the subject is exposed to the experimental stimulus has already been discussed. In addition to this, there are time relations among the stimulus units within an experimental sitting and time relations among the several experimental conditions, both of which may present serious problems of control. We shall here be concerned with the time characteristics of procedures within a given experimental sitting.

In psychophysical experiments, variations may occur in the rate at which experimental stimuli are changed and the length of time given to the subject for expressing his judgment. This is readily seen in the method of constant stimulus differences. Several comparison stimuli are separately presented with the standard. The time of exposure plus the time between exposures is the time the subject has for appreciating the stimuli and making his judgment. Any variation in these times is to be referred to the experimenter's inability to manipulate the apparatus correctly. Extended preliminary practice by the experimenter will minimize variation of this kind.

Variation in the time interval between successive stimulus phases in learning experiments may contribute significantly to the results. For example, varying the interval between the conditioned stimulus and the unconditioned stimulus is an important factor in determining the rate of formation and the strength of the conditioned response. Time intervals between trials in learning experiments may be a few seconds, as in most conditioning experiments and discrimination-learning experiments, or they may be a number of hours, as in some maze experiments. In nearly all instances the elimination of variation in between-trial intervals rests with the experimenter and can be achieved by a rigorous following of an appropriate experimental procedure.

Minimizing the Contribution of Factors Arising from the Order of the Experimental Conditions. This temporal factor differs from those already considered in that we are here interested in the temporal ordering of experimental conditions rather than in the ordering of elements within an experimental condition. The problem of correctly arranging the temporal order of the experimental conditions is encountered in nearly every investigation in which the subject must contribute performance in more than one condition. Very frequently the testing of an experimental variable requires reactions to various gradations of the stimulus. Where some change, in the form of practice, knowledge, memory, fatigue, skill, and the like, is carried forward from one gradation or condition to another, it is necessary to effect a balancing of this effect among the experimental conditions so it will contribute uniformly to every one.

In investigating the use of the prone position by the pilot in flying aircraft, the authors wanted to learn the forces that could be applied by a person in executing different kinds of movements by the arms and hands in different variations of the prone position. Three movements of a wheel-type control column were selected for study, as follows: a push-pull motion, an up-down steering-wheel motion, and a right-left sideways swing movement of the whole column. The prone-position bed was varied in height by using three levels: low, medium, and high. The subject's body was positioned at three distances from the control column: close, medium, and far. The number of experimental conditions that could be formed by combining the three types of movements with the three bed heights and the three distances from the control column was $3 \times 3 \times 3$, or 27. Actually, the number of conditions was greater than 27 because it was desirable to test the movements from more than the central position of the control column, e.g., with the control column swung out to one side of the mid-line of the bed-control column axis.

It was impossible within the time available to investigate all of the combinations, and so nine conditions were selected, among which each of the three characteristics was represented in different values. These conditions were then arranged in a modified random order, and this order was varied for different subjects by having them begin each day's work at a different point in the series. The reason for randomizing and then counterbalancing the order of the conditions was twofold: first, fatigue arising within a daily session would be dispersed equally to all of the experimental conditions; and second, practice or learned effects carried from one condition to the next or from one sitting to the next would be evenly dispersed to all of the conditions.

The counterbalancing of the temporal order of conditions is especially important in experiments in memory and in work, in which practice and fatigue effects may occur within short periods of activity. In studies on work using expert craftsmen as subjects, it might be supposed that we are dealing with perfected habits, but this is not true. If an experiment involves the tasks of a factory job, say operating a drill press, and we use as subjects workers who have been on the job a number of years, we would presume that there would be no effects from further practice of the tasks. As a matter of fact, psychological functions seem never to reach this perfected practice state, regardless of the amount of past training. This is true even though the functions are simple in nature and are used many times daily by the subject, as, for example, simple coordinated reaching movements of the fingers, hand, and arm. In any experiment on work it is necessary to take into account the possible effects of practice, and when the study requires the subject to perform in more than one experimental condition, the counterbalancing of the order of the conditions is a standard procedure for achieving an equilibration of this practice effect.

Counterbalancing of the Order of Experimental Conditions through Their Random Assignment to Subjects. This method needs only to be discussed briefly, because it is very similar in purpose and result to counterbalancing experimental conditions in time. In fact, it is frequently combined with the temporal procedure, as was done in the experiment on prone-position responses.

In the present procedure, the order of the experimental conditions is varied by assigning a different order to each subject or group of subjects. Suppose the experimental conditions are a, b, and c, and it is suspected that a practice effect might occur between adjacent conditions. The possible orders of the three conditions are as follows: a, b, c; b, c, a; c, a, b; b, a, c; a, c, b; and c, b, a. If there are six subjects, then the orders are assigned randomly to them.

In this hypothetical example we could have used only the first three orders of the conditions, on the assumption that practice effect is determined by position in the series and therefore is equated when each condition occupies each position in the series. For most experiments this procedure is sufficient. Occasionally, and especially in experiments on work, it may be suspected that the effects differ for different temporal arrangements of adjacent conditions. For example, the learning of task A previous to the learning of task B might give a different effect than if we have the subjects learn the tasks in the reverse order. This probably would be the case when task A is similar but considerably more difficult than task B. When we suspect variations in effects of this kind, all possible orders of the experimental conditions are utilized.

This procedure of counterbalancing the order of the experimental conditions through the random assignment of the different orders to the subjects is the only method that can be used when all of the work required of a subject is to be accomplished in a single session.

SELECTED READINGS

Festinger, L.: Laboratory Experiments, in L. Festinger and D. Katz (eds.), "Research Methods in the Behavioral Sciences," chap. 4, The Dryden Press, Inc., 1953. This selection deals with problems encountered in conducting laboratory experiments in the area of social psychology. Major topics covered are the nature of laboratory experimentation, the design of laboratory experiments, the execution of laboratory experiments, the content and form of the experimental situation, techniques for the control and manipulation of variables, and opportunities for measurements in laboratory experimentation.

Thurstone, L. L.: Psychophysical Methods, in T. G. Andrews (ed.), "Methods of Psychology," chap. 5, John Wiley & Sons, Inc., 1948. A brief description is given of the process of measuring subjective phenomena by means of several of the commonly used psychophysical methods. It is pointed out that these methods have become important tools in the solution of problems in political and social behavior in addition to serving as major procedures in quantifying responses in the classical fields of experimental psychology.

Underwood, B. J.: "Experimental Psychology," chap. 10, Appleton-Century-Crofts, Inc., 1949. This chapter describes two basic designs that may be utilized when the same subjects participate in all phases of an experiment. The methods are used for controlling the possible effects of certain variables operating during the conduct of a study. The two designs involve a counterbalancing of the experimental conditions and a systematic randomization of the conditions.

CHAPTER 13

The Subject in Psychological Experiments

In the preceding chapter we considered problems in experimental methodology that are connected with the physical testing situation. We explored the factors in this situation that affect the production and control of the experimental variables being used to test the theorem and the factors that are involved in controlling and minimizing sources of variation that are not a part of the experimental test of the theorem. In the present chapter we are concerned with problems of experimental methodology that are associated with the responding subject. Again we shall explore factors that are manipulated in order to produce the experimental variables selected for testing a theorem and factors that need to be controlled and minimized as sources of error variation.

PRODUCING EXPERIMENTAL VARIABLES THROUGH MANIPULATING PREDISPOSING PSYCHOLOGICAL FACTORS

Behavior cannot be attributed solely to physical stimuli. The nature and amount of response is, in part, a function of the psychological predispositions of the subject. In general terms, psychological predispositions can be defined as tendencies to behave in certain ways because of the particular manner in which inheritance and past experience have set the physiological mechanisms to respond. The physical stimulus arouses to activity mechanisms already conditioned or set to respond in certain ways. The characteristics of the resulting behavior change cannot then be entirely explained in terms of the various attributes of the physical stimulus eliciting the response.

As determiners of behavior, the psychological predispositions of the subject can be studied as experimental variables and used for testing theorems. It is obvious that we cannot achieve the same precision of control in manipulating these variables that we attain in the manipulation of the physical stimulus. We are not always able to produce the variables at our own convenience or in the amounts we desire. It is possible, however, to control them as experimental variables in testing theorems, thus gaining knowledge about hypotheses we are interested in confirming.

Some Predisposing Psychological Factors. There is insufficient space to describe all of the many different predisposing psychological factors that condition behavior. Four general categories deserve to be mentioned, namely, interest, attitude, ability, and past experience.

Interest. Interests are predispositions that influence us to pay attention to certain kinds of environmental situations, such as sports, politics, or automobile repairing. Environmental objects become associated with the satisfaction of our many different needs. They then take on a high stimulating value for us, and we acquire an interest in them; we pay attention to them and spend much time in seeking them.

It should be obvious that interests function as determinants of behavior because they determine in part the kinds of physical-stimulus situations to which we readily respond. Interests also condition the length of time we respond, the intensity of our response, and other characteristics. In this way interests are related to motivation. For example, we tend to continue making a response if we are interested in it.

Interests are formed in conjunction with all of our needs, therefore they are legion in number. They furnish an extensive background of predispositions that can be studied in the role of determinants of behavior and therefore in the role of experimental variables useful for testing theorems.

Attitude. This term refers to an enduring predisposition to react either in a favorable or unfavorable way toward a given type of person, social group, political issue, and the like. Attitudes are pro-and-con predispositions. They are closely associated with interests—they may develop from interests or they may be influential in the development of interests. Bias and prejudice are two forms of expression of attitude.

Attitudes are important determinant predispositions because they may condition the behavior we make to any type of stimulus. We can have attitudes about anything—any kind of behavior, issue, person, group, object, and so on.

Attitudes vary in what can be called psychological strength; that is, an attitude may be manifest in terms of behavior that varies in some intensive way, as illustrated in the vehemence of the expression, the loudness of the voice, the intensity of the response, the prolongation of the argument. We usually have little difficulty in observing differences in intensity of attitude, yet it is a difficult characteristic to describe. We note that Jones is more outspoken than Smith, that Johnson sticks to his point regardless of opposition, that Rogers is always appreciative of any help given him. These characterizations are manifestations of what we have called the psychological strength of attitude, and although they are not difficult to perceive, they are very difficult to describe and quantify.

Ability. This is another term that is used to stand for a great many specific kinds of predispositions. Ability refers to power to perform a response. In general usage it includes potential power as well as present facility. By power to perform is merely meant that resident in the individual's sensori-neuro-muscular equipment is an established or potentially establishable organization by which a given reaction is or can be made.

We need not take time to describe the many different abilities possessed by a person or the various ways in which his abilities determine his behavior. Suffice it to say that ability underlies every response an individual performs; it makes possible the response and therefore is an important determinant of the response. As a determiner of behavior it can be studied as an experimental variable in testing theorems.

Past Experience. All change that is introduced into the organization of the individual's sensori-neuro-muscular equipment because of previous behavior is to be included in the expression past experience. The mere act of responding changes the physiological organism in ways that are stable in time and thus they are carried forward to affect subsequent behavior. Everything we do, then, registers its influence upon future responses.

By controlling experience it is possible to manipulate it as an experimental variable in testing theorems. In respect to any given type of adaptive situation there are wide variations in the past experiences of different persons. It is possible to utilize these variations in past experiences as experimental variables. Past experience becomes the experimental variable whenever a given theorem is testable by comparing the performance of two or more groups of individuals which vary systematically in their past experience in some relevant area of behavior.

Interrelationships among Psychological Predispositions. From the beginning we must realize that all psychological predispositions are inextricably and very complexly interrelated. This is in fact what we refer to when we talk about the individual as an integrated personality. The tremendous complexity of the neural connections provided in the central nervous system makes this integration not only possible but actually a matter of fact. It is, then, necessary for us to bear in mind the possibility of error in thinking that predispositions can be readily isolated and brought under observation in some simple and pure form.

Interests, attitudes, abilities, and past experiences are interrelated in many complicated ways. Our attitudes are conditioned by our experiences, our experiences are conditioned by our interests, our interests are conditioned by our abilities. This statement can be repeated with each one of these types of predispositions occupying any point in the sequence.

For example, we can write the statement over as follows: our experiences are conditioned by our abilities, our abilities are conditioned by our attitudes, our attitudes are conditioned by our interests. The most complex way in which we can imagine these predispositions to be interrelated will still probably not equal the degree of complexity actually involved.

With an enormous number of psychological predispositions interdependently related, it becomes a difficult task for the scientist to control any particular predisposition for experimental study. He is confronted with the identical problems that we have repeatedly mentioned; namely, he must isolate, manipulate, and measure certain predispositions as experimental variables while at the same time keeping constant the effect of other predispositions functioning as unwanted systematic or as unsystematic variables. With less direct control over these variables than is possible in the manipulation of the physical-stimulus situation, he must depend more upon the methods of selection and statistical analysis for effecting the relationships necessary for his comparisons. These methods, when appropriately and adequately applied, achieve the precision of control required for experimentally testing theorems.

The Use of Predispositions as Experimental Variables. In the last chapter we examined procedures by which change in behavior can be elicited by manipulating the external stimulating situation. Variation in the stimulus can then be correlated with the resulting variation in the response. From the interrelationships discovered between the stimulus and response changes it is possible to make inferences about the psychological processes of the responding subject. The responses of the subject are considered to reflect directly fundamental psychological predispositions as these are brought into activity by the stimulus. The primary purpose is to study a given predisposition as a psychological process in order to learn its nature; that is, what it is as a functioning psychological process in the subject, what its constituents are, what its precursors are, what variation is possible in its amount or frequency of occurrence. The responses reflecting the predisposition are the center of attention.

In the present chapter we are interested in predispositions as experimental variables; that is, we are interested in determining how variation in a given predisposition affects some other psychological process. There is an active psychological process, represented objectively in some pattern of response, which we examine in order to determine if it changes when we introduce variation in some predisposition that we wish to study. Of course, this psychological process itself is a predisposition reflected in the subject's behavior, but it is not the predisposition in which experimentally controlled variation is introduced. Rather, it is the variable that is expected to register a change when purposeful variations are made in the experimentally controlled predisposition. We are interested in measuring the nature of any change in the active psychological process in terms of amount, intensity, or frequency as we introduce change in kind, amount, or frequency in the experimental predisposing factor. An example would be determining the relationship between various amounts of religious training and incidence of juvenile delinquency. The religious-training variable is the experimental predisposition; juvenile delinquency is the active psychological process.

The Isolation of Predisposing Psychological Factors. *Isolating the Predisposing Factor as Part of a Complex.* It was indicated earlier that psychological predispositions are complexly interrelated and that it is very difficult to isolate a particular predisposition for experimental study. In most instances, the best we can do is to make the predisposition to be examined the predominant one within the complex of variables that we find reflected in the behavior. In other words, production of the experimental predispositional variable in pure form is usually impossible, so we must endeavor to get it to predominate in a complex that we isolate. It must be the most important determinant in the complex so we can be assured that, for the most part, any results obtained can be attributed to it.

Discovering Signs of Predispositions. To isolate a predisposing psychological factor we must work with signs or indices of its existence. We cannot directly observe the predisposition, so we must infer its existence from various kinds of manifestations that can be logically linked with it. Such signs can be past achievements of an individual that may be found in work records, school records, judgments of acquaintances, or even statements made by the individual. Performances currently obtained in a situation that reveals the predisposition are also valuable signs. Such performances can be measured by means of tests, inventories, or ratings.

Steps in Isolating Predispositions for Study. Several steps are involved in the procedure of isolating a psychological predisposition as an experimental variable. First, it is important to define as accurately as possible the specific psychological predisposition that is to be studied. It is through careful definition that the interrelationships of the given predisposition with others are revealed. Often it is possible by careful definition to discover signs that minimize any unwanted interrelationships.

Secondly, signs must be found for detecting the predisposition as defined. Not just any past occurrence that was a manifestation of the predisposition can be used. The more closely the signs conform to the definition, the greater the chances of freeing the experimental predisposition from other potentially interfering predispositions.

The third step is to locate subjects in whose history we can find the signs that we have selected. This in itself may be either an easy or a difficult task, depending on the particular predisposition being studied.

For example, if the predisposition is revealed in the amount of schooling in the first 8 years of life, there are many persons available for study in whom this sign can be found. If the predisposition is revealed in such a variable as religious bigotry, it might be very difficult to find subjects in whom the accepted signs can be found.

The Measurement of Predisposing Psychological Factors. *The Problem.* To obtain the most accurate description of the predisposing factor we must find ways for quantifying it. Most predispositions can be considered to be magnitudes and to vary in terms of amount. The problem is to find signs that are quantitative in nature and that at the same time accurately reveal the predisposition. For many predispositions, it is not a difficult task to divide them into the two quantitative categories of presence and absence and use one group of subjects that possesses the predisposition and another group that does not possess it. It is sometimes a difficult task, however, to devise accurate descriptions of different levels of amount by which we can accurately quantify any functional relationship that is brought under study.

The Use of Descriptive Indices. Many descriptive indices vary in amount, thus making a quantification of the predisposition possible. Furthermore, with many of these indices it is safe to assume that the quantitative variation in the index is revealing of quantitative variation in the predisposition. There are exceptions, however, and the scientist must be on the alert to detect instances in which the quantitative change in the sign does not correspond with the quantitative change in the predisposing factor. For example, the length of a course studied in school does not necessarily accurately indicate the amount of experience gained and retained by a student. An individual may take a course with little intent to learn, and so what little he does learn is not accurately reflected in the amount of time spent in training. However, duration of exposure to some types of experience is often a sound index for revealing quantitative variation in predispositions. Some examples are the length of time spent on a certain job, the number of years of attendance in school, the number of months spent as an apprentice, the tenure in an office, etc.

Level of past achievement is another sign that can be used to reveal variation in amount of a predisposing factor. For example, the level of past achievement may be used to indicate the amount of a psychological predisposition in the form of an ability. In general, this is probably true for scholastic ability. On the average, a high school diploma represents a higher amount of scholastic ability than does an eighth-grade certificate. A college degree represents higher scholastic ability than does a high school diploma. In a university the doctorate degree represents higher scholastic ability than does the master's degree, and this latter represents higher ability than does the bachelor degree.

When the sign of the predisposition is being quantified, it should be apparent that the units of measurement may be crude and approximate, and there may be times when the sign is not even applicable to a particular individual. These difficulties, however, do not make measurement impossible.

The Use of Measuring Devices. Measuring devices that give a quantitative description of present ability can be used to assess predispositions. The effectiveness of present performance can be assumed to reflect the amount of the predisposition. If one person is shown to be superior to another when assessed by some proficiency measure such as a mental test, then it is fairly safe to argue that there are corresponding quantitative differences in the predispositions of the two persons. Inaccuracy arises in the relationship between the present performance measure and the predisposition. If the performance measure can be demonstrated to be closely associated with the defined predisposition, little error will be introduced in estimating the quantity of the predisposing factor.

The inaccuracy of the gross units characterizing many descriptive indices may sometimes be reduced by using measuring devices for estimating the amount of the sign. In the construction of tests, inventories, and questionnaires we can usually devise more precise units of measurement than is possible in commonly used descriptive indices like years in school. With the greater precision in the units there naturally follows an increased accuracy in measurement of the sign, and consequently a more accurate description of the predisposing factor. For example, a work-sample machinist test may give a more accurate measure of a person's mechanical know-how than the number of years spent in jobs in the area of mechanics.

Manipulating Predisposing Psychological Factors by Manipulating Persons. In previous sections references were made to the problem of discovering signs in the experimental subjects that reveal the predispositions that we desire to investigate. It was stated that persons could be selected for study who differed in terms of the accepted signs and therefore varied in the predisposing factor. This is one of the key ways of controlling predispositions in their role as experimental variables. The manipulation of the factor is accomplished through the manipulation of persons. If persons differ in respect to a predisposition, then separating the persons according to the signs being used accomplishes a division of the predisposition in terms of kind, level, or amount, depending on the nature of the breakdown within the signs or indices. Although this may seem to be an obvious procedure, it is well to realize that for some predispositions it is the only procedure available for isolating and manipulating predisposing factors for study as experimental variables.

From the nature of the above procedure for manipulating predisposing factors, it should be apparent that knowledge about the experimental subjects is of primary concern. Having defined the predisposition and determined the nature of the signs that will reflect it, the next important task is to find persons in whom the signs can be clearly discovered in the forms and amounts required. Knowledge of persons is the avenue through which we eventually gain control of the predisposing factor. Failure to get comprehensive and accurate knowledge about potential subjects relative to the signs of the predisposition will inevitably introduce error. Such error is difficult to appraise and therefore difficult to remove because the nature and amount of its effect on the experimental variable cannot be determined. It is a far sounder procedure to avoid such error by accurately assessing the potential subjects relative to the signs being used to reflect the predisposition.

Subjects used in the experiment must be selected carefully. The criteria of selection are usually readily verbalized but are frequently difficult to apply. Subjects should be selected for study in whom the signs reflecting the predisposition are accurately discernible and in whom the signs meet the characteristics of kind, amount, frequency, etc., prescribed in the experimental design. Carelessness in the selection of the subjects spells failure to manipulate the predisposing variable in accordance with the experimental design.

An Example. Consideration of an example will help to highlight some of the points made in the preceding sections. Suppose there is an industrial training program to be set up for the job of machinist. The following are relevant facts: (1) there is an appreciable number of new employees to be trained each year; (2) the employees range in background from novice to expert, but the largest number have had considerable machine-work experience although usually not of the special kind required by the job; (3) there are three different training methods that can be utilized; (4) these training methods vary considerably in cost and in the time away from the job required of the worker during training; (5) it is believed that the effectiveness of the several methods is a function of the previous training and experience of the trainees; (6) it is believed that cost of training might be kept at a minimum if certain particular kinds and amounts of previous training and experience were required of the prospective trainee.

The predisposing variable is the previous training and experience of the prospective trainees who will be selected for training from among applicant workers. Evaluating variation in this predisposition requires a consideration of both formal and informal training, experience gained on jobs, achievements in terms of characteristic rates of work or quality of work, ability and experience in repairing machines as well as in operating them, and other relevant signs. All such characteristics should be examined in the process of defining the predisposing factor and in discovering means for quantifying it.

The variable in which we look for change when we introduce different values in the experimental predisposition is the training-methods variable. What we are interested in determining is the effect that differences in the amount of previous training and experience have on the relative effectiveness of the several training methods. If it is found that differences in the predisposing factor affect one training method more significantly than another, this will furnish the information needed. This information, together with information on the relative effectiveness and relative costs of the methods, will enable management to decide which training method to adopt and what training and experience to require of the worker who is recruited for the training program.

PRODUCING EXPERIMENTAL VARIABLES THROUGH MANIPULATING ANATOMICAL-PHYSIOLOGICAL FACTORS

All behavior, in whatever form it is observed, is dependent upon tissue changes in the body. Knowledge about behavior will then be increased through a study of the nature of the tissue changes that underlie it. In all previous discussions in this text, whether it has been made explicit or not, it has been assumed that between what we commonly call the external physical stimulus and the resulting change in behavior as observed either in experience or in overt movements, there is activity in the complex mechanisms of the sense organs, the nervous system, the glands, and the muscles. Behavior is the functioning of these mechanisms.

The General Problem. Studying the correlation of changes in the sense organs and the nervous system with changes in behavior is one of the oldest research areas in both physiology and psychology. In recent years there has been an accelerated interest in the area as a result of the great strides made in the improvement of experimental procedures. Developments in the field of electronics have been adapted to the measurement of the micropotential changes found in sense organs, nerves, and muscles. Quantitative techniques for measuring molar types of behavior have significantly added to the tools required for studying functional relationships between integrative behavior and the underlying changes in the response mechanisms.

In most studies involving the anatomical-physiological mechanisms of response, the hypotheses revolve around two problems, namely, the problem of the "where," and the problem of the "how." The first concerns the localization of the change underlying the response. A typical problem concerning the nervous system would be the determination of the particular part of the brain of a rat that is required for the learning of the maze. The problem of the how concerns the nature of the activity underlying the response. For example, we could ask: What particular electrical and chemical changes take place in the cortical fields that are active during a given response? To date, the attention of the psychologist has been primarily directed to the problem of the locus of the tissue change underlying behavior.

We are here concerned with reviewing some of the procedures by which the anatomist, physiologist, and psychologist have endeavored to find explanations of behavior through the study of response mechanisms. We must restrict our discussion to those procedures directly concerned with producing change in behavior by manipulation of these mechanisms. There are important subsidiary procedures, such as those of histology, anesthesiology, encephalography, etc., by which greater precision is gained in the description and quantification of the behavior changes. It is not possible for us to give space to the description of all of these procedures.

Some Procedures Used in the Study of the Nervous System. We can profitably begin our study of experimental procedures for manipulating response mechanisms by a consideration of those that are used in the investigation of the nervous system. Many of the procedures that are used in studying the nervous system are also applicable to nonneural response mechanisms.

The Procedure of the Nerve-muscle Preparation. The neuron is the smallest structural unit of the nervous system, and to study its functions is to study the mechanics of behavior in their most rudimentary phases. The activity of neurons can be studied in the nerve-muscle preparation. This preparation consists of a given motor nerve with its attached muscle fibers. Sometimes the preparation is removed from the body; at other times the experiment is conducted with the nerve and muscle *in situ.* The application of electrodes on the nerve permits control of the duration and intensity of the electrical charge used as a stimulus. Other electrodes placed on the nerve or on the muscle enable an accurate record to be taken of the nerve-fiber response. Several hypotheses concerning the electropotential characteristics of nervous action have been investigated, using the nerve-muscle preparation.

The Procedure of the Spinal Preparation. At the reflexive level, we study the mechanisms involved in simple muscular movements. The simplest form of reflex response is observable in spinal preparations. In this preparation the spinal cord is transected in the cervical region, thus removing the nervous centers below the cut from communication with the higher brain centers. The neural centers below the level of the transection remain functional and can be stimulated to activity through the afferent nerves serving them. The muscles below the transection also remain functional and serve as a means by which the changes in the neural centers can be studied. It should be remembered that we cannot directly observe the central nervous changes underlying responses. We must infer the nature of these changes from the characteristics of the stimulus used to elicit them and from the nature of the resulting responses.

Three very significant hypotheses for explaining simple coordination of response, which have been confirmed by many experiments using spinal preparations, are the reciprocal innervation of antagonistic muscles, the central excitatory state of the motor neuron, and the central inhibitory state of the motor neuron. It would take us too far afield to describe these hypotheses.

The Procedure Involving Surgical Lesions in the Higher Integrative Centers. In this procedure the nervous mechanism to be studied is rendered partially or totally inoperative. This change in the functional condition of the mechanism is the experimental variable. The effect of the change is then noted in some form of behavior, such as sensory experience, motor coordination, emotional expression, or activity required to learn or solve a problem. The surgery is done under aseptic conditions, with the animal under deep anesthesia. The same attention is given to the animal as if the operation were being performed on a human being in a well-equipped hospital.

In studying the nervous mechanisms involved in the higher mental processes, lesions are produced in cortical and subcortical regions of the brain. The tissue can be destroyed by cutting, but it is more frequently destroyed by thermocoagulation, using an electric current. Investigations of the functional importance of localized parts of the cortex and subcortex have required procedures for effecting circumscribed lesions within very restricted areas or regions. One procedure devised for this purpose uses a goniometer manipulator for controlling the movement of the electrodes used in coagulating the tissue. The goniometer includes devices for stabilizing the animal's head in reference to axes in the three planes of space and for inserting and positioning a point electrode in the subcortex or positioning paired electrodes on the cortex in reference to these same three axes. The amount of destruction is controlled primarily through the duration of the coagulating current. Without some kind of instrument for controlling the movement of the electrodes and the size of the lesion, the investigator cannot achieve comparable lesions in different animal subjects.

In these investigations on the functions of the brain, the experimenter must train his animals on a maze, problem box, or other apparatus used for measuring response, and evaluate the animals' behavior as in any other animal experiment. He then sacrifices the animals, histologically examines the parts of the brain that were affected by the operation, and maps and quantitatively describes the regions destroyed. Only by meticulously following each of these steps is it possible to obtain reliable facts from which accurate statements can be made concerning the functional importance of brain regions.

Some hypotheses that have been investigated by this procedure are: mass action (that the effectiveness of behavior is a function of the amount of cortical tissue being activated); equipotentiality of brain tissue (that the cortex is undifferentiated in so far as higher mental activities are concerned; i.e., that one part of the cortex is as important as any other part); cerebral dominance (that in a given response the cortical centers are prepotent over the subcortical centers).

The Procedure of Stimulation. This is one of the oldest procedures for experimentally studying brain functions. The brain is exposed under aseptic conditions and electrodes are gently applied to the region to be stimulated. Response in the muscles is used as a means of discovering and describing any discharges in the motor nerves produced by the stimulus. Occasionally with human subjects—persons who are undergoing brain surgery and consent to having their brain cortex electrically stimulated— it is possible to record changes in subjective feelings, particularly changes in sensory experience.

Stimulus experiments have been conducted on deeper nuclei of the brain by inserting needle electrodes into these deeper tissues. Peripheral nerves have also been studied in vivo by the method of electrical stimulation.

The Electrical-potential-recording Procedure. The development of electronics has made it possible to record accurately electrical-potential changes from individual nerves, from the deeper nuclei of the brain, and from the surface of the cortex of the brain through the skull. The eel has been a favorite animal in the study of the functions of the optic nerve, and the cat a favorite subject in the study of auditory-nerve potentials. Naturalistic stimuli of light and sound are used. The electrical discharges along the nerve and from surrounding tissues are registered and photographed. In some experiments, the experimental variable consists of changes in one or more characteristics of the external stimulus. In others, the experimental variable consists of changes produced in the tissue by surgery or drugs.

The electrical-potential changes recorded from the cortex through the skull are called brain waves. In humans these waves are studied in connection with the subject's mental activity, emotional condition, or purposely introduced changes in sensory stimulation. In the operated animal the introduction of stimuli in various parts of the nervous system makes possible the study of facilitation, inhibition, and blocking.

Changes in electrical potential of various rates have been recorded.

When the human subject is in the resting state the rate of change in the brain waves is about 10 per second. This is called the alpha rhythm. Other rhythms, both slower and faster than the alpha rhythm, have been found.

Some Procedures Used in the Study of Sense Organs. It is not possible, in the limited space available, to describe the many procedures that have been evolved for studying the functions of sense organs. As stated earlier, methods involving electronic devices have greatly improved the recording of sense-organ responses. Changes in sensory nerves, as electronically registered, are used to reveal what occurs in the sense organ itself. Much knowledge about the eye, the ear, touch endings, and kinesthetic endings has been discovered through this procedure.

Present discussion is limited to a consideration of the cutaneous senses. In the study of these endings, several procedures have been evolved that we have not yet described.

The Problem. In early studies on the nature of the sensory responses of the skin, a question arose concerning the existence of specialized kinds of end organs for mediating the different experiences of pressure, warmth, cold, and pain. Opposed to this theory is the explanation that each different kind of stimulus sets up a distinct pattern of excitement in the sensory nerves which is then interpreted by the brain. It would appear that there are facts to support each point of view, which leads to the conclusion that probably both discreteness of anatomical tissue and distinctness of neural reaction underlie the responses of the skin sense organs.

Identifying Cutaneous Endings by Correlating Psychological and Anatomical Findings. Two facts underlie this procedure. First, there is the punctate distribution of sensitivity in the skin. By this is meant that the skin is not uniformly sensitive to different stimuli. If a given area of the skin is explored, it will be found that some spots or points are sensitive to warmth, others to cold, others to pressure, and still others to pain. Secondly, the anatomist has been able to identify several different kinds of encapsulated endings in the skin that could serve as sensory end organs. In addition, the skin is richly served with free nerve endings that could also function as sensory end organs. These various endings, particularly the encapsulated ones, are not uniformly distributed throughout all skin areas. The method of correlation endeavors to determine for a given skin area the relation of the location and density of the endings to the location and density of the pointlike experiences. This approach is not entirely satisfactory, as the correlation is not usually based on findings from the same subjects; that is, the anatomical results discovered on one person are associated with the psychological reactions discovered on another person.

The Surgical Procedure of Identifying Cutaneous Endings. In this procedure a careful study is made of the experiences arising from a given skin area, all points of experience being carefully mapped. Then the skin is excised, stained, and examined under a microscope. The points of sensation marked on the skin are then examined in connection with any sensory endings found nearby. It has not been possible by this method to establish a one-to-one correlation between the different types of sensory experience and the different kinds of sensory ending.

The Vital-staining Procedure of Identifying Cutaneous Endings. Sensory endings can be identified and accurately delimited by vital-staining procedures. Although the end organs are desensitized by injecting the dye under the skin, sensation returns after a few hours, so that experiments can be conducted while the endings are still identifiable. Some correlation between type of sensory experience and type of end organ has been found by this method, but the facts do not support a one-to-one relationship.

Procedures Using Loss and Recovery of Sensation. In these procedures the sensory endings are made nonfunctional and then allowed to recover. It is argued that if the sensory experiences are lost and recovered in a precise order, this would be evidence that there is a distinct anatomical structure for each experience. Loss of sensory experience may be produced by sectioning the peripheral nerve, by cocaine anesthesia, by freezing, or by asphyxia brought on by cutting off the blood supply long enough to cause oxygen want. Before the loss in sensation is produced, the skin area to be affected is carefully mapped in regard to the different cutaneous experiences. In all procedures except the one involving the sectioning of the peripheral nerve, the rate of loss of the several sensory experiences is carefully determined. In every method the time and rate of recovery of the different sensory experiences is recorded. Results from the different methods are not in complete agreement. For example, the order of loss under cocaine anesthesia is first cold, then warmth, and last pressure, with the time of disappearance of pain varying in different experiments. In the method of asphyxia, the order of loss is first light pressure, then cold, then dull pressure, then warmth, and finally pain.

The Manipulation of Anatomical-physiological Mechanisms by the Use of Drugs. *Some Uses of Drugs.* We have already alluded to the use of drugs in the study of cutaneous sense organs. Drugs have also been used widely to desensitize, block, excite, and otherwise affect different response mechanisms. In experiments with animals, curare has been an invaluable aid in work with muscles. For example, it has been used in paralyzing somatic muscles in experiments on conditioning. It has also been used as a cortical depressant. The effects of Benzedrine have been studied in connection with the higher mental functions. The effects of caffeine, alcohol, and the barbiturates have been studied on a wide variety of responses. Glandular products have been used in investigations of certain kinds of emotional reactions.

Controlling the Factor of Suggestion. One of the most stubborn problems that has confronted the experimenter in the use of drugs on human subjects is the control of the stimulating or inhibiting effect that is suggested by the use of the drug. The subject, being aware, at least in part, of the nature of an experiment, may react to the administration of the drug in terms of what he believes the effect should be. This is to say that when the drug is given, he may deliberately try to be affected in the direction that is in agreement with his own ideas about the drug's effect. For example, if an individual believes that a drug like alcohol does not have a deleterious effect on performance, then when he is given a task such as mental arithmetic he will work extra hard on the problems in order to demonstrate that he is not affected by the drug.

Various procedures have been devised for disguising the administration of drugs. Caffeine is administered in the form of pills rather than in coffee, and a placebo, looking exactly like the caffeine pill, is alternated with it so the subject never knows when he is being given the drug. No satisfactory control of suggestive effects has been found for alcohol.

An Example of Controlling Suggestion. In one experiment on the effect of smoking on certain kinds of responses, the investigator constructed a false pipe to alternate with a regular pipe. The false pipe was a regular pipe so modified that the subject drew in warm air as he puffed on it. He was blindfolded during the actual time of using either pipe so he could not tell in a given condition whether he was smoking warm air or drawing smoke from a pipe bowl filled with tobacco. In order to control olfactory stimuli, the experimenter smoked at appropriate times so that the subject was aware of the odor of burning tobacco any time he was drawing on a pipe.

MINIMIZING THE CONTRIBUTION OF IRRELEVANT PSYCHOLOGICAL FACTORS

The Problem. From previous discussions it is obvious that the particular behavior that will be elicited by the stimulating situation organized by the scientist to test his theorem is not going to be determined solely by the various characteristics that he purposely presents in the physical-stimulus situation. Actually, the particular effect that an experimental stimulus will have will be determined by the various psychological factors that are acting on the response mechanisms through which the effect of the physical stimulus must be manifest. It is, then, sound experimental design to plan procedures by which unwanted factors will be prevented from exercising a determinant effect upon the measures selected for evaluating the experimental variable.

For purposes of description, some of the major psychological factors needing to be controlled and procedures used in dealing with them are considered under three headings; namely, motivation of the subject, facility of the subject in adapting to the experimental conditions, and predisposing background factors of the subject.

The Control of Motivational Factors. Special procedures for maintaining high motivation in the subject are important for obtaining a representative performance. The subject's response to the physical stimulating situation is in part determined by his desire, willingness, or even compulsion to react.

Animal Subjects. In animal experiments, hunger, thirst, and pain are the principal drives that are manipulated to motivate the subject to respond. The degree of the subject's hunger can be crudely controlled by regulating the amount of food. Thirst is manipulated by regulating the amount of water. In either case, within limits, the longer the incentive is withdrawn, the more likely is the animal to respond to the experimental conditions presented to him. The usual effect of electric-shock stimuli is to increase the motivation of the animal to respond, but control of the level of motivation is much more difficult than with food or water. There are wide differences in susceptibility to shock stimuli among different subjects (both human and animal). Also, within a given experimental period the sensitivity to shock of the same subject may change markedly.

Human Subjects. The problem of getting representative performances in human subjects is also closely associated with their motivation. Humans usually volunteer to be subjects and are not under compulsion to cooperate. This does not mean, however, that they are equally motivated to respond under the experimental conditions set for them. Subjects approach the task given them with different motives, sets, and intents. Furthermore, differential change in their motivation occurs as the experiment proceeds, some showing more cooperation, some showing less.

The factor of the individual's aspirations and prestige is important in nearly all experiments involving the higher mental processes. Individuals differ greatly in their aspirations. Some set high aspirations in most tasks they undertake; others do not. Some do their best in nearly every task they perform; others do not. In most experiments the subject wants to know about the quality of his performance and how it compares with that of other subjects. Some individuals develop anxiety when they are not satisfied with their performance.

The experimenter's control over the motivation of human subjects is usually by way of instructions, although he can also utilize some forms of reward. Children can be highly motivated if promised desired objects like candy. Adults can often be highly motivated by being promised a complete description and explanation of the results following completion of the experiment.

Special sets and intents are controlled by standardized instructions. The use of such instructions guarantees that everyone will be given the same explanation, and thus no subjects will have an advantage over others because they received extra aid. The instructions should be comprehensive, covering all areas wherein the subject must respond. They should be written at a level that comes within the understanding of the particular subjects to be used. They should be given a tryout in a pilot study to determine if they actually function in a satisfactory way.

Provision should be made for giving special instructions when the subject's interest flags. The experimenter should prepare ahead of time and put into standardized form the type and amount of extra stimulation he believes it possible to give a subject whose interest is flagging. Leaving such special instruction to the exigencies of the moment when they are urgently needed runs the risk of changing the experimental conditions and invalidating the testing of the theorem.

The Facility of the Subject to Adapt to the Experimental Conditions. *The Problem.* In most psychological experiments there will be features of the procedures, materials, or apparatuses that will be totally unfamiliar to the subject, and this unfamiliarity should not function as a determinant variable. Many subjects will not have had experience with specific tasks comparable to those they will be called upon to perform. For example, in an experiment on concept formation the subject will bring to the laboratory his past experience with concepts, abstractions, and the like, but in addition he may be exposed to the relatively unfamiliar stimuli of Chinese characters, printed marks called radicals, memory exposure devices, and other content features peculiar to the experiment. We must be aware of the fact that different subjects will not adjust to these unfamiliar features with the same ease and readiness and that because of these features the subjects may face the experiment with different amounts of understanding concerning their role as subjects. These variations may then function in a systematic manner. Similarly, attitudinal and ability factors may change during the experiment in ways not associated with the particular variables under study. Special steps must then be taken for anticipating and controlling such unwanted variations as may arise within the particular investigation being conducted.

The Procedure of Preliminary Practice. If the design of an experiment requires the subjects to be equally conversant and facile with the particular materials and procedures to be used, then the subjects are given preliminary practice on these or similar materials and procedures before being actually started on the experiment. The purpose of the preliminary training is to bring subjects to a comparable level of familiarity before the experiment.

Suppose that the experiment demands that a subject operate two control wheels similar to those found in a machine lathe. For example, the two-hand motor coordination test requires the subject to manipulate two control wheels, one with each hand. The task confronting the subject is to keep a movable pointer, which is controlled by these wheels, in contact with a target that is made to move automatically at varying rates through a prescribed irregular course. Left and right movement of the pointer is controlled by the left-hand wheel and forward and backward movement of the pointer by the right-hand wheel. It is very difficult to learn how to operate this test merely from written or oral instructions. A minute's practice manipulating the controls, however, is usually sufficient to develop an understanding in the subject of what he is expected to do.

Very few experiments are so simple in design that all subjects are ready to perform the required tasks without practice. Nearly always, then, a fore-exercise, practice exercise, or preliminary training is given before the subject is required to respond to the experimental conditions in which the theorem is under test.

The Procedure of Completed Practice. The purpose of this procedure is to bring the subject to a level of performance where no further improvement is expected from additional practice. If the experimental stimulus is likely to have only a slight effect on behavior, great difficulty may be encountered in detecting this effect and in separating change resulting from the experimental variable from change resulting from other determinants. Any particular response to be used as a test of the experimental variable should then be well established in order to minimize changes in it from irrelevant determinants. For example, if the rate of the color-naming response is to be used to study the possible deteriorating effect of the ingestion of alcohol, it is necessary to remove other factors affecting the rate of color naming, such as practice effect, fatigue, boredom, attitude of subject toward use of alcohol, etc. One of these factors, namely practice effect, is controlled by the method of completed practice.

In the case of complex tasks it is doubtful if a subject can be trained to a maximum of his performance within the limited time at the disposal of both experimenter and subject. In conducting an experiment on the effects of high temperatures on mental performance, one of the authors found it very difficult to get the subjects trained to a stable practice level. The task was the addition of two 1-place numbers, which actually is very simple in nature as mental tasks go. The individual problems were arranged 15 to the row and 25 rows to the page, and several pages were prepared with different combinations and sequences of problems in order to prevent memorizing of sequences of answers. The subjects were practiced 20 minutes a day.

In the case of one subject, six distinct practice levels were attained and surpassed. After practice was extended through about 3 months, the subject was still showing improvement. Needless to say, the subject was not used in the experiment. But suppose he had been exposed to a high-temperature environment while working on the addition problems, and suppose that there was no difference in his performance between the high-temperature and normal-temperature conditions; it could not be concluded that the high temperature had had no effect because it could have been possible that a deleterious effect from the high temperature was canceled by further improvement in the function of addition. Inasmuch as any effect from high temperature was expected to be rather small, it was extremely important that a stable practice level be reached by the subject.

Minimizing Variation in Predisposing Psychological Factors. *The Problem.* In every experiment there will be predisposing psychological factors that should be prevented from exercising a determinant effect upon the measure used for evaluating the experimental variable. We have previously described the four most common predisposing factors of interest, attitude, ability, and past experience. Although each of these terms stands for a generalized concept, we shall mean by them the specific interests, attitudes, abilities, and past experiences operating in any given study. It is almost certain that all four types of factors are represented in some form in every investigation. The problem then is one of keeping them constant rather than one of eliminating them. Manipulation of these conditioners of response is achieved in many different ways, some of them being very simple procedures.

The Control of Attitude. Factors conditioning attitude are not difficult to manipulate in most experimental studies. The scientist usually has no particular ax to grind, so he does not have to point his investigation toward satisfying any ulterior ends. He can choose any individuals he wishes to act as his subjects. That these subjects may be white rats, adolescent youths, or gray-bearded adults need not deter him one whit from his course toward gaining further knowledge. All he needs from a subject is a willingness to cooperate to the extent of following the directions of the experiment and to respond to the best of his knowledge and ability to the various tasks that are set for him. Such cooperation can be obtained by asking human subjects to volunteer their services. If a subject happens to become uncooperative, or if he is too ignorant to perform the tasks involved, the experimenter can dismiss him.

If the attitude of subjects has a direct bearing on the nature of the investigation—as, for example, stereotyped racial attitudes in a study involving judgments about the behavior of different racial groups—the experimenter can often manipulate this attitude to equalize its contribution among the several conditions of his investigation by a random selection and assignment of the subjects to the different experimental conditions. In the discussion of the use of alcohol, the attitudinal factor of suggestion was mentioned. Left uncontrolled this suggestion factor probably would contribute as an unwanted systematic attitudinal variable in most experiments in which human subjects were used. Control of this factor by means of random selection and assignment of subjects to the experimental conditions does not remove the effects of suggestion but distributes them randomly to the several conditions.

The Control of Interest, Ability, and Past Experience. In contrast with attitude, factors conditioning interest, ability, and past experience are not so readily held constant, and frequently special precautionary procedures must be taken to control their possible determining influence. For many investigations dealing with the nature of psychological variables, it is sufficient to follow the rule of selecting subjects who have the minimum of interest, ability, and past experience required by the tasks of the experiment. For example, the rule of minimal facility is usually used in studying the characteristics of sensory experience and the sensory thresholds, the basic facts of learning, the laws of memory, and similar topics. The interest, ability, and experience of the subject are then supposed to contribute to the understanding of the procedures to be followed by him; but they are not supposed to contribute differentially to the nature of the results unless they themselves are part of the experimental variable under study.

When comparisons are to be made concerning the relative effectiveness of two methods, such as two methods of learning poetry, the interests, abilities, and experiences of the subjects have a high likelihood of affecting the results. It is then necessary to follow a manipulatory procedure that will distribute these effects equally to all phases of the investigation. Some of the better-known procedures for achieving this distribution will now be considered.

Procedures for Equating Interest, Attitude, Ability, and Past Experience. *The Procedure of Matched Groups.* In research with human subjects the procedure involving matched or equated groups is very frequently used. When we are interested in discovering the effects on behavior of controlled variation in a specific factor to which we purposely expose our subjects, we want to be assured that the results obtained can be unquestionably attributed to the variation that we experimentally introduce. To achieve this we utilize two groups of individuals in one of which we introduce the variation and in the other of which no variation is allowed. The group in which the variation is introduced is called the experimental group, while the other is called the control group.

Suppose we are interested in knowing if 2 years of college training is conducive to faster learning in aircraft pilot training. We would form two groups matched on such factors as age, intelligence, mechanical ability, etc., one of which would have 2 years of college training (the experimental group), the other of which would be high school graduates with no college training (the control group). It is obvious that any differences found between the two groups in their rate of learning to be pilots cannot be attributed to their differences in respect to the experimental variable of college training unless we make sure that the two groups are alike with respect to other relevant factors that conceivably might contribute to these differences (age, intelligence, mechanical ability, etc.).

The fundamental purpose in forming matched groups is to gain greater control over the relevant factors that might enter the experiment to produce a specific bias in the results or to increase the sampling error. We want to obtain two groups that are homogeneous with respect to all variables that might produce differences in behavior that will affect in any way the difference to be expected from the experimental variable. It is apparent that if two groups are homogeneous in respect to relevant characteristics at the beginning of an experiment and a difference between them occurs after the introduction of an experimental variation, then the difference must be ascribed to this variation. In using the method of matched groups the problem is to determine the particular relevant factors that, when used as a basis for equating the individuals, will produce the greatest homogeneity with respect to the unwanted relevant factors that might contribute a systematic effect.

To equate two groups in such factors as interest, attitude, ability, and past experience, special procedures are used in assembling the two groups. One procedure is to randomly assign the subjects to the control and experimental groups. The assumption is made that through a random assignment of the subjects the chances are about equal that any relevant factors will be dispersed in the two groups to about the same extent. A second procedure requires the forming of pairs of individuals who are about equal in terms of experience, ability, etc. Then by random assignment, an individual of each pair is placed in each of the two groups.

A special form of the matched-group procedure is that of consanguineous pairing, in which siblings, fraternal twins, or identical twins become the pairs, each pair then being divided between the control and experimental groups by some random method of assignment.

The Procedure of Self-control. Another procedure for manipulating relevant disturbing factors involves using the participating subjects as their own controls. In this procedure the performance of the same individuals is measured under all experimental conditions, and any differences in behavior are ascribed to the differences among the two experimental conditions. The effect of relevant disturbing factors in the form of interest, attitude, ability, and experience is largely equated by using the subjects in every condition. Other disturbing factors may arise, however, such as those of fatigue and practice effect, and these must be held constant or eliminated before the findings can be attributed to the differences introduced in the experimental conditions.

The Procedure of Successive Practice. This is an adaptation of the procedure of self-control. The subject engages in the several conditions of the experiment, repeating them several times in different orders so as to equalize the effects of fatigue, practice, changes in incentive, and the like which arise during the experiment. The factors of interest, attitude, ability, and past experience are presumed to be held constant through self-control. It will be noted that the procedure discussed in Chap. 12, of counterbalancing experimental conditions to minimize factors arising in the order of these conditions, exploits the method of successive practice in distributing equally to all conditions any variation arising from factors not part of the experimental variable. Predisposing interest, attitude, ability, and experience factors are held constant through the procedure of self-control.

The procedure of successive practice is used in experiments on transfer of training. Here the problem is to find whether training on task A influences the performance on task B. If the transfer and control groups are matched, then the transfer group performs task A followed by task B, whereas the control group performs only task B. The procedure of self-control is functioning in the transfer group. In some transfer experiments it may be impossible to form matched groups, in which case it is necessary to devise and utilize equated tasks. The procedure of self-control must then be used, the subjects performing task A and then task B. It should be apparent that under these conditions the two tasks of A and B must be equated, otherwise there is no way of determining whether any obtained difference is a transfer effect or is due to a variation in the tasks.

SELECTED READINGS

Buxton, C. E.: Studying Memory and Transfer, in T. G. Andrews (ed.), "Methods of Psychology," chap. 3, John Wiley & Sons, Inc., 1948. Basic experimental designs are described for the areas of learning, retention, and transfer. For each of these areas examples are presented illustrating how different kinds of variables can be manipulated for measurement purposes. Variables that are illustrated are found in the learner, the learning task, the practice conditions, the retention test, the retention period, and the transfer task.

Hovland, C. I., A. A. Lumsdaine, and F. D. Sheffield: Experiments on Mass Communication, vol. 3, Appendix C, of "Studies in Social Psychology in World War II," Princeton University Press, 1949. This appendix presents a comparison of the *before-after* and the *after-only* methods of experimental design, and discusses the types of analyses possible with the two methods.

Lindsley, D. B.: Studying Neuropsychology and Bodily Functions, in T. G. Andrews (ed.), "Methods of Psychology," chap. 15, John Wiley & Sons, Inc., 1948. A brief review is given of some of the methods used in the investigation of the relationships between behavior and different structural and functional aspects of nervous processes and other bodily functions. Procedures discussed include those used in studying the development of the nervous system, behavioral changes correlated with delimitation of the nervous system brought about by pathology or special operative techniques, changes incident to stimulation of selected parts of the nervous system, electropotential changes detected along nervous pathways during various forms of response, and behavioral changes correlated with various conditions in the internal environment of the body.

CHAPTER 14

Some Procedures for Quantifying Behavior

The most profitable form of description involves the measurement of the phenomenon under study. Measurement requires us to apply some meaning of numbers to the phenomenon. In order to measure we must discover a characteristic of the phenomenon that exists in more than one value or amount, that is, a characteristic that has magnitude, and then we must express the amount of the characteristic in some acceptable unit of measurement. If the characteristic is amenable to the number meaning that we wish to apply, then by expressing the characteristic in quantitative terms we achieve a form of description of the phenomenon upon which wide agreement can be obtained.

Before discussing specific quantitative procedures, we should have in mind what is meant by the phrase behavior change. Interpreted broadly, we mean any change we can observe in the individual. There is then a very wide variety of responses for which we shall need quantitative procedures. We shall need to measure objectively expressed behavior, that is, all kinds of overt responses, and we shall need to measure subjectively expressed behavior, that is, all kinds of experience. We shall need to subdivide the overt responses into many classes, which extend along a continuum of complexity from the simple reflexes at one end to the very complex behaviors observed in the interpersonal relationships of social adjustment at the other end. We shall also need to subdivide the subjective reactions into many classes, which extend from the sensory experiences of the more simple type to the complex mental processes involved in the highest forms of reasoning.

At the outset we should understand that the accuracy of measurement is directly conditioned by the particular nature of the behavior we wish to quantify. In contrasting objective and subjective behavior, we shall find the objective more amenable to measurement. In contrasting motor and mental behavior, we shall find the motor more amenable to measurement. In contrasting reflexive and interpersonal behavior, we shall find the reflexive more amenable to measurement. In contrasting the measurement of single isolated characteristics with the measurement of integrated molar forms of behavior, we shall find the former more amenable to measurement.

It is not our intention in this chapter to describe a particular measurement procedure for every one of these several kinds of behavior change. Rather, the principal types of measurement will be discussed within which various adaptations can be found that are applicable to the many kinds of behavior change that will need to be measured.

SOURCES OF ERROR IN QUANTIFYING PSYCHOLOGICAL VARIABLES

We can better understand measurement procedures if we are aware of some of the ways through which error may be introduced. Several times in previous chapters we have had occasion to indicate how mistakes may occur in the application of the scientific method. When committed, many of these mistakes will be reflected as errors in the quantitative description of the variables.

The Definition and Delimitation of the Variables as a Source of Error. We should carefully define and delimit the behavior to be studied before selecting the appropriate measurement procedures. It might be said that we cannot measure any behavior that we do not understand. This statement is not entirely correct. One purpose of quantifying a variable is to gain a better understanding of it. Measurement is a step on the way to understanding. It is necessary to try our hand at measuring a poorly defined variable as a means of gaining an improved definition of it. Right from the beginning, however, the behavior to be quantified should be described as accurately as possible.

Inadequate definition of the problem means errors in determining the appropriate responses to be observed. Having decided what kind of behavior we are going to study, we must then determine what specific responses are expressions or samples of this behavior and carefully define and describe these responses. It is through these individual responses that we measure the predispositions involved in testing the theorems of the problem.

Since the conduct of the study may require the utilization of several observers, we must make the descriptions so clear and comprehensive that any qualified observer can understand them and thus can gain an exact knowledge of the specific responses he is to describe. It should not be left to the observer to decide during the course of an observation whether or not a given response being noted fits into the categories worked out for the investigation. Opportunity to make such errors should not arise, for they will adversely affect the accuracy of measurement of the variables.

Let us illustrate a problem in definition from the field of attitude measurement. In the use of attitude scales, the specific attitude to be measured must be selected and defined by the experimenter. Accuracy of measurement is dependent upon having a single attitude represented on the continuum. All statments on the scale must revolve around one and only one attitude. If more than one attitude is represented on the continuum, then the particular response called out from a given subject by the scale will be a function of which attitude is activated at the time the subject makes his decision. For example, in reference to such an issue as prohibition there may be several attitudes. An individual may interpret the statements in terms of the issue of individual freedom and be unfavorable toward prohibition because it is restrictive of the rights of the individual. Or he may interpret the statements in terms of public morals and be favorable toward prohibition because he feels it would curb drunkenness. Or he may interpret the scaled items in terms of the prescriptions of his religion and favor prohibition because it agrees with his religious creed. These three reactions reflect three different attitudes, not one. Which one of the three will be reflected in the subject's responses to a set of scaled statements can be controlled to a large extent by adequately defining and delimiting the attitude variable. Further control is achieved in a careful selection of the statements. This selection should be based on quantitative procedures for determining the validity and consistency of each item and not upon subjective judgments made by the investigator about the validities and consistencies of the items.

The Registration of the Behavior Change as a Source of Error. As we learned earlier, registration refers to the procedure of making a record of what happens in an experiment. A broad interpretation of registration would include a consideration of the rigor with which the whole experimental procedure is followed.

Obviously, registration must be made of the behavior changes that follow from the variations introduced in the experimental variables. The particular meanings that can be applied to these changes are those made possible through the records. This is to say that changes in behavior that are not registered are lost, and therefore no meanings about these changes become available for subsequent analysis. Only those meanings made permanent by registration are manipulable in the logical and statistical analyses through which generalizations are evolved from the experimental results. Registration, then, directly shapes the particular quantitative description that can issue from any study.

Registration is involved in the appropriate presentation of the experimental stimuli. It has to do with the determination of the type of stimuli to be presented and with all of the characteristics of these stimuli, such as duration, position, amount of exposure, etc. It thus determines in an important way how successfully the desired behavior will be elicited for observation and measurement.

Registration is associated with the standardization of the experimental conditions so that a representative sampling of the behavior of each subject is obtained. It aids in minimizing variations in experimental procedures which might result in differences in exposure to crucial experimental stimuli. It thus determines how accurately the behavior of each subject is represented in the quantitative analysis.

In addition to recording the functioning of systematic variables, registration includes the recording of changes resulting from unsystematic variables. It thus is part of the procedure by which chance factors are brought under control for purposes of evaluation. It is the basis on which the chance factors are separated from the experimental factors, a step that must be taken before any quantitative evaluation can be made of the theorem being tested.

With this broader conception of registration it should be apparent that errors of registration can directly result in errors of measurement. Failure to register accurately the quantitative variation in either the experimental stimuli or the consequent responses makes possible errors in the measurement of the functional relationships under study. Failure to record variations in factors not part of the experimental variables results in error in the evaluation of chance factors. The quantitative changes that might be attributed to the experimental variables remain muddied by the possible effects of these other factors. It becomes impossible to determine the magnitude of the chance errors and thus it is impossible to make an accurate quantitative analysis of the effects of the experimental variables.

MEASUREMENT BY FREQUENCY OF OCCURRENCE

The use of frequency of occurrence in measuring behavior change was discussed in Chap. 6. It is briefly mentioned again because of its widespread usefulness in the quantitative description of behavior.

The Unit of Measurement in the Method. The amount characteristic involved in this method is the frequency of occurrence of some given unit of behavior. The behavior may be either an overt response or a subjective experience. The unit of behavior—the response or the experience—becomes the unit of measurement. In determining the number of occurrences of this unit of behavior all manifestations that satisfy the definition of the unit are considered equal for purposes of being counted. We are not to infer that these manifestations are equal in terms of all of their characteristics. They must be equal only in those meanings used to define the behavior for counting purposes. For example, the number of times a worker is late for work can be used as a measure of his effectiveness. The behavior of "being late for work" is first precisely defined.

Then every occurrence of lateness satisfying this definition is considered to contribute equally to the judgment about the worker's effectiveness. If the length of time the worker is late is made part of the definition, then the occasions of lateness are classified according to amount, using some such categories as the following: 0–5 minutes, 6–10 minutes, over 10 minutes. Here an amount characteristic is being used in association with the frequency of occurrence of the late behavior.

The Importance of Accurately Defining the Variable. This point needs little further amplification. It should be obvious that if the unit of behavior is the unit of measurement, there can be accurate measurement only when there is accurate definition of the unit of behavior. Accurate observation of the frequency of occurrence of the behavior is impossible when the behavior to be recorded is ambiguously defined. If we are to count the manifestations of a given unit of behavior we must know exactly what it is that we are observing and counting.

The Widespread Use of the Method. The method of measurement by frequency of occurrence is useful in measuring all forms of behavior change. Its application in measuring subjective experience is seen in the determination of sensory thresholds. The frequencies of occurrence of the judgments "sensation present" and "sensation absent" in association with variations in the intensity of the physical stimulus give the necessary data for the computation of the absolute intensity thresholds of sensation. The use of the method in the measurement of higher mental processes is seen in the counting of the number of right answers in tests of intelligence or the number of correct solutions of problems in reasoning. The use of the method in studying motor coordination is seen in the measurement of the time involved in the performance of a reaction, or the number of correct responses performed in a given time period.

The method of frequency of occurrence is basic to most other measurement procedures, as will be made apparent in the following sections.

MEASUREMENT BY MEANS OF HIGHLY STRUCTURED TESTS

In previous discussions we have described the procedures involved in the testing of theorems and have referred to the situations created for this purpose as tests. In the present section we shall use the word test in the sense of meaning the problematic situations devised for the purpose of measuring ability. This use arose in connection with the efforts of the psychologist to measure intelligence, and is now applied to the evaluation of all kinds of ability.

The word structure refers to the degree to which the responses of the subject are determined and channeled by the nature of the stimulating situation presented to him. In highly structured tests the responses of the subject are forced to follow certain patterns and therefore take on the particular characteristics required by the test situation. When relatively unstructured situations are used the subject is allowed great freedom in his response, and therefore the behavior he manifests is less determined by the nature of the external stimuli and more determined by the particular organization of his personality.

Tests as Measures of Psychological Predispositions. In most interpretations of test theory the objective of testing is to measure fundamental predispositions to respond, both those that are little affected by past experience and those that have been greatly influenced and shaped by past experience. The responses of an individual in any test situation can be referred to the following general factors: the current sensory stimulation, both external and internal, including symbolic stimuli; the potentials for response and the predispositions to respond that are attributable to natural endowment; and the variations and changes in natural endowment effected through the past experiences of the individual.

It should be obvious that in the testing situation the investigator is limited to manipulating certain segments of the current sensory stimulation. Through these manipulations he endeavors to introduce control over the overt and subjective responses of the subject. Most of the internal sensory stimuli in the form of intraorganic processes are beyond the experimenter's direct manipulation.

What a subject does in a test situation is supposed to be a direct function of the predispositions to respond that fall in the specific narrow areas represented in the test items. Actually, the responses of the subject are also a function of three other factors, namely, predispositions other than those being measured, internal stimuli of intraorganic origin, and objective sensory stimuli not directly associated with the test items. Each of these three factors is a potential determiner of behavior in any test situation, and when any one of them is known to have significantly contributed to the subject's performance it is usually impossible to determine the exact meaning of the test results.

Areas of Measurement by Tests. The scientific psychologist has evolved a variety of names to represent the many different predispositions to respond that he has isolated and measured. Some of the major areas in which measurements have been developed are here briefly described.

Ability. Ability is a general term that refers to the power of the individual to respond. It is used to include all other more restrictive terms that refer to the individual's response power.

Proficiency. Proficiency stands for what the individual can do at any moment, that is, without further preparation. No reference is made to whether the response is primarily determined by inherited endowments or by the experiences of the past. In proficiency we are interested in finding out what power to respond the individual can manifest at the moment.

Potentiality. This ability refers to reactions that the individual can learn to make if given the experience or training necessary but that at the moment he cannot perform. It signifies future promise, and is primarily, but not exclusively, conditioned upon inherited endowments.

Capacity refers to the highest level of ability to be expected from an individual after ample training and experience. It also is used in the sense of promise.

Aptitude. Aptitude is a broader term than potentiality. In addition to potential ability, it includes factors of proficiency, personality, temperament, and interests. It is the meaning usually applied when we speak of the promise of an individual to succeed in some global stimulus-response situation like a vocation.

Personality. Personality is the sum total of an individual's characteristics that summarizes his unique adjustments to his environment. It includes character, temperament, and, at times, attitude and interest. Behavior involved in interpersonal relationships with other members of society is an important aspect of personality. Sometimes personality is conceived as a collection of interrelated traits; at other times as a unitary whole with many divergent modes of expression.

Attitude. Attitude is defined as the way a person looks at some aspect of the world around him. It is an organization of all the perceptual, emotional, motivational, and cognitive processes resulting from his experience with that aspect and with phenomena related to it. For example, the attitude of an individual toward war is an organization of the psychological processes resulting from his past experiences in which he was exposed to situations related to war.

Interests. Organizations of motives that predispose an individual to pay attention to certain features of his environment rather than other features are called interests. They involve inherited predispositions as well as the varied past experiences associated with the particular environmental features.

The above are general categories of response. Tests are directed toward the measurement of rather specific types of responses within the broad categories considered above. An example of the more restricted areas of testing developed in the field of ability is found in the subcategories of intellectual tests developed in the Aviation Psychology Program during the Second World War. Each of the subcategories, of course, can be further subdivided into less inclusive areas. The subcategories are verbal ability, mathematics, reasoning, visualization, mechanical ability, information, perception, perceptual speed, form perception, size and distance estimation, spatial ability, orientation, set, and attention.

The Manipulation of Physical Stimuli as Test Objects. In some testing situations manipulation of physical stimuli plays the determinant role in eliciting the desired psychological behavior. For example, in tests of sensory response the quality of the stimulus usually automatically determines the sense modality of the reaction, and other characteristics of the response are associated with such features of the stimulus as its intensity, duration, location, distance, speed, repetitive nature, etc.

Manipulation of the physical aspects of the stimulating situation is necessary in the measurement of muscular activities, such as those involved in tests of motor speed, muscular coordination, and muscular strength. The timing of the response is in part a function of the speed of presentation of the stimulus. This is particularly true in pursuit tasks in which radical changes in the rate of the response can be produced by variations in the rate of movement of the stimulus target. The difficulty of the task in tests of muscular response is conditioned by the speed of movement required of the subject. Tasks requiring excessive speed may eventually produce incoordination, fatigue, anxiety, and emotional upset; a spread of change in response far beyond the rate and accuracy of the response that are actually under study.

Test situations in which manipulation of the stimulus is accomplished by means of apparatus range from simple sensory tests in which a single stimulus is presented requiring merely a verbal report from the subject to complex configurations of stimuli requiring the subject to perform simultaneously several closely interrelated and precisely timed movements of eyes, hands, and feet. In the following tests, manipulation of the stimulus by apparatus control is very important: two-hand coordination, rotary pursuit, arm-hand steadiness, self-paced path tracing, bimanual planned pursuit, blindfold bimanual coordination, visual-coincidence reaction, motor judgment, conflicting manipulations, peg moving, dial setting, speed of manipulation, triform pegboard reaction, controls-confusion response, foresight and planning maze reactions, kinesthetic discrimination, sway compensation, and stability of orientation.

The Manipulation of Symbolic Stimuli as Test Objects. Either verbal or pictorial stimuli may be used to arouse inferential meanings. The particular meanings assigned to the symbols by the subject will determine the nature of the predisposition that will be expressed and measured. It is important then that we use symbols that are understandable to the subject. Unless the test is aimed at measuring verbal ability, the symbols must be understood by the subject or the test is not measuring the particular ability for which it is intended.

Level of difficulty in a psychological ability being measured is controlled by the nature of the inferential meanings aroused by the symbols. Difficulty is a function of several characteristics of meaning, prominent among which is that of abstractness. This abstract nature of meaning always involves relationships, and so the experimenter can use relationships between symbols as the means for introducing greater and greater degrees of abstractness into the test items. A level of abstractness characterizing relationships among higher order conceptual meanings can be found that will challenge even the most brilliant minds.

The factor of difficulty requires careful study in the preparation of any symbolic test of ability because of the probability that it might elicit interfering emotional reactions. When the difficulty extends much beyond the ability of the subject, anxiety, worry, discouragement, and the like may result. In this instance the subject's responses are being partly determined by emotional predispositions rather than being solely determined by the ability predispositions which the test was designed to measure.

Literally dozens of different kinds of symbolic verbal test items have been devised for eliciting expressions of predispositions. It is possible to mention only a few of them. The following ones should be sufficiently familiar to the reader to need no further explanation: mathematical problems, reasoning problems, word-meaning puzzles, synonyms-antonyms, analogies, proverbs, substitution problems, object identification, speed of perceptual motion, problems of recall and recognition, problems of set and attention, and problems of information.

Some types of items require the use of pictorial presentation. Photographic reproductions of objects, people, machinery, landscapes, etc., may be used. Maps and charts are other media that have proved extremely successful. In order to elicit the particular type of discriminatory response that is to be evaluated, the pictorial representation is accompanied by verbal test items which are used to focus the attention of the subject on the particular concepts that he is to manipulate.

Some Response Characteristics Requiring Measurement. As we have noted, the nature of the subject's response is a function of the kind of stimuli presented, including the kind of materials or apparatus that he must manipulate. In some test situations the primary purpose is to measure the overt response for its own sake, and in others the overt response is used as an indication of the effectiveness of some sensory-intellectual judgment that is reflected in the response. For example, in testing hand steadiness, we are interested in observing the actual amount of movement in the hand itself, whereas, in testing the accuracy of response in solving reasoning problems, the overt behavior is used as a basis for making inferences about the mental processes called reasoning.

Different problems require the quantitative description of different response characteristics. A few examples will make this clear. In the simple reaction-time test, the speed of movement is primary, the direction and extent of movement are unimportant. In the simple discrimination-reaction-time test, speed and direction of movement are important and extent is unimportant. In certain more complex discrimination-reaction tests, all three characteristics of response are important. In pursuit responses, the rate and direction of movement are of primary concern, extent being of minor importance. In the steadiness test, avoidance of movement or the maintenance of a constant position is the important function.

In most tests of intellectual ability, interests, attitudes, and personality, the overt responses are reduced to very simple forms so the subject can concentrate on evolving answers to the problems presented to him. It is unnecessary to review the characteristics of predispositional responses in these areas that need description, as they have been referred to in previous discussions. Suffice it to say that the following are important characteristics: the nature or kind of response, the rate of response, the accuracy of response, and the level of difficulty at which the subject can respond satisfactorily.

The Recording of the Subject's Response. The recording of the subject's reactions is not a major problem in pencil-and-paper types of tests. The response usually consists of making some simple mark, such as a number or check, in an appropriate space near the test item.

In apparatus tests, registration sometimes may become a very difficult problem to solve. The nature of the recording procedure depends upon the type of response to be registered. Photographic and polygraphic techniques give the best continuous recording of movements. In the polygraphic method, one or more writing pens register on a continuously moving paper tape. One pen is connected with a timer and registers a time line in appropriate units such as fifths or halves of a second. Other pens can be activated by the subject as he responds to the problem he is solving. The experimenter also may use some of the pens to record facts about the subject's behavior. The analysis and evaluation of the records are a very time-consuming task, particularly if many subjects are tested. In a relatively short experimental sitting several yards of tape per subject may be accumulated. Variations in the recordings of each pen must be measured and read off accurately, which requires much time.

Sometimes different components of a complex response are measured separately, while at other times a single score is used to represent the total performance, each component making its contribution to this single score. Separately measuring the work performed by different muscle groups that are coordinated in the execution of a complex movement may be of considerable aid in understanding the effectiveness of response in work situations. For example, in assembly jobs the worker may use each hand to manipulate parts of the object being assembled, and he may at times introduce foot movements to control a lever that holds the partly assembled object in place while the hands are manipulating additional parts. The over-all effectiveness of job performance may be handicapped by ineffective reactions in some part function, and such ineffectiveness may be revealed if the part functions are scored separately.

The Evaluation of the Subject's Responses. The meaning of the test performance of any individual or group of individuals is determined by comparing it with what are called norms of performance. Test norms are the cumulative test performances of many individuals with prescribed characteristics. The value of the norms lies not simply in the numerical scores but also in the particular characteristics of the persons supplying the performances. The value of a test is a direct function of the degree to which the norm populations contain the characteristics that are meaningful for the new individuals on whom the test will be used. If we are trying to learn about the intelligence of a college freshman and use norms of an intelligence test that are based on the performance of high school freshmen and sophomores, the meaningful information we can get from his test score is extremely limited. It is the obligation of the constructor of a test to collect and supply norms from the performances of individuals representative of the groups of persons for which the test is constructed.

Various kinds of scores are available in terms of which the individual's performance can be cast. These were discussed earlier in Chap. 10 in connection with the measurement of level of achievement.

MEASUREMENT BY MEANS OF INVENTORIES AND QUESTIONNAIRES

Like tests, inventories and questionnaires are a means of presenting a series of standardized stimuli to a subject for the purpose of eliciting certain kinds of response. The term questionnaire as used here refers to the highly standardized instrument that is carefully constructed for measurement purposes, and not to the more commonly used assemblage of questions hurriedly put together merely to collect information.

Contrasted with tests, which in the main are concerned with abilities, inventories and questionnaires are focused on discovering the preferences of the individual. In the use of these procedures the emphasis is upon attributing the response to some condition within the individual which is more or less enduring in nature. This is to say that the responses are elicited and studied as indices of some fundamental predisposition within the individual which functions as a determiner of his preferences.

The Logic of Measurement by Means of Inventories and Questionnaires. Doubt has been expressed that these instruments can be used to measure behavior, and so it is appropriate that we here briefly restate certain arguments presented earlier. Inventories and questionnaires can be used to quantify responses by the procedure of frequency of occurrence. Only in the sense that units of behavior are being counted and these counts used to describe and compare differences in the behavior represented are we justified in attributing measurement to these two procedures.

Doubt also has been expressed that a predisposition to respond can be reflected in the replies made to items of the type used in these procedures. Admittedly, there is a distinct difference between a question that presents a problem for which the subject must supply a solution (as in ability tests) and a question that requires the person to reveal a preference or make a statement of fact connected with his past behavior (as in inventories and questionnaires). The difference, however, is not one between measurement and nonmeasurement. In either instance a series of responses is elicited from the subject and these responses are counted and evaluated as descriptions of certain of his predispositions. The logic underlying the two types of measurement is the same.

Two objectives must be realized in order to accomplish measurement by inventories and questionnaires; namely, items must be devised that elicit replies that are valid reflections of the given predispositions to be measured, and items must be devised that elicit replies that are representative of the predispositions of the individual being examined. If these two conditions are realized, then measurement by frequency of occurrence is justified in inventory and questionnaire procedures.

The Validity of Items. An inventory or a questionnaire is a valid instrument of measurement only when it has been empirically demonstrated to be so. This principle immediately removes from consideration as measuring instruments inventories and questionnaires that base their usefulness solely on the judgment and beliefs of the persons who construct them. These latter devices can be used to collect information, but statistical treatment of the data for the purpose of quantitatively assessing individual behavior is not justified.

Empirical validation demands that the scores derived from an inventory or questionnaire be demonstrated to agree highly with some other reliable device that measures the differences or the relationships involved in the description. A simple illustration will make this clear. Suppose we wish to measure differences in vocational interests in reference to the medical profession. First we learn the various ways in which interests in medicine are expressed and select those that can be represented in terms of verbal statements. These statements are then tried out on physicians who are known by acceptable criteria to be successful and on other vocational groups having interests divergent from those of physicians. Those items are retained on which physicians score high and other vocational groups score low. An individual whose score on these items agrees with the scores of successful physicians is said to have the interests common to the medical profession. Individuals will vary in the degree to which their scores agree with those of successful physicians, and this variation in frequency of occurrence of similar responses is interpreted as representing differing amounts or degrees of interest in medicine. Only in this sense are we justified in claiming that we are measuring interests in medicine.

The Representativeness of the Subject's Responses. When it has been demonstrated that an inventory or questionnaire is valid, accurate measurement of a particular person's predispositions depends upon the degree to which his responses truly represent his predispositions. The items must elicit responses that reflect his predispositions, and these responses must accurately and comprehensively reveal the nature and organization of these predispositions. Any purposeful distortion of the responses by the subject in order to conceal his predispositions results in invalid measurement. This way of responding is called faking.

Faking refers to the attempt on the part of the subject to manifest responses that do not accurately reflect his predispositions. We know that on many of the occasions in which measures of predispositions are needed, the subject is being evaluated in reference to some subsequent adjustment situation, such as entrance into a school to which he has applied, or being hired for a job that he desires, or selecting a permanent vocational career, etc. It is quite natural for him to want to give the best performance he can. For some subjects this means that the replies should be oriented toward making the best impression relative to the subsequent adjustment situation rather than toward revealing accurately the predispositions under study. This faking or cheating results in unrepresentativeness in the responses and therefore invalid measurement.

Although this source of error should be eradicated, it should not be interpreted as making measurement impossible. We must keep in mind the fact that there are many situations in which inventories and questionnaires are used where the subjects give honest answers and do not endeavor in any way to manipulate their replies for ulterior purposes. Furthermore, faking may be minimized by using items in which the content cannot readily be associated by the subject with the particular predispositions being measured. In some of the better inventories procedures have been evolved for detecting faked responses.

Types of Stimulus Items. In using an inventory or questionnaire the usual procedure is to present the subject with a list of statements or questions and ask him to check those that describe activities that he likes to perform or that characterize his behavior. Sometimes an item will allow the subject to make one of three responses such as like, indifferent, or dislike. Another type of three-choice-response situation is illustrated by an item from an inventory on suggestibility. The subject was required to select one of the following three possible answers:

In complete agreement with the experts
Agree with the experts, but with reservations
Disagree with the experts

In adjustment inventories, statements are selected that reflect behavior found in major life-adjustment situations, such as the home, the school, the play yard, etc. The statements are so framed as to represent different kinds of adjustive responses, and the subject selects the responses that characterize his own behavior. Following are some sample items:

Do you sleep well at night?
Are you annoyed when people push ahead of you in a line?
Would you rather read a book or go to baseball game?

Items are sometimes formed of pairs of statements, the subject being required to select one statement of each pair. This type of item is used in some vocational-interest inventories. A number of vocational pursuits are arranged in pairs, each vocation being paired with every other one. The subject is required to indicate in each pair the vocation he would prefer to follow. His vocational interests can then be described by determining the particular vocations that have the highest preference ratings.

The Evaluation of the Subject's Responses. A subject's responses to an inventory or questionnaire are quantitatively expressed by using the method of frequency of occurrence. An evaluation of his responses consists in comparing them with norms collected from populations having the particular characteristics that are being described. For example, in measuring interest in the medical profession, the subject's responses are interpreted in terms of their similarity with the responses of successful physicians.

Successful evaluation depends upon obtaining adequate population norms, for it is through these norms that the necessary meanings are obtained for understanding the subject's responses. Both the qualitative and quantitative meanings of the subject's score depend upon their relation with the norms. The kinds of answers made to the items by an appropriate comparison population aids in interpreting the qualitative nature of the subject's performance and thus minimizes the need for the subjective interpretations of the investigator. Similarly, the full quantitative meaning of the subject's score is unknown without the norms from a comparison population. Suppose a person answers seven out of ten items on an adjustment inventory in a manner indicating that he might be having difficulty in his social adjustments. The full meaning of 7 in 10 cannot be determined simply from these two numbers. Without a comparable population norm for these items, meaning can be evolved only by imposing the subjective judgment of the investigator. This, of course, is subject to grave unreliability.

MEASUREMENT BY MEANS OF UNSTRUCTURED STIMULUS SITUATIONS

Measuring instruments in which there is little attempt to set up prescribed stimulus-response relationships are described as unstructured. Actually, all measuring situations are structured to some degree for the subject. What is meant by unstructured is really a relatively low degree of structuring of the stimulus situation.

Unstructured testing situations are primarily concerned with discovering the organization underlying the predispositions that form an individual's personality. The organization of the personality is presumed to be revealed in the observable behavior of the individual. To get this organization reflected in behavior it is necessary to use unstructured situations. The subject's behavior will then be determined by the relative strengths and interrelationships of his predispositions rather than by the structure imposed by the test situation. These unstructured situations are commonly called projective tests.

The Purpose of Using Unstructured Stimulus Situations. The primary aim of unstructured situations is to observe personality in action, to provide a stimulating situation that will encourage the subject to project the thoughts, feelings, motivations, attitudes, etc., that are characteristic of his personality. In order to do this the experimenter and the test situation should contribute as little as possible to the nature of the specific responses. The fewer the restrictions placed upon the responses, the greater will be the chances of eliciting behavior that is representative of the personality of the subject. Although unstructured test situations do not provide opportunity for completely free responses, the stimuli they do provide are near-natural in character, and thus the situations tend to elicit near-natural types of responses.

One of the primary objectives of unstructured tests is to reduce the subject's purposeful control of his responses. The tests are planned to minimize the possibility of the subject's selecting and manifesting only those responses that are of the socially approved type or which in some way are satisfactory to him but not representative of his personality and inhibiting other forms of response that are not socially approved or which at that moment are not satisfying to the subject. What is wanted are responses characteristic of the inner dispositions and not just responses that the individual is willing to put on display for others to observe. What is needed, then, is a form of stimulating situation that will elicit a very wide range of responses which will reflect the many facets of the personality. The wider the range of responses, the higher the chances of eliciting behavior that is representative of the personality.

Inasmuch as the subject may be wary of revealing any responses that are in any sense unsocial, it is desirable to prevent him from knowing the particular purpose of the testing. If his cooperation can be elicited without his becoming concerned with the nature of the situation to which he is asked to respond, purposeful control of his responses will be greatly reduced. The more the test situation is structured, the more readily can the subject discern the possible uses that might be made of his performance, and the greater the likelihood that he will introduce conscious control over his responses.

Sometimes inner motivating conditions are active without the individual's being conscious of them; that is, there are features of behavior that even the individual cannot trace to known purposes or desires on his part. It is important that these features of personality be studied, and it is doubly difficult to detect and describe them when the subject purposely decides on the type of response he is going to make.

The Structuring of the Situation by the Subject. It should be remembered that the word structure refers to the meaningfulness of the stimulating situation that is determined by the organization imposed on the stimulus elements. With unstructured stimuli, a minimum of organization of the stimulus elements is imposed by the experimenter. Great freedom is allowed the subject to structure the situation for himself. The specific meanings assigned the stimulus elements are largely contributed by the subject in terms of his own perceptual, emotional, rational, attitudinal, etc., predispositions.

Kinds of Stimuli. A wide variety of verbal and pictorial stimuli have been utilized in projective tests. Only a few can be described here. One of the very early types of verbal stimulation is the list of stimulus words used in the free-association test. The nature and relationships of the "deeper" characteristics of the personality are presumably exposed in the meaningfulness exhibited in the stimulus-response relationships that the subject forms by his replies and by other characteristics of his behavior that reveal emotional disturbances connected with certain stimulus areas. A more complex verbal type of test situation requires the subject to tell a story, which is then used as a means of interpreting his personality. The nature of the content of the story, the plot, the characters, the manner of telling it, and any other aspects of the story situation are studied in order to discover the make-up of the subject's personality.

A form of pictorial stimulus, which is relatively unstructured, is the cloud pictures. There are three pictures, each consisting of cloudlike masses shaded in different tones of gray, nonsymmetrical in shape and indefinite in outline. The subject is shown a picture and asked to tell what he sees. The meaningless nature of the forms is conducive to a wide range of responses. Another unstructured stimulus consists of photographs of ambiguous pictures, usually containing human figures. The blurring of the outline of the objects represented, the indefiniteness of design, and the lack of detail make the pictures rather ambiguous in meaning. The subject is asked to tell the story that he thinks a picture depicts. The Thematic Apperception Test is a widely used test of this kind.

Kinds of Responses Observed. There are no restrictions on the kinds of responses that the investigator may use in his analysis of the personality. Overt movements, subtle gestures, inflections of voice, signs of inhibiting response, as well as the content of verbal expressions contribute to the analysis.

The uniqueness of a subject's responses is of vital concern. If the personality of a given individual is to be understood, we must learn how he differs from other individuals. It is important then to discover the unique meanings that a given individual places upon the stimulus-response relationships of the test situation. The investigator must closely observe in a subject the interplay among the perceptual, emotional, rational, and other forms of response if he is to determine successfully the meaning any given response has for the subject at the time it is manifest.

The Recording of the Subject's Responses. No attempt is made to obtain a record of all the subject's responses, but permanent registration of the more significant phases of his responses is attempted. If the subject does not make a record of his performance, as in a written completion of a story, the investigator usually takes notes. Forms for recording responses by shorthand symbols make possible rather full accounts of the behavior. It is necessary that the activity of recording not contribute significantly to the structuring of the test situation; therefore, there is little use made of any kind of instrumental registration unless it is accomplished without disturbance to the subject.

The Evaluation of the Subject's Responses. In an unstructured stimulus situation, the responses are studied not in their own right as adaptive responses to prescribed stimuli, but as indices of the more general personality organization that presumably pervades all of the individual's responses. The meaning to be assigned any given response is determined primarily in terms of its integration with other responses comprising the personality, and so this meaning will vary with changes in the specific conditions under which the response occurs. It is then possible for the same response to have different meanings in different contexts even though it is a manifestation of the same personality.

The responses observed in an unstructured stimulus situation are specific in nature; the personality to be described is general in nature. The responses are then rationally manipulated in ways that promise to shed light on the nature of the inner personality mechanisms. This is accomplished by means of rational constructs derived to a large extent through the intuitive judgment of the experimenter. Some of these constructs are far removed from empirically observed facts, as, for example, the concept of reified unconscious. Other constructs hew closer to empirical evidence and get their characteristic meanings primarily from observable data, as, for example, the concept of conflict.

For the most part, procedures for scoring and evaluating the subject's responses are not highly standardized. For most test situations, the norms are not objectively and statistically derived as in tests of ability. Rather, they are frequently based upon the subjective values found in the psychological, logical, and philosophical points of view of the investigator. These subjectively derived norms are applied to the responses during the rational analysis. Not being objectified, they cannot be readily submitted to empirical check by other investigators. Admittedly, a great amount of research must still be accomplished on projective-test situations before they can be accepted as reliable and valid scientific measuring instruments.

MEASUREMENT BY MEANS OF RATINGS

Rating procedures are primarily concerned with obtaining accurate quantitative descriptions of global types of behavior. Some notion of the widespread use of ratings can be obtained from the following types of response to which they have been applied: attitudes, opinions, beliefs, preferences, personality traits, character traits, abilities, and interests. In some procedures the behavior to be rated is elicited by means of experimentally controlled stimuli, and in others the behavior results from uncontrolled naturalistic stimuli.

Kinds of Measurement in Rating Procedures. *Expert Judgment Based on Observation of Behavior.* In this procedure the quantifying of the behavior is based on the judgment of a so-called expert, e.g., a teacher in a schoolroom, an officer in a military unit, a foreman in a working gang. More than one judge is usually necessary to get an accurate measurement. A rating scale may be used. This consists of a series of statements or paragraph descriptions describing the characteristics of the responses that the judge is to evaluate. The scale may provide a line on which the judge indicates the quantitative value of the response, or it may provide a series of categories representing different amounts, and the judge chooses that category that best describes the subject being rated.

In this procedure the judge making the rating must have had the opportunity of observing the specific responses to be evaluated as they were performed by the particular individual being assessed. This requirement can be met in two ways. In one procedure, acquaintance judges are used; that is, persons do the rating who through their past associations with the subject have observed him behave in situations in which the responses being measured would normally be expressed. In the other procedure, an experiment is devised in which the subjects are placed in a stimulating situation that would normally call out the behavior to be assessed, and the judge observes a subject respond before making an evaluation of him.

Self-appraisal. In this procedure the subject rates or judges himself. With adults, some form of scale is used to represent or portray the response to be evaluated, and the subject checks that point on the scale that he thinks best represents his own behavior. Self-appraisal may be used with children by presenting behavior situations in the form of descriptive statements in which some personal characteristic is being varied and asking the child to select the statement that best describes his own way of doing things. Self-appraisal procedures have significant application when the child's notions about himself are being studied.

Many attitude scales utilize the self-appraisal method. The individual examines a list of scaled statements and selects those that he considers represent his own thinking and convictions on the issue involved.

Comparison of Products with Scaled Samples. This procedure contains two parts, namely, a sample response or product made by the subject who is to be evaluated, and a set of samples of the same type of response, which have been scaled on a particular continuum in terms of their quality, excellence, or some other similar meaning. The task of the rater is not one of estimating the quality of the subject's sample but rather of determining that specimen on the scale that is most nearly like the sample product of the subject. The score given to the subject's response is the score of the scaled specimen that the judge selects.

Two Types of Stimuli in Rating Procedures. In using rating procedures it is necessary to distinguish two types of stimuli, namely, those that elicit the behavior in the subject who is to be rated, and those influencing the judge at the time he is making his evaluation. When an experimental situation is created to elicit the behavior to be rated, both types of stimuli are present in the measurement situation. Of particular importance is the fact that the judge is in the situation and gets firsthand and immediate observational data for his rating. When a judge is asked to rate a person from his past acquaintance with him, the stimuli on the rating scale or rating form are used to aid the judge in understanding the behavior to be evaluated so he will be more likely to recall from his past experience those particular responses of the subject that are pertinent. Of course, the stimuli that led the subject to make the particular responses recalled by the judge are usually unknown and indeterminable.

In measurement by use of ratings, the purpose of the general instructions of the rating procedure and of the specific items on any scale that is used is to acquaint the judge with the characteristics of behavior that are to be rated. It is intended that these verbal stimuli will elicit recall and evaluative reactions in the judge and will direct and restrict these recall and evaluative reactions to the particular behavior to be measured. These stimuli then contribute significantly to the determination of the particular responses that are rated, even though they are not the stimuli that elicited responses in the subject himself.

The two types of stimuli are found in attitude measurement. The area of attitude being measured is delineated by general descriptions of the scale and by the individual statements comprising the scale. These stimuli, however, do not determine the attitude of the subject; they merely function to elicit reactions of recall, reasoning, comparison, etc., by which the subject determines those items that depict an attitude in agreement with his own.

An Illustration of an Experimental Situation for Rating Behavior. An experimental situation created to present stimuli to subjects so their behavior can be observed and rated is illustrated in the play yard of a nursery school. In the experimental play yard, stimuli are presented in the form of toys, swings, other children, etc., which are known to elicit the responses that are to be evaluated. The judge observes the behavior of a given child as he responds to the stimuli and describes the various characteristics of the child's responses, such as kind, frequency, intensity, duration, etc. Immediately after the observation period the judge rates the child on the particular behaviors under study.

The Recording of the Subject's Responses. In most rating situations, records of the subject's responses that are to be rated are not available. The judge is usually dependent upon the accuracy of his recall of concrete expressions of the responses as he remembers them performed by the subject. Actually, what frequently happens is that the judge, being an acquaintance of the subject, has already formed certain general notions about him, and these general notions form the basis of the evaluation. This is one of the significant sources of error in the use of various rating procedures when experimental situations are not used. Unless the general notions of the rater have been accurately formed and directly concern the particular responses that are to be evaluated, they will inevitably lead to an unreliable and invalid evaluation of the subject.

In recent years, motion-picture cameras and sound-recording devices have made possible rather comprehensive records of behavior, which can then be observed many times before any final judgment is formulated. Such instrumental registration, however, can be used in only a small proportion of the total number of situations for which the rating method of measurement is applicable.

The Accuracy of Measurement by Ratings. The accuracy of measurement by ratings depends directly upon getting the judge, or the subject if he is functioning as a judge, to do a conscientious job of evaluation. It is possible to get a measure that is completely fictitious. For example, in attitude measurement not every individual who is measured on a particular attitude scale has crystallized his attitude on the issues being represented. The question arises as to what is measured when an individual responds to an attitude scale when he really has not formed an attitude about the issue. Similarly, in the use of ratings by expert judges, a rater may not have an adequate understanding of the responses being assessed, or if he has an adequate understanding he may not have had an opportunity to observe the individual being rated in the appropriate situations reflecting these responses. Yet in either case he will follow the prescribed rating procedures and evolve an evaluation of the subject. Again, the question arises as to what has been measured in such an instance.

THE INTERVIEW AS A DATA-COLLECTING PROCEDURE

Like the other procedures thus far discussed, the interview is a means of collecting data about a subject's behavior. The term interview stands for a generic concept which includes a variety of procedures used in collecting data through a person-to-person contact between an interviewer and a respondent. An interview may be conducted in a casual manner and the respondent may then not even be aware that he is being interviewed, or it may be highly formalized, requiring special physical facilities and adhering to a thoroughly standardized routine.

The Scientific Status of Interviewing Procedures. Interviewing varies widely in respect to its scientific worth. As a method for studying the determinant relationships of a given behavior phenomenon, it is a difficult procedure and subject to many pitfalls. In the hands of an untrained person an interview is worthless, being reduced to a biased selection of replies made to a series of questions the stimulating value of which is to a large extent unknown and unknowable.

We are interested in the interview as a scientific instrument. When carefully planned in regard to purpose, questions, observations, record taking, and analysis of results, the interview assumes the characteristics of a scientific procedure. Unplanned, with variable purposes and questioning procedures, with biases of the interviewer entering into the selection, recording, and analysis of the material, it may become completely unreliable and invalid. It then cannot be dignified with the name of science.

Some Advantages of Interview Procedures. One advantage of the interview is its flexibility. For certain kinds of fact collecting it is very desirable to have a procedure that can be varied to meet the demands of the moment. In measuring human behavior it is not possible to solve all problems by exposing every individual to standardized and invariable procedures. Differences are sometimes more readily detected by varying the measuring procedure than by keeping it constant. It is true, of course, that in the process of varying the procedure the measurement ceases to be identical for different individuals. The resulting error may or may not be of serious consequence. Comparisons of different persons will be adversely affected, and when quantitative values are involved such comparisons are not justified. In the evaluation of a given person, the errors may be inconsequential. This is true when we need to obtain all of the knowledge we can about an individual. For example, we may primarily want to know about John Smith as an individual, and not about John Smith as a member of a group.

Another significant characteristic of the interview is that it provides a situation for gaining knowledge about behavior that is closely associated with underlying personality predispositions. As in the case of unstructured stimulus situations, this behavior is considered a manifestation of inner conditions which can be reached only by inference through rational analysis. Any conclusion is then subject to the errors of the intuitive judgment of the interviewer.

A further advantage is the possibility afforded in the interview situation of gaining ideas about the interrelatedness and interactions of responses of different kinds. The human personality is to be interpreted as a unified whole, but the structure of that unity is not easy to discover. In the interview the interplay of different stimulus-response relationships may be revealed, thus giving knowledge of the inner organization of the personality structure. Again, the accuracy of interpreting the results rests largely on the skill of the interviewer.

The Stimulus Situation in Interviewing Procedures. There are many kinds of questions that can be used in interviewing. One characteristic of all questions is the degree to which they structure the respondent's replies. Two forms of questions that represent the two extremes of this characteristic are the fixed-response question and the free-response question. Degrees of structuring, of course, exist between these two extreme forms. The fixed-response question affords greatest control over the stimulus-response relationships that are to be elicited. Its main deficiency is a tendency for it to arouse defense reactions in the respondent when the content of the question concerns personal-social behavior. The free-response question overcomes this limitation in some measure, but in so doing it produces an unstructured situation in which the control of the stimulus-response relationships passes from the interviewer to the respondent. The meanings of the responses must then be interpreted in terms of their own interrelationships rather than in terms of a known objective set of stimuli provided in the form of precise questions.

The interviewer plays a very significant role in the stimulus situation. Even when his primary job is to administer a set of highly standardized questions, his manner of executing the procedures can have a definite effect upon the nature of the results obtained. His influence on the recall, thinking, and verbalization of the respondent can have a determinant effect on the particular sequences of behavior that are revealed. It is then of prime importance to have well-trained interviewers.

The Response Situation in Interviewing Procedures. When a highly structured interview is conducted, a direct control is presumed to be effected over the stimulus-response relationships that are elicited. This is true if there is no prefabrication of erroneous responses or if there are no defensive replies that distort the responses from those characteristic of the respondent. When there is no structuring of the interview, any manipulation of the respondent's replies is accomplished after the interview is completed. By a process of selection those responses pertinent to the particular problem being investigated are discovered and subjected to special analysis.

It is often important that a full record be made of what transpires in an interview situation. The immediate use made of the collected material is not the only use that may be made of it. Individuals other than the interviewer may have to evaluate the material, and they can do an adequate job only if they have a fairly comprehensive record of the interview proceedings.

The Evaluation of the Respondent's Replies. Highly structured interviews are amenable to quantitative treatment. The method of measurement by frequency of occurrence is applicable if the conditions of this method are met. For example, in consumer-research investigations it is possible to design interviews so that statistical methods can be applied to measure the effects of different factors on the purchasing and use of a given commodity. It is known that economic level, amount of education, age, number of persons in the family, and similar factors influence the buying of goods. By correctly designing the study and interviewing a sample of consumers in whom these several factors are found as they occur in the actual market situation, we can determine the relationships between the factors and consumer-buying behavior as these relationships are revealed in the use of a particular brand of some commodity.

In the unstructured interview the evaluation of the respondent's replies depends on the subjective judgment of the interviewer. Obviously, accurate quantitative description of the respondent's behavior is difficult, if not impossible, to achieve.

SELECTED READINGS

Goodenough, F. L.: The Measurement of Mental Growth in Childhood, in L. Carmichael (ed.), "Manual of Child Psychology," 2d ed., chap. 8, John Wiley & Sons, Inc., 1954. Many of the early developments in quantifying global types of behavior were made in devising measures of intelligence for children, and a large proportion of the concepts in psychological measurements are associated with intelligence tests. In this chapter the author gives a brief survey of the results of measurement studies on the mental growth of children. Among the topics discussed are the following: the nature and organization of intelligence, the quantification of intellectual performance, mental growth curves, and the modifiability of intelligence.

Guilford, J. P.: "Psychometric Methods," 2d ed., chap. 15, McGraw-Hill Book Company, Inc., 1954. The logic underlying the construction and evaluation of mental tests and attitude scales is presented. The reader can understand much of this logic without working through the more technical mathematical parts of the discussion.

Jahoda, M., M. Deutsch, and S. W. Cook: "Research Methods in Social Relations," vol. 1, chaps. 6 and 7, The Dryden Press, Inc., 1951. Chapter 6 deals with interviews, questionnaires, and scaling techniques. Chapter 7 provides descriptions of disguised methods including the projective techniques.

CHAPTER 15

Scientific Method in Field-type Studies

In order to perfect their methods, the earlier scientists went "indoors" and set up laboratories where they could create simple experimental situations that would yield to the analytical approach. Above all else, experimentation demands control of variables, and science was developed in a restricted environment in order to achieve this goal. The outcome was what we know as modern laboratory science.

Laboratory experimentation has proved itself a forceful method for attacking behavior problems. It has pioneered the way in nearly every phase of psychological science. Through it enormous numbers of facts have been collected, scores of procedures have been devised, thousands of determinant variables have been evaluated, and large numbers of explanatory concepts and principles have been evolved.

With the formulation of a large number of dependable procedures the scientific psychologist in recent years has broadened his interest to include problems that are not amenable to study in the rigorous laboratory environment. Laboratory experimentation is still vigorous and fertile in achievement, but today, with greater refinement in methods, the psychologist is directing his attack upon the more intangible and global complexes of behavior that are not readily re-created in a laboratory.

The present chapter is concerned with nonlaboratory or field-type studies. First we shall consider factors that historically have led to the application of scientific method to field-type problems. In the remainder of the chapter four field-type experiments are described. The first investigation is developed in a step-by-step progression to illustrate the application of scientific methodology under nonlaboratory conditions. The problem dealt with is the evolution and validation of a program for the selection and classification of workers. The next two examples illustrate how well-designed experiments can be executed under variable conditions in the field. The first describes an investigation of two methods used in the treatment of schizophrenia. The second is a study of human motivation in a factory. The fourth investigation is included to illustrate how ingenious procedures can be devised to overcome deficiencies of field conditions. A method is described for effecting constant stimulus conditions in a group experiment involving social interaction.

SOME HISTORICAL ANTECEDENTS OF FIELD-TYPE STUDIES

The Problem of Controlling Variables. In the beginning the psychologist utilized the physical control procedures of the natural sciences. His problems were centered on the analysis of sensation; and the light, sound, and other stimuli he used were generated and measured by the then known procedures of physical science. Procedures for registering responses were required, and he again adapted those that the natural scientists had devised.

In the areas of the more complex mental responses, the psychologist seldom could achieve the control he desired simply through the manipulation of the physical stimulating situation. As we learned in earlier chapters, he had to invent means for equating the past experiences and schooling of the subjects he used. He had to make sure that his subjects were representative of the groups that he wanted to describe. He had to isolate for separate study such global factors as home environment, economic status, and the like. He then devised procedures for controlling variables through the selection of his subjects, his materials, and his data, and by adapting to his variables the logic and analysis of mathematical statistics.

With the growth of the science, psychology developed a large number of specialized control procedures which, when they were perfected, opened up new vistas for the application of the scientific method.

The Distortion of Variables under Laboratory Conditions. When the psychologist took his problems into the laboratory, he sometimes found that the variables he studied were not exactly the same as the variables he had intended to study. The constricted and rigid conditions of the experimental laboratory had distorted the expression of the variables from that which would have been expected to occur under natural conditions. By "natural conditions" are meant the conditions under which the variables are found before action is taken to study them by scientific procedures. The controls the psychologist had so earnestly sought in the laboratory had introduced changes in the variables themselves, so they were forced to operate in ways not characteristic of their natural occurrences. For example, controls that were introduced in order to prevent variation in all but a single experimental variable prevented the simultaneous functioning of variables that normally are found operating together. Such rigorous control prevented interaction between these factors and thus freed the experimental variable from the influence of the other variables. With less rigorous physical manipulation of the factors, interaction among the variables would have contributed to the over-all effect that any variable would have manifested. Experimental variables in the laboratory were then not always representative of natural experimental variables.

From purely scientific motives the psychologist proceeded to study his variables under conditions more nearly like those of natural situations. In so doing he modified his familiar laboratory procedures and devised many new ones that were more serviceable under the new conditions.

The Inapplicability of Laboratory Methods to Some Problems. The scientific psychologist, in expanding the application of his experimental procedures, encountered situations that he could not reproduce in the laboratory. For example, the study of newborn children and the study of crowds imposed conditions that were impossible to achieve in the laboratory. The psychologist therefore took his laboratory procedures to the nursery and to the street. He proceeded to set up field studies. In some instances, as in the studies of young infants, he could duplicate his laboratory in nearly all respects; in others, such as in the study of crowds, the conditions were so radically different that the procedures developed no longer resembled those of the laboratory.

In the field situation the problem of finding the relative importance of the several factors conditioning an event still remained central. The psychologist still wanted to separate the more important factors from the less important and to discover the functional relationships existing among the more important determiners. In many field situations these problems proved insoluble by application of available laboratory procedures, but eventually statistical methods provided means for their solutions.

The Development of Interest in Applied Science. Not only did psychologists want to study behavior under more natural conditions of expression, they also desired to study variables that would immediately and directly further the understanding of problems in applied science. They endeavored to transfer to applied problems the procedures developed in laboratory experimentation. After some modification, many of these procedures operated successfully, but additional procedures had to be devised to meet the distinctive features of the applied situations.

Within many applied areas the use of scientific procedures has resulted in marked improvement in the control, prediction, and understanding of behavior. Applications in the area of education came early. Many laboratory psychologists were professionally working in this area as teachers and took advantage of the facilities that the classroom situation offered. The possibility of applying psychological techniques was soon recognized in other areas, such as in law, medicine, industry, and vocational counseling.

A comment needs to be made here concerning the application of scientific method to practical problems of behavior. We are primarily interested in the basic research phases of these problems. A distinction can be made between the task of discovering the principles of organization underlying the predispositions by which individuals achieve satisfactory adjustment in any type of behavior situation and the task of discovering the best method for applying these principles to the adjustment problems of a given individual or group of individuals in a specified type of situation. The first task is the problem of the scientist, the second is the problem of the practitioner. Obviously, we must understand a principle before we can apply it accurately. This understanding is gained from executing basic research studies under the conditions that are operative in the practical situation. Let us not make the error of thinking that basic research can be done only in a laboratory, that the basic nature of a study is a function of the place in which it is conducted. The purpose of the study and the nature of its methodology are the factors by which we determine whether or not it can be classified as basic research. The examples described in the following pages belie the statement that basic research can be conducted only under the rigorous controls of the experimental laboratory.

AN EXPERIMENTAL STUDY OF THE SELECTION AND CLASSIFICATION OF WORKERS

The selection and classification of men for jobs presents the psychologist with a difficult practical problem on which he can try out his scientific procedures. It is important to both management and the worker to know at the time of hiring if the applicant is capable of effective performance on the job. Success on the job is a function of the abilities, knowledges, and skills of the worker as they relate to the kinds of behaviors required by the job tasks. Knowledge of the psychological predispositions prerequisite for a job and the availability of procedures by which these predispositions can be assessed in applicant workers make possible the organization of a highly successful selection and classification program.

To illustrate the several phases of basic research involved in selection and classification, references will be made to the Aviation Psychology Program conducted during the Second World War. This program, under the direction of the Air Surgeon, was responsible for the basic research involved in developing procedures for the selection and classification of aircrew, particularly in the officer ratings of pilot, bombardier, and navigator.

The Dual Problems of Selection and Classification. There are two problems in adjusting workers to jobs, namely, selection and classification. In selection we discover the workers who have the necessary talents to perform effectively on a job. In classification we discover the assignments of workers to jobs that will achieve the highest over-all utilization of the available manpower. These two concepts are closely related and thus often confused. Frequently, the emphasis is on worker selection to the complete neglect of worker classification. In general, the goal toward which society is striving is full employment, and therefore the greater emphasis should be placed on worker classification.

In selection, we are dealing with the problem of finding workers to fill a certain job. The emphasis is upon getting the job filled, and our concern is with learning if a worker applicant can perform the job. Usually there is only one job under consideration but many applicant workers to be evaluated. We are then oriented toward the job. We ask that the person to be hired be capable of doing the best work. We seldom are concerned with whether the worker is better fitted for other jobs and whether another job would offer more challenge to his abilities and prove more interesting to him than the job for which he is being considered.

In classification, there are several jobs under consideration, as well as many workers to be evaluated. There is the problem of matching the workers and the jobs. The jobs must be filled by competent workers so there will be effective performance. Also, each worker must be placed in a job in which his abilities will be challenged and effectively used. The problem is not one of finding the particular worker who can best perform a particular job; neither is it the problem of finding the particular job that a particular worker can best perform. There is a compromise between these two approaches. There being several jobs and several workers, no one job can be considered to the exclusion of the others, nor can one worker be considered to the exclusion of the others. The objective is to achieve the best possible job performance and the best possible worker adjustment when all jobs and all workers are considered as parts of the same problem.

The Area of Hypotheses in Worker Selection and Classification. The problem of matching jobs and workers offers a rich area in which to develop hypotheses. These hypotheses revolve primarily around the psychological predispositions that underlie successful job performance.

The Definition of a Job. The first problem of definition concerns the job itself. It is essential for us to know the requirements of the job; what kinds of tasks are performed, what kinds of responses a worker must use in order to achieve success, etc. When the job involves skilled responses the task of definition is somewhat less difficult than when it is of the administrative or executive type involving the use of judgmental responses.

The method of analyzing and defining a job is called job analysis. Several well-developed procedures are available for discovering and evaluating information about job requirements and job tasks.

In the Aviation Psychology Program the first problem of definition concerned the kinds of responses required of the pilot, of the bombardier, and of the navigator. To be a successful pilot a person must know when the plane is operating correctly, must effectively adjust the various controls by which the plane is maneuvered, must correctly interpret the information provided him on the control panel, must make decisions involving the relations of the plane with the crew, weather, and mission objective, and must make many other responses too numerous to list here. Similar behaviors are required of the bombardier and of the navigator, except that the responses will not be exactly the same as those of the pilot. There will be some responses common for the three aircrew positions, but there will be many responses unique for each of the positions. One of the early tasks of the aviation psychologists was to make comprehensive job analyses of the three aircrew positions.

The Definition of the Psychological Predispositions. With knowledge of what the job requires, our next task is to discover the psychological predispositions that are involved in performing the job responses. The job responses are translated into the abilities, interests, attitudes, skills, etc., of the worker. The procedures of worker analysis are available for this purpose. The term worker analysis does not refer to the study of any given individual worker but to the determination of the qualifications of the hypothetical successful worker.

There are two major objectives to be achieved in worker analysis, namely, the definition of the essential worker characteristics and the determination of the relative weights to be assigned the several characteristics in formulating an over-all evaluation. Any job requires many responses that are of little significance in discriminating between successful and unsuccessful workers. What we need to know are the characteristics that sharply discriminate the two groups. The identification of potentially successful workers is a function of how well we are able to select the essential worker predispositions. In the process of discovering the essential predispositions we also discover their relative importance in successful job performance. It should be apparent that not all essential worker characteristics contribute equally to successful job performance. We are here dealing with a composite in which interaction and interrelation of responses are important variables. It is the composite picture, with each worker characteristic given its appropriate weight, that will enable us to delimit the appropriate psychological predispositions of the successful worker.

In the Aviation Psychology Program, the job responses of the three aircrew positions had to be translated into psychological characteristics in the form of interests, abilities, attitudes, and the like. From the knowledge then available about airplane pilots and navigators it was possible to make accurate judgments about many of the predispositions for these positions. Less information was available on the characteristics of bombardiers. Rather than make a piecemeal attack on the worker characteristics, however, a systematic approach was evolved by organizing psychological research units for broad areas of predispositions and charging each unit with making a comprehensive study of the predispositions within the area assigned to it. These research units were located at cadet classification centers. Four primary research areas were selected, as follows: (1) information, judgment, and intellectual ability, (2) alertness, observation, and speed of perception, (3) motor coordination and visual-motor skill, and (4) personality, temperament, and interest. Each psychological research unit concerned itself with developing procedures for identifying and evaluating psychological predispositions within its general area which were essential to the successful performance of the jobs of pilot, bombardier, and navigator.

The Formulation of Hypotheses. Simultaneously with the determination of the job requirements and the translation of the job responses into worker predispositions, many ideas arise about possible relationships between the predispositions and successful performance on the job. Hypotheses then are formulated as functional relationships between the psychological predispositions of the worker and successful execution of the job responses.

From the job analyses and worker analyses of the pilot, navigator, and bombardier came ideas about what kinds of motor skills, intellectual judgments, personality traits, and the like would be required to successfully pilot an airplane, navigate a course in the sky, or make the necessary adjustments of a bombsight to effect a direct hit of a target. As the aviation psychologist pondered about these interrelationships he developed hypotheses for possible investigation.

The Evolving of Theorems. *Identifying Responses That Reflect Predispositions.* The functional relationships between psychological predispositions and job performance evolved at the hypothetical level must be expressed in tangible forms that lend themselves to empirical verification. After studying the available facts about the job responses and the worker characteristics, we hypothesize that certain predispositions underlie certain successful job responses. We must then determine what kinds of behavior can be used to reflect the predispositions we think are essential to the job responses. Obviously, we can try out the worker on the job, but this is wasteful of time and money. The *raison d'être* of a selection and classification program is that it is a faster and cheaper means of identifying and measuring the predispositions of the successful worker.

In previous chapters several short-cut procedures for learning about predispositions were described. One of the fastest and most reliable procedures is the use of various kinds of ability tests. Another is to get a record of the worker's relevant past experiences. This is often done by the interview method. Other short-cut procedures include the use of inventories and ratings.

In the selection and classification of pilots, bombardiers, and navigators, pencil-and-paper tests and apparatus-psychomotor tests were the chief means of measuring the selected predispositions. These instruments were supplemented by information obtained through ratings and through interviewing the cadets. Following are some of the more effective pencil-and-paper tests: arithmetic reasoning, dial-and-table reading, spatial orientation, biographical data, numerical operations, reading comprehension, judgment, general information, instrument comprehension, mechanical principles, mechanical information, and speed of identification. Some of the more effective psychomotor tests were rotary pursuit, two-hand coordination, complex coordination, rudder control, discrimination-reaction time, and finger dexterity.

Not all of the tests were used for any one of the aircrew positions. The weights of the tests used for each position were empirically determined. The relative importance of the tests common to all three positions was not the same for the several positions. The selection of the tests most highly predictive of an aircrew position and the determination of the relative weight of any test were based on measures of job performance obtained after the cadet had completed certain phases of his specialized training, e.g., graduation from primary pilot school.

Stating the Consequences of a Theorem. A very important aspect of any theorem is the statement of the consequences. It will be remembered that the general formulation of a theorem states that given certain M conditions then certain X consequences will occur. In the selection and classification problem our hypothesis may state that certain predispositions are involved in successful job performance. Our theorem then makes this more definite by defining behaviors that can be used to identify the predispositions. But the theorem must go further; it must define the behavior that will identify the change in job responses brought about by the conditions of the theorem. That is, the theorem must include a statement of the consequences.

The theorem sets up a functional relationship between certain manifestations of the hypothesized predispositions and certain manifestations or measures of effectiveness in job performance. A measure of the effectiveness in job performance is just as important as a measure of the be-havior selected to reflect the predispositions. Without either measure we cannot empirically examine the theorem.

In the area of matching workers and jobs, the measure of job success by which differences in job performance are detected and evaluated is called the criterion. The criterion is usually a reliable and valid practical measure of job performance, such as the productiveness of performance on the job itself. The criterion should be quantitative in nature and easy to obtain.

Although the most valid measure of the effectiveness of an air-force pilot, bombardier, or navigator is how well he performs his job in combat, the use of combat criteria for evaluating the selection and classification program was not possible because of difficulties of obtaining measures of combat performance in time of war. Partial and intermediate criterion measures of performance in training schools were the principal ones used. Performance in operational training—training just preceding assignment to combat duty—was available in the later stages of the war. A simple index of effectiveness of performance in navigation training was the student's rank in his class at the time of graduation. In pilot training the student's success or failure in graduating from primary training, basic training, and advanced training was used. In bombardier training the student had to complete several aerial missions on which a certain number of bombs were dropped. His average circular error was then a measure of his performance as a bombardier. In all three positions class grades in various required courses also were available as criteria.

The Empirical Testing of the Theorem. *The General Nature of the Testing Situation.* A theorem is confirmed if empirical evidence support-ing its consequences can be found. In the problem of matching workers and jobs the theorem states that certain test responses as manifestations of certain predispositions are valid indices of successful job responses and that the consequence of using these test responses in selecting and classifying the workers would be an improvement in job performance. The empirical testing of the theorem is accomplished when test scores measuring the predispositions are collected, the persons are allowed to perform on the job, the job-performance measures are obtained, and the job-performance measures are checked against the test scores. If there is a positive relationship between the two sets of measures, then the test scores are an index of job responses. The higher this relationship is, the higher will be the validity of the index.

In the Aviation Psychology Program a large number of tests were constructed in order to assess the predispositions. Not all of these tests were actually used. Similarly, in order to assess the job responses many criteria were investigated; only a few of these were found to be reliable.

The cadets were given the written and apparatus psychological tests and thorough physical examinations at the classification centers. They were then sent to various aircrew training schools. At the completion of each major phase of training, measures of their success in school were formed into training criteria. These were the job-performance measures. The test scores and the job-performance measures were then correlated to determine the predictive effectiveness of the various tests.

The Validation Group. It is important that representative workers form the group on which the empirical testing is done. The importance of this is readily seen when we consider the possibility of immediately using the tests for selecting new workers. But it is also important from the point of view of the basic design of the research. The theorem states a relationship between two sets of measures. Both of these measures are in part determined by the characteristics of the group on which they are obtained. In setting up the hypothesis and deriving the theorem, certain defined jobs and certain defined workers are studied and evaluated. If an adequate test is to be made of the theorem it is necessary that the subjects be representative of these workers in order that the conditions of the theorem can be translated into an empirical testing stituation.

We can use two types of groups for validating selection and classification procedures. One is composed of applicants for jobs, the other is composed of workers already on the job. If applicants are used then we obtain information about their predispositions by means of tests, ratings, interviews, etc., before they are hired. They are then assigned to the job. After they have worked long enough to have been able to develop relevant job responses, measures are made of the effectiveness of their job performance. In the second procedure workers already employed are given the tests designed to reveal differences in the essential predispositions. They are also evaluated in terms of their effectiveness on the job.

In the selection and classification of aircrew the applicant method was used. The aviation cadets were the applicants. They were given a day and a half of psychological tests and a thorough physical examination. A composite score, called a stanine, was computed for each aircrew position. This score was a combination of the scores from several tests selected for a given position, each test being assigned its appropriate weight. Every cadet received three stanine scores, one for pilot, one for navigator, and one for bombardier. These three scores, together with the results of the physical examination, formed the basis for the final selection, classification, and assignment of the cadets, subject, of course, to overriding factors arising from the fortunes of the war. As stated previously, job-performance measures in the form of training criteria were obtained at different stages in the cadet's training program.

The number of cadets used in validation studies totaled many thousands. The number actually tested and classified was over 600,000.

The Measurement of the Functional Relationships. The final check of the theorem is made by quantifying the degree of relationship existing between the measures of the predispositions and the measures of the job responses. If both variables are quantitative in nature, this step is greatly simplified by using an appropriate statistical equation. When the validation group is comprised of job applicants there is usually a wide range

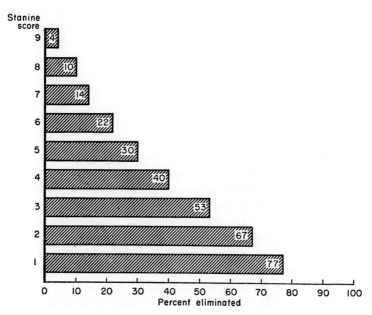

Fig. 12. Per cent of cadets eliminated from primary pilot training, based on the records of 185,367 cadets.

of variation in both the predisposition scores and the job-performance scores. The appropriate statistic is then some measure of correlation.

In the Aviation Psychology Program, coefficients of correlation were computed between the criteria obtained from the different phases of training and the three stanine scores. Similar coefficients were computed between the criterion measures and the scores on each of the tests. Such coefficients are known as validity coefficients. Near the end of the war the validity coefficients of the stanines for the three aircrew positions were for pilot .58, for navigator .61, and for bombardier .38. Graphs were also made, diagramming the relationship existing between the rate of elimination and the stanine scores. The relationship found between the pilot stanine and elimination from primary pilot training is presented in Fig. 12. It will be seen that there is a high positive relationship between the stanine score and the proportion of cadets eliminated from further pilot training.

Both the correlation coefficients and the graph provide evidence that the selection and classification of aviation pilots achieved remarkable success. Comparable evidence also was obtained for the positions of navigator and bombardier.

AN EXPERIMENTAL STUDY OF METHODS OF TREATING SCHIZOPHRENIA

Schizophrenia is a mental disturbance with widespread involvement of the personality. Characteristic symptoms are a loss of interest in external happenings, tendency toward peculiar mannerisms, inappropriateness between emotional expressions and the stimuli eliciting them, emotional apathy, negativism, frequent fantasy, delusions, and hallucinations. This psychosis does not readily yield to treatment and the prognosis is not as high as for other mental disturbances. Over the years many kinds of treatment have been tried to effect release from the symptoms, which in certain forms of the disease are extremely traumatic to the patient. None of the present methods of therapy is highly effective, so the search for improvement in treatment continues to be an active program among psychiatrists and psychologists.

One method that has received widespread attention in recent years is called shock therapy. Shock can be produced either electrically or by means of drugs. In the study to be described the use of insulin shock was investigated. From the point of view of experimental design this study is among the better ones thus far conducted.

The Problem. Schizophrenia is interpreted by some authorities as an abnormal formation of habit patterns. Treatment of the disease has often been directed toward a breaking-up of the abnormal habit patterns and the establishing of adjustive modes of behavior. The conservative method of psychotherapy frequently has contributed little relief to the patient. To explain this failure it is argued that the malformed habit patterns are so intensively established that they are little affected by psychological procedures. It is further argued that shock treatment can be used to break up the nervous organization underlying the malformed habits, allowing older more effective responses to become active again, or providing an interval of time in which to reeducate the patient in more adaptive responses. The present experiment was organized to compare the two treatments of psychotherapy and insulin shock.

Factors That Required Control. Inasmuch as two experimental treatments were to be studied, it was necessary to use two groups of patients. This then demanded that factors other than the treatment differences be kept as constant as possible. The procedure used for achieving this constancy was through the selection and assignment of the patients to the two experimental groups. An attempt was made to control the following factors by this procedure:

1. Policy of admission to the hospital
2. Criteria used in diagnosis
3. Relative percentages in the experimental groups of different forms of the disease
4. Freedom of the subjects from other kinds of disease
5. Racial composition of the groups
6. Age and sex composition of the groups
7. Economic, occupational, and educational levels of the groups

The Criterion Used for Evaluating Differences between Treatments. The effects of the two treatment methods were measured in terms of the rate of remission, that is, the degree of improvement shown at the end of a period of time following release from the hospital. Two classifications were used for measuring the extent of the improvement. Patients who fully recovered or recovered sufficiently to adjust socially at approximately their former level were placed in one category. Patients who continued to show defects but were able to live in the community at a somewhat lower level than previously, and those who showed no improvement, were placed in a second category. To determine if the effects of the treatments varied with the type of onset of the disease, each treatment group was divided into those manifesting acute onset and those manifesting gradual onset, and a comparison was made of the rates of remission. A further division of the two treatment groups was made in terms of the length of the illness, and comparisons were made in terms of the remission rate. These comparisons were done to check on the statement often made that early treatment of schizophrenia with insulin shock produces a higher remission rate than similar early treatment by more conservative procedures.

Procedures of the Experiment. Sixty-six patients, in whom typical symptoms of schizophrenia were manifest, comprised the insulin-shock group. Each patient was given progressively larger amounts of insulin until the dose was sufficient to produce coma within 2 or 3 hours after injection. He was allowed to remain in the coma from 1 to 3 hours. During the experiment each patient was subjected to 30 periods of coma at the rate of 6 per week.

One hundred and thirty-two patients constituted the psychotherapy group. Each one was given a psychiatric examination to determine the specific problems and conflicts that might have bearing on his maladjustment. An attempt was made to understand the development of his personality in terms of the difficulties he experienced in making social adjustments. Whenever possible, individualized social-adjustment programs combined with psychotherapy were given to help the patient solve his conflicts and develop adequate social responses. Not all patients were exposed to a full program of reeducation or rehabilitation owing to factors limiting their stay in the hospital.

Follow-up clinical evaluations of each patient's condition were made at intervals of 6 months for a period of from 1 to 4 years. The clinical examination revealed the presence of any psychotic symptoms, the seriousness of these symptoms, signs of further deterioration, the success with which the patient was adjusting in his family and community, his current level of adjustment as compared with his former adjustment in the hospital and before treatment was begun, and other similar information.

A Comparison of Insulin and Psychotherapy Treatments in Terms of Rate of Remission. The findings indicate no significant differences in the rate of remission between the two treatment groups. The per cents falling in the two categories used for measuring the degree of improvement, based on the last clinical examination, are given in Table 6. It will be

Table 6. Comparative Effects of Treatment of Schizophrenic Patients by Insulin Shock and Psychotherapy

Treatment	Per cent fully or socially recovered	Per cent not or slightly improved
Insulin shock.......	35	64 *
Psychotherapy......	33	64 *

* Per cents do not add to 100 because of deaths.

seen that the differences in per cent between the two groups are not statistically significant.

To determine if there was differential recovery under the two treatments in terms of the type of onset, the results of Table 7 were prepared. Again we see no significant differences between the two groups in either acute onset or gradual onset.

The patients in each treatment group were divided into three subgroups in terms of the duration of the illness. Comparisons of corresponding subgroups in terms of rate of remission again showed no significant differences between the two methods of treatment.

Generalizations from the Study. From the data collected the following generalizations are substantiated:

1. Insulin-shock treatment of schizophrenic patients, as administered in this experiment, does not increase the remission rate of patients above

Table 7. Comparative Effects of Treatment of Schizophrenic Patients by Insulin Shock and Psychotherapy Analyzed in Terms of Type of Onset

Onset	Treatment	Per cent fully or socially recovered	Per cent not or slightly improved
Acute......	Insulin shock	45	55
	Psychotherapy	45	55
Gradual....	Insulin shock	26	72 *
	Psychotherapy	29	67 *

* Per cents do not add to 100 because of deaths.

that resulting from the use of the more conservative treatment of psychotherapy.

2. The relative curative effects of insulin shock and psychotherapeutic treatments of schizophrenic patients are not related with the type of onset of the disease.

3. Early treatment of schizophrenics by insulin shock does not produce a higher rate of remission than early treatment by psychotherapy.

AN EXPERIMENT ON HUMAN MOTIVATION

The psychological predispositions underlying human motivation have been difficult to subject to experimentation. In this area laboratory control procedures modify the natural-type variables that the psychologist really wants to study. Motivational processes operating under natural life conditions have proved difficult to analyze. Despite deficiencies in the control of these variables, however, some progress is being made. In the following pages a brief description is given of part of a study conducted on motivating factors operating in an industrial situation.

The Problem. One determinant factor in worker motivation that has received delayed recognition but one that probably pervades all types of job performances from the least skilled worker to the highest administrator, is that of identification with the job and the organization. This identification can be developed by the worker in many different ways. In recent years it has been shown to be frequently associated with the degree to which he participates in the formulation and organization of the conditions under which he works. It is difficult to reduce this psychological factor to rigorous control, and we cannot expect in an actual industrial situation to achieve the degree of control that characterizes a laboratory experiment. In the present study, however, a very sound experimental design was used, and the facts collected add significant meanings about the motivational processes characteristic of many industrial workers.

Evolving the Hypothesis. *The Source of the Problem.* In a sewing factory employing mostly women workers, it became necessary to transfer some of the workers from their accustomed jobs to other jobs that were sometimes considerably different and to require some of the workers to adopt new kinds of working procedures. The workers resisted the changes in several ways. Although the new jobs were not necessarily more difficult than the old ones or the new procedures more difficult than the customary ones, the production of the workers dropped off markedly after the changes were made. Resentment toward management was clearly manifest and the rate of labor turnover rose significantly.

In analyzing the various innovations usually made, management came to the conclusion that the workers' difficulties were probably not due to any technical changes introduced, as these appeared not to make increased demands upon the workers' skills. It was decided that the negative reactions of the workers were probably traceable to motivational factors.

The Hypothesis. It appeared to the management that some of the complaints of the workers were related to the way in which the changes were brought about. Apparently, in the manner that has been traditional in some industries, the changes in jobs, methods, rates of pay, etc., were developed by the production department and given to the workers in completed form without opportunity for them to criticize or contribute. Although this was only one of several possible explanations of the workers' negative reactions, it was judged worthy of investigation. The general hypothesis was evolved that the decreased effectiveness in performance of the employees following the change in working conditions was a motivational and morale problem. The workers did not identify individually with the changes that were made; they did not identify with the new goals that were imposed on them. The new jobs and new methods were not theirs, and therefore they were not motivated to achieve high performance.

The Theorem. Increasing the participation of the workers in evolving and formulating the necessary changes appeared to be one method by which to encourage them to identify with the desired changes in jobs and working conditions. The logic underlying this approach is that a worker's identification with his job is a function of the degree to which he makes a personal contribution in shaping it. The more the new goals are accepted as of his own making, the more readily will he adapt to the changes introduced. It was decided that a study should be conducted in which the workers would be given a better understanding of the reasons underlying the changes and be allowed to assist in evolving new jobs and new kinds of procedures. Accordingly the following theorem was investigated: worker participation in evolving the necessary changes in procedures and jobs will result in a higher level of motivation and therefore no slump in production will occur after the changes are introduced.

The Testing Situation. Three conditions were organized, representing three levels of participation of workers in determining and planning the changes to be made in jobs and working procedures. Four groups of workers were studied (two groups were assigned to condition three), and an attempt was made to match the groups in general level of proficiency and other relevant factors. The following experimental conditions were set up:

1. Control Group. Management merely announced the changes to the workers as in the customary manner. In this condition the worker was allowed minimum participation.

2. Group I. Management conferred with the workers some time before the changes were made. The changes were explained in a dramatic fashion and management tried to get the workers to come to a general agreement that changes were necessary. The workers chose representatives to cooperate with management in planning the needed changes in jobs and procedures.

3. Groups II and III. The procedure was similar to that for group I with the exception that all members of the groups participated in designing the new jobs and procedures. For instance, every worker contributed performance in establishing the piece-rate pay for the changed conditions.

On both the old and the new jobs the workers were paid by piece rate, so objective criteria were provided for evaluating the workers' performance and for serving as a basis for comparing the performances under the several conditions. Another available criterion was the rate of labor turnover.

The Confirmation of the Hypothesis. The quantitative measurement of output for the four groups is presented in Fig. 13, in which production before the changes were instituted is compared with production after the changes. The control group showed the usual drop in production and failed to manifest later recovery. Group I (some participation) dropped in performance following the changes, continued for about 10 days at a lower level of output, but then improved in effectiveness for the next 20 days. Groups II and III, in which every worker helped to design the changes in jobs and procedures, showed only a slight drop at the time the changes were made. After about the third day these groups started to increase their production and at the thirty-second day were around 10 units per hour higher than before the changes were instituted.

Other criteria for evaluating the workers' performance showed similar trends. Worker discontent was far greater in the control group than in the other groups, and similarly, the control group manifested the greatest increase in labor turnover after the changes were effected.

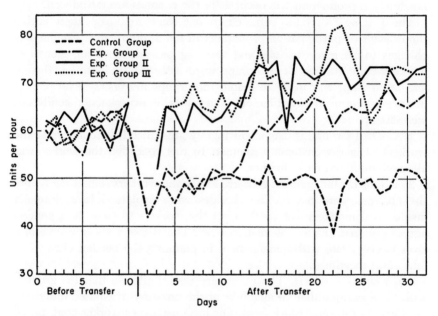

FIG. 13. The effects of participation through representation (Group I) and of total participation (Groups II and III) on recovery after an easy transfer.

AN EXPERIMENT ON THE MEASUREMENT OF SOCIAL INTERACTION

To obtain an accurate measurement of an individual's personality it is necessary to observe him interacting with others. The predispositions underlying personality are reflected in these interpersonal relationships. In social-interaction situations, as in laboratory experimentation, we are faced with the problem of keeping stimulating conditions constant when we want to compare the behavior of different individuals. To ascribe accurately a difference in behavior to differences in personality, we must be sure that the behavior difference cannot be explained by differences in the stimulating situation. In the study of social behavior in unstructured situations, as, for example, in the rating of the effectiveness of perform-ance of an individual from observing him participating in a group discussion, the stimulating conditions are continuously changing and are markedly inconstant for the various participants.

In the experiment to be described the stimulating conditions were kept relatively constant within a specially designed social-interaction situation called the group squares test. The experiment was conducted to measure the personality responses of individuals who were placed in a conflict situation in which their willingness to cooperate to achieve a group goal was placed in competition with their desire to satisfy an immediate individual goal. This study, for the first time, sets up a situation of social interaction in which the stimulating conditions for each individual are identical.

The primary purpose in describing the experiment is to show how an ingenious procedure was devised to effect constancy in the physical and symbolic stimuli of a group-interaction situation. We shall therefore dispense with a detailed consideration of the hypothesis and theorems involved in the study and concern ourselves with the procedural characteristics of the group squares testing situation.

The Objectives to Be Achieved in the Experimental Situation. The several objectives to be achieved in the experimental situation can be stated very briefly as follows:

1. That the situation be one in which social-interaction behavior between several persons is elicited

2. That there be a common group task in which each subject is invited to participate

3. That each subject be given an identical individual task to perform that can be accomplished in consonance with or in opposition to the achieving of the group goal

4. That the problems presented to the subjects, the stimulating materials used, and the communication among the subjects be held constant for every subject

5. That the behavior be describable in quantitative terms

The Nature of the Subjects' Task. The problem presented to the subjects was similar to the familiar jigsaw puzzle, in which variously shaped pieces of cardboard are fitted together to form a pattern or picture. In the group squares test the subject formed a 4-inch square from three pieces of cardboard that differed in respect to both size and shape. The goal of each subject was to complete his square.

The group task consisted in the subjects' cooperating with each other to the end that all subjects could complete their squares. Each subject was to assist the others by giving up pieces he had that might aid another to complete his square. The group goal was achieved when every subject's square was completed.

The Procedure for Keeping the Stimulating Situation Constant. The stimulating situation was made constant for all subjects by the following procedure:

1. Presenting every subject with exactly the same number and same shaped pieces of cardboard at the beginning of the test

2. Providing every subject with pieces of identical shapes for trading purposes during the process of completing his square

3. Requesting every subject to give up pieces of exactly the same shape after he has completed his square, in order to assist another subject

Constancy of the stimulating conditions was achieved by the experimenter as he dealt with each subject individually. The subjects (in this study there were five participants) sat in tablet armchairs formed in a large circle, their backs toward the center so they could not observe each other at work. The space between chairs was made large enough to enable the experimenter to move in behind the subjects when he needed to change the stimulus materials. At the beginning of the experiment the subject drew his three cardboard pieces from envelopes, each piece from a different envelope. Although it appeared to the subject that he was drawing pieces randomly, the experimenter had arranged the pieces in the envelopes so that without knowing it each subject drew pieces with identical shapes. Only two of the three pieces drawn by a subject fitted together.

By means of a large tray the experimenter made it possible for the subjects to exchange pieces, to signal their needs, and to give up pieces to others. The subjects were not allowed to converse with each other, but made requests and answered requests via the experimenter's tray. On the front section of the tray, pieces were placed for exchange purposes. On the rear section of the tray, pieces were manipulated for communication purposes. On this section there were 14 pieces with variable shapes, all painted white on the underside. To make a request for a certain shaped piece, the subject merely turned over the piece of corresponding shape in the rear section so its white side was in view. If a subject wished to answer a request he took from his square the piece that was requested and placed it on the front section of the tray.

It will be apparent from the above procedure that all communication among subjects is under the control of the experimenter inasmuch as he is in possession of the tray at all times. Thus the procedure enables the experimenter to make identical requests of every subject and to answer every subject's requests by providing pieces of identical shape.

The Sequence of Trials. The general scheme followed was to allow each subject, in turn, to complete his square, and then to request each one to give up a certain shaped piece from his completed square. In the first trial, two pieces were placed on the front section of the tray, neither one of which could be used by the subject. The subject usually made no exchange but did make known his request on the rear section of the tray. In the second trial the piece was provided by which the subject could complete his square. Through the next four trials two request pieces appeared on the rear section of the tray, but these pieces were always different from any held by the subjects. These four trials forced upon each subject the notion that, although he had completed his square, the other subjects still appeared to be working on theirs.

The seventh trial was the first critical one. The subject was requested to give up a certain piece from his completed square. This placed him in a conflict situation, his desire to meet the request conflicting with his desire to maintain the completed square. This situation presented an opportunity for the subject to cooperate with the others or to maintain a more individualistic approach of maintaining his own square intact. If he did not meet the request on this trial, then the request was repeated on each subsequent trial until he answered it. The score given the subject was the number of that critical trial on which he yielded the requested piece. After a subject had met the request, he was allowed to complete his square on the next trial. The experimenter then kept him active in the situation until all squares were completed by presenting him with requests for pieces that he did not have.

The Hypothesis and Theorem of the Experiment. The particular experiment being reported was part of a larger personality assessment program in which the definition, analysis, and prediction of effective performance was being studied. One of the general hypotheses underlying the study was that behavior manifested by an individual in a group-interaction situation is prognostic of his personality. Personality was more specifically defined as effective performance, and the group squares test was devised as a particular kind of social-interaction situation. Effective performance was further analyzed into three variables, namely, (1) promise of success in a professional field, (2) originality as a scholar or scientist, and (3) soundness as a person. Ratings on these variables constituted the criteria. The theorem tested was that the group squares test scores are predictive of the three measures of effective performance. The experimental subjects were graduate students in a university.

The Results of the Experiment. The validity of the group squares test can be studied in terms of the mean ratings on the criteria for different ranges of scores on the test, and also by correlating the test scores with the criteria ratings. These two types of statistical measures are presented in Table 8. Those subjects who met the request by breaking their squares on the first critical trial (seventh) are called the "fast" group, those who broke their squares on the second and third critical trials the "medium"

Table 8. Relation of Group Squares Test Scores to Potential
Success, Originality, and Soundness

Rating	Fast N = 15	Medium N = 12	Slow N = 10	Eta *
Potential success.......	49.7	55.3	48.0	.28
Originality............	51.2	59.1	45.6	.41
Soundness as a person..	46.5	54.8	46.7	.38

* Correlation coefficient for nonlinear relationships.

group, and those who broke their squares from the fourth to the twentieth critical trial the "slow" group. From an examination of the mean scores of these three groups on each of the three criterion measures, it will be seen that the highest scores were obtained by the medium group. These results indicate that the most effective performers did not break too quickly or too slowly, which is a significant finding meriting further investigation. From the column of coefficients it will be noted that the scores on the group squares test are positively and significantly related with each of the criteria, the coefficients for originality and soundness being very promising.

The results of the experiment clearly point to this form of group-interaction measure as an acceptable diagnostic and predictive instrument for assessing personality as it is expressed in terms of the effectiveness of performance of the individual.

SELECTED READINGS

Bechtoldt, H. P.: Selection, in S. S. Stevens (ed.), "Handbook of Experimental Psychology," chap. 33, John Wiley & Sons, Inc., 1951. This chapter surveys the problems, methods, and some of the theory of selection and classification. Among the topics covered are the following: steps in selection research, the classification problem, criterion measures, and the prediction problem.

French, J. R. P., Jr.: Experiments in Field Settings, in L. Festinger and D. Katz (eds.), "Research Methods in the Behavioral Sciences," chap. 3, The Dryden Press, Inc., 1953. Many of the problems confronting the experimentalist in investigating social behavior are presented. Specialized procedures to be used in solving these problems are described under the following three general rubrics: the constitution of a field experiment, the planning of a field experiment, and the execution of a field experiment.

Hovland, C. I., A. A. Lumsdaine, and F. D. Sheffield: "Experiments on Mass Communication," vol. 3, chap. 5, of *Studies in Social Psychology in World*

War II, Princeton University Press, 1949. This chapter presents descriptions of several experimental studies made to compare the relative effectiveness of different types of presentations of materials to groups of servicemen. The studies discussed are, *The Comparative Effectiveness of a Sound Motion Picture and a Film-strip Presentation*, *the Comparative Effectiveness of Documentary and Commentator Radio Presentations, and Comparison of Introducing Supplementary Material at the Beginning and the End of a Training Film.*

Index